lonely planet

Buenos Aires

Wayne Bernhardson

LONELY PLANET PUBLICATIONS
Melbourne · Oakland · London · Paris

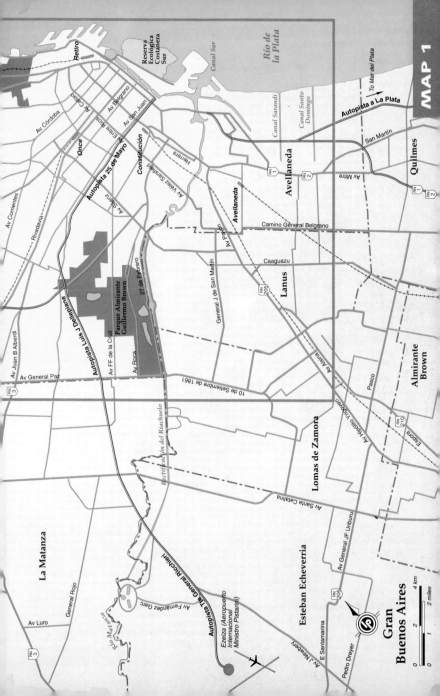

MAP 1

Retiro

Reserva Ecológica Costanera Sur

Río de la Plata

Canal Sur

Canal Sarandí

Canal Santo Domingo

To Mar del Plata

Autopista a La Plata

San Martín

Av Córdoba

Av Corrientes

Rivadavia

Av Callao

Av Entre Ríos

Av Belgrano

Av San Juan

Once

Autopista 25 de Mayo

Constitución

Herrera

Av Sáenz

Av Vélez Sársfield

Avellaneda

Camino General Belgrano

Av Mitre

Quilmes

RN 1

RN 2

RN 1

RN 2

Avellaneda

Caaguazu

Lanus

Av Juan B Alberdi

Av General Paz

Autopista Luis J Dellepiane

Parque Almirante Guillermo Brown

27 de Febrero

Av FF de la Cruz

Av Roca

General J de San Martín

RN 205

Av Alsina

10 de Setiembre de 1861

Rectificación del Riachuelo

Almirante Brown

Pasco

Av Hipólito Yrigoyen

RN 210

Esperia

La Matanza

General Rojo

Av Luro

RN 3

Río Matanza

Autopista Tte General Ricchieri

Av Fernández Garc

Ezeiza (Aeropuerto Internacional Ministro Pistarini)

Lomas de Zamora

Av Santa Catalina

Esteban Echeverría

Av General JF Uriburu

Av E Santamarina

Pedro Dreyer

Av J Newbery

RN 205

Gran Buenos Aires

0   2   4 km

0   1   2 miles

Buenos Aires
2nd edition – May 1999
First published – May 1996

Published by
Lonely Planet Publications Pty Ltd A.C.N. 005 607 983
192 Burwood Rd, Hawthorn, Victoria 3122, Australia

Lonely Planet Offices
Australia PO Box 617, Hawthorn, Victoria 3122
USA 150 Linden St, Oakland, CA 94607
UK 10a Spring Place, London NW5 3BH
France 1 rue du Dahomey, 75011 Paris

Photographs
Bill Bachmann/Comesaña, Frank S Balthis, Wayne Bernhardson, Sally
Black/Blacklight, Victor Englebert, David R Frazier, Robert Frerck/
Odyssey Productions/Chicago, Robert Fried, Gustavo Gatto, Library
of Congress, Brian McGilloway/Robert Holmes Photography, Allan
Philiba, Robert Rattner, Sylvia Stevens, Randy Wells

Some of the images in this guide are available for licensing from
Lonely Planet Images.
email: lpi@lonelyplanet.com.au

Front cover photograph
La Boca (Corbis/Enzo Ragazzini)

ISBN 0 86442 643 7

text & maps © Lonely Planet 1999
photos © photographers as indicated 1999
climate charts compiled from information supplied by Patrick J
Tyson, © Patrick J Tyson 1999
chapter endings from paintings by Florencio Molina Campos, previously published in *Cowboys of the Americas*, by Richard W Slatta

Printed by Colorcraft Ltd, Hong Kong

Contents

1

The Author

Wayne Bernhardson

Wayne Bernhardson was born in Fargo, North Dakota, grew up in Tacoma, Washington, and earned a PhD in geography at the University of California, Berkeley. He has traveled extensively in Mexico and Central and South America, and lived for extended periods in Chile, Argentina and the Falkland (Malvinas) Islands. His other LP credits include *Argentina, Uruguay & Paraguay*, *Chile & Easter Island*, *South America on a shoestring*, *Baja California*, and *Mexico*. Wayne currently resides in Oakland, California, where his Alaskan malamute Gardel smiles every bit as charismatically as his legendary *porteño* namesake.

FROM THE AUTHOR

Special mention to Fito and Mary Massolo of Olavarría, Buenos Aires province, my Argentine family for so many years.

Many others in Buenos Aires were exceptionally helpful and hospitable in the process of pulling this all together. The list could be even longer, but special mentions go to the following Buenos Aires residents: Federico Kirbus; Joaquín Allolio; Dori Lieberman; Michael Soltys and Andrew Graham-Yooll of the *Buenos Aires Herald*; Diego Curubeto of *Ambito Financiero*; Ernesto Seman of *Clarín*; Mario Banchik of Librerías Turísticas; Monique Larraín of the *Guía Argentina de Tráfico Aéreo*; and Armando Schlecker of the *Guía Latinoamericana de Transportes*. A huge and special thanks to Georges and Marion Helft of San Telmo for their willingness to permit photography of their extraordinary collection of modern Argentine art.

In Uruguay, I appreciate the help from Manuel Pérez Bravo of the Asociación de Hoteles y Restaurantes del Uruguay.

In Oakland, thanks to James T Smith for paying my bills and to María Laura Massolo for permission to adapt material from her contribution to LP's *Travel with Children*. Thanks also to Miguel Helft of San Francisco.

Thanks again to Tony and Maureen Wheeler for keeping me employed these several years.

This Book

FROM THE PUBLISHER

This book was edited in Lonely Planet's Oakland office by Robert Reid. Vivian Numaguchi helped edit. Paige Penland, Julie Connery, David Peterkofsky and Brigitte Barta proofed. Many thanks to Brigitte for her patient guidance and advice. Thanks also to Jacqueline Volin, Susan Charles, Kate Hoffman and Joslyn Leve for advice and help, and to Carolyn Hubbard for impromptu Spanish lessons.

Tracey Croom drew the maps, with guidance from Alex Guilbert. Illustrations were researched and created by Hayden Foell, along with Hugh D'Andrade and Mark Butler. Wendy Yanagihara designed and laid out the book, with guidance from Scott Summers. Rini Keagy designed the cover. Josh Schefers helped get the photographs.

THANKS

Many thanks to following travelers who used the last edition and wrote to us with helpful hints, useful advice and interesting anecdotes:

C Gabriel Alperovich, Charles Anderson and Julian Anderson, Cherie Anderson and Dairne Fitzpatrick, Matt Anderson, Claus B Andersson, Valeria Axelrad. Jerry Azevedo, Christine Badre, Bernard Badzioch, Carolyn Barnato, Craig Barrack and Carolyn Johnson, Dom Barry, Lee Barry, John Beaven, Anja Behrendt and Alexander Sturm, Steve Bergren, Góran Berntsson, Ragnhild and Antoon Beyne-Pille, Loretta Biasutti, Colleen Blake, Christoph Braun, Gert-jan Bremer, Marianne Brito, Linda Broschofsky, Matthew Burke, Stephen D Busack, Jasper F Buxton, Carmel Castellan and Alexandra Taylor, Mike Cavendish, Dale and Kevin Coghlan, Pat Coleman and Sara Tizard, Anne Cook, Aaron Corcoran, Bryce Coulter, Keith Crandall, Paula Crotty, Paul Crovella and Julia Pike, Sebastián Cwilich, Phillip A Dale, Myriam Deshaies, Jason Diautz, Juan Carlos Dima, Carole Dixon, Marion Drexler, Bernd Ebner, Dana Ellerbrock, Marie Engelstad, Donald C Erbe, Igor Fabjan, Gustavo Faigenbaum, Michael Falk, Douglas Fears, Carolyn Foreman, John L Franklin, Jonathan Freeman, Roberta Friend, Anne Geddes, Klaus Gierhake, Juan Bernardo Gimelli Santos, Thomas and Alke Girtz, Christian Ezequiel Golman, Lorenzo Gordon, Moira Greaven, David P Grill, Danile Grujic, Michael K Gschwind and Valentina Salapura, Wade Guthrie, Patrick Hagans, Christiane Hanstein, James Hardy, Lynda Harpley, Bill Hart, Holger Hartmeier, Boris Hasselblatt, Michelle Hecht and Bob Redlinger, Darlene R Hector, Michele Heymann, Julius Heinis, Elisabeth Herrería, Jochen Hoettcke, Andrew Holmes, Russell Hopp, Bernhard Humpert, Lyndsay Humphries, David L Huntzinger, Ernestien Idenburg, Nuria Ivorra and Michiel Kraak,

Felicia Jalomo, Marie Jenneteg, Keith Johnson, Ripton Johnson, Kristine Jürs, Dale Kabat, Harry Kangassolo, Wolfgang Kessler, Bernd Klett, Josef Klimek, Steven Koenig, Daniel Alberto Korman, Thomas Krusekamp, Peter Kunkel, Oda Karen Kvaal and Gavin Tanguay, Fred 'Chico' Lager, Nadia Landolt, Julianne de Lange, Eric and Brenda Legget, Brian and Lorna Lewis, Federico Lifsichtz, John Lilley, Jill Liu, Karl H Loring, Jessica Lowe and Nathan Kesteven, Francesco Lulli, DF Luond, Tamsin Lyle, Iain Mackay, Will Markle, William Massie, Luis Mazarrasa, Denise and Malcolm McDonough, Jane McKenzie, Martie Meyer and Albert van der Rooy, Patrick Miller, Chris and Janet Morris, Lori Murphy, James Musick, Gavin Nathan, Bruce and María Nesbitt, Leo and Marita Niemenen, Anna Noakes, Shannon. Orton, Eric Otterson, Olav Østrem, Anthony Palmer, Patrick Paludan, Julie and Spiros Pappas, Gennaro Pastore, Marc Peake, Neil Pepper, Marco Perezzani, Alison Peters, Andreas Poethen, Michale Pößl, Julianne Power, Tatiana Prowell, Marcus Pussel, Juliet Rhodes, Amy E Risley, Doug Robinson, Vanessa Rodd, Roy and Becey Rogers, Jorge A Romero Lozano, Egon Conti Rossini, Hans R Roth, Roberto F Salinas, Dirk Scharlevsky, Josee and Manfred Schick, Doreen Schreiber and René Sorbe, Henrik Schinzel, Toralf Schriner, Lisa Schroeder, Martin Sczendziva, Franz and Gabi Seibold, Jerome Sgard, Daniel Sherr, Tira Shubart, Vlad Sinayuk, Clark Smeltzer, Charlotte Snowden, Erland Sommerskog, Robert E Sonntag, Sebastian Sorge, Paul Stang, Urs Steiger, Patrick Sterckx, Ralph E Stone, Mark and Kathie Sund, Alison Teeman and G Michael Yovino-Young, Andreas Tölke, Arnood Troust and Fenna den Hartog, CA Veerman, Nicole Washburn, JP Watney, Jonathan Weber, Judit Wessel, Rob and Lee Williams, Anne Wilshin, Monty Worth.

Foreword

ABOUT LONELY PLANET GUIDEBOOKS

The story begins with a classic travel adventure: Tony and Maureen Wheeler's 1972 journey across Europe and Asia to Australia. Useful information about the overland trail did not exist at that time, so Tony and Maureen published the first Lonely Planet guidebook to meet a growing need.

From a kitchen table, then from a tiny office in Melbourne (Australia), Lonely Planet has become the largest independent travel publisher in the world, an international company with offices in Melbourne, Oakland (USA), London (UK) and Paris (France).

Today Lonely Planet guidebooks cover the globe. There is an ever-growing list of books and there's information in a variety of forms and media. Some things haven't changed. The main aim is still to help make it possible for adventurous travelers to get out there – to explore and better understand the world.

At Lonely Planet we believe travelers can make a positive contribution to the countries they visit – if they respect their host communities and spend their money wisely. Since 1986 a percentage of the income from each book has been donated to aid projects and human rights campaigns.

Updates Lonely Planet thoroughly updates each guidebook as often as possible. This usually means there are around two years between editions, although for more unusual or more stable destinations the gap can be longer. Check the imprint page (following the color map at the beginning of the book) for publication dates.

Between editions up-to-date information is available in two free newsletters – the paper *Planet Talk* and email *Comet* (to subscribe, contact any Lonely Planet office) – and on our website at www.lonelyplanet.com. The *Upgrades* section of the website covers a number of important and volatile destinations and is regularly updated by Lonely Planet authors. *Scoop* covers news and current affairs relevant to travelers. And, lastly, the *Thorn Tree* bulletin board and *Postcards* section of the site carry unverified, but fascinating, reports from travelers.

Correspondence The process of creating new editions begins with the letters, postcards and emails received from travelers. This correspondence often includes suggestions, criticisms and comments about the current editions. Interesting excerpts are immediately passed on via newsletters and the website, and everything goes to our authors to be verified when they're researching on the road. We're keen to get more feedback from organizations or individuals who represent communities visited by travelers.

Lonely Planet gathers information for everyone who's curious about the planet – and especially for those who explore it firsthand. Through guidebooks, phrasebooks, activity guides, maps, literature, newsletters, image library, TV series and website we act as an information exchange for a worldwide community of travelers.

Research Authors aim to gather sufficient practical information to enable travelers to make informed choices and to make the mechanics of a journey run smoothly. They also research historical and cultural background to help enrich the travel experience and allow travelers to understand and respond appropriately to cultural and environmental issues.

Authors don't stay in every hotel because that would mean spending a couple of months in each medium-sized city and, no, they don't eat at every restaurant because that would mean stretching belts beyond capacity. They do visit hotels and restaurants to check standards and prices, but feedback based on readers' direct experiences can be very helpful.

Many of our authors work undercover, others aren't so secretive. None of them accept freebies in exchange for positive write-ups. And none of our guidebooks contain any advertising.

Production Authors submit their raw manuscripts and maps to offices in Australia, USA, UK or France. Editors and cartographers – all experienced travelers themselves – then begin the process of assembling the pieces. When the book finally hits the shops, some things are already out of date, we start getting feedback from readers and the process begins again…

WARNING & REQUEST

Things change – prices go up, schedules change, good places go bad and bad places go bankrupt – nothing stays the same. So, if you find things better or worse, recently opened or long since closed, please tell us and help make the next edition even more accurate and useful. We genuinely value all the feedback we receive. Julie Young coordinates a well-traveled team that reads and acknowledges every letter, postcard and email and ensures that every morsel of information finds its way to the appropriate authors, editors and cartographers for verification.

Everyone who writes to us will find their name in the next edition of the appropriate guidebook. They will also receive the latest issue of *Planet Talk*, our quarterly printed newsletter, or *Comet*, our monthly email newsletter. Subscriptions to both newsletters are free. The very best contributions will be rewarded with a free guidebook.

Excerpts from your correspondence may appear in new editions of Lonely Planet guidebooks, the Lonely Planet website, *Planet Talk* or *Comet*, so please let us know if you *don't* want your letter published or your name acknowledged.

Send all correspondence to the Lonely Planet office closest to you:

Australia: PO Box 617, Hawthorn, Victoria 3122
USA: 150 Linden St, Oakland, CA 94607
UK: 10A Spring Place, London NW5 3BH
France: 1 rue du Dahomey, 75011 Paris

Or email us at: talk2us@lonelyplanet.com.au

For news, views and updates see our website: www.lonelyplanet.com

HOW TO USE A LONELY PLANET GUIDEBOOK

The best way to use a Lonely Planet guidebook is any way you choose. At Lonely Planet we believe the most memorable travel experiences are often those that are unexpected, and the finest discoveries are those you make yourself. Guidebooks are not intended to be used as if they provide a detailed set of infallible instructions!

Contents All Lonely Planet guidebooks follow the same format. The Facts about the Country chapters or sections give background information ranging from history to weather. Facts for the Visitor gives practical information on issues like visas and health. Getting There & Away gives a brief starting point for researching travel to and from the destination. Getting Around gives an overview of the transport options when you arrive.

The peculiar demands of each destination determine how subsequent chapters are broken up, but some things remain constant. We always start with background, then proceed to sights, places to stay, places to eat, entertainment, getting there and away, and getting around information – in that order.

Heading Hierarchy Lonely Planet headings are used in a strict hierarchical structure that can be visualized as a set of Russian dolls. Each heading (and its following text) is encompassed by any preceding heading that is higher on the hierarchical ladder.

Entry Points We do not assume guidebooks will be read from beginning to end, but that people will dip into them. The traditional entry points are the list of contents and the index. In addition, however, some books have a complete list of maps and an index map illustrating map coverage.

There may also be a color map that shows highlights. These highlights are dealt with in greater detail later in the book, along with planning questions and suggested itineraries. Each chapter covering a geographical region usually begins with a locator map and another list of highlights. Once you find something of interest in a list of highlights, turn to the index.

Maps Maps play a crucial role in Lonely Planet guidebooks and include a huge amount of information. A legend is printed on the back page. We seek to have complete consistency between maps and text, and to have every important place in the text captured on a map. Map key numbers usually start in the top left corner.

Although inclusion in a guidebook usually implies a recommendation we cannot list every good place. Exclusion does not necessarily imply criticism. In fact there are a number of reasons why we might exclude a place – sometimes it is simply inappropriate to encourage an influx of travelers.

Introduction

One of Latin America's great cities, Buenos Aires was arguably once its greatest. The region's first city to have a million inhabitants, the sprawling Argentine metropolis (sometimes known as the 'Paris of the South') is a contradictory place that retains many aspects of the Gran Aldea (Great Village) of the late 19th century in its intimate *barrios* – boroughs or neighborhoods – whose inhabitants rarely move more than a few blocks beyond their place of birth. Among many *porteños*, as inhabitants of this port city are known, there survives a remarkable and reassuring local spirit, encouraging a livability that may provide lessons for troubled cities elsewhere.

Buenos Aires' attractions are manifold. Beyond the bustling downtown, with its theater district and soaring hotels, lie the colonial quarter of San Telmo; the colorful working-class neighborhood of La Boca; the chic barrio of Recoleta with its sumptuous restaurants; the spacious parks and open spaces of Palermo and the riverside Costanera; and the suburban grace of Belgrano. The grandeur of Buenos Aires may now be a little faded, but enough survives to offer the visitor a rich and unique urban experience.

Since the restoration of democracy in 1984, Buenos Aires is once again a lively place despite lingering economic problems. Political and public dialogue are freewheeling, the publishing industry has rebounded, and the arts are flourishing.

Only a few hours outside Buenos Aires are intriguing towns and cities perfect for day trips and weekends away. To the north, porteños head to the waterways of the Delta del Paraná and Tigre to escape the frenetic pace of city life. From Tigre, travelers can hop a ferry to Isla Martín García, a peaceful island offering historic attractions and scenic trails. To the southeast of Buenos Aires the grandiose public buildings of La Plata, the provincial capital, line streets patterned after those of Washington, DC.

Sixty-five km west of Buenos Aires, Luján attracts thousands of pilgrims seeking the intercession of La Virgen, an image housed in a neo-Gothic basilica. Another 50km west lies the gaucho capital of San Antonio de Areco. East of Buenos Aires in Uruguay, Colonia and the capital, Montevideo, are only a short ferry ride across the Río de la Plata.

The sophistication of Buenos Aires and the allure of easy day trips in any direction should keep visitors happily occupied for weeks, or months, on end.

Facts about Buenos Aires

HISTORY
Origins

Buenos Aires dates from 1536, when Spanish explorer Pedro de Mendoza camped on a bluff above the Río de la Plata, possibly at the site of present-day Parque Lezama. Mendoza's oversized expedition of 16 ships and nearly 1600 men – nearly three times the size of Hernán Cortés' forces that conquered the Aztecs – arrived too late in summer to plant crops, and the area's few Querandí Indian hunter-gatherers reacted violently when the Spaniards forced them to provide food. Lacking provisions and facing incessant Querandí opposition, some members of the expedition sailed up the Río Paraná, where they founded the city of Asunción (in present-day Paraguay) among the more sedentary and obliging Guaraní peoples. Within five years, the remaining Spaniards, so short of supplies that some resorted to cannibalism, abandoned Buenos Aires to the Querandí, leaving only the name 'Puerto Nuestra Señora Santa María del Buen Aire' behind.

Nearly four decades passed before an expedition from Asunción, led by Juan de Garay, reestablished Spain's presence on the west bank of the Río de la Plata in 1580. Buenos Aires, at the terminus of a cumbersome supply line stretching from Madrid via Panama and Lima, was clearly subordinate to Asunción. The Spaniards in Buenos Aires survived but did not flourish. Garay himself died at the hands of the Querandí only three years later. Buenos Aires long remained a backwater in comparison to Andean settlements in present-day Argentina such as Tucumán (founded in 1571), Córdoba (1573), Salta (1582), La Rioja (1591) and Jujuy (1593).

Over the next two centuries, Buenos Aires grew slowly but steadily on the basis of the enormous feral herds of cattle and horses that began to proliferate when the first Spaniards abandoned them on the lush pastures of the surrounding Pampas. As local frustration over Spain's mercantile restrictions grew, merchants began to smuggle contraband from Portuguese and British vessels on the river. In 1776 Buenos Aires became capital of the new Virreinato del Río de la Plata (Viceroyalty of the River Plate), which included the famous silver district of Potosí (in present-day Bolivia). For many of its residents, the new status as a capital was palpable recognition that the adolescent city was outgrowing Spain's parental authority.

British invasions in 1806 and 1807 were a major turning point in late colonial times. Forces of *criollos* (American-born Spaniards) feigned cooperation with British forces occupying Buenos Aires, and then repelled them. Only three years later, on May 25, 1810, influential criollos confronted and deposed the viceroy, on the pretext that Spain's legitimate government had fallen. As described by American diplomat Caesar Rodney, the architects of the revolution and the people of the city showed remarkable restraint and maturity:

At some periods of the revolution, when the bands of authority were relaxed, the administration actually devolved into the hands of the inhabitants of the city. Hence, it might have been imagined, endless tumult and disorder would have sprung up, leading directly to pillage and bloodshed. Yet no such disturbances ever took place; all remained quiet ...The people have in no instance demanded victims to satisfy their vengeance; on the contrary, they have sometimes, by the influence of public opinion, moderated the rigor with which their rulers were disposed to punish the guilty.

Growth & Independence

Six years later, on July 9, 1816, in the northern Argentina city of Tucumán, outlying areas of the viceroyalty declared independence from Spain and founded the Provincias Unidas del Río de la Plata (United Provinces of the River Plate), Argentina's direct forerunner. The young union, however, failed to resolve the conflict between two elite sectors: 'Federalist' landowners of the interior provinces, who were concerned with preserving their autonomy and economic privileges, and the 'Unitarist' *porteños* (residents of Buenos Aires, literally 'residents of the port') who maintained an outward orientation toward overseas commerce and European ideas.

After more than a decade of violence and uncertainty, Federalist *caudillo* (provincial strongman) Juan Manuel de Rosas finally asserted authority over Buenos Aires when he became governor of the province in 1829.

When Charles Darwin visited Buenos Aires in 1833, shortly after the ruthless Rosas took power, he was impressed that the city of 60,000 was

large; and I should think one of the most regular in the world. Every street is at right angles to the one it crosses, and the parallel ones being equidistant, the houses are collected into solid squares of equal dimensions, which are called quadras. On the other hand the houses themselves are hollow squares; all the rooms opening into a neat little courtyard. They are generally only one story high, with flat roofs, which are fitted with seats, and are much frequented by the inhabitants in summer. In the center of the town is the Plaza, where the public offices, fortress, cathedral, &c., stand. Here also, the old viceroys, before the revolution had their palaces. The general assemblage of buildings possesses considerable architectural beauty, although none individually can boast of any.

Rosas' reign lasted 23 years during which time Buenos Aires' influence grew despite his (perhaps opportunistic) Federalist convictions. He required all overseas trade to be funneled through the port city, rather than proceeding directly to the provinces, and set ominous political precedents, creating the *mazorca* (his ruthless political police) and institutionalizing torture.

The Roots of Modern Argentina

Rosas' overthrow in 1852 ushered in a new era of Argentine development, resulting in the Constitution of 1853 (still in force today despite frequent suspension), and opening the city to European immigration. The population grew from 90,000 in 1854 to 177,000 in 1869 to 670,000 by 1895. By the turn of the century, Latin America's largest city boasted more than a million inhabitants.

By the end of the 1850s, Buenos Aires had become the de facto seat of government after the defeat of a rival government in Entre Ríos province. In the 1880s, when the city became the official federal capital, the indignant authorities of Buenos Aires province moved their government to a new provincial capital at La Plata. Still, as agricultural exports boomed and imports flowed into the country, the port city became even more important. In the words of British diplomat James Bryce, none of the leaders of Glasgow, Manchester or Chicago 'shewed greater enterprise and bolder conceptions than did the men of Buenos Aires when on this exposed and shallow coast they made alongside their city a great ocean harbour.'

Physical development of the port area east of Plaza de Mayo was, however, a controversial and corruption-plagued enterprise that reinforced the power of downtown commercial interests at the expense of the traditional port areas of Barracas and La Boca. Immigration and growth brought serious social problems too, as families crowded into substandard housing, merchants and manufacturers suppressed wages, and labor became increasingly militant.

The establishment of universal male suffrage, under the 1912 Sáenz Peña law, altered the balance of political power, giving the new Unión Cívica Radical (UCR) political party a foothold in the government. In 1919, under pressure from landowners and other elite sectors, the Radical government of President Hipólito Yrigoyen ordered the army to suppress a metalworkers' strike in what became known as La Semana Trágica (the Tragic Week), setting an unfortunate precedent for the coming decades.

In the 1930s, ambitious municipal administrations undertook a massive downtown modernization program, obliterating many of Buenos Aires' narrow colonial streets to make way for broad avenues like Santa Fe, Córdoba and Corrientes.

The Peróns & the Post-War Capital

After WWII, the rise of Lieutenant-General Juán Perón, who used an obscure post in the Labor Ministry as a power base, and his glamorous, ambitious mistress (soon-to-be-wife) Eva Duarte, a onetime radio soap opera star, earned Buenos Aires international fame (or notoriety). Borrowing freely from Nazi Germany and Fascist Italy in their use of public spectacle, the Peróns created a populist movement known formally as 'Justicialism.' Known more enduringly as 'Peronism,' it appealed to underrepresented sectors of society, particularly labor unions (whose General Confederation of Labor, or CGT, soon became one of Argentina's most powerful – and corrupt – institutions) and women, who finally obtained the vote in 1947.

Eva Perón

Elected president in 1946 and re-elected in 1952, Juan Perón, along with 'Evita,' reshaped the country and the city in many ways. The Plaza de Mayo, always the center of the urban life, became the focus of countless, vociferous pro-Perón demonstrations that terrified the traditional oligarchy and the middle classes. Until her death from cancer in 1952, Evita's powerful but unaccountable Fundación de Ayuda Social (Social Assistance Foundation, later renamed the Fundación Eva Perón), promoted the construction of schools, hospitals and other important public projects, using them as a means to expand Peronist political influence.

Peronist rule left a visible impact on the cityscape through monumental architecture like the Fundación's headquarters, now the Facultad de Ingeniería (Engineering School), described by English writer Gerald Durrell as 'a cross between the Parthenon and the Reichstag.' Another impact – literally – was created by bullets that struck the Economy Ministry and other downtown buildings when the military overthrew Perón in 1955, midway through his second term. Returning from exile in 1973, an ailing Perón won a third term but died less than a year later.

During and after Perón's rise, sprawling Gran Buenos Aires (Greater Buenos Aires) grew rapidly through spreading shantytowns, absorbing many once-distant suburbs. Though long surpassed in population by Mexico City and São Paulo, the capital remains Argentina's dominant economic, political and cultural center, home to nearly a third of the country's population.

Like the rest of the country, Buenos Aires suffered during the succession of military coups and dictatorships that culminated with the so-called Proceso de Reorganización Nacional of 1976-83. Ostensibly an effort to remake Argentina's political culture and modernize the economy, the Proceso was in practice an exercise in state terrorism against political dissidents. It resulted in at least 30,000 deaths and 'disappearances' during the Guerra Sucia (Dirty War). The horrors of the Proceso finally came to international attention thanks to the efforts of individuals like Nobel Peace Prize winner Adolfo Pérez Esquivel and groups like the Madres de la Plaza de Mayo, who marched in front of the presidential palace weekly demanding information on their 'disappeared' children. The Dirty War ended only after a desperate military, seeking to divert public attention from the Proceso's failures, undertook a foolhardy and unsuccessful invasion of the British-governed Falkland Islands (claimed by Argentina since 1833) in 1982.

Widespread corruption during the Proceso resulted in massive public works projects, many of them never completed, whose funding often found its way to the Swiss bank accounts of officials who solicited development loans from international agencies. At the same time, the dictatorship neglected the capital's physical and social problems, so that a city that once prided itself on European sophistication and living standards now shares the same dilemmas as other Latin American megacities – pollution, noise, decaying infrastructure and declining public services, unemployment and underemployment, and spreading shantytowns.

State of the City

Not all signs are negative, though. President Carlos Menem's economic reforms have improved communications and other services through privatization, though at very high cost. The Menem administration has also reduced a bloated public sector and devised an effective tax collection system to support public services, and certain sectors of the economy, most notably finance and services, are prospering. While nationwide unemployment may be high, around 14%, it is notably lower in the capital.

Recent constitutional reforms have given the city representative self-government, through an elected mayor and city council, for the first time. The privatized subway system has expanded and improved service after decades of neglect. Certain neighborhoods have seen changes for the better, such as the once abandoned Puerto Madero complex on the waterfront, now undergoing redevelopment for upscale lofts, offices, restaurants, a yacht harbor and open space. The country's continuing economic difficulties make the future unpredictable, but Buenos Aires remains a vibrant combination of international capital, with all the cultural diversity that implies, and traditional barrio life.

GEOGRAPHY

At the continental edge of Argentina's Pampas heartland, an almost completely level plain of wind-borne loess and river-deposited sediments once covered by lush native grasses and now occupied by grain farms and ranches, low-lying Buenos Aires sprawls along the west bank of the Río de la Plata, which discharges its thick sediments here and far out into the South Atlantic

Ocean. The city's highest elevation is only 25m, and much of it is barely above sea level.

Politically, in addition to the Capital Federal, Gran Buenos Aires encompasses the partidos of Almirante Brown, Avellaneda, Berazategui, Estéban Echeverría, Florencio Varela, General San Martín, General Sarmiento, La Matanza, Lanús, Lomas de Zamora, Merlo, Moreno, Morón, Quilmes, San Fernando, San Isidro, Tigre, Tres de Febrero and Vicente López.

CLIMATE

Buenos Aires' climate is humid, with an annual rainfall of 900mm spread evenly throughout the year. The changeable spring, hot summer and mild autumn resemble New York City's seasons, but winter temperatures are moderated by the South Atlantic, and – for city with a relatively low latitude (34° 37′ S) – are more comparable to Los Angeles, Sydney or Cape Town. Frosts are rare – the lowest temperature ever recorded is -5.4°C (22.3°F) – while snow has fallen only once this century, in 1918. It's unlikely to fall again, much less stick, because of the heat generated by the densely built city.

The hottest temperature ever recorded was 43.3°C (109.9°F), but much lower temperatures can seem oppressive when humidity is high. Occasional *pamperos* (cold fronts from the southwest) can lower the ambient

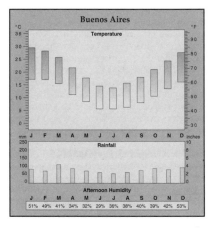

temperature dramatically. From the other direction, occasional *sudestada* (southeasterly) combines with high tides and heavy runoff in the estuary of the Río de la Plata, flooding low-lying neighborhoods like La Boca.

ECOLOGY & ENVIRONMENT

Buenos Aires' dense concentration of population and industry in a very small area has caused serious environmental problems. The most noticeable example is the visible contamination of waterways like the Riachuelo in the barrio of La Boca, but the concentration of industrial chemicals and heavy metals in the sediments beneath the surface is even more serious than floating oil slicks. Supposedly, the Riachuelo is the Carlos Menem administration's number one environmental priority, but nobody takes environment secretary María Julia Alsogaray's pledge, to swim in the river when the cleanup finally ends, seriously.

Diesel-spewing buses, fleets of taxis and countless private vehicles have the usual impact on air quality, though frequent rains clear the air with some regularity. One real plague is the seemingly infinite number of feral cats dumped into virtually any green space and fed by bag ladies. Schools, for instance, must post signs asking people not to abandon cats on their property. The impact on songbirds around the city is obvious.

Like other world megacities, Buenos Aires long ago outgrew local energy resources; despite Argentina's self-sufficiency in petroleum and abundant (if sometimes remote) hydroelectric capacity, Argentine governments have promoted nuclear power since 1950. The 344Mw Atucha I reactor near Buenos Aires has supplied energy to the capital since 1974, but it operated at only half-capacity through the 1980s because cheaper hydroelectricity made nuclear power less competitive.

GOVERNMENT & POLITICS

It is difficult to separate Buenos Aires politics from Argentine politics at large because most national and local government institutions – not to mention economic and financial actors – reside here. Even most porteños

admit that the concentration of political and economical power in the capital is undesirable, while many residents in the provinces (especially from important cities like Córdoba and Rosario) vigorously oppose the capital's primacy.

Even so, when the Radical government of President Raúl Alfonsín proposed moving the seat of government to the small northern Patagonian city of Viedma in Río Negro province in the 1980s, powerful opposition forced him to abandon the plan. Though the project probably would have been at least as costly and no more successful than Brazil's attempt to reduce the influence of Rio de Janeiro and São Paulo by creating Brasilia in 1960, Alfonsín's failure vividly illustrated Buenos Aires' persistent dominance.

Like Washington, DC, and Mexico City, Buenos Aires is a federal district administratively distinct from Argentina's other 23 provinces. (Unlike Washington, DC, however, Buenos Aires enjoys voting representation in the Argentine congress). Traditionally, the country's president appointed the mayor, but constitutional reform in 1996 permitted Fernando de la Rúa, of the Radical party (a middle-class party with a misleading name), to become the city's first mayor elected by majority vote. By virtue of his influential position, De la Rúa is a leading opposition presidential candidate for 1999.

The 1996 reforms also replaced the corruption-ridden Concejo Deliberante (city council) with a 60-member Poder Legislativo (legislature), elected by proportional representation for four-year terms, with the possibility of re-election for an additional term. Half the seats are up for election every two years. After completing two consecutive terms, neither the mayor nor any legislator may run for the same office again until four years have elapsed.

In late 1998, the Poder Legislativo's Alianza majority consisted of 19 Radicals and 18 members of the left-leaning Frepaso (Frente de Pais Solidario; including many ex-Peronists). The remaining legislators included 11 Peronists, 11 ex-Peronists belonging to Gustavo Béliz's Nueva Dirigencia (New Leadership; a repudiation of Peronist corruption), and a single member of the Bloque Porteño (Porteño Block).

The reform of municipal government has not been free from conflict. The Alianza (Alliance; a coalition of the Radical and Frepaso parties), wrested control of the city from the Peronists in the 1996 elections, then cut back the number of *ñoquis* (ghost employees) appointed under the Peronist administration. (Ñoquis employees are named after the potato pasta traditionally served in Argentine homes on the 29th of each month, implying the employees show up at work once a month – to pick up their paychecks.) The Peronists, in turn, accused the Alianza of arbitrary dismissals and subsequent replacement of discharged employees by political cronies.

The new legislature has nevertheless undertaken bold but controversial reforms, such as decriminalizing prostitution and public drunkenness in order to curb police abuses such as bribery and brutality. At the same time, offenses like desecration of tombs, soccer hooliganism and firearms violations will be taken more seriously. Still, the corrupt justice system will need more than just paper reforms.

ECONOMY

A character in Osvaldo Soriano's novel *Shadows* relates the tale of a relative who found an unusable 'treasure' of 10 billion old pesos in the mountains of Córdoba, who remarks that 'a country where finding a fortune is a waste of time isn't a serious country.' Indeed, Argentina's inability to achieve its potential – despite its abundant natural resources and highly literate and sophisticated population – has mystified outside observers for decades. Burdened with a monstrous foreign debt that is unlikely ever to be repaid, its middle class is shrinking, while the working class and the poor have little hope of advancement. Despite the recent stability of the Menem administration, it is difficult to find any Argentine truly optimistic about the country's future.

With a per capita GDP of nearly US$8900 (a misleading figure because of an overvalued peso and unequal income distribution),

When Carlos Menem's presidency ends in 1999, many Argentines fear the stability he helped build may end as well.

Argentina is one of Latin America's wealthiest countries. Its modern economic history, however, has been one of astronomical inflation amid corruption and perpetual chaos.

Lieutenant-General Juan Perón's rise to power after WWII demonstrated that the export-oriented rural economy was too one-dimensional for broader prosperity: Argentina needed to develop its industrial base and workers needed to share in the development. At the time, there was little alternative to state involvement in industry, given the national budget surplus and the impossibility of capital infusions from war-ravaged Europe. Over succeeding decades, however, the state's dominance in the economy outlived its usefulness. Many state enterprises became havens for corruption, including the proliferation of 'ñoquis,' or ghost employees, under the Perón administration.

Ñoquis contributed to inflation rates often exceeding 50% per month (the government turned on printing presses for money to pay government employees). The Peronist Menem administration has been able to break the inflationary spiral over the past several years by reducing public sector employment, selling off inefficient state enterprises and restricting labor union activities. The key measure, however, was former economy minister Domingo Cavallo's 'convertibility' law, which pegged the peso at parity with the US dollar, in effect establishing a gold standard. The government could print no more pesos than represented by hard currency reserves. Persistently low inflation figures since the policy came into effect in 1991 reflect the success of Cavallo's policies, continued by his successor, Roque Fernández.

The selling off of state assets like Aerolíneas Argentinas, the state petroleum enterprise YPF and the phone company ENTel was a one-time bonanza that reduced or eliminated short-term budget deficits. Increased productivity and a more efficient tax system will have to be the keys to economic prosperity in the future. The legacy of state domination has fostered a large informal sector that operates parallel to the official economy in providing goods and services. One study claimed that only 40% of Argentina's workers functioned in the 'official' economy; the remainder labored independently, were often paid in cash and avoided taxes entirely.

The reduction of the state sector created other costs that often do not fit into conventional accounting systems. In April 1995, for instance, the privatized YPF dumped waste oil into the Río de la Plata near Buenos Aires' popular Reserva Ecológica Costanera Sur, on the rationale that they 'had to get rid of the waste somehow and this looked like the only solution.' Although a state-controlled YPF might not have done things any differently, this intentional discharge also came at a time when the company had contracted to clean up the area's waters.

Whether Menem and Cavallo's 'rationalization' of the Argentine economy will bring lasting success is uncertain, but many similar measures in the recent past have failed. One side effect of privatization is increasing unemployment, which the government sees as an essential structural adjustment but which ordinary people worry may be a more enduring problem. In mid-1995, official unemployment figures in Argentina hit 12.2%, with a probable undercount in rural areas, then rose to nearly 20% as the economy slowed down in the aftermath of President Menem's re-election. By late 1997, unemployment dropped to about 13%, but even the government admitted that many of these new jobs were temporary, earning modest wages. The legal monthly minimum salary is only about US$200 in a country where living expenses are not much lower than in Europe or North America.

The economy of the Capital Federal remains largely administrative and financial, supporting the export-oriented rural economy. The city is also the country's major entrepôt for imports and exports, leading to grandiose and controversial plans for a new integrated rail, road, sea and air 'omniport' to be built on the landfill opposite the current port. There is a large service-oriented sector as well, but the industrial suburbs of Gran Buenos Aires, such as Avellaneda, are the primary sites of blue-collar jobs.

The tourist trade is a major contributor to Buenos Aires' relative prosperity, keeping unemployment and underemployment considerably lower than in the provinces. In 1996, the city received more than 10 million foreign tourists, nearly a million of them Europeans and North Americans; in the summer of 1997-98 alone, 2.5 million tourists spent nearly US$900 million. Nearly 200,000 came from overseas, another 500,000 from neighboring countries and the remainder from within Argentina.

POPULATION & PEOPLE

According to the 1991 census, 8.3 million people, more than a quarter of Argentina's 32.3 million people, reside in Gran Buenos Aires, which includes the densely populated Capital Federal (with a population of more than three million) and contiguous suburbs in Buenos Aires province. Beginning in the mid-19th century, a trickle of European immigrants became a flood, as Italians, Basques, Welsh, English, Ukrainians and immigrants of other nationalities inundated Buenos Aires, just as they did New York. Italian surnames are still more common than Spanish ones, though Italo-Argentines do not constitute a cohesive, distinctive group in the way that Italian-Americans do in many North American cities.

Some immigrant groups, most notably Anglo-Argentines throughout the country, have retained a distinctive cultural identity.

Buenos Aires' flourishing Jewish community of about 400,000, the world's eighth-largest, drew international attention in the wake of the 1992 bombing of the Israeli embassy, which killed 29 people, and the 1994 bombing of the Asociación Mutua Israelita Argentina (AMIA), which leveled the Jewish cultural center, killing 87 people.

Middle Eastern immigrants, though not so numerous, have political influence disproportional to their numbers. Their most prominent figure is President Carlos Menem, of Syrian ancestry. Argentines refer indiscriminately to anyone of Middle Eastern ancestry (except Jews or Israelis) as a *turco* (Turk), sometimes, but not always, with racist connotations.

Non-European immigrants have generally not been welcome in Argentina, and despite major upheavals in Asia the over past decade, only a relative handful of immigrants from that region have entered the country. There is a conspicuous Japanese community in the suburb of Escobar and a small 'Chinatown' in Belgrano, where scores of Chinese restaurants have opened in the past decade. The Korean surname Kim fills nearly a page in the Buenos Aires telephone directory; 'Coreatown' is around Av Cobo in the southern barrio of Nueva Pompeya.

Some 18,000 Bolivian highlanders have come to Buenos Aires over the past decade; most work in the construction industry and live around Nueva Pompeya's Av Fernández de la Cruz. About 29,000 Paraguayans, 40,000 Peruvians and 40,000 Uruguayans also reside permanently in Argentina. Buenos Aires also has a small and barely visible population of urban Indians, most from the Andean Northwest and from Patagonia.

ARTS

In the 19th and early 20th century, Buenos Aires self-consciously emulated French cultural trends in art, music and architecture, thereby earning its nickname the 'Paris of the South.' Many Argentine intellectuals and artists have been educated in European capitals, particularly Paris, and several performers have made their mark outside the country's borders.

Music & Dance

Music and dance are difficult to separate in Buenos Aires. The palatial Teatro Colón, home to the Buenos Aires opera, is one of the finest facilities of its kind in the world. Classical music and ballet, as well as modern dance, appear here and at similar venues like the Teatro Avenida.

Tango Probably the best known manifestation of Argentine popular culture is the tango, both as music and dance. Important figures like the legendary Carlos Gardel, the late Julio Sosa and Astor Piazzola, and contemporaries like Susana Rinaldi, Eladia Blásquez and Osvaldo Pugliese have brought tango to the world. Tango is constantly on the radio (particularly on the 24-hour, all-tango station, FM Tango 92.7), tops the bill at the capital's finest nightclubs and can even be heard in the streets. (For more on the history of tango, see Gardel & The Tango.)

Tango enthusiasts can ask for a free sample copy of the monthly newsletter *El Firulete* (☎ 408-720-9506, fax 732-2690, tangoman@hooked.net), 1111 W El Camino Real, Suite 109, Sunnyvale, CA 94087 USA.

Jazz Internationally, Argentina's best known jazz musician is probably Rosario-born saxophonist Gato Barbieri, though he rarely plays in Buenos Aires. Nevertheless, there are many jazz venues in the city, mostly in the Microcentro and San Telmo (see the Entertainment chapter).

Best known for his Hollywood soundtracks, porteño composer and pianist Lalo Schifrin moved to the United States in the 1950s to play with jazz legends like Dizzy Gillespie and Eric Dolphy.

Folk Music The late Atahualpa Yupanqui was a giant of Argentine folk music, which takes much of its inspiration from the northwestern Andean region and countries to the north, especially Bolivia and Peru. Los Chalchaleros, a northern Argentine folk institution, recently celebrated their 50th anniversary.

Gardel & the Tango

In June 1935, a Cuban woman committed suicide in Havana, while a woman in New York and another in Puerto Rico tried to poison themselves, all over the same man – whom none of them had ever met. The man, whose smiling photograph graced their rooms, had just died in a plane crash in Medellín, Colombia. On his body's long odyssey to its final resting place in Argentina, Latin Americans thronged to pay him tribute in Colombia, New York, Rio de Janeiro and Montevideo. Once in Buenos Aires, his body lay in state at Luna Park stadium before a horse-drawn carriage took him to the Cementerio de la Chacarita (Map 4). The man was tango singer Carlos Gardel, *El Zorzal Criollo*, the songbird of Buenos Aires.

Carlos Gardel

Tango originated around 1880, only a decade before Gardel's birth. It was considered the vulgar dance and music of the capital's *arrabales* (fringes), blending gaucho verse with Spanish and Italian music. Gardel created the *tango canción*, the tango-song, taking it out of Buenos Aires' brothels and tenements to New York and Paris. Only after Gardel had won over audiences in North America and Europe did the Argentine elite deign to allow it into their salons.

It was no accident that the tango grew to popularity when it did. In the late 19th century, the Gran Aldea (Great Village) of Buenos Aires was becoming an immigrant city where frustrated and melancholy Europeans displaced gaucho rustics, who retreated gradually to the ever more distant countryside. The children of those immigrants became the family's first generation of porteños, and the tango-song summarized their new urban experience.

Permeated with nostalgia for a disappearing way of life, the melancholy tango-song expressed the anxieties of individuals. Its themes ranged from mundane pastimes like horse racing to more profound feelings about the changing landscape of neighborhood, the figure of the mother, betrayal by women, and friendship. English musician Robert Fripp has compared the relationship between Argentines and tango to that of North Americans and the blues.

The inevitable transformations of La Boca's Caminito *peatonal* (pedestrian mall) mirrored the changes in Gardel's own life:

Caminito que entonces estabas	Caminito of what you once were
bordeado de trébol y juncos en flor	bordered by clover and flowering rushes
una sombra ya pronto serás	a shadow you soon will be
una sombra, lo mismo que yo . . .	a shadow just like me . . .

Though born in France, Gardel came to epitomize the porteño. When he was three, his destitute, single mother brought him to Buenos Aires, where he passed his formative years in a neighborhood near the Mercado de Abasto – a produce market near a Subte (underground) station now named after Gardel. In his youth, he worked at a variety of menial jobs but also entertained neighbors with his singing. His performing career began after he befriended Uruguayan-born José Razzano. They formed the popular duo Gardel-Razzano, which lasted until Razzano lost his voice.

From 1917 onward, Gardel performed solo. His voice and charisma made him an immediate success in Argentina and other Latin American countries, although the Argentine elite still despised the music and what it stood for: the rise of a middle class that challenged its monopoly on power. Building on this popularity, Gardel sang regularly on the radio and soon became a recording star. To broaden his appeal, he traveled to Spain and France, where widespread acceptance finally made him palatable even to the elite sectors of Argentine society, which once were scandalized by the tango's humble origins and open sensuality. Later he began a film career that was cut short by his death.

Gardel's untimely death rescued him from aging, allowing his iconic figure to dominate Argentine popular culture. One measure of his immortality is the common saying that 'Gardel sings better every day.'

Photographs of Gardel, with his unmistakable smile, can be seen throughout Argentina. (One photo lab in Buenos Aires sold more than 350,000 pictures in the first two decades after his death.) The large, devoted community of his followers, known as *gardelianos*, cannot pass a day without listening to his songs or watching his films.

Daily, a steady procession of pilgrims visit his plaque-covered tomb in the Cementerio de la Chacarita where, often, a lighted cigarette rests in the hand of his life-size statue. On December 11, 1990, the centenary of his birth, it was smothered in floral tributes.

For an excellent account of Gardel's life in English, get Simon Collier's *The Life, Music and Times of Carlos Gardel*, a serious biography that refrains from the most romantic exaggerations of the singer's fanatical devotees.

Folk singer Mercedes Sosa

Other contemporary performers include Mercedes Sosa of Tucumán (probably the best known Argentine folk artist outside South America), Suna Rocha (also an actress) of Córdoba, Antonio Tarragó Ross, León Gieco (modern enough to adopt and adapt a rap style at times) and the Conjunto Pro Música de Rosario.

Rock & Pop Rock musicians such as Charly García (formerly a member of the pioneering group Sui Generis) and Fito Páez (dismissed by some as excessively commercial) are national icons. García's version of the Argentine national anthem does what Jimi Hendrix did for 'The Star-Spangled Banner,' but it earned him a court appearance for allegedly lacking 'respect for national symbols.' When a judge dismissed the lawsuit, the *Buenos Aires Herald* celebrated García's defense as a victory over 'extremist nationalist sectors' which had too long 'imposed their warped and often authoritarian views on the rest of society.'

The band Les Luthiers satirize those nationalist sectors, primarily in the middle class or military, with irreverent songs played with unusual instruments, many of which the band built from scratch.

Other performers are more conventional and derivative, but before you report an Elvis sighting in Buenos Aires, make sure it isn't Sandro, a living Argentine clone of the King. The advent of Sandro impersonators in the raucous *boliches* (nightclubs) of La Boca may be sending a message to Sandro, known to his devotees as 'El Maestro.'

Popular Argentine groups playing 'rock nacional' include the recently defunct Soda Stereo, Los Divididos (descendants of an earlier group known as Sumo), the wildly unconventional Babasónicos, Patricio Rey y Sus Redonditos de Ricota and Los Ratones Paranóicos, who in 1995 opened for the Rolling Stones' spectacularly successful five-night stand in Buenos Aires. (One of the Ratones' albums was produced by early Stones associate Andrew Loog Oldham.) Also on the bill with the Stones were Las Pelotas and local blues artist Pappo.

Los Fabulosos Cadillacs (winners of a Grammy in 1998 for best alternative Latin rock group and a favorite crossover act among Anglophone audiences) have popularized ska and reggae, along with groups like Los Auténticos Decadentes, Los Pericos, Los Cafres and Espías Secretos. Almafuerte, descended from the earlier Hermética, is Buenos Aires' leading (but surprisingly literate) heavy metal band. Actitud María Marta is a young but politically conscious rap group whose songs are about the children of the Disappeared during the Dirty War and other controversial topics.

Porteño blues band Memphis La Blusera, a credible live act, has worked with North American legend Taj Mahal. (The current fashionability of blues in Buenos Aires perhaps adds a new dimension to the old question 'Can blue men sing the whites?') Las Blacanblus is a female vocal ensemble doing humorous, nearly a-cappella-style versions of blues standards.

Singer Patricia Sosa's closest counterparts in the English-speaking world would be Janis Joplin or, perhaps, Melissa Etheridge. The appropriately named Dos Minutos emulate punk-rock legends Ramones, who themselves played Buenos Aires several times.

Painting

Like much of Argentine culture, the visual arts express a tension between European derivative and criollo originality. The European influence has been so powerful that porteño art critic Jorge Glusberg argued that the 'colonial period' in Argentine art lasted into the mid-20th century, severed only by the outbreak of WWII. Nevertheless, there exists a thriving alternative and unconventional art scene, only grudgingly acknowledged (if at all) by the arbiters of official taste, who tend to be middle class and conservative. Many of the most innovative artists must go abroad – usually to Europe or North America – to make a living.

Early Argentine painting can pride itself on figures like self-taught Cándido López. This 19th-century military officer lost his right hand in the war against Paraguay but rehabilitated himself well enough to paint more than 50 extraordinary and historiographically valuable oils on the conflict. The many Argentine artists who studied in France or Italy produced work with European themes, but some local manifestations of their work are more memorable, such as the restored ceiling murals of Antonio Berni, Lino Spilimbergo and others in the Galerías Pacífico shopping center on Florida in the Microcentro. The late Benito Quinquela Martín, who put the working-class barrio of La Boca on the artistic map, painted brightly colored oils of life in the factories and on the waterfront.

Contemporary painting has eschewed the romantic without abandoning its regard for the countryside. Tucumán-born Víctor Hugo Quiroga's paintings, for instance, deal with provincial rather than porteño themes, but they successfully reflect the impact of modern global developments on criollo life. Porteño painter Guillermo Kuitca makes an imaginative use of cartographic images by integrating them with events like the genocide of European Jews in works like Kristallnacht II. Graciela Sacco is a multimedia artist who incorporates audio and video narratives into her arrangements of ready-made objects like plastic spoons and bar codes.

Contemporary Argentine art has gained recognition in international markets. Berni's 1954 painting Juanito Laguna bañándose entre latas (Juanito Laguna washing amongst the trash), a protest against social and economic inequality, sold in New York for US$150,000 in 1997. Another Berni painting, Emigrantes, sold for US$500,000 in 1996.

For an up-to-date listing of events, get the monthly newsletter Arte al Día at galleries and museums throughout the city. (See the Shopping chapter for a list of suggested art galleries; see Books in the Facts for the Visitor chapter for books on Argentine art.)

Sculpture

Given its French origins, official public art tends toward hero worship and the pompously monumental, expressed through equestrian statues of military figures like José de San Martín, Justo José Urquiza and Julio Argentino Roca. A welcome exception is the work of the late Rogelio Yrurtia, some of whose works deal sympathetically with the struggles and achievements of working people. (See his Canto al Trabajo on the Plazoleta Olazábal on Av Paseo Colón at Av Independencia in San Telmo; Map 8.)

An even stronger counterpoint to nationalist idolatry are modern works by individuals like sculptor Alberto Heredia, whose pieces ridicule the solemnity of official public art and even figures like national icon José de San Martín. Heredia's powerful and controversial statue El Caballero de la Máscara depicts a 19th-century caudillo as a headless horseman. During the military dictatorship of 1976-83, this sculpture could not be exhibited under its original title El Montonero, which authorities thought implied associations with guerrilla forces that had nothing to do with the artist's theme. Heredia has also dealt with environmental issues in works like the ghostly Chernobyl.

Another overtly political sculptor is Juan Carlos Distéfano, whose disconcerting El Rey y La Reina (The King and the

Queen) shows two figures shot to death in the front seat of an automobile; it actually appeared in a downtown gallery on Florida during the dictatorship. For comic relief, the surrealistic junk sculptures of Yoël Novoa appeal to audiences of almost any age or political persuasion.

Folk Art

Visitors should not overlook the often anonymous folk art in the streets – even political graffiti can be remarkably elaborate and eloquent. Of particular interest is *filete*, the ornamental line painting that once graced the capital's horsecarts, trucks and buses (see Filete & Its Future in the Shopping chapter).

Architecture

Buenos Aires' reputation as the 'Paris of the South' would lead travelers to expect European styles, and in fact many of the capital's turn-of-the-century buildings would not be out of place across the Atlantic in Europe. There may even be a better representation of early 20th-century Western European styles here than in many parts of Europe, since the latter suffered the devastation of WWII. (Buenos Aires, by contrast, suffers from erosion through economic decline.) Many public buildings, like the landmark Palacio de las Aguas Corrientes on Av Córdoba (Map 6), are remarkable examples of a European style that, despite features like French mansard (two-tier) roofs, seems appropriate here. Others, however, such as the Biblioteca Nacional in Palermo, are pharaonic monuments to the corruption and excesses of military dictatorships.

Buenos Aires retains a sample of valuable colonial and post-independence architecture in the barrio of San Telmo, one of the city's best walking areas. There is also a wide variety of vernacular architecture. San Telmo is famous for its *casas chorizos* (sausage houses) – so-called for their long, narrow shape (some have a 2m frontage on the street) – while the barrio of La Boca derives much of its unique personality from its brightly painted corrugated-metal dwellings.

(See Books in the Facts for the Visitor chapter for a guide to the capital's architecture.)

Literature

Primarily porteños, Argentine writers of international stature include Jorge Luis Borges, Julio Cortázar, Ernesto Sábato, Manuel Puig, Osvaldo Soriano, Adolfo Bioy Casares, and Victoria Ocampo. Many of their works are available in English. Publication dates given here are for Spanish-language originals unless otherwise indicated.

By far the country's most famous literary figure is Borges, best known for his short stories though he was also a poet. His material often deals with simple, everyday porteño and rural life, but his erudite language and references sometimes makes his work inaccessible to readers without a solid background of the classics. British author James Woodall recently analyzed (in almost every sense of the word) Argentina's most famous writer in *Borges: a Life*, originally published in Britain under the title *The Man in the Mirror of the Book*.

Sábato's *On Heroes and Tombs* (1961), a psychological novel that explores people and places in Buenos Aires, has remained a cult favorite among Argentine youth. Also try *The Tunnel* (1950), Sábato's engrossing novella of a porteño painter so obsessed with his art that it distorts his relationship to everything and everyone else.

Cortázar was a Parisian expatriate for most of his life but emphasized clear Argentine characters in novels like the experimentally structured *Hopscotch* (1963) and *62: A Model Kit* (1968). The landmark 1960s film *Blow-Up* was based on his short story of the same name.

Puig's novels, including *Kiss of the Spider Woman, The Buenos Aires Affair* (1968) and *Betrayed by Rita Hayworth* (1968), focus on the ambiguous role of popular culture in Argentina. His *Pubis Angelical* (1986), merges contemporary Argentine sexual politics and science fiction.

Bioy Casares' hallucinatory novella *The Invention of Morel* (1985) deals with an inability or unwillingness to distinguish between fantasy and reality; it was a partial inspiration for the highly praised film *Man Facing Southeast*. His *Diary of the War of the Pig* (1972) is also available in translation.

The late Soriano, perhaps Argentina's most popular contemporary novelist, wrote *A Funny Dirty Little War*, later adapted into a film, and *Winter Quarters* (1989). In Soriano's *Shadows* (1993), the English translation of *Una Sombra Ya Pronto Serás* (whose title is the lyric of a popular tango), the protagonist is lost in an Argentina where the names are the same, but all the familiar landmarks and points of reference have lost their meaning. The story was later made into a film.

Buenos Aires Herald editor Andrew Graham-Yooll recently made a foray into fiction with his novel *Goodbye Buenos Aires* (1997) which, despite its title, is at present available in Spanish only. (An English version is making the rounds of publishers in London and New York.)

Far fewer women writers have appeared in English translation than their male counterparts, but Doris Meyer's biography *Victoria Ocampo: Against the Wind and the Tide* (1990) contains a selection of Ocampo's essays for English readers. Borges edited many issues of Ocampo's literary magazine *Sur*, which was a beacon for Spanish-language writers in the first half of the century and also proved influential among writers in other languages, including England's Bloomsbury group.

A guide to Buenos Aires bookshops appears in the Shopping chapter.

Film

Despite the limited budgets available to directors, Argentine cinema has achieved international stature, especially since the end of the military dictatorship of 1976-83. Many Argentine films, made both before and after the Dirty War, are available on video.

María Luisa Bemberg, one of Argentina's best-known contemporary directors, died of cancer in 1995. Her historically based films often illuminate Argentine experience, particularly the relationship between women and the Church. *Camila* (nominated for an Oscar for best foreign-language film in

1984) recounts the tale of Catholic socialite Camila O'Gorman, who ran away from Buenos Aires with a young Jesuit priest in 1847, an act that incited Rosas' ruthless mazorca to hunt them down. Bemberg's English-language film *Miss Mary* (1986), starring Julie Christie, focuses on the experience of an English governess in Argentina. Her last directorial effort, *I Don't Want to Talk About It* (1992), is a bizarre love story starring Marcelo Mastroianni. Filmed in Colonia, Uruguay, across the river from Buenos Aires (see the Excursions chapter), it metaphorically explores issues of power and control in a provincial town.

Director Luis Puenzo's *The Official Story* (1985) deals with a delicate, controversial theme of the Dirty War – the adoption of the children of missing or murdered parents by those responsible for their disappearance or death. It stars Norma Leandro, a popular stage actress who has also worked in English-language films in the US. Some critics, however, rebuked Puenzo for apparently implying that Argentines were innocently ignorant of the flagrant atrocities of the time. The film won an Oscar for best foreign-language film.

Eliseo Subiela's *Man Facing Southeast* (1986) takes part of its inspiration from Adolfo Bioy Casares' ingenious novella *The Invention of Morel*. Uruguayan poet Mario Benedetti has a cameo in Subiela's *The Dark Side of the Heart* (1992), a compelling and melancholy love story with a surprise ending set in Buenos Aires and Montevideo.

Born in Buenos Aires, Héctor Babenco directed the English-language *Kiss of the Spider Woman* (1985), starring William Hurt and the late Raúl Julia. Set in Brazil but based on porteño Manuel Puig's novel, it's an intricate portrayal of the way in which the police and military abuse political prisoners and exploit informers. Babenco, who has spent most of his career in Brazil, also directed the engrossing *Pixote* (1981), a brutally frank drama about Brazilian street children.

Director Fernando 'Pino' Solanas politicized the tango in *Tangos – The Exile of*

Gardel (1985), dealing with the disrupted lives of a group of displaced Argentines during the Dirty War. The film's Parisian setting was ironically apropos for Francophile Argentina. (Solanas lived in exile in Paris following the military coup in 1976.) The late tango legend Astor Piazzola composed the soundtrack and appears in the film.

Marcelo Piñeyro's *Wild Horses* (1995) is, despite the director's denials, a road movie that starts with a curious Robin-Hood-style bank robbery in Buenos Aires and ends with a chase in the province of Chubut. It stars veteran actor Héctor Alterio.

Héctor Olivera's *The Night of the Pencils* (1986) retells the notorious case of half a dozen La Plata high school students abducted, tortured and killed by the military during the Dirty War. Olivera also adapted Osvaldo Soriano's satirical novels to the big screen in *A Funny Dirty Little War* (1983) and *Una Sombra Ya Pronto Serás* (1994). Despite its title, the former has almost nothing to do with the horrors of the military dictatorship, except perhaps indirectly.

One of Argentina's best internationally-known actors is Federico Luppi, who plays the lead in Mexican director Guillermo del Toro's *Cronos* (1992), an offbeat science-fiction gangster film, and in US director John Sayles' *Men with Guns* (1997), an allegorical exploration of political violence in Latin America.

Argentina has also left its mark on Hollywood and vice-versa, as Carlos Gardel flashed his smile in several Spanish-language films, including *El Día Que Me Quieras* (1935). Hollywood also used Argentina as a location under forced circumstances; when Juan Perón's policies prohibited American studios from exporting box-office profits, some made a virtue of a necessity by using the money to film in Argentina. The epic *Taras Bulba*, for instance, was filmed partly around Salta in northwest Argentina.

Although not a filmmaker himself, porteño composer Lalo Schifrin wrote much of the music for which Hollywood is best known, including themes and soundtracks for *Mission Impossible*, *Bullitt*, *Cool Hand Luke* and *Dirty Harry*, among many others.

For video versions of Argentine films (without English subtitles), check Alquileres Lavalle (☎ 4476-1118) at Lavalle 1199 in San Nicólas (Map 5). Note that Argentine videos use the PAL system and are incompatible with North American video technology, unless converted.

(For books on Argentine cinema, see Books in the Facts for the Visitor chapter.)

Theater

Buenos Aires has a vigorous theater community, equivalent in its own way to New York, London or Paris. It began in colonial times, a few years after the city became the viceregal capital in 1776, and continued in the 19th century with *sainete*, informal dramas focusing on immigrants and their dilemmas. Formally, though, the theater really took off in the late 19th century through the artistic and financial efforts of the Podestá family, (whose name graces theaters in Buenos Aires and La Plata), and playwrights like Florencio Sánchez, Gregorio de Laferrere and Roberto Payró. Legendary Argentine performers include Luis Sandrini and Lola Membrives; famous European writers like Federico García Lorca and Jean Cocteau have explored the Buenos Aires theater scene. Probably Argentina's most famous contemporary playwright is Juan Carlos Gené, who was the director of the Teatro General San Martín until recently.

The theater season is liveliest in winter, from June through August, but there are always performances on the docket. Av Corrientes (between Avs 9 de Julio and Callao) is the capital's Broadway or West End, but large and small theater venues and companies dot the city. Some are very improvisational and unconventional: some rent houses to stage performances, others act in plazas and parks, and one truly 'underground' company performs in subway stations. Generally, the difference between official and unconventional theater is the quality of production rather than the actors, who are professional at all levels. The number of companies and the proliferation of those offering acting lessons seem extraordinary, though participation can also be an exercise in therapy. (Buenos Aires is renowned for the concentration of shrinks in its so-called 'Barrio Freud'; see Villa Freud in the Things to See & Do chapter.) Many of the capital's most popular (and vulgar) shows move to the provincial beach resort of Mar del Plata for the summer.

Unlike stage actors in some countries, those in Argentina seem to move seamlessly among stage, film and television. Perhaps performers like Norma Leandro, Federico Luppi and China Zorrilla feel less self-conscious about moving among the various media, since the Argentine public is smaller and work opportunities fewer than in global communications and entertainment centers like London, New York and Los Angeles. Some 150 Argentine plays have passed from the theater to film since the silent era.

SOCIETY & CONDUCT

English-speaking visitors may find Buenos Aires more accessible than other Latin American cities because of its superficial resemblance to their own societies. In contrast to cities with large indigenous populations, like Lima and La Paz, foreign travelers are relatively inconspicuous and can more easily integrate themselves into everyday life. Argentines, in general, are gregarious and, once you make contact, much likelier to invite you to participate in their daily activities than, say, a Quechua llama herder in Bolivia.

Argentines are more physically demonstrative than most North Americans and Europeans, and regularly exchange kisses (on the cheek) in greeting – even among men. In formal situations, though, it is better to go with a handshake unless you are certain of the appropriate gesture.

Sport is extremely important to Argentines. Most visitors will be familiar with Argentine athletes through its World Cup champion soccer teams, featuring players like Daniel Batistuta, Diego Maradona and Daniel Passarella (who is now coach of the national team), and with tennis stars like Guillermo Vilas and Gabriela Sabatini, but

rugby, polo, golf, skiing and fishing also enjoy great popularity. Soccer, though, is the national obsession – River Plate (from the elite barrio of Núñez) and Boca Juniors (based in the working-class immigrant barrio of La Boca) are nationwide phenomena in a rivalry comparable to that of the New York Yankees and Brooklyn Dodgers in the 1950s.

Traditional Culture

One traditional activity, which visitors should not refuse, is the opportunity to *tomar un mate*, or drink *yerba mate* (pronounced **mah**tay). Also known as Paraguayan tea, the drinking of mate is an important ritual throughout the Río de la Plata region, but especially so in Argentina, where it serves as a social glue that transcends class. (For details, see Mate & Its Ritual.)

The *asado*, the famous Argentine barbecue, is as much a social occasion as a meal. An important part of any meal, whether at home or in a restaurant, is the *sobremesa*, dallying at the table to discuss family matters or other events of the day. No matter how long the lines outside, no Argentine restaurateur would even dream of nudging along a party that has lingered over coffee long after the food itself was history.

Dos & Don'ts

During the military dictatorship of 1976-83, Argentina was a forcibly conformist society: police or military personel who saw a man or boy with hair thought to be too long would abduct him to shave it off – or worse. Fortunately, in the aftermath of the Proceso regime, unconventional appearance barely raises eyebrows, and many Argentine men of all ages now sport ponytails (even pierced body parts are not unusual). Still, being polite goes a long way in any encounter with Argentine officialdom – or with any ordinary Argentine for that matter. Do not forget to preface any request with the appropriate salutation – *buenos días* (good morning), *buenas tardes* (good afternoon) or *buenas noches* (good evening) – and use *usted* (the formal mode of address) unless you are certain that informality is appropriate.

Mate & Its Ritual

Nothing captures the essence of *argentinidad* ('argentinity') as well as the preparation and consumption of *mate* (pronounced **mah**tay), perhaps the only cultural practice that transcends barriers of ethnicity, class and occupation. More than a simple drink like tea or coffee, mate is an elaborate ritual, shared among family, friends and coworkers. In many ways, sharing is the whole point.

Yerba mate is the dried, chopped leaf of *Ilex paraguayensis*, a relative of the common holly. Also known as 'Paraguayan tea,' it became commercially important during the colonial era on the plantations of the Jesuit missions in the upper Río Paraná. Europeans quickly took to the beverage, crediting it with many admirable qualities. The Austrian Jesuit Martin Dobrizhoffer wrote that mate 'provokes a gentle perspiration, improves the appetite, speedily counteracts the languor arising from the burning climate, and assuages both hunger and thirst.' Unlike many American foods and beverages, though, mate failed to make its mark in Europe.

After the Jesuits' expulsion in 1767, production declined, but has increased dramatically since the early 20th century.

Argentina is the world's largest producer and consumer of yerba mate. Argentines consume an average of 5kg per person per year, more than four times their average intake of coffee. It is also popular in parts of Chile, southern Brazil, Paraguay and, in particular, Uruguay, which consumes twice as much yerba mate per capita as Argentines.

Preparing mate is a ritual in itself. In the past, upper-class families even maintained a slave or servant whose sole responsibility was preparing and serving it. Nowadays, one person, the *cebador* (server), fills the mate (gourd) almost to the top with yerba, heating but not boiling the water in a *pava* (kettle) and pouring it into the vessel.

While porteños dress casually for most recreational activities, informal dress is normally inappropriate for business, some restaurants, casinos and events like the symphony or opera. Some places that are informal by day may become very formal by night.

RELIGION

Inattention to the role of religion will limit any visitor's understanding of Argentine society. Roman Catholicism is the official state religion, but probably less than 20% of Argentines attend mass regularly. As in many other Latin American countries, evangelical Protestantism is making inroads among traditionally Catholic believers – especially among the working class. In parts of the city, street preachers are a common sight, and many former cinemas and storefronts now serve as churches or, at least, centers for evangelical gatherings.

Within the Catholic religion, popular beliefs are increasingly diverging from official doctrine. One of the best examples is the cult of the Difunta Correa. Based outside

Drinkers sip the liquid through a *bombilla*, a silver straw with a bulbous filter at its lower end that prevents the leaves from entering the tube.

Gourds can range from simple calabashes to carved wooden vessels to the ornate silver museum pieces of the 19th century. Bombillas also differ considerably, ranging in materials from inexpensive aluminum to silver and gold with intricate markings, and in design from long straight tubes to short, curved ones.

There is an informal etiquette for drinking mate. The cebador pours water slowly near the straw to produce a froth as he or she fills the gourd. The gourd then passes clockwise and this order, once established, continues. A good cebador will keep the mate going without changing the yerba for some time. Each participant drinks the gourd dry each time. A simple *gracias* will tell the server to pass you by.

There are marked regional differences in drinking mate. From the Pampas southwards, Argentines take it *amargo* (without sugar), while to the north they drink it *dulce* (sweet) with sugar and *yuyos* (aromatic herbs). Purists, who argue that sugar ruins the gourd, will keep separate gourds rather than alternate the two usages. In summer, Paraguayans drink mate ice-cold as *tereré*.

An invitation to mate is a sign of acceptance and should not be refused, even though mate is an acquired taste and novices may find it bitter and very hot at first. On the second or third round, both the heat and bitterness will diminish. It is poor etiquette to hold the mate too long before passing it on. Drinking it is unlikely to affect either your health or finances, despite Dobrizhoffer's warning that

by the immoderate and almost hourly use of this potation, the stomach is weakened, and continual flatulence, with other diseases, brought on. I have known many of the lower Spaniards who never spoke ten words without applying their lips to the gourd containing the ready-made tea. If many topers in Europe waste their substance by an immoderate use of wine and other intoxicating liquors, there are no fewer in America who drink away their fortunes in potations of the herb of Paraguay.

Buenos Aires in San Juan province, hundreds of thousands of professed Catholics make annual pilgrimages and offerings, despite the Church hierarchy's aggressive campaign against the Difunta Correa's veneration.

Like other Argentine institutions, the Church has many factions. During the late 1970s and early 1980s, the Church generally supported the de facto military government despite persecution, kidnapping, torture and murder of religious workers. Most of these victims, adherents of the 'liberation theology'

movement, worked among the poor and dispossessed in both rural areas and the *villas miserias* (shantytowns) of Buenos Aires and other large cities.

Such activism has resumed in today's more permissive political climate, but the Church hierarchy remains obstinate. The late Cardinal Antonio Quarracino of Buenos Aires, for example, publicly defended President Menem's pardon of the convicted murderers and torturers during the Dirty War, and it appears that official chaplains acquiesced in the atrocities by counseling the perpetrators.

Spiritualism and veneration of the dead have remarkable importance in a country that prides itself on European sophistication. Novelist Tomás Eloy Martínez observed that Argentines honor national heroes like San Martín not on their birthday, but on the anniversary of their death. Visitors to Recoleta and Chacarita cemeteries in Buenos Aires – essential sights for comprehending Argentine culture – will see steady processions of pilgrims going to the resting places of icons like Juan and Eva Perón, psychic Madre María, and tango singer Carlos Gardel; visitors come to communicate by laying their hands on their tombs and leaving arcane offerings.

LANGUAGE

Spanish is the official language, but some immigrant communities retain their language as a badge of identity. Italian, the language of the largest immigrant group, is widely understood. The use of English extends beyond the relatively small number of native speakers in the capital's Anglo-Argentine community. Many porteños study English as a second language, and it is widely understood in the tourist and financial sectors of the city's economy. German speakers are numerous enough to support a weekly newspaper, *Argentinisches Tageblatt*.

For useful phrases in Argentine Spanish, see the Language chapter.

Facts for the Visitor

WHEN TO GO

For residents of the Northern Hemisphere, a visit to Argentina offers the inviting possibility of enjoying two summers in the same year, but the country's great variety makes a visit during any season worthwhile. In the southern winter (June, July, August) or spring, the heat and humidity are usually less oppressive than in summer (December, January, February), though Buenos Aires' urban attractions transcend the seasons. Some visitors have found the capital very crowded during the Argentine winter holidays, usually the first two weeks of July, when modest accommodations like hostels are likely to be full of energetic students.

ORIENTATION

At first glance, Buenos Aires seems as massive and imposing as New York or London. Celebrated Argentine writer Jorge Luis Borges once described his birthplace as 'such an outrageous city that nobody can ever learn it.' Still, for most visitors, a brief orientation suffices for the city's compact downtown grid and most frequented *barrios* (boroughs or neighborhoods).

The Capital Federal – bounded by Río de la Plata and its tributary, plus the ring roads, Avs 27 de Febrero and General Paz – consists of 48 distinct barrios, some very small and others quite large (Map 3). These barrios have rigid, formal limits, but informal boundaries (more common in everyday usage) are rarely congruent and often contradictory. The line between Palermo and Recoleta is unclear, while the Av Córdoba boundary between Balvanera and Recoleta so clearly demarcates two distinct parts of the city that every *porteño* who crosses the street acknowledges the division.

Other factors complicate the city's geographical organization. Few locals refer to the downtown barrio of San Nicolás as such, instead using the term Microcentro for roughly the area north of Av de Mayo (in

Montserrat), east of Av 9 de Julio and south of Av Santa Fe in Retiro. Many important commercial and entertainment areas are strung along its Avs Corrientes, Córdoba and Santa Fe, plus the Florida and Lavalle *peatonales* (pedestrian malls). Much of the

Law of the Indies

Perceptive visitors to Buenos Aires and other Latin American cities will immediately notice their structural similarity. Except in the seats of the great empires of Mexico and the Andes, where the Spaniards adapted indigenous cities to their own society's needs, the colonial Leyes de Indias (Law of the Indies) decreed the imposition of a regular grid pattern traceable to Roman times.

The Spaniards were largely an urban people and drew on their European experience to build the new colonial settlements. In Spain, the slow-growing medieval city had resulted in dispersal of major urban institutions like the *Cabildo* (town council), the church and the market, but in the colonies all of these clustered around the central plaza. Because of the plaza's defensive functions on the frontier, settlers often called it the 'Plaza de Armas.' As the leading Spanish citizens settled near the institutions of power, the plaza became the city's economic and social center.

There were exceptions to the rule, of course. Officials were directed to choose town sites in open, level areas, but the spontaneous development and irregular topography of many ports and mining towns discouraged uniform application of the system. Nevertheless, the rectangular grid system became the template for urban development throughout the region. Especially in Argentina, this legacy greatly simplifies the task of orientation for visitors.

western half of San Nicolás and parts of neighboring barrios Montserrat and Balvanera make up another area, popularly known as Congreso. Another informal barrio, Barrio Norte is a vaguely defined neighborhood, comprising mostly residential parts of Recoleta and Retiro barrios. The northern reaches of the barrio of Palermo are sometimes closely associated with Belgrano.

The maps and organization of this book follow the formal extents of city barrios. Visitors should be aware that the vernacular extents may differ – even porteño sources sometimes disagree about precise boundaries. The major divisions used here are San Nicolás and the Microcentro (including parts of Congreso); Montserrat (sometimes known as Catedral al Sur) and Balvanera (the two barrios comprising most of Congreso); San Telmo; Constitución (including parts of Barracas); La Boca; Retiro and Recoleta (the two barrios making up Barrio Norte); Palermo (including parts of Colegiales); and Belgrano (including the Costanera, which provides access to the Río de la Plata). There is also a map for Caballito, Almagro and Parque Chacabuco barrios.

The traditional focus of activity is the Plaza de Mayo, straddling the Microcentro and Montserrat, opposite the Casa Rosada presidential palace (Map 7). Both the Catedral Metropolitana and portions of the original Cabildo (colonial town council) are also here, at the east end of Av de Mayo. Street names change and street numbers rise on each side of Av de Mayo, while numbers on east-west streets rise from zero near the waterfront.

An ordeal for pedestrians, the broad Av 9 de Julio forms a north-south axis, simultaneously encompassing Cerrito and Carlos Pellegrini north of Av de Mayo, and Lima and Bernardo de Irigoyen south of Av de Mayo. It runs from San Telmo's Plaza Constitución in the south to Recoleta's Av del Libertador, which continues to the city's exclusive northern suburbs and spacious parks.

MAPS

The municipal Dirección General de Turismo distributes a free *Plano Turístico* which includes most of the central barrios and an up-to-date Subte (underground) diagram. The downtown area, however, is cluttered by 3-D representations of certain buildings and other features, to the detriment of its usability.

Metrovías, the private operator of the Subte, publishes a very good pocket-size map of the area it serves, which includes most of the capital's tourist attractions. Available free from most public information offices, it's the most convenient map to carry around.

Covering a smaller area on a larger scale, Guías Taylor's *Plano Turístico de la Ciudad de Buenos Aires* focuses on the Microcentro, San Telmo, La Boca, Recoleta and Palermo. Widely available from kiosks along Florida peatonal, it also contains a useful Subte diagram, but oversized symbols for some landmarks detract from the map's readability. A smaller bilingual version is available free from tourist offices. Another common giveaway called *The Golden Map Buenos Aires* has similar virtues and shortcomings.

For visitors spending some time in Buenos Aires, the best resources are Lumi Transportes' *Capital Federal* and *Capital Federal y Gran Buenos Aires*, both in compact ringbinder format, with all city streets and bus routes indexed. A similar worthwhile acquisition is the *Guía Peuser*. In a foldout format is Argenguide's *Capital Federal/Ciudad de Buenos Aires*, with a separate index for streets and bus routes.

Automapa publishes *Gran Buenos Aires*, a foldout map of the capital and its suburbs, with a street index, at a scale of 1:40,000. This, however, is more awkward than the Lumi series. YPF's Buenos Aires *Turístico y Alrededores* is a Spanish-language guidebook that includes detailed large-scale maps, but it's increasingly difficult to find.

For topographic maps of Argentina, visit the Instituto Geográfico Militar (☎ 4576-5576), at Av Cabildo 381 in Palermo (Subte: Ministro Carranza; Map 13). It's also reached by bus No 152 and is open 8 am to 4 pm weekdays.

The Automóvil Club Argentino (ACA; ☎ 4802-6061), Av del Libertador 1850 in Palermo near Recoleta (Map 13), publishes the *Carta Vial de Buenos Aires y Alrededores*, which is useful beyond the city center.

Its detailed provincial road maps are imperative for motorists planning to leave the capital and useful for anyone else. You may also find them at specialty bookstores like Stanfords in London, or in the map rooms of major university libraries. Members of foreign automobile clubs can purchase these maps at discount prices in Argentina.

ACA has branch offices in Congreso (☎ 4372-5283; Map 7) at Av Belgrano 1749, in Palermo at Godoy Cruz and Demaría (☎ 4771-9158; Map 13), and in Belgrano at the corner of Av Cabildo and Virrey Arredondo (☎ 4785-2934; Map 14). See the Getting There & Away chapter for more on ACA.

TOURIST OFFICES
Local Tourist Offices
The Dirección Nacional de Turismo (☎ 4312-2232), Av Santa Fe 883 in Retiro (Map 11), is open 9 am to 5 pm weekdays; there's a branch (☎ 4480-0224) at Aeropuerto Internacional Ministro Pistarini (Ezeiza; Map 1). Both have helpful English-speaking staff.

More convenient are two locations in San Nicolás (Map 5): the municipal tourist kiosk at the intersection of the Florida peatonal and Diagonal Roque Sáenz Peña (open 10 am to 6 pm weekdays, 2 to 6 pm weekends and holidays), and its office in the Galerías Pacífico, at Av Córdoba and Florida (open 10 am to 4 pm weekdays, 11 am to 6 pm Saturdays). Both distribute excellent pocket-size maps in English and Spanish, as well as other brochures.

For more detailed information on the city, visit the Dirección General de Turismo de la Municipalidad de Buenos Aires (☎ 4476-3612, 4371-1496), in the Centro Cultural San Martín, 5th floor, Sarmiento 1551 in Congreso (Map 5). This office sometimes organizes free weekend guided walks. It also distributes brochures on walks and tours in barrios beyond the usual tourist circuit.

Readily available around town is the glossy bilingual (English-Spanish) *BA Guide*, which contains information on basic visitor services and current events, despite the flagrant commercialism of its restaurant and shopping listings. Equally commercial, but with superior content, is *Aires Viajero*.

Tourist Offices Abroad
The larger Argentine consulates (see Embassies & Consulates later in this chapter), such as those in New York and Los Angeles, usually have a tourist representative. Local offices of Aerolíneas Argentinas often have similar information at their disposal.

DOCUMENTS
Passports are obligatory for all visitors except citizens of bordering countries. Argentina presently enjoys a civilian government, and the police and military presence is subdued, but the police can still demand identification at any moment. In general, officials are very document-oriented, and passports are essential for cashing traveler's checks, checking into hotels and other routine activities.

Visas
Argentina has eliminated visas for many but not all foreign tourists. In theory, upon arrival all non-visa visitors must obtain a free tourist card, good for 90 days and renewable for 90 more. In practice, immigration officials issue these only at major border crossings, such as airports and on the ferries and hydrofoils between Buenos Aires and Uruguay.

Although you should not toss your card, losing it is no major catastrophe. At most exit points, immigration officials will provide immediate replacement; that is, the bureaucracy may require you to fill one out even though you're leaving the country.

Nationals of the USA, Canada and most Western European countries, including Britons, do not need visas. Australians no longer need visas. New Zealanders, however, do need visas and must submit their passports with a fee of US$24; some immigration officials may ask to see a return or onward ticket. Usually, the visa will be ready the following day. Verify whether the visa is valid for 90 days from date of issue, or 90 days from first entry.

Children under the age of 14 traveling without both parents theoretically need a parent's consent form, but the author's 10-year-old daughter has traveled many times to and from the country with only one parent and has never been asked for such a form.

EMBASSIES & CONSULATES

The following are most likely to be useful to intending visitors. See also the Tourist Offices Abroad entry.

Argentine Embassies & Consulates
Argentina has diplomatic representation throughout Latin America, North America, Western Europe and many other regions, including Australia.

Australia
Embassy:
(☎ 02-627-39111)
1st floor, MLC Tower,
Woden, ACT 2606

Consulate:
(☎ 02-9251-3402,
fax 251-3405)
Gold Fields House,
1 Alfred St, Sydney,
NSW 2000

Bolivia
(☎ 02-353233, 417737)
Sánchez Lima and Aspiazú,
La Paz 64

Brazil
Consulates:
(☎ 021-533-1569)
Entrepiso, Praia de Bota-
fogo 228, Rio de Janeiro

(☎ 011-285-2274)
9th floor, Av Paulista 1106,
São Paulo

Canada
Embassy:
(☎ 613-236-2351)
90 Sparks St, Suite 620,
Ottawa, Ontario L1B 5P4

Consulates:
(☎ 416-955-0232)
1 First Canadian Place,
Suite 5840, Toronto,
Ontario M5X 1K2

(☎ 514-842-6582)
2000 Peel St, Montréal,
Quebec H3A 2W5

Chile
(☎ 2-222-6853)
Vicuña Mackenna 41,
Santiago

France
(☎ 01 45 53 27 00)
6 Rue Cimarosa, Paris
75116

Germany
(☎ 030-220-2621)
Dorotheenstraße 89, 3rd
floor, Berlin-Mitte 10117

Paraguay
(☎ 021-442151)
Banco Nación, Palma 319,
1st floor, Asunción

UK
Embassy:
(☎ 020-7318-1300)
65 Brook St, London
W1Y 1YE

Consulate:
(☎ 020-7318-1340)
27 Three Kings Yard,
London W1Y 1FL

USA
Embassy:
(☎ 202-238-6460)
1600 New Hampshire Ave,
Washington, DC 20009

Consulates:
(☎ 202-238-6460)
1718 Connecticut Ave NW,
Washington, DC 20009

(☎ 213-954-9155)
5550 Wilshire Blvd,
Suite 210,
Los Angeles, CA 90036

(☎ 305-373-1889)
800 Brickell Ave,
Penthouse 1,
Miami, FL 33131

(☎ 312-819-2610)
205 N Michigan Ave,
Suite 4209,
Chicago, IL 60601

(☎ 212-603-0403)
12 W 56th St,
New York, NY 10019

(☎ 404-880-0806)
245 Peach Tree Center
Ave, Suite 2101,
Atlanta, GA 30303

(☎ 713-871-8935)
1990 Post Oak Blvd
Suite 770,
Houston, TX 77056

Uruguay
(☎ 02-903-0084)
Wilson Ferreira Aldunate
1281, Montevideo

Embassies & Consulates in Buenos Aires

As a tourist, it's important to realize what your own embassy can and can't do.

Generally speaking, it won't be much help in emergencies if the trouble you're in is remotely your own fault. Remember that you are bound by the laws of the country you are in. Your embassy will not be sympathetic if you end up in jail after committing a crime locally, even if such actions are legal in your own country.

In genuine emergencies you might get some assistance, but only if other channels have been exhausted. For example, if you need to get home urgently, a free ticket home is exceedingly unlikely – the embassy would expect you to have insurance. If you have all your money and documents stolen, it might assist with getting a new passport, but a loan for onward travel is out of the question.

Australia
(☎ 4777-6580)
Villanueva 1400, Palermo

Belgium
(☎ 4331-0066)
Defensa 113, Montserrat

Bolivia
(☎ 4381-0539)
Av Belgrano 1670, 1st floor, Montserrat

Brazil
(☎ 4394-5264)
Carlos Pellegrini 1363, 5th floor, Retiro

Canada
(☎ 4805-3032)
Tagle 2828, Palermo

Chile
(☎ 4394-6582)
San Martín 439, 9th floor, San Nicolás

Denmark
(☎ 4312-6901)
Leandro N Alem 1074, 9th floor, Retiro

France
(☎ 4312-2409)
Santa Fe 846, 3rd floor, Retiro

Germany
(☎ 4778-2500)
Villanueva 1055, Palermo

Ireland
(☎ 4325-8588)
Suipacha 1380, Retiro

Israel
(☎ 4342-6932)
Av de Mayo 701, 10th floor, Montserrat

Italy
(☎ 4816-6132)
MT de Alvear 1149, Retiro

Japan
(☎ 4318-8220)
Bouchard 547, 15th floor, San Nicolás

Mexico
(☎ 4821-7170)
Larrea 1230, Recoleta

Netherlands
(☎ 4334-4000)
Ave de Mayo 701, 19th floor, Montserrat

Norway
(☎ 4312-2204)
Esmeralda 909, 3rd floor, Retiro

Peru
(☎ 4811-4619)
Av Córdoba 1345, Retiro

Paraguay
(☎ 4812-0075)
Viamonte 1851, Balvanera

Spain
(☎ 4811-0078)
Guido 1760, Recoleta

Sweden
(☎ 4342-1422)
Tacuarí 147, Montserrat

Switzerland
(☎ 4311-6491)
Santa Fe 846, 10th floor, Retiro

UK
(☎ 4803-7070)
Dr Luis Agote 2412, Palermo

Uruguay
(☎ 4807-3040)
Las Heras 1907, Recoleta

USA
(☎ 4777-4533)
Colombia 4300, Palermo

Argentina has a wide network of embassies and consulates, both in neighboring countries and overseas. Some are very accommodating, while others (most notably those in Colonia, Uruguay, and La Paz, Bolivia) may treat your visit as a major nuisance.

Individuals born in Argentina, even of foreign parents, are considered Argentines and may encounter difficulties entering the country with non-Argentine documents. In one instance, officials harassed a retired US army colonel, who was born in Buenos Aires, for lacking proof of completing obligatory military service in Argentina. Argentine passports renewed overseas expire upon re-entry into Argentina, and renewing them with the Policía Federal can be a tiresome process on a short trip.

Visa Extensions Argentine tourist cards are valid for 90 days. For a 90-day extension, visit the Dirección Nacional de Migraciones (☎ 4312-8661) at Av Antártida Argentina 1355 in Retiro (Map 11). There may be a nominal charge. In areas where the police are unaccustomed to dealing with immigration, the process can be tedious and time-consuming. Renewing a nearly expired visa outside the country at a consulate other than the one that issued it can be almost impossible; it is easier to get a new passport and then request a new Argentine visa.

Travelers wishing to stay longer than six months will find it simpler to cross the border into a neighboring country for a few days and then return for an additional six months. Although it is possible to obtain residence, leaving the country then becomes problematic and you cannot take advantage of tourist regulations with respect to Argentine customs and duties. (Tourists are able to bring in items, such as laptop computers and cameras, without the scrutiny that Argentines and permanent residents must endure.)

Travel Insurance
In addition to health and accident insurance, a policy that protects baggage and valuables such as cameras is a good idea. Keep insurance records separate from other possessions in case you have to make a claim.

Driver's License & Permits
Motorists need an International or Interamerican Driving Permit to complement their national or state licenses, but drivers should not be surprised if police at the numerous roadside checkpoints do not recognize it or, worse, claim it is invalid and try to exact a bribe. Politely refer them to the Spanish translation.

Hostel Card
The Red Argentina de Albergues Juveniles (RAAJ; ☎ 4511-8712, fax 4312-0089, raaj@hostels.org.ar) is part of Argentina's energetic nonprofit student travel agency Asatej, Florida 835, 3rd floor, in Retiro (Map 11). It sells the Hostelling International card for US$20. RAAJ is rapidly displacing the moribund Asociación Argentina de Albergues de la Juventud (AAAJ; ☎ 4476-1001), Talcahuano 214, 2nd floor, in Congreso (Map 5), which also sells the card.

There are now several Buenos Aires hostels, not all of which require the Hostelling International card, but hostels in the provinces generally do. The two hostel representatives have slightly different networks of hostels throughout the country, though there is some overlap. The standards of RAAJ-affiliated hostels are generally higher.

Student & Youth Cards
The International Student Identity Card (ISIC), available from RAAJ and Asatej (see Useful Organizations, later in this chapter), can help travelers obtain discounts on public transportation and museum admissions, but virtually any official-looking university identification may be an acceptable substitute.

Seniors' Cards
Travelers over the age of 60 can sometimes obtain *tercera edad* (senior citizen) discounts on museum admissions and the like. Usually a passport with date of birth will be sufficient evidence of age.

Photocopies
In the event of loss or theft, it's a good idea to keep photocopies of important documents

such as passport, plane ticket, traveler's checks, credit cards and the like. Store copies separately from the originals.

CUSTOMS

Though infamous for corruption because of the so-called *aduana paralela* (parallel customs), Argentine officials are generally courteous and reasonable toward tourists. Nevertheless, travelers who cross the border frequently and carry equipment such as cameras or a laptop computer may find it helpful to have a typed list of equipment, including serial numbers, to be stamped by authorities. Officials at Buenos Aires' Ezeiza airport often ask about such goods, which are much more costly in Argentina than overseas.

Depending on where you have been, officials focus on different things. Travelers southbound from the central Andean countries may be searched for drugs, while those from bordering countries will have fruit and vegetables confiscated. *Never* carry firearms.

MONEY

For visitors unaccustomed to hyperinflation and without sufficient zeros on their pocket calculators, Argentine money traditionally presented real problems; when Argentine economists spoke hopefully of single-digit inflation, they meant *per month*. Since the institution of former economy minister Domingo Cavallo's convertibility policy in early 1991, however, inflation has fallen to record lows, and the peso has remained at parity with the US dollar. Still, given Argentina's history of financial instability, travelers should keep a close watch on exchange markets and current economic events. It is still not advisable, and not really necessary, to keep large amounts of cash in local currency.

Currency

The past decade of economic stability has all but closed the former revolving door of Argentine currencies. The present unit is the peso ($), which is at par with the US dollar; it replaced the inflation-ravaged *austral* on January 1, 1992. The austral had replaced the *peso argentino* in 1985, which had replaced the *peso ley* in 1978, which had replaced a previous *peso* some years earlier. One new peso equals 10,000 australs.

Paper money comes in denominations of 2, 5, 10, 20, 50 and 100 pesos. One new peso equals 100 *centavos*; coins come in denominations of 1, 5, 10, 25 and 50 centavos, and one peso. Few merchants want anything to do with one-centavo coins, and even five-centavo coins get scant attention.

At present, US dollars are de facto legal tender almost everywhere, but it's wise to carry some pesos; institutions like the post office and some bus companies, as well as a few nationalistic merchants, refuse to accept US currency.

Tattered, nearly shredded Argentine banknotes seem to stay in circulation for decades, but few banks or businesses accept torn, worn or defaced US dollars. Counterfeiting, of both local and US bills, has become a problem in recent years, and some merchants may be skeptical of large denominations.

Exchange Rates

Despite the current stability, for most of the past half-century exchange rates have been volatile. In mid-December 1990 the dollar sank below 5000 australs until a minor economic crisis and intensified domestic demand drove the rate up dramatically. By September 1991, the rate was just below 10,000 australs per US dollar.

country	unit		peso
Australia	A$1	=	Arg $0.64
Bolivia	Bol$1	=	Arg $0.18
Brazil	BraRl 1	=	Arg $0.83
Canada	C$1	=	Arg $0.66
Chile	Chi$1000	=	Arg $2.16
euro	€ 1	=	Arg $1.16
France	1FF	=	Arg $0.18
Germany	DM1	=	Arg $0.59
Italy	It£1000	=	Arg $0.60
Japan	¥100	=	Arg $0.89
New Zealand	NZ$1	=	Arg $0.54
Paraguay	Par₲1000	=	Arg $3.55
United Kingdom	UK£1	=	Arg $1.66
United States	US$1	=	Arg $1
Uruguay	Ur$10	=	Arg $0.94

Exchanging Money

Although convertibility has reduced the need to change money, dozens of *casas de cambio* (exchange bureaus) still line the Microcentro's San Martín – Argentina's counterpart of Wall St – south of Av Corrientes (Map 5). There are many more cambios north of Av Corrientes, along Av Corrientes and on the Florida peatonal. Cambio hours are generally 9 am to 6 pm weekdays, but a few are open Saturday mornings.

Prices in this book are quoted in US dollars, a common standard throughout Latin America.

Cash Cash can be exchanged at banks, cambios, hotels, some travel agencies and often in shops or even on the street. Since the peso is at par with the US dollar, however, most merchants use the two currencies interchangeably, so most visitors will find it pointless to change cash except for paying postal charges or local bus fares. US coins are not accepted.

Travelers confident of their ability to carry cash safely will find it a much better alternative than traveler's checks, which often carry commission charges of up to 10% or more. Hard currencies other than US dollars will find a market in Buenos Aires, though they are less convenient; outside Buenos Aires, they are difficult to exchange.

Traveler's Checks Travelers' checks are easier to change in Buenos Aires than elsewhere in the country, but they are increasingly difficult to cash anywhere and specifically *not* recommended; an ATM card is a far better alternative. American Express, Arenales 707 near Plaza San Martín in Retiro (Map 11), will change its own traveler's checks without commission. Many places charge up to 10% or more to change traveler's checks. It's best to avoid bringing checks in currencies other than US dollars.

ATMs While traveler's checks can be problematic, *cajeros automáticos* (ATMs) are increasingly abundant, and many can also be used for cash advances on major credit cards like MasterCard and Visa. ATMs are so ubiquitous that it would be pointless to mention any in particular. Many but not all dispense either US dollars or Argentine pesos.

Credit Cards The most widely accepted credit cards are Visa and MasterCard, though the latter (affiliated with the local Argencard) is the most useful. Travelers with UK Access should insist on their affiliation to MasterCard. American Express, Diner's Club and others are also valid in many places. Because lost or stolen credit cards are vulnerable to abuse, credit card holders should consider enrolling in a protection plan to insure themselves against serious financial loss.

Some businesses add a *recargo* (surcharge) of 10% or more to credit-card purchases to recoup high bank charges and the loss of interest between the time of sale and their own receipt of payment. This practice is less common than in the past, but still exists. (The flip side is that some merchants give a discount of 10% or more for cash purchases.)

Also, the actual amount customers pay depends upon the exchange rate not at the time of sale, but when the purchase is posted to an overseas account, often weeks later.

If the Argentine peso is depreciating, the price may be a fraction less of the dollar cost calculated at the time of purchase. On the other hand, a strong local currency may mean that the cost in dollars (or other foreign currency) will be significantly greater than expected. At present, this is not an issue for travelers whose overseas accounts are in US dollars, but those whose purchases are converted to other currencies should be alert to changes.

Travelers using their credit cards to pay for restaurant bills should be aware that, as a rule, tips may *not* be added to the bill, so keep some cash on hand for gratuities. Some private tour companies will not accept credit cards, so confirm before booking.

Holders of MasterCard and Visa can also get cash advances at most downtown banks between 10 am and 4 pm, but most ATMs will do the same.

The following local representatives can help travelers replace lost or stolen credit cards or traveler's checks:

American Express
  (☎ 4312-1661) Arenales 707, Retiro
Diner's Club
  (☎ 4379-4545) Carlos Pellegrini 1023, Retiro
MasterCard
  (☎ 4331-2088) Perú 143, Montserrat
Visa
  (☎ 4379-3300) Corrientes 1437, 3rd floor,
  San Nicolás

International Transfers For travelers running out of money, American Express Money Gram is a quick and efficient (if costly) means of transferring funds from their home country to Argentina. American Express has a major office in Retiro and representatives throughout the country.

Black Market At present there is no black market and there are few restrictions on changing money freely, but in times of crisis visitors should stay aware of the so-called *mercado paralelo* (parallel market). For the most up-to-date information, see the English-language daily *Buenos Aires Herald* or *Ambito Financiero*, Argentina's counterpart to the *Wall Street Journal* or *Financial Times*.

Costs

During periods of economic instability, which occur often, Argentines panic and buy US dollars, the exchange rate collapses, and the country can become absurdly cheap for the visitor with hard currency. At present, though, the economy is relatively stable due to the stringent convertibility policy, making Buenos Aires nearly as expensive as European or North American cities. Inflation has remained relatively high in some sectors, so that prices for transportation, accommodations and meals have risen more rapidly than other sectors in the economy at large. (In 1994, when the aggregate inflation rate was only 4%, transportation costs increased by nearly 19%.) Some Argentines even prefer to take their holidays in countries like the USA where certain products (particularly electronics) are much cheaper; these Argentine travelers have acquired the ironic nickname *démedos* because, on their visits to Miami

for example, they find consumer items so cheap that they tell the clerk to 'give me two.'

This does not make budget travel impossible. Certain costs, such as modest lodging, food and some transportation, will be lower than in Europe or North America even if they are higher than in surrounding countries. After overcoming the initial shock, travelers arriving from inexpensive countries like Bolivia should be able to spend a rewarding time in Buenos Aires by adapting to local conditions. By seeking out cheaper lodging and dining selectively, judicious travelers can control costs. In particular, those accustomed to eating every meal in a restaurant in neighboring countries will not be able to do so in Argentina; consider sandwich fixings from the market and splurge on an occasional treat elsewhere.

Still, everyone but compulsive shoestring travelers should allow a minimum of US$35 to US$40 per day for food and lodging, and pat themselves on the back if they can get by on less. It's possible to spend much more, and prices in this book are subject to fluctuation.

Tipping & Bargaining

In restaurants, it is customary to tip about 10% of the bill, but in times of economic distress Argentines frequently overlook the custom. In general, waiters are ill paid, so if you can afford to eat out, you can afford to tip. Even a small *propina* will be appreciated, but note that restaurant tips may *not* be added to a credit-card bill. Cinema ushers also receive a tip of 25 or 50 centavos.

Bargaining is not the way of life as it is in Bolivia or Peru, but artisans' markets and downtown shops selling leather and other tourist goods will consider offers.

Discounts

Late in the evening, some hotels may give a break on room prices; if you plan to stay several days, they almost certainly will. Many better hotels give discounts up to 30% for cash payment. Students, teachers and senior citizens with appropriate identification may obtain discounts on long-distance buses and admission to museums.

Taxes & Refunds

One of Argentina's primary state revenue earners is the 21% value-added tax known as the *Impuesto de Valor Agregado* (IVA). Under limited circumstances, foreign visitors may obtain IVA refunds on purchases of Argentine products upon departing the country. A 'Tax Free' window decal (in English) identifies participants in this program, but always verify the shop's status before making your purchase.

Tax refunds can be obtained for purchases of US$200 or more at one of the participating stores. To do so, present your passport and tourist card to the merchant, who must enter the amount of the refund on the reverse of the invoice and paste an equivalent quantity of stamps on the provided form, whose triplicate you will also receive. On leaving the country, keep the purchased items separate from the rest of your baggage; a customs official will check them and seal the invoice.

With this invoice, branches of Banco de la Nación at Buenos Aires' Ezeiza, Aeroparque Jorge Newbery (for flights to some neighboring countries), and the capital's river ports at Dársena Norte and Dársena Sur will refund the money in pesos and then convert it to US dollars. These branch banks are open 24 hours daily.

POST & COMMUNICATIONS
Postal Rates

Argentina's postal rates are among the world's most expensive. Domestic letters weighing 150g or less cost US$0.75, while postcards cost US$0.50. International letters weighing 20g or less cost US$0.75 to bordering countries, US$1 to elsewhere in the Americas and US$1.25 to outside the Americas.

Certified and international express mail services are more expensive but a better value because of their dependability. Certified letters start at US$2.75 for up to 20g, while international express service begins at US$5.50 for up to 100g.

Airmail packages are expensive, while surface mail is much cheaper but less dependable.

Ernesto *Che* Guevara   75c

República Argentina

Dis. G.Brea   Casa de Moneda 97

Sending Mail

Correo Argentino (also known as Encotesa), the privatized postal service, occupies the distinctive Correo Central, Sarmiento 189, which fills an entire block along Av Leandro N Alem between Av Corrientes and Sarmiento in the Microcentro (Map 5). Open 9 am to 7:30 pm weekdays, it does not accept US dollars.

For international parcels weighing over 1kg, go to the Correo Internacional, on Antártida Argentina across from Plaza Canadá near the Retiro train station (Map 11). It's open 11 am to 5 pm weekdays.

Branch post offices are scattered throughout the city; one of the most central is below street level in the Galería Buenos Aires, on Florida between Av Córdoba and Paraguay in Retiro, but Correo Argentino offices are so numerous now that it is no longer an effort to find them.

Send essential overseas mail *certificado* (registered) or *puerta a puerta* (express, literally 'door to door') to ensure its arrival. Mail may be opened and the contents appropriated if it appears to contain money or anything else of value, though this is less common than it once was.

When writing to addresses in Buenos Aires, bear in mind that Argentines commonly refer to the city as the 'Capital Federal.' Porteños often shorten this term to 'la capital.'

Receiving Mail

Travelers can receive mail via Lista de Correos or Poste Restante, both equivalent to general delivery, at any Argentine post office. Instruct correspondents to address letters clearly and to indicate a date on the envelope until which the post office should hold them; otherwise they will be returned or destroyed. Letters should be addressed as follows:

    Albert JONES (last name in capitals)
    Lista de Correos
    Sarmiento 189
    1003 Buenos Aires
    ARGENTINA
    (day-month-year)

Post offices impose heavy charges (up to US$1.50 per letter) on poste restante services. To avoid this costly and surprisingly bureaucratic annoyance, arrange to have mail delivered to a private address such as a friend or a hotel.

Private Mail Services

Correo Argentino (formerly Encotel) no longer has a monopoly on postal services, and private-run international and national services are considerably more dependable but much more expensive. Federal Express (☎ 4393-6054) is at Maipú 753 in the Microcentro (Map 5); DHL International (☎ 4347-0600) is at Moreno 967 in Montserrat (Map 7). OCA (☎ 4771-1068), which makes domestic connections for several international couriers, is at Av Santa Fe 4535 in Palermo and at Viamonte 526 in the Microcentro (Map 5). Private international mail services accept US dollars and international credit cards.

Telephone

Argentine telephone rates remain very high, despite the prospect of cheaper calls with the end of the Telecom/Telefónica duopoly at the end of 1999. Some rates, however, have fallen and making international collect calls or calls by credit card is not necessarily cheaper than calling from long-distance offices. There are no domestic collect calls within Argentina.

Argentina's two phone companies, Telecom and Telefónica, have split the city down the middle at Av Córdoba; theoretically, everything north belongs to Telecom, while everything south is the responsibility of Telefónica, but occasionally there's overlap.

The Number You Dialed . . .

In January 1999, the Argentine telephone system made major changes. All numbers throughout the country added the initial 4 so that, for example, the seven-digit numbers in Gran Buenos Aires became eight-digit numbers. (The number for Asatej student travel agency was ☎ 311-6953, but is now ☎ 4311-6953.) Simultaneously, an initial 1 was added to the Gran Buenos Aires area code, making the new area code ☎ 11.

Outside Gran Buenos Aires, area codes were also changed and all ordinary numbers added the initial 4. In Telecom services, generally north of Buenos Aires, an initial 3 was added, so that Córdoba's ☎ 51 area code became ☎ 351. In Telefónica's service areas, generally south of the capital, an initial 2 was added to the area code, so that La Plata's ☎ 21 became ☎ 221.

Toll-free numbers now repeat their initial digit three times. For instance, MCI Worldphones' ☎ 51002 became ☎ 555-1002. Cellular phones in Buenos Aires added an initial 4, while those in the provinces added an initial 2 or 3, depending on whether they are based in Telecom or Telefónica service areas.

A transition period followed January 1999, when old numbers simultaneously worked with new ones. All numbers listed in this book are of the new format. If you have any dated numbers in Buenos Aires, add an initial 4 to ensure your call will go through.

Despite some improvements in service, the antiquated infrastructure bequeathed by the former state monopoly ENTel will probably plague the city for decades. In theory, local calls should be simple, but callers often find that, even if the call gets through, the person at the other end is unable to hear. Repairs can take weeks, and coordination between the two companies is very poor.

Most public telephones, at least, are now functional. To make a local call, purchase *cospeles* (tokens) for about $0.25 each, or more convenient *tarjetas telefónicas* (magnetic phone cards) from almost any kiosk, or from street vendors. Callers fortunate enough to get through will only be able to speak for about two minutes, so carry lots of cospeles. There are different types of cospeles for local and long-distance calls.

Long-distance offices are usually very busy, especially during evening hours (from 10 pm to 8 am) and weekend discount hours when overseas calls are more reasonably priced. Telefónica's most convenient and efficient office, at Av Corrientes 701 (Map 5), is open 24 hours a day. There are two kinds of booths to make long-distance calls. The booths with direct connections to operators in North America, Europe, Japan and neighboring countries greatly simplify collect and credit-card calls – and you won't be charged to use them. Otherwise, a cashier will give you a ticket for a booth, where you can either dial directly or ask for operator assistance. When you complete the call, pay the cashier. Telecom has a comparable office at Av Córdoba 379 in Retiro (Map 11), but it keeps shorter hours, from 9 am to 11 pm only.

Since the demise of ENTel, numerous other private *locutorios* (long-distance telephone offices) have sprung up around central Buenos Aires, so it is usually not necessary to go much out of your way to make a long-distance call, or to send or receive a fax. However, some locutorios do not care to handle collect or credit-card calls, which must be placed at a Telecom or Telefónica office, or from a private telephone. If you're calling from a private phone, use Discado Directo Internacional (International Direct Dialing), which provides direct access to home-country operators for long-distance collect and credit-card calls.

Argentina's country code is ☎ 54; Buenos Aires' area code is ☎ 11. The Spanish term for area code is *característica*.

The following toll-free numbers provide direct connections to home-country operators. If you're calling from a public telephone, dial the first listed number; from a private telephone, dial the second number. (For other countries dial Telintar at ☎ 000 – a number blocked at many locutorios that do permit access to 800 numbers.)

Australia
  ☎ 0-800-555-6100
  ☎ 006-180-666-111
Canada
  ☎ 0-800-555-5500
  ☎ 001-800-222-1111
France
  ☎ 0-800-555-3300
  ☎ 0033-800-999-111

DAVID R FRAZIER

Purchasing a phone card

Germany
☎ 0-800-555-4900
☎ 00449-800-99111

Italy
☎ 0-800-555-3900
☎ 0039-800-555-111

United Kingdom (British Telecom)
☎ 0-800-555-4401
☎ 0044-800-555-111

United Kingdom (Mercury)
☎ 0-800-222-4400
☎ 0044-800-333-111

USA (AT&T)
☎ 0-800-222-1001, 0-800-555-4288
☎ 001-800-200-1111

USA (MCI)
☎ 0-800-555-1002
☎ 001-800-333-1111

USA (Sprint)
☎ 0-800-555-1003
☎ 001-800-777-1111

Fax & Telegraph

International telegrams, telexes and faxes can be sent from Encotel, still a state monopoly, at Av Corrientes 711 next door to the main Telefónica office (Map 5). Many locutorios also offer fax services.

Rates for international telegrams of up to seven words start at US$2 for neighboring countries, US$4 for the rest of the Americas and US$7 for the rest of the world. Rates more than triple for up to 25 words, double again for up to 50 words, and rise more slowly thereafter.

Email

Online services, including Internet cafés, are becoming more and more common in Buenos Aires and larger provincial cities. They are still, however, very expensive in comparison with those in the US or Europe. Recent reductions in phone charges for Internet connections, however, may result in reduced costs for end-users.

The 2600 Internet Café (☎ 4807-4929), Scalabrini Ortiz 3191 in Palermo (Map 13), charges US$8 per hour; it's open 11 am to midnight Monday through Thursday, 11 am to 1:30 am Friday and Saturday, and 6 pm to midnight Sunday. Other possibilities include the Leru Bar (☎ 4383-4940) at Rivadavia

1475 between Paraná and Uruguay in Congreso (Map 5) and the Cybercafé (☎ 4775-9440) at Maure 1886 in Palermo, on the border of Belgrano (Map 13).

Two of Palermo's major shopping centers have Internet cafés: the Web Café (☎ 4827-8000) at the Alto Palermo Shopping at Coronel Díaz and Arenales (Map 13), where the US$11 hourly charge includes coffee and an *alfajor* (a biscuit filled with, usually, *dulce de leche* or caramel), and Cybermanía (☎ 4804-9666) at the Paseo Alcorta, Av Presidente Figueroa Alcorta and Salguero (Map 13). The latter has only two computers, however.

BOOKS

There is a tremendous amount of literature on Argentina, much of it by porteño authors, so readers can afford to be selective. Many key writers, such as Jorge Luis Borges, Julio Cortázar, Adolfo Bioy Casares, Ernesto Sábato, Osvaldo Soriano and Manuel Puig have been translated into English. (For examples of their work, see Literature in the Facts about Buenos Aires chapter.) Buenos Aires is one of the Spanish-speaking world's major publishing centers and has many excellent bookstores on or near Av Corrientes, which is a delightful area to browse. (For suggestions, see the Shopping chapter.)

Most books are published in different editions by various publishers in different countries. As a result, a book might be a hardcover rarity in one country while it's readily available in paperback in another. Fortunately, bookstores and libraries search by title or author, so your local bookstore or library is the best place to find out about the availability of the recommendations below.

Lonely Planet

Other guidebooks can supplement and complement this one, especially for travelers visiting areas outside Buenos Aires or countries other than Argentina. Two good choices are the *Argentina, Uruguay & Paraguay*, also by Wayne Bernardson, and *South America on a Shoestring*. The *Latin American Spanish Phrasebook* is a handy pocket-sized guide for words and phrases.

Internet Resources

Argentina – and Buenos Aires in particular – has spawned a growing mass of Internet resources. In this fast-moving field, however, change is the rule and addresses and content can change quickly. Remember that there is a great deal of inaccurate information on the Internet, and that some websites are updated far less frequently than guidebooks (including this one!).

Government & Information

Cancillería Argentina
www.mrecic.gov.ar/pag1/pagina.htm
Argentina's foreign ministry home page, with up-to-date information on diplomatic missions, including both embassies and consulates, and visa requirements.

Centers for Disease Control & Prevention
www.cdc.gov/travel/index.htm
Official US government website with worldwide information on travel-related health issues.

Dirección General de Museos
www.buenosaires.gov.ar/cultura/museos/html/index.html
Current information on Buenos Aires museums.

Gobierno de la Ciudad de Buenos Aires
www.buenosaires.gov.ar
General information on Buenos Aires, including government, tourism, business and the like.

Grippo – El Directorio de Argentina
www.grippo.com/
Private Argentine Internet directory with huge numbers of links organized by category, including arts and humanities, news and media and science. In Spanish and English.

Instituto Nacional de Estadísticas y Censos
www.indec.mecon.ar/default.htm
Homepage for Argentine federal government's major statistical agency, though the on-line census material is insufficiently organized to be very useful.

Páginas Amarillas
www.paginasamarillas.com.ar
Searchable business phone directory, but may not include all the phone numbers you need.

Language Schools

Instituto de Lengua Española para Extranjeros
www.studyabroad.com/ilee

Tradfax
www.anunciar.com/tradfax

Lonely Planet

www.lonelyplanet.com
The Lonely Planet website has succinct summaries on traveling to most places on earth, postcards from other travelers and the *Thorn Tree* bulletin board, where you can ask questions before you go or dispense advice when you get back. You can also find travel news, updates and links to the most useful travel resources on the web.

Media

Ambito Financiero
www.ambitofinanciero.com
The website for Buenos Aires' leading financial daily.

Buenos Aires Herald
www.buenosairesherald.com
Abbreviated but still informative weekly version of the capital's venerable English-language daily. The classified section posts (often expensive) short and long-term apartment rentals.

Clarín
www.clarin.com.ar
Very complete version of the world's largest-circulation Spanish-language daily, but graphics overkill often means very slow downloading.

La Nación
www.lanacion.com.ar
Homepage of one of Buenos Aires' oldest and most prestigious dailies.

Página 12
www.pagina12.com
Left-of-center daily known for the capital's best investigative journalism.

UkiNet
www.ukinet.com/
Human-rights-oriented website by a committed and talented independent journalist.

Travel & Tourism
Aerolíneas Argentinas
www.aerolineas.com.ar/
Homepage for Argentina's traditional flag carrier.

Business Travel to Argentina
www.invertir.com/12busin.html
Information slanted toward business-oriented visitors to Buenos Aires and some provincial cities.

Council Travel
www.counciltravel.com/
Homepage for widespread network of student discount travel agencies, which also includes information on study programs.

José de Santis
www.argentinae.com/desantis/
Information on tourist-oriented *estancias*,

mostly in the Buenos Aires province, in the vicinity of the capital.

Red Argentina de Alojamiento para Jóvenes (RAAJ)
www.hostels.org.ar
Official website for local affiliate of Hostelling International.

STA Travel
www.sta-travel.com/index.html
Similar to Council Travel, a widespread network of student discount travel agencies.

Uruguay
Dieciocho – Gran Directorio de Recursos
Uruguayos en Internet
www.civila.com/uruguay/
Guide to Uruguayan Internet resources.

Mercopress News Agency
www.falkland-malvinas.com/index.html
Montevideo-based Internet news agency covering politics and business in the Mercosur countries of Argentina, Brazil, Uruguay and Paraguay, but also including both Chile and the Falkland/Malvinas Islands as well. Articles appear in English and Spanish.

Montevideo Comm
www.montevideo.com.uy/
Uruguayan Internet provider with a good choice of links for content.

Usenet Discussion Groups
Soc.culture.argentina
Wide-ranging, sometimes trivial, but often polemical and irritating discussion group.

Rec.travel.latin-america
Regional travel discussion group with frequent though not numerous items on Buenos Aires and Argentina.

Guidebooks

The *APA Insight Guides* series has volumes on Buenos Aires and Argentina which are excellent in cultural and historical analysis, but weak on practical information. They're filled with superb photographs and are better for pre-trip familiarization than use on the road. Many typographical errors mar the Argentina volume.

Readers competent in Spanish will find *La Guía Pirelli, Buenos Aires, Sus Alrededores y Costas del Uruguay* (1993) full of illuminating historical and cultural material on the capital and nearby areas, but the woefully incomplete maps are barely suitable even for orientation. It also seems to assume every visitor has a new BMW and stays in five-star hotels. (By their standards, the US$140 rooms at the Hotel Plaza Francia rate as budget accommodations.) Pirelli also publishes a guide to the entire country with the same strengths and shortcomings. Both are available in English, but can be hard to find; the English language editions are less up-to-date than the Spanish versions.

For a distinct specialized audience, there's always Raquel Orella and Marcela Osa's *Guía Erótica de Buenos Aires* (1994).

History

The late James Scobie's *Argentina: A City and a Nation*, which has gone through many editions, is the standard Buenos Aires-biased account of the country's development. Even more closely focused on the capital is Scobie's *Buenos Aires: Plaza to Suburb, 1870-1910* (1974), which focuses on the city's social evolution during the period of its greatest growth.

The most comprehensive English-language history of the country is David Rock's *Argentina 1516-1987: From Spanish Colonization to the Falklands War and Alfonsín* (1987). Visitors interested in the capital's sizable Jewish community should acquire Víctor Mirelman's *Jewish Buenos Aires, 1890-1930: In Search of an Identity* (1990). Mirelman did his research in the archives of the Asociación Mutual Israelita Argentina (AMIA), since destroyed by a terrorist bomb in 1994.

Arts & Architecture

For a brief survey of modern Argentine art in English, look for Jorge Glusberg's *Art in Argentina* (1986). Readers who understand Spanish can try Rafael Squirru's *Arte Argentino Hoy* (Ediciones de Arte Gaglianone, Buenos Aires, 1983), a selection of work from 48 contemporary painters and sculptors illustrated in color.

Readers who know Spanish may enjoy Diego Curubeto's entertaining *Babilonia Gaucha* (1993), which explores the relationship between Hollywood and Argentina. Curubeto, a film critic at the Buenos Aires business newspaper *Ambito Financiero*, also authored *Cine Bizarro* (1996), an account of offbeat films from Argentina and other countries.

Though selective in its coverage, the multiauthored *Buenos Aires: Guía de Arquitectura* (1994) is a superbly written and illustrated guide to the city's architecture, with outstanding B&W photographs. Eight suggested walking tours focus on some of the city's most notable buildings and public spaces. It also offers a representative selection of activities and places to dine. Although expensive at nearly US$40, it's highly recommended for travelers spending any length of time in the city. Even those with limited Spanish will find it a useful resource.

FILMS

A truly creepy English-language film with a Dirty War theme, Martin Donovan's *Apartment Zero* (1989) depicts many amusing aspects of porteño life as it follows an Anglo-Argentine film buff (played by Colin Firth) who takes a morbid interest in his mysterious North American housemate.

Fay Dunaway's salary probably absorbed 90% of the budget in the appalling *Eva Perón* (1981), an NBC-TV miniseries now trying to recover costs in video release. Even worse, though filmed in Buenos Aires (and Budapest) on a much larger budget, is Alan Parker's *Evita* (1996), a cheesy effort confirming Mick Jagger's judgment that Madonna was 'a thimbleful of talent in an ocean of ambition.' Even more recently,

Buenos Aires gets obliterated in the cartoonish sci-fi epic *Starship Troopers* (1997), whose heroes are porteños, and parts of the Brad Pitt epic *Seven Years in Tibet* (1997) were shot in Argentina's Mendoza province, near the Chilean border.

(For a listing of Argentine directors and films, see Film in the Facts about Buenos Aires chapter.)

NEWSPAPERS & MAGAZINES

Argentina is South America's most literate country, supporting a wide spectrum of newspapers and magazines despite unceasing economic crisis. Freedom of the press is far greater than under the military dictatorship of 1976-83, but abuses still occur. The present administration, for instance, has withheld government advertising from newspapers that have investigated official corruption too vigorously for its taste, and the administration even won a libel suit against the respected weekly magazine *Noticias* despite everyone's admission that the facts of the case – the birth of a son to President Menem out of wedlock – were in fact true. The unsolved 1997 murder of *Noticias* photographer José Luis Cabezas, which was linked to shady businessman Alfredo Yabrán (who had ties to President Menem), is an issue that refuses to go away.

Buenos Aires nonetheless has a thriving daily press of 11 nationwide dailies, several of them now online, with unambiguous political leanings. Part of a multimedia consortium that also includes radio and TV stations, the centrist tabloid *Clarín* sells about 600,000 copies daily and more than a million Sunday papers – the largest circulation of any newspaper in the Spanish-speaking world. It has an excellent Sunday cultural section and is also the publisher of the new sports-oriented daily *¡Olé!* (circulation 60,000).

La Nación, founded in 1870 by former president Bartolomé Mitre, has moved from the right toward the center, but has come to resemble some of its less thoughtful competitors in the process. Its circulation is about 200,000 daily, double that on Sundays. *La Prensa* is equally venerable, but less influential.

The tabloid *Página 12* provides refreshing leftist perspectives and often breaks important stories that mainstream newspapers are slow to cover, but it has lost much of the innovative fervor that characterized its early years in the aftermath of the military dictatorship. Many articles are long and repetitive, but political columnist Horacio Verbitsky is widely acknowledged as the best in the country. Circulation is about 30,000 weekdays, 45,000 Sundays; it does not publish Mondays.

The tabloid *Crónica*, which has a weekday circulation of 400,000, is the counterpart to the USA's *National Enquirer* or Rupert Murdoch's *Sun*. Its circulation diminishes on weekends, since most of its public read it on the way to work.

Ambito Financiero, the morning voice of the capital's financial community and a strong supporter of the Menem administration's economic policies, also has an excellent entertainment and cultural section. *El Cronista* is its afternoon rival. Both have circulations of around 30,000 and, along with the less influential *Buenos Aires Económico*, appear weekdays only.

Weekly magazine *Noticias* is the local equivalent to *Time* or *Newsweek*, while the recent startup *Trespuntos* takes a more aggressive, investigative stance. Monthlies like *La Maga* and *El Porteño* offer a forum for Argentine intellectuals and contribute greatly to the capital's cultural life. The monthly *Humor* caricatured the Argentine

Weighty Journalism

According to statistics from porteño journalist Ernesto Seman, hauling around Buenos Aires' eight Sunday papers might make a good workout. Each Sunday, an average 1500 pages (weighing 4.8kg) are published – equivalent to the amount of paper needed for nearly 19 average-sized books. The largest newspapers are *Clarín* (414 pages, 1.03kg) and *La Nación* (360 pages, 1.11kg). *Página 12* brings up the rear (84 pages, 300g).

military during the Dirty War and even during the early nationalist hysteria of the Falklands conflict. In safer times, it has lost much of its edge but is still worth reading. Avoid its soft-porn spin-off *Humor Sexo*. Strangely, in a country known for conservative Catholicism and male machismo, downtown kiosks sell (or at least display) a surprising amount of gay pornography.

The English-language daily *Buenos Aires Herald* covers Argentina and the world from an Anglo-Argentine perspective, emphasizing commerce and finance, but its perceptive weekend summaries of political and economic developments are a must for visitors with limited Spanish; its Sunday edition now includes Britain's *Guardian Weekly* (see The *Herald* & Its History). *Argentinisches Tageblatt* is a German-language weekly that appears Saturdays.

North American and European newspapers like the *New York Times*, *USA Today*, the *Guardian* and *Le Monde* are available at kiosks at the corner of Florida and Av

The *Herald* & Its History

Ever since its debut under Scottish founder William Cathcart in 1876, the *Buenos Aires Herald* has played a critical, activist role in times of crisis, while Argentina's Spanish-language press has often been timid or sycophantic. The *Herald* could do this in part because it appears in English, but that did not insulate it against official and extra-official hostility. During the Dirty War of 1976-83, the newspaper was outspoken in condemning military, paramilitary, police and guerrilla abuses. When the dictatorship decreed that only official notices regarding the Disappeared could be published, the *Herald* responded by printing requests for habeas corpus.

Not surprisingly, editor Robert Cox and his family became the focus of threats that forced them into exile, as did current senior editor Andrew Graham-Yooll. Nationalist hysteria during the Falklands/Malvinas War of 1982 led Cox's successor James Neilson to move himself and his family across the river to Uruguay for the duration of the conflict. Still, the paper never backed off from its independent editorial stance.

These were not the paper's first encounters with political coercion. In the early 1950s, Juan Perón's government forced the paper to sell its printing plant in an effort to control production, distribution, and (indirectly) editorial policy. By 1975, though, the paper had built new offices and a printing plant only a few blocks from the Casa Rosada presidential palace.

In the interest of being accessible to all Argentines, the *Herald* publishes its editorials in both English and Spanish. Several sections, including regular aviation and shipping features, reflect the commercial interests of the Anglo-Argentine community, though much of the paper's advertising also appears in Spanish. The current owner is the Evening Post Publishing Company of Charleston, South Carolina, which in 1968 purchased a controlling interest from the Italo-British Rugeroni family, who had owned it since 1925 and recently sold their remaining 40%.

Although the Herald had a circulation as large as 50,000 in the 1930s, today it is only about 9000. However, with increased news coverage and the addition of several supplements, particularly foreign business, finance and tourism, the paper hopes to nearly double its circulation within two years. The *Herald's* readers comprise a varied lot from traditional Anglo-Argentines to international business impresarios to students and teachers of English, as well as tourists.

Most of the *Herald's* staff are Argentines, from the secretarial staff and gofers to the editor-in-chief, and there's a scattering of other nationalities, including British, American and Australian. Attentive readers will notice irregularities and idiosyncrasies that set the paper apart from its overseas counterparts. The typesetting, for example, often reflects Spanish rather than English syllabification.

Córdoba – at premium prices (US$10 or more for the Sunday *New York Times*, for example). Magazines like *Time*, *Newsweek* and the *Economist* are also easy to obtain.

RADIO & TV

In the post-Proceso years, the end of government monopoly in the electronic media opened up the airwaves to a greater variety of programming than in the past. The most popular station, the nationwide Radio Rivadavia, is a combination of Top 40 and talk radio, but there are many other choices on the AM band, including Radio Mitre (AM 800). Dozens of FM stations specialize in styles from classical to pop to tango – FM Tango 92.7 has tango all day, every day. Radio Nacional (FM 96.5), widely diffused throughout the country, has good news coverage.

As in other countries, media conglomerates have great influence. *Clarín* is only the print flagship of a group that includes Radio Mitre, two TV stations and other outlets. Likewise, *El Cronista*'s holding company controls two major TV stations and a substantial amount of cable service throughout the country.

Legalization of privately owned television companies and the cable revolution, however, have brought a wider variety of programming to the small screen. To be sure, there are countless game shows, dance parties and soap operas *(novelas)*, but there is also serious public-affairs programming on major stations at prime viewing times like Sunday evening. English-speakers can tune to CNN for news and ESPN for sports. Spanish and Chilean stations are also available.

PHOTOGRAPHY & VIDEO

Kinefot (☎ 4374-7445), Talcahuano 248 in Congreso (Map 5), has fast, high-quality developing of E-6 slide film, but is not cheap. For prints, try Le Lab (☎ 4322-2785) at Viamonte 624 or Laboclick at Esmeralda 444, both in the Microcentro of San Nicolás (Map 5).

For minor camera repairs, visit Gerardo Föhse (☎ 4311-1139), in the basement at Florida 835, Local 37 in Retiro (Map 11). For fast, reliable service on more complex problems, contact José Norres (☎ 4373-0963), Oficina 403, 4th floor, Lavalle 1569 in San Nicolás (Map 5).

TIME

Argentina is three hours behind GMT/UTC; the country no longer observes daylight-savings time (summer time).

ELECTRICITY

Electric current operates on 220 volts, 50 cycles. Travelers bringing appliances from countries that use the 100-volt system, such as the USA, can find a large concentration of shops specializing in transformers and adapters on Talcahuano, south of Av Corrientes in San Nicolás (Map 5).

WEIGHTS & MEASURES

The metric system is universal, but a few vernacular measures survive. *Manos* (hands) are used to measure horses and *leguas* (leagues) to measure distances in the countryside, while carpenters often use English units. Tire pressure is commonly measured in pounds per square inch. There's a conversions chart inside the back cover of this book.

LAUNDRY

In recent years, laundromats have become much more common in Buenos Aires, but they tend to be more expensive than their equivalents in the USA or Europe. (Figure about US$6 to US$8 per load, washed, dried and folded.) Some inexpensive hotels have spots where you can wash your own clothes and hang them to dry. Some hotels offer laundry service at reasonable prices, but agree on charges in advance.

RECYCLING

Most beer and soft-drink bottles purchased at markets and grocery stores are reusable, and merchants collect a small deposit for them. They usually only reimburse customers for bottles purchased from their own store, but accept bottles from other sources in exchange for a new bottle deposit. At the junction of the Florida and Lavalle peatonales in the Microcentro (Map 5), there are containers for recycling aluminum and colored glass.

TOILETS

In terms of sanitation, public toilets are probably better than in most of South America, but there are certainly exceptions. For the truly squeamish, the better restaurants and cafés are good alternatives. Always carry your own toilet paper, since it often seems to run out in public restrooms.

HEALTH

Buenos Aires' Hospital Municipal Juan Fernández (☎ 4801-5555) is at Av Cerviño 3356 in Palermo (Map 13), but there are many others, including the highly regarded British Hospital (☎ 4304-1081) at Perdriel 74 in Barracas, several blocks southwest of the Constitución train station (Map 9). The reader-recommended Hospital Alemán (☎ 4821-1700) is a private facility at Av Pueyrredón 1640, Recoleta (Map 12).

WOMEN TRAVELERS

In Argentina, attitudes to women remain traditional, and International Women's Day becomes yet another occasion to 'send her flowers.' For women traveling alone, the country is probably safer than Europe, the USA and most other Latin American countries, but Buenos Aires is notorious for annoyances such as unwelcome physical contact, particularly on crowded buses or trains. If you're physically confident, a slap or a well-aimed elbow should discourage any further contact. If not, a scream can be very effective.

Other nuisances include crude language and *piropos*. There is no universally accepted definition of a piropo, but most Argentine males consider it the art of approaching a woman in public and commenting on her femininity or attractiveness. This is idealized – piropos are most often vulgar, although some are creative and even eloquent. (One cited in the *Buenos Aires Herald* was 'Oh God, the sky is parting and angels are falling.') Crude language, generally in the presence of other males, usually emphasizes feminine physical attributes. If you respond aggressively ('Are you talking to me?'), you will probably shame the aggressor. One clever New Yorker found that a bogus wedding ring helped discourage unwanted admirers, but some porteños would consider this a challenge rather than a deterrent.

While verbal aggression can be irritating, it rarely becomes physical. On occasions when persistent suitors trail you for blocks, the best means of discouraging their pursuit is to completely ignore them.

Single women checking in at budget hotels may find themselves objects of suspicion, since prostitutes may frequent such places. If you otherwise like the place, ignore this and the suspicions will evaporate. You should interpret questions as to whether you are running away from parents or husband as expressions of concern.

GAY & LESBIAN TRAVELERS

While Argentina is a strongly Catholic country and homosexuality is taboo, there are enclaves of tolerance in Buenos Aires (particularly along Av Santa Fe and in Recoleta), the Delta del Paraná and some other areas. Argentine males are often more physically demonstrative than North American and European males, so behaviors such as kissing (at least on the cheek in greeting) or a vigorous embrace may seem innocuous even to those who express unease with homosexuals. Lesbians walking hand-in-hand should attract little attention, since heterosexual Argentine women frequently do so, but this would be very conspicuous behavior for males. When in doubt, it's better to be discreet.

As everywhere, the gay community has its own slang. Heterosexuals are *gente nada que ver* (literally, 'people nothing to see') or *paquis* (the latter short for *paquidermos* or pachyderms). Closeted male homosexuals are *chongos*, while lesbians may be called *locas* (crazies). Very masculine lesbians may be called *bomberos* (firemen) or *camioneros* (truckers).

There are now several organizations of particular interest to gay visitors. In addition to HIV/AIDS support groups (see Useful Organizations later in this chapter), there are the Comunidad Homosexual Argentina (CHA; ☎ 4393-9736) at Viamonte 611, 9th floor in the Microcentro (Map 5); Gays por Derechos Civiles (☎ 4381-2327)

Buenos Aires' *porteños*

ALLAN PHILIBA

ROBERT FRERCK

ROBERT FRERCK

GUSTAVO GATTO

WAYNE BERNHARDSON

Looking toward Av de Mayo from the Palacio del Congreso

ROBERT FRERCK

Up all night: Calle Lavalle in the Microcentro

ROBERT FRERCK

Teatro Colón

ROBERT FRIED

Browsing at a downtown kiosk

RANDY WELLS

Argentine landmarks: the national flag and the Obelisco on Av 9 de Julio

Palacio del Congreso

at Virrey Cevallos 463, 1st floor, Oficina B, in Montserrat (Map 7), which advises gays hassled or arrested by the police; and Lesbianas a la Vista (☎ 4307-6656), Piedras 1170, 1st floor, in Constitución (Map 9). Together, these groups sponsor a small Marcha de Orgullo Gay (Gay Pride Parade) from the Plaza de Mayo to Congreso in late June.

DISABLED TRAVELERS

Travelers with disabilities will find things difficult at times. The wheelchair-bound in particular will find Buenos Aires' narrow, often broken sidewalks difficult to negotiate. Crossing streets is also a problem, since Argentine drivers can be a challenge to even world-class gymnasts. Nevertheless, Argentines with disabilities do get around. One of the most famous works of contemporary Argentine fiction is Ernesto Sábato's *On Heroes and Tombs*, which includes the extraordinary 'Report on the Blind' based, in part, on the author's Buenos Aires observations. (The now elderly Sábato, however, is not blind).

SENIOR TRAVELERS

Senior travelers should encounter no particular difficulties in Buenos Aires, where older citizens traditionally enjoy a great deal of respect; on crowded buses, for instance, most Argentines will readily offer their seat to an older person. Senior discounts on transportation and most other services are, however, virtually a thing of the past.

Certain areas, such as the city's many plazas and, specifically, the chess tables in Parque Lezama in San Telmo (Map 8) are hangouts for seniors. In general, though, Argentines do not segregate themselves by age either formally or informally, and cross-generational communication is excellent.

BUENOS AIRES FOR CHILDREN

Although it's a major megalopolis, Buenos Aires is remarkably child-friendly. Once children are old enough to cross the street safely and find their way back home, porteño parents don't hesitate to send unaccompanied preadolescents on errands or on visits to friends or neighbors. While most visiting parents are not likely to know the city well enough to feel comfortable doing this, they can usually count on their children's safety in public places.

Porteños are very helpful on public transport. Often someone will give up a seat for a parent and child, but if that does not occur an older person may offer to put the child on his or her lap. Sometimes this is so spontaneous that foreigners find someone pulling the child out of their arms. This is also a country where people frequently touch each other, so your children may be patted on the head or gently caressed.

Basic restaurants provide a wide selection of food suitable for children (vegetables, pasta, meat, chicken, fish), but adult portions are normally so large that small children rarely need a separate order. Waiters are accustomed to providing extra plates and cutlery for children, though some places may add a small additional charge. Argentina's high-quality ice cream is a special treat.

Breast-feeding in public is uncommon, but mothers can always retreat into a café and cover themselves with a baby blanket during feedings.

Poorly maintained public bathrooms may be a concern for some parents. Always carry toilet paper, which is rarely stocked. While a woman may take a young boy into the ladies' room, it would be socially unacceptable for a man to take a girl of any age into the men's room.

Buenos Aires' numerous plazas and public parks, many with playgrounds, are popular gathering spots for families; the most attractive are the wide open spaces of Palermo (Map 13). Plaza Alemania, fronting on Av del Libertador between Cavia and Av Casares in Palermo, is where porteño skateboarders go to show their moves; younger children also bicycle and rollerblade in the area.

Ambito Financiero, the capital's financial newspaper, publishes an excellent Friday cultural section with listings of children's activities, including films, music and theater presentations. Many of these activities take place during winter recess (early to mid-July) and are very crowded.

USEFUL ORGANIZATIONS

Asatej (☎ 4311-6953, fax 4311-6840), Argentina's nonprofit student travel agency and an affiliate of STA Travel, is at Florida 835, 3rd floor, in Retiro (Map 11). The organization is eager to encourage budget travelers, and you need not be a student to take advantage of their services. Asatej is also affiliated with Hostelling International through the Red Argentina de Albergues Juveniles (RAAJ; see Hostel Card, earlier in this chapter), and is helping to expand and promote the Argentine hostel system. For other Asatej locations, see Travel Agents in the Getting There & Away chapter.

Travelers can also contact the Asociación Argentina de Albergues de la Juventud (AAAJ; ☎/fax 4476-1001), 2nd floor, Oficina 6, Talcahuano 214, 1013 Buenos Aires (Map 5), for information on Argentine youth hostels. This office also serves as a travel agency, issues international student cards, and maintains a message board for travelers (mostly young Argentines) seeking companions for extended trips. AAAJ is, however, moribund in comparison with Asatej and RAAJ. The two hostel representatives overlap affiliations with some hostels, but also represent others exclusively.

The Administración de Parques Nacionales (APN; ☎ 4312-0783), Av Santa Fe 690 in Retiro (Map 11), provides information on national parks and stocks a small number of publications interesting to conservationists and wildlife enthusiasts. Inquiries out of the ordinary, however, usually draw blank stares.

Another address of interesting to conservationists is the pro-wildlife organization Fundación Vida Silvestre Argentina (☎ 4331-4864), Defensa 245, just south of Plaza de Mayo in Montserrat (Map 7). Membership starts at US$35 per year and includes a subscription to the foundation's newsletter, *Otioso*; US$60 membership includes the group's magazine, *Revista Vida Silvestre*. It's open 9:30 am to 6 pm weekdays.

Bird watching enthusiasts can contact the Asociación Ornitológica del Plata (☎ 4312-8958) at 25 de Mayo 749, 2nd floor, in the Microcentro (Map 5); hours are 3 to 9 pm

weekdays. The Argentine affiliate of Greenpeace (☎ 4962-2291) is at Lucio N Mansilla 3046, a few blocks from the Agüero station on Línea D of the Subte (underground) in Recoleta (Map 12).

Buenos Aires has two AIDS-related support organizations. Cooperación, Información y Ayuda al Enfermo de SIDA (Coinsida; ☎ 4304-6664) is an information and assistance center for people with AIDS and HIV at Dr E Finocchietto 1263 in Barracas (Map 9). Línea SIDA (☎ 4922-1617) is at Zuviría 64 (Subte: Av La Plata) in the barrio of Parque Chacabuco, near Caballito (Map 15).

LIBRARIES

At Agüero 2502 in Recoleta, the Biblioteca Nacional (National Library; ☎ 4806-9764), is open 8 am to 9 pm Monday through Saturday, 11 am to 7 pm Sundays. Guided visits take place at 4 pm weekdays. The library is also the site of frequent literary events and free concerts.

The United States Information Agency has moved its excellent Biblioteca Lincoln, which carries the *New York Times*, the *Washington Post* and English-language magazines, to the Instituto Cultural Argentino-Norteamericano (☎ 4322-3855, 4322-4557), Maipú 672 in the Microcentro (Map 5).

CULTURAL CENTERS

One of Buenos Aires' finest cultural resources is the high-rise Centro Cultural San Martín (☎ 4374-1251), with free or inexpensive galleries, live theater and lectures. Most visitors enter from Av Corrientes, between Paraná and Montevideo in Congreso (Map 5), but the official address is Sarmiento 1551, where the Plaza Cubierta has rotating exhibitions of outdoor sculpture and occasional free concerts on summer evenings and weekends. Films are shown at the Sala Leopoldo Lugones – visited by more than 80,000 moviegoers in 1997 – while photographers display their work at the basement Fotogalería. Ask at the front desk for a monthly list of events, or check the boards outside the Corrientes entrance.

At Junín 1930 in Recoleta (Map 12), the Centro Cultural Ciudad de Buenos Aires

(☎ 4803-1041) also offers free or inexpensive events, including art exhibitions and outdoor films on summer evenings. At the southeast corner of the Galerías Pacífico, at the corner of Viamonte and San Martín in the Microcentro (Map 5), the new Centro Cultural Borges (☎ 4319-5359) features art exhibits. It's open Monday through Thursday 10 am to 9 pm, Friday through Sunday 10 am to 10 pm. Admission costs US$2.

A similar facility is the Complejo Cultural Ricardo Rojas (☎ 4953-0390) at the Universidad de Buenos Aires, Av Corrientes 2038 in Balvanera (Map 6), open 10 am to 10 pm Monday through Saturday. The Centro Cultural del Sur (☎ 4306-0301), on the border between Constitución and Barracas at Av Caseros 1750 (Map 9), has live music, food, juices and the like, open 4 to 9 pm daily.

There are also several foreign cultural centers in the Microcentro (Map 5), such as the Instituto Cultural Argentino-Norteamericano (☎ 4322-3855, 4322-4557) at Maipú 672; the *Alianza Francesa* (☎ 4322-0068), Av Córdoba 936; the Instituto Goethe (☎ 4315-3327), Av Corrientes 319, 1st floor, offers German-language instruction, lectures, films and even concerts.

The Asociación Argentina de Cultura Inglesa/British Arts Centre (☎ 4393-6941), Suipacha 1333 in Retiro (Map 11), is open 3 to 9 pm weekdays, 11 am to 1:30 pm Saturdays, but is closed in January and February. Admission is free. At Av Casares 3015 in Palermo (Map 13), the Fundación Cultural Japonés (☎ 4804-4922) showcases Japanese art and promotes cultural contacts with Argentina.

DANGERS & ANNOYANCES

While violent crime is relatively rare, and personal security is a lesser concern than in most other Latin American cities, parts of the barrio of La Boca have seen armed robberies against visitors. As in most places, travelers cannot afford to be complacent with their possessions: pickpockets and purse-snatchers certainly exist.

Watch particularly for diversions like the 'inadvertent' collision that results in ice cream or some substance being spilled on an unsuspecting visitor, who loses precious personal possessions while distracted by the apologetic perpetrator working in concert with a thief. (One LP reader eloquently called them 'mustard artists.') Some travelers have had similar problems with ambulatory street vendors at sidewalk cafés.

Porteño drivers, like most Argentines, jump the gun when the traffic signal is about to change to green. Be especially wary of vehicles turning right; even though pedestrians at corners and crosswalks have legal right-of-way, almost nobody behind the wheel respects it. In 1997, 423 pedestrians died in traffic accidents – a figure roughly equal to the number of citations issued for failure to cede right-of-way – and approximately 10 times that of pedestrian traffic deaths in Paris or Madrid.

Other troublesome and even potentially deadly hazards include potholes and loose tiles on city sidewalks, which can also be slippery when wet; pedestrians have died after falling and striking their heads.

US residents concerned with domestic travel conditions in Argentina or any country can obtain recorded travel information from the US Department of State Bureau of Consular Affairs (☎ 202-647-5225).

Police & Military

Travelers may find the police, who are not above petty harassment, of more concern than common criminals. The Buenos Aires provincial police is the country's single most notoriously corrupt force, though members of the capital's Policía Federal are no angels. For motorists, so-called safety campaigns often result in citations for minor equipment violations, such as a malfunctioning turn signal, that carry very high fines. In most cases, corrupt officers will settle for less expensive *coimas* (bribes), but this requires considerable caution and tact. A discreet hint that you intend to phone your consulate may minimize or eliminate such problems: often the police count on foreigners' ignorance of Argentine law. Another tactic, whether you know Spanish or not, is to pretend you don't understand what an officer is saying.

Avoid military installations, which still often display the warning 'No stopping or photographs – the sentry will shoot.' Though a military coup or similar emergency may seem unlikely, state-of-siege regulations suspend all civil rights; carry identification at all times, and make sure someone knows your whereabouts. If you have more problems with police and want more information on Argentine laws, contact your embassy or consulate for advice.

Fireworks

A major cause for concern is the widespread availability of fireworks, which are high-powered, poorly regulated and very dangerous. Especially around holidays such

as Christmas and New Year's, arrested-development cretins set off firecrackers in the streets and even toss them from high-rise apartments. (When these go off between tall buildings, the echo-chamber effect mimics the bombing of Dresden or Hanoi.) It may be better to stay off the streets at these times.

Terrorism

The state terrorism of the 1970s and 1980s has subsided, but deadly attempts on Jewish and Israeli centers in Buenos Aires in 1992 and 1994 raised questions about the government's commitment to public safety. In the months prior to the bombings, anti-Semitic incidents were increasingly common, and most Jewish community landmarks are now heavily fortified with concrete barriers, some of them thinly disguised as planters.

In late 1997, an Argentine congressional committee learned that a Buenos Aires provincial policeman charged in connection with the 1994 Asociación Mutual Israelita Argentina (AMIA) bombing, for which Islamic Jihad claimed responsibility, re-

ceived US\$2.5 million just prior to the act. Police officers provided the still unidentified perpetrators with a stolen van.

In late 1997 and early 1998 there were incidents of vandalism in Jewish cemeteries in and around Buenos Aires, some linked to the provincial police.

Tobacco

Many Argentines are heavy smokers, even though most will acknowledge the habit is unhealthy. (If lung cancer death rates are not higher than in other cities, it's only because so many porteños perish in traffic accidents first.) In what might be the ultimate example of 'unclear on the concept,' the author once saw a porteño jogger with a lighted *pucho* in his mouth.

Nevertheless, long-distance and local buses, the Buenos Aires Subte and some other areas are legally smoke-free, even if enforcement is lax. All domestic flights are now smoke-free as well.

Under municipal legislation, many restaurants and *confiterías* have set aside smoke-free areas, but this is optional. Travelers bothered by second-hand smoke in an inappropriate setting, such as a taxi, will find it more productive to appeal to common courtesy by pleading *alergia* (allergy) than to get indignant.

BUSINESS HOURS

Traditionally, business hours commence by 8 am and break at midday for three or even four hours, during which time people return home for lunch and a brief siesta. After the siesta, shops reopen until 8 or 9 pm. This schedule is still common in the provinces, but government offices and many Buenos Aires businesses have adopted a more conventional 8 am to 5 pm schedule in the interests of 'greater efficiency' and, especially in the case of government, reduced corruption.

PUBLIC HOLIDAYS & SPECIAL EVENTS

Government offices and businesses are closed on the numerous national holidays, which include:

January 1
  Año Nuevo – New Year's Day
March/April
  Viernes Santo/Pascua – Good Friday/Easter
May 1
  Día del Trabajador – Labor Day
May 25
  Revolución de Mayo – May Revolution
June 10
  Día de las Malvinas – Malvinas Day
June 20
  Día de la Bandera – Flag Day
July 9
  Día de la Independencia – Independence Day
August 17
  Día de San Martín – Date of San Martín's death
October 12
  Día de la Raza – Columbus Day
December 25
  Navidad – Christmas Day

Visitors spending an extended period in Buenos Aires should ask the municipal Dirección General de Turismo for its annual booklet listing special events in the city. (One section covers January through June, while the other covers July through December.) It also lists congresses and conventions due to take place in the capital, but probably only a handful of readers will be interested in events like the annual plastic-surgery congress. For short-term visitors, *Turismo's* quarterly brochure of activities – including current exhibits, concerts and other items – is a valuable resource.

Restricted to a small area on Av de Mayo between Bolívar and Luis Sáenz Peña in Montserrat, Buenos Aires' official Carnaval is a very modest celebration by Brazilian standards (even Montevideo's is more impressive), but it appears to be growing in size and importance despite its flagrant commercialism. Taking place on weekends only, most festivities in this slow-moving event consist of spraying passersby with canned foam which, fortunately, leaves no permanent stains on clothing (bring a towel or handkerchief to wipe it from your eyes or off your glasses). Visiting *comparsas* (troupes) from Carnaval hotbeds like Corrientes and Gualeguaychú, however, may be well worth seeing.

In late March, horse lovers flock to Palermo for the Exposición de Otoño de la Asociación Criadores de Caballos Criollos, showcasing Argentine-bred equines. It takes place at the Predio Ferial de la Sociedad Rural Argentina on Av Sarmiento (Subte: Plaza Italia; Map 13); for details, contact the Asociación Criadores de Caballos Criollos (☎ 4961-2305), Larrea 670, 2nd floor, in Balvanera (Map 6).

Buenos Aires' annual book fair, the Feria del Libro, attracts more than a million patrons during the first three weeks of April. Most exhibitors come from Latin America, but by no means all; in 1995, there were displays from England, China, France, Ukraine, Norway, Armenia and other countries. It takes place at the sprawling Centro Municipal de Exposiciones (☎ 4374-1251, ext 208) at Av Figueroa Alcorta and Av Pueyrredón in Recoleta (Map 12), and is so important that the president of the country gives the opening address. Admission costs US$4 or US$5, depending on the day, but many bookstores give away tickets.

Though porteño motorists seem to be constantly in training for the Gran Prix Fórmula 1, the capital's major auto race officially takes place in early to mid-April at the Autódromo Municipal Oscar Gálvez (☎ 4638-1995), on the outskirts of the Capital Federal, at Av General Paz and Av Coronel Roca in the barrio of Villa Riachuelo (Map 2).

The local art world's counterpart to the Feria del Libro is mid-May's Feria de Galerías Arte BA, a rapidly growing event that now features more than 80 different galleries. Having started small in 1991, it recently moved from the Centro Cultural Ciudad de Buenos Aires in Recoleta to the much larger Centro Municipal de Exposiciones (Map 12).

June 24 is the Día de la Muerte de Carlos Gardel, the anniversary of Gardel's death in a plane crash in Medellín, Colombia. Numerous tango events during the week bookend pilgrimages to the singer's tomb in the Cementerio de la Chacarita (Map 2).

Winter's biggest celebration is July's Exposición Internacional de Ganadería,

Agricultura y Pesca, the annual agricultural exhibition organized by the Sociedad Rural Argentina (☎ 4326-5095). It takes place at the Predio Ferial in Palermo (Map 13).

Though not a formal holiday, November 11 is the Día de San Martín de Tours, the capital's patron saint. In late November, runners can try the Maratón Internacional de la Argentina (☎ 4753-9040, ext 248), which draws up to 15,000 participants. It starts at 8 am in the 3800 block of Av Figueroa Alcorta in Palermo (Map 13).

Día del Tango commemorates Gardel's birthday December 11. There are many tango events around this informal holiday, and the singer's tomb at Chacarita draws further crowds of pilgrims.

The spring polo season culminates in December's Campeonato Abierto Argentino de Polo (Argentine Open Polo Championship), taking place at Palermo's Campo Argentino de Polo (☎ 4774-4517), at Av del Libertador and Dorrego (Map 13). For details, contact the Asociación Argentina de Polo (☎ 4343-0972), Hipólito Yrigoyen 636 in Montserrat (Map 7).

Around the same time, the gaucho sport of pato holds its Campeonato Argentino Abierto de Pato (Argentine Open Pato Championship); for details, contact the Federación Argentino de Pato (☎ 4331-0222), Av Belgrano 530, 5th floor, in Montserrat (Map 7).

DOING BUSINESS

Foreign businesses in Argentina generally enjoy the same legal status as local businesses, with very few exceptions, and there are no restrictions on movement of capital into and out of the country. Argentina's relative economic stability and freemarket privatization policies have encouraged foreign investment in recent years, but some observers still harbor doubts about long-term prospects. Businesses still encounter instances of inconsistent regulations, fraud and corruption, and there have been cases of gullible foreign firms – even large and sophisticated ones – getting scammed by unscrupulous opertors. In 1998, an international survey of foreign and national businesspeople ranked Argentina as the 16th most corrupt of 54 countries evaluated. Customs procedures, in particular, are expensive and time-consuming, and the so-called aduana paralela (parallel customs) has been a major scandal. Before signing contracts, consult a lawyer recommended by your embassy or consulate.

Credit remains expensive, particularly for smaller businesses. Intellectual property rights, especially for computer software and entertainment items like sound and video recordings, have been a serious international issue, and Argentina has drawn criticism for failure to protect these rights as well.

Besides the porteño business newspapers *Ambito Financiero* and *El Cronista*, the magazines *Apertura*, *Mercado* and *Negocios* are the most important sources of business information. At present, according to the US embassy, the best potential for nonagricultural goods and services exists in the following areas: travel and tourism services, electric power generation and transmission equipment, medical equipment, franchising services, oil and gas field machinery, telecommunications equipment, airport and ground support equipment, construction and building materials, packaging equipment and pollution control equipment.

Business Etiquette

More so than in North America or Europe, business negotiations depend on personal contacts, which can take some time to establish. Before making a business call, it is advisable to set up an appointment. Business dress, appearance and general approach are traditionally conservative, but things are changing; it's not all that rare, for instance, to see youthful male bankers with ponytails, though they still may wear tailored suits. Many Argentine businesspeople speak good English, but foreigners who manage Spanish well will make a good impression.

Since Argentines usually take their vacations in the summer months of January and February, business travelers may find it difficult to conduct business during that time without making preparations far in advance. The best months for business travel are April through November.

Useful Addresses

The following contacts may prove useful for business travelers in Buenos Aires.

Administración Nacional de Aduanas (customs)
   (☎ 4343-0661, fax 4331-9881)
   Azopardo 350, Montserrat

Bolsa de Comercio de Buenos Aires (Buenos
Aires Stock Exchange)
   (☎ 4311-5231, fax 4312-5010)
   Sarmiento 299, 1st floor

Cámara Argentina de Comercio (Argentine
Chamber of Commerce)
   (☎ 4343-9423, fax 4331-8051)
   Av Leandro N Alem 36, ground floor

Cámara de Comercio de los Estados Unidos en
Argentina (US Chamber of Commerce in
Argentina)
   (☎ 4371-4500, fax 4371-8400)
   Viamonte 1133, 8th floor

Cámara de Importadores de la República
Argentina (Argentine Chamber of Importers)
   (☎ 4342-1101, fax 4345-3003)
   Av Belgrano 427, 7th floor

Sociedad Rural Argentina (Argentine Agricultural
Association)
   (☎ 4322-3431, fax 4325-8231)
   Florida 460

WORK

It's not unusual for visiting travelers to work as English-language instructors in Buenos Aires, but wages are much lower than in the US or Europe, even for certified teachers. The city's high cost of living is also a major discouragement. Check the classified section of the *Buenos Aires Herald*. Residence and work permits are relatively easy to obtain, but the effort may not be worth it.

Getting There & Away

Buenos Aires has a bewildering variety of transportation options. Most daily newspapers, including the English-language *Buenos Aires Herald*, publish lists of arriving and departing international flights, and air and bus schedules are fairly easy to come by. Bus services are frequent to most major domestic destinations, and there are also ferry and hydrofoil services to Uruguay across the Río de la Plata.

AIR

There are often significant seasonal discounts, so try to avoid peak travel times such as Christmas and New Year's or Easter. Advance purchase of a ticket for a given period of time, usually less than six months, often provides the best, most flexible deal.

Advance Purchase Excursion (Apex) tickets can be a good deal for travelers who know exactly where they will be going and how long they will be staying, but must be bought well before departure. Also, such tickets have minimum and maximum-stay requirements, rarely allow stopovers, and are difficult or impossible to modify without incurring monetary penalties.

Valid for 12 months, economy-class (Y) tickets have the greatest flexibility within their time period. However, travelers who try to extend their stay beyond a year will have to pay the difference of any interim price increase.

Discount fares are often available from travel agents but are less common in Latin America, though they do exist between Buenos Aires and Santiago, Chile. One of the cheapest means of getting to South America is via courier flights, in which travelers surrender all or part of their baggage

---

Travel Agencies in Buenos Aires

Asatej (☎ 4311-6953, fax 4311-6840), the Argentine affiliate of STA Travel, has its main offices on the 3rd floor, Oficina 319-B, at Florida 835 in Retiro (Map 11). Open 9 am to 6 pm weekdays, it has the cheapest air fares available (the US$159 roundtrip to Santiago, Chile, is only slightly more than the equivalent bus fare, though airport taxes are additional). Asatej also publishes a brochure of discount offers at hotels, restaurants and other businesses in the city and throughout Argentina for holders of international student cards. It has branch locations at Av Santa Fe 2450, 3rd floor, Local 93 in Recoleta (☎ 4821-2126; Map 12), and at Echeverría 2592, Planta Alta, in Belgrano (☎ 4511-7800; Map 14).

Another youth and student-oriented travel agency is the Asociación Argentina de Albergues de la Juventud (AAAJ; ☎/fax 4476-1001), 2nd floor, Oficina 6, Talcahuano 214 in San Nicolás (Map 5). It issues hostel memberships and international student cards, and has a message board for travelers (mostly young Argentines) seeking companions for extended trips.

Yet another student-oriented agency is Turismo Unión Buenos Amigos (TUBA; ☎/fax 4953-3773), Sarmiento 1967, first floor, in Congreso (Map 6). The local affiliate of Council Travel is AB Travel/TIJE (☎ 4322-7372), in the Galería Jardín at Florida 537, Local 333, San Nicolás (Map 5).

American Express (☎ 4312-0900, fax 4315-1866), Arenales 707 west of Plaza San Martín in Retiro (Map 11), cashes its own traveler's checks without additional commission, and offers many other services. Reader-recommended Swan Turismo (☎/fax 4816-2080), Cerrito 822, 9th floor, in Retiro (Map 11), will help renegotiate air passes and make connections with LADE or other airlines for which timetables are not easily available outside the country.

allowance and accompany business equipment or documents in return for a highly discounted fare. The major drawbacks, in addition to being limited to carry-on baggage, are the often short travel period allowed and the limited number of gateway airports in Europe and North America.

Some travelers take advantage of Round-the-World (RTW) fares to visit widely separated places (such as Asia and South America) on the same trip. For example, a Qantas-Aerolíneas Argentinas ticket lets travelers circle the globe with stops in New Zealand, Europe and Southeast Asia. Aerolíneas also has RTW agreements with Air New Zealand, British Airways, Cathay Pacific, KLM, Malaysia Airlines, Singapore Airlines, Swissair and Thai Airways International. Similar 'Circle Pacific' fares allow excursions between Australasia and South America.

The cost of domestic flights has risen dramatically in recent years. One alternative on some airlines is *banda negativa*, in which limited seats on a selected list of flights every month are available for discounts of about 40%. These excellent bargains are often (but not always) night flights and require advance purchase. Ask about other discount fares available through advance purchase, and to the cities of Córdoba and Mendoza (the most competitive routes in Argentina). Sample one-way domestic air fares can vary widely: Buenos Aires to Córdoba costs US$49 to US$148; to Mar del Plata, US$39 to US$93; to Mendoza, US$59 to US$196; and to Tucumán, US$79 to US$228.

Departure Tax

International passengers leaving from Aeropuerto Internacional Ministro Pistarini (commonly known as Ezeiza) pay a US$18 departure tax, also payable in local currency. On flights of less than 300km to neighboring countries, such as Uruguay, the tax is only US$5, while the tax for domestic flights is US$3. Note that 21% IVA has recently been applied to airport taxes.

Other Parts of Argentina

Commonly known as *vuelos de cabotaje*, nearly all domestic flights (as well as some regional ones) leave from Aeroparque Jorge Newbery, a short distance north of downtown, but a few depart from Ezeiza.

Argentine air traffic, routes and fares have undergone a major transformation since the privatization of Aerolíneas Argentinas, which handles domestic as well as international routes, and its close partner Austral Líneas Aéreas, which handles domestic routes only. While these two airlines have the most extensive and numerous services, some secondary airlines have expanded routes, and others have come into existence, undercutting the very high fare structure of the established carriers. In response, Aerolíneas and Austral have introduced a supplementary fare system that offers cheaper alternatives with some restrictions. Aerolíneas and Austral serve nearly every major Argentine city between Bolivia and the Beagle Channel.

Andesmar, a recent startup subsidiary of a well-established bus company, serves northern and western cities (Rosario, Córdoba, Mendoza, La Rioja, Tucumán and Salta) and Buenos Aires provincial beach resorts (Villa Gesell, Mar del Plata, Miramar).

Having recently expanded routes, Dinar Líneas Aéreas still flies mostly to the northwestern Argentine destinations of Tucumán, Salta, and Jujuy, but also to Córdoba, Mendoza, Mar del Plata and Comodoro Rivadavia.

Líneas Aéreas del Estado (LADE) refuses to die in the face of budget cutbacks and privatization. It is the Air Force's commercial service and serves southern Buenos Aires province and Patagonian destinations only. Líneas Aéreas de Entre Ríos flies to Mesopotamian destinations in Entre Ríos and Corrientes, and to Santa Fe, La Pampa and coastal Buenos Aires province.

Líneas Aéreas Privadas Argentinas (LAPA) continues to expand routes to compete with Aerolíneas and Austral. Its capacity is still smaller than its competitors, and flights are often booked far in advance, especially those with discount fares. LAPA also provides regional services to Punta del Este, Uruguay.

Southern Winds, a Córdoba-based startup links the capital with Córdoba, Río Cuarto,

Mendoza, Salta and Tucumán. In summer, Transporte Aéreo Cost Atlántica (TACA) flies small planes to Atlantic coastal destinations, Mesopotamia, Puerto Iguazú and Bariloche.

The USA

The principal gateways are Miami, New York and Los Angeles. Aerolíneas Argentinas (☎ 800-333-0276 in North America) is the flag carrier, but other airlines serving Buenos Aires include American Airlines, British Airways, Japan Airlines, Korean Air, LanChile, Lloyd Aéreo Boliviano (LAB), United Airlines and Varig. Most other South American flag carriers have northbound connections from Buenos Aires via their own capitals.

Aeroperú (☎ 800-777-7717 in North America) offers a Visit South America fare that includes a roundtrip flight from the US to Lima, and four or six coupons for flights within the continent to any of the following: Buenos Aires, Guayaquil, La Paz, Rio de Janeiro, Santiago and São Paulo. Valid for 60 days and available only in the USA, four-coupon tickets cost US$799 from Miami, and US$999 from Los Angeles, while six-coupon tickets cost US$1299 from Miami, and US$1499 from Los Angeles.

Most major airlines have ticket 'consolidators' offering substantial discounts on fares to Latin America, but things change so frequently that even weekly newspaper listings are soon out of date. Among the best sources of information on cheap tickets are the Sunday travel pages of major US newspapers, such as the *New York Times*, *Miami Herald*, *Los Angeles Times* and *San Francisco Examiner*. Travelers can also check the local affiliate of the Council on International Education & Exchange (CIEE or Council Travel) or the Student Travel Network (STA); student status is not necessary to take advantage of their services.

Council Travel (☎ 800-226-8624 in the USA, cts@ciee.org) has agencies in the following cities and in many other college towns:

Austin, TX
  (☎ 512-472-4931) 2000 Guadalupe St
Berkeley, CA
  (☎ 510-848-8604) 2486 Channing Way
Boston, MA
  (☎ 617-266-1926) 273 Newbury St
Denver, CO
  (☎ 303-571-0630) 900 Auraria Parkway, Tivoli Bldg
Los Angeles, CA
  (☎ 213-208-3551) 10904 Lindbrook Drive
Miami, FL
  (☎ 305-670-9261) 9100 S Dadeland Blvd, Suite 220
New York, NY
  (☎ 212-822-2700) 205 E 42nd St, ground floor
Pacific Beach (San Diego), CA
  (☎ 619-270-6401) 953 Garnett Ave
San Francisco, CA
  (☎ 415-421-3473) 530 Bush St
Seattle, WA
  (☎ 206-632-2448) 1314 NE 43rd St, Suite 210
Washington, DC
  (☎ 202-337-6464) 3300 M Street, NW, 2nd floor

Like Council Travel, the Student Travel Network (STA; ☎ 800-777-0112) has offices in the following cities plus many other college towns:

Berkeley, CA
  (☎ 510-642-3000) ASUC Travel Center, Univ of California
Boston, MA
  (☎ 617-266-6014) 297 Newbury St
Chicago, IL
  (☎ 312-786-9050) 429 S Dearborn St
Coral Gables, FL
  (☎ 305-284-1044) Univ of Miami, 1306 Stanford Dr
Los Angeles, CA
  (☎ 213-934-8722) 7202 Melrose Ave
  (☎ 310-824-1574) 920 Westwood Blvd
New York, NY
  (☎ 212-627-3111) 10 Downing St
Philadelphia, PA
  (☎ 215-382-2928) 3730 Walnut St
San Francisco, CA
  (☎ 415-391-8407) 51 Grant Ave
Seattle, WA
  (☎ 206-633-5000) 4341 University Way NE
Washington, DC
  (☎ 202-887-0912) 2401 Pennsylvania Ave, Suite G

In the USA, New York and Miami are the only cities with courier flights to South

America. For the widest selection of destinations, try Now Voyager (☎ 212-431-1616, fax 334-5253), 74 Varick St, Suite 307, New York, NY 10013; or Air Facility (☎ 718-712-1769), 153 Rockaway Blvd, Jamaica, NY 11434.

For up-to-date information on courier and other budget fares, send US$5 for the latest newsletter or US$25 for a year's subscription from Travel Unlimited, PO Box 1058, Allston, MA 02134. Another source of information is the International Association of Air Travel Couriers (☎ 561-582-8320, fax 582-1581, iaatc@courier.org), PO Box 1349, Lake Worth, FL 33460; its US$45 annual membership fee includes the monthly newsletter *Shoestring Traveler* (not related to Lonely Planet).

Canada

Canadian Airlines' Toronto-Buenos Aires route offers the only direct flights to Argentina (daily except Thursday), but numerous airlines make connections in New York, Miami and Los Angeles. The Brazilian airline Vasp, which flies five times weekly from Toronto, is the only other carrier that flies to Buenos Aires, after changing planes in Rio de Janeiro or São Paulo.

Travel Cuts, the Canadian national student travel agency, is the Canadian counterpart of Council Travel and STA. Travel Cuts (☎ 888-838-2887 toll-free, 416-977-2185, fax 977-4796) is located at 243 College St, 5th floor, Toronto, Ontario M5T 2Y1.

Mexico

Aeroméxico, Aeroperú and Mexicana run daily 'Alas de América' service from Mexico City, sometimes via Cancún. Some LanChile flights from Buenos Aires go to Mexico City after Santiago. American, Avianca, Cubana, Lloyd Aéreo Boliviano (LAB) and Varig provide less direct services.

Aerolíneas Argentinas flies twice weekly to and from Cancún. LAB and Varig also fly to Cancún, but with stopovers.

Neighboring Countries

Bolivia La Paz is the principal gateway, but some flights go via Santa Cruz de la Sierra (also known as Viru Viru after the name of its airport). Lloyd Aéreo Boliviano (LAB) flies from La Paz and Santa Cruz, as does Varig (though it's necessary to change planes in São Paulo).

Brazil Rio de Janeiro and São Paulo are the main gateways to Ezeiza for many airlines, including Aerolíneas Argentinas, Canadian Airlines, Japan Airlines, KLM, Korean Air, LAB, Swissair, TAM (via Asunción), TAP (Air Portugal), Trans Brasil, Varig and Vasp. The latter three carriers have the greatest number of flights from cities beyond the two Brazilian megalopolises.

Pluna flies to Ezeiza from Rio de Janeiro and Salvador via Montevideo, and to Aeroparque Jorge Newbery from Florianópolis, Porto Alegre, São Paulo and Rio, also via Montevideo. LAB flies to Ezeiza from Manaus via Santa Cruz.

Chile Many airlines fly between Ezeiza and Santiago, a route on which heavily discounted tickets are available. Asatej offers the cheapest, at US$159 roundtrip. (For more information, see Travel Agencies in Buenos Aires.)

Paraguay Asunción is Paraguay's only city providing air connection with Buenos Aires; flights arrive at both Aeroparque Jorge Newbery and Ezeiza (US$181 one-way). The only direct carriers are Aerolíneas Argentinas and TAM, though Pluna has connections in Montevideo.

Uruguay There are numerous flights between Aeroparque Jorge Newbery and Montevideo, while a few long-distance international flights arriving at Ezeiza continue to Montevideo. (Services from Aeroparque tend to be cheaper and more efficient than the major airlines at Ezeiza.) From Aeroparque, the only other Uruguayan destination is Punta del Este, with LAPA (twice on Fridays and twice on Sundays) and more frequently with Aerolíneas Argentinas.

The UK & Europe

Direct services to Buenos Aires are available with Argentina's principal carrier Aerolíneas

Air Travel Glossary

Bucket Shops These are unbonded travel agencies specializing in discounted airline tickets.

Bumped Just because you have a confirmed seat doesn't mean you're going to get on the plane (see Overbooking).

Cancellation Penalties If you have to cancel or change a discounted ticket, there are often heavy penalties involved; insurance can sometimes be taken out against these penalties. Some airlines impose penalties on regular tickets as well, particularly against 'no-show' passengers.

Check-In Airlines ask you to check in a certain time ahead of the flight departure (usually one to two hours on international flights). If you fail to check in on time and the flight is over-booked, the airline can cancel your booking and give your seat to somebody else.

Confirmation Having a ticket written out with the flight and date you want doesn't mean you have a seat until the agent has checked with the airline that your status is 'OK' or confirmed. Meanwhile you could just be 'on request.'

Courier Fares Businesses often need to send urgent documents or freight securely and quickly. Courier companies hire people to accompany the package through customs and, in return, offer a discount ticket that is sometimes a phenomenal bargain. In effect, what the companies do is ship their freight as your luggage on regular commercial flights. This is a legitimate operation, but there are two shortcomings – the short turnaround time of the ticket (usually not longer than a month) and the limitation on your luggage allowance. You may have to surrender all your allowance and take only carry-on luggage.

Full Fares Airlines traditionally offer 1st class (coded F), business class (coded J) and economy class (coded Y) tickets. These days there are so many promotional and discounted fares available that few passengers pay full economy fare.

ITX An ITX, or 'independent inclusive tour excursion,' is often available on tickets to popular holiday destinations. Officially it's a package deal combined with hotel accommodations, but many agents will sell you one of these for the flight only and give you phony hotel vouchers in the unlikely event that you're challenged at the airport.

Lost Tickets If you lose your airline ticket, an airline will usually treat it like a traveler's check and, after inquiries, issue you another one. Legally, however, an airline is entitled to treat it like cash; and if you lose it, then it's gone forever. Take good care of your tickets.

MCO An MCO, or 'miscellaneous charge order,' is a voucher that looks like an airline ticket but carries no destination or date. It can be exchanged through any International Association of Travel Agents (IATA) airline for a ticket on a specific flight. It's a useful alternative to an onward ticket in those countries that demand one, and is more flexible than an ordinary ticket if you're unsure of your route.

No-Shows No-shows are passengers who fail to show up for their flight. Full-fare passengers who fail to turn up are sometimes entitled to travel on a later flight. The rest are penalized (see Cancellation Penalties).

On Request This is an unconfirmed booking for a flight.

Onward Tickets An entry requirement for many countries is that you have a ticket out of the country. If you're unsure of your next move, the easiest solution is to buy the cheapest onward ticket to a neighboring country or a ticket from a reliable airline that can later be refunded if you do not use it.

Open Jaw Tickets These are return tickets on which you fly out to one place but return from another. If available, these can save you backtracking to your arrival point.

Overbooking Airlines hate to fly with empty seats and since every flight has some passengers who fail to show up, airlines often book more passengers than they have seats. Usually excess passengers make up for the no-shows, but occasionally somebody gets bumped. Guess who it is most likely to be? The passengers who check in late.

Point-to-Point Tickets These are discount tickets that you can buy on some routes in exchange for waiving your right to a stopover.

Promotional Fares These are officially discounted fares, available from travel agencies or direct from the airline.

Reconfirmation At least 72 hours prior to departure time of an onward or return flight, you must contact the airline and 'reconfirm' that you intend to be on the flight. If you don't do this, the airline can delete your name from the passenger list and you could lose your seat.

Restrictions Discounted tickets often have various restrictions on them – such as advance payment, minimum and maximum periods you must be away (eg, a minimum of two weeks or a maximum of one year) and penalties for changing the tickets.

Round-the-World Tickets RTW tickets give you a limited period (usually a year) in which to circumnavigate the globe. You can go anywhere the carrying airlines go, as long as you don't backtrack. The number of stopovers or total number of separate flights is decided before you set off, and they usually cost a bit more than a basic return flight.

Stand-By This is a discounted ticket on which you fly only if there is a seat free at the last moment. Stand-by fares are usually available only on domestic routes.

Travel Agencies Travel agencies vary widely and you should choose one that suits your needs. Some simply handle tours, while full-service agencies handle everything from tours and tickets to car rental and hotel bookings. If all you want is a ticket at the lowest possible price, then go to any agency specializing in discounted tickets.

Transferred Tickets Airline tickets cannot be transferred from one person to another. Travelers sometimes try to sell the return half of their ticket, but officials can ask you to prove that you are the person named on the ticket.

Travel Periods Ticket prices vary with the time of year. There is a low (off-peak) season and a high (peak) season, and often a low-shoulder season and a high-shoulder season as well. Usually the fare depends on your outward flight – if you depart in the high season and return in the low season, you pay the high-season fare.

Argentinas (☎ 020-7494-1001 in London), as well as Aeroflot, Air France, Alitalia, British Airways, Iberia, KLM, Lufthansa, Pluna, Swissair, TAP (Air Portugal) and Trans Brasil. Varig has easy connections via Rio de Janeiro and São Paulo.

London's so-called 'bucket shops' can provide the best deals; check out newspapers or magazines such as the Saturday *Independent* or *Time Out* for suggestions. Currently the cheapest fares from London to Buenos Aires run about £357 one-way (£581 return) in low season (March 1 to June 30), and £424 one-way (£702 return) the rest of the year.

Since bucket shops come and go, it's worth inquiring about their affiliation with the Association of British Travel Agents (ABTA), which will guarantee a refund or alternative if the agent goes out of business. The following are reputable London bucket shops:

Campus Travel
(☎ 020-7730-3402)
52 Grosvenor Gardens, London SW1W 0AG
Journey Latin America
(☎ 020-8747-3108)
16 Devonshire Rd Chiswick, London W4 2HD
Passage to South America
(☎ 020-8767-8989)
Fovant Mews, 12 Noyna Rd, London SW17 7PH
South American Experience
(☎ 020-7976-5511)
47 Causton St, London SW1
STA Travel
(☎ 020-7361-9962)
86 Old Brompton Rd, London SW7 3LQ
Trailfinders
(☎ 020-7938-3939)
194 Kensington High St, London W8
(☎ 020-7938-3366)
42-50 Earls Court Rd, London W8

In Berlin, check out the magazine *Zitty* for bargain-fare ads. In Berlin and other European cities, the following agencies are good possibilities for bargain fares:

France
(☎ 01 44 41 89 80) Council Travel, 1 Place de l'Odéon, 75006 Paris
Germany
(☎ 030-283-3903) STA Travel, Marienstraße 25, Berlin

(☎ 069-430191) STA Travel, Bergerstraße 118, Frankfurt
Ireland
(☎ 01-602-1600) USIT Travel Office, 19 Aston Quay, Dublin
Italy
(☎ 06-462-0431) CTS, Via Genova 16, Rome
Netherlands
(☎ 020-642-0989) NBBS, Rokin 38, Amsterdam
(☎ 020-623-6814) Malibu Travel, Damrak 30 Amsterdam
Spain
(☎ 91-347-7778) TIVE, José Ortega y Gasset 71, Madrid
Switzerland
(☎ 01-297-1111) SSR, Leonhardstraße 10, Zürich

Travelers interested in courier flights between Europe and South America should contact British Airways (☎ 020-8564-7009), which has roundtrips to Buenos Aires for £400, taxes included. More information is available by sending a stamped, self-addressed envelope to British Airways Travel Shop, World Cargo Centre, Export Cargo Terminal, S 126 Heathrow, Hounslow, Middlesex TW6 2JS.

Australia & New Zealand

The most direct service is Aerolíneas Argentinas' Tuesday, Thursday and Saturday transpolar flight from Sydney via Auckland, which is an obvious connection for buyers of the Qantas-Aerolíneas RTW fare. Aerolíneas has a Sydney office (☎ 02-9283-3660). Otherwise, LanChile's trans-Pacific flights from Tahiti to Santiago (including a possible stopover on Easter Island) have easy connections to Buenos Aires, but some travelers have found it cheaper to go via London or Los Angeles.

For travelers starting in Australia, the combined Qantas-Aerolíneas RTW ticket allows stopovers in Auckland, London, Paris, Bahrain, Singapore and other cities, but you must arrange the itinerary in advance. The Qantas-Aerolíneas ticket costs A$3299 in Sydney or US$3218 in Buenos Aires. (The price in Sydney is about 39% less.)

STA Travel (☎ 1-800-637-444) is a good place to inquire for bargain air fares; student status is not necessary to use their services. There are STA offices in the following cities in Australia:

Adelaide
(☎ 08-8223-2426) 235 Rundle St
Brisbane
(☎ 07-3221-9388) Shop 25-26,
Brisbane Arcade, 111 Adelaide St
Canberra
(☎ 02-6247-8633) 13-15 Garema Place
Melbourne
(☎ 03-9349-2411) 220 Faraday St, Carlton
Perth
(☎ 08-9227-7569) 100 James St, Northbridge
Sydney
(☎ 02-9281-5259) 730 Harris St, 1st floor,
Ultimo, Sydney

STA also has offices at the following New Zealand locations:

Auckland
(☎ 09-307-0555) Union Bldg, 2nd floor,
Auckland University
Christchurch
(☎ 03-379-909) 90 Cashel St
Wellington
(☎ 04-385-0561) 233 Cuba St

Asia & Africa

Japan Airlines and Korean Air serve Buenos Aires directly from Asia, though usually via North America. Varig and Vasp also have good connections from Tokyo and Seoul via Rio de Janeiro or São Paulo.

Malaysia Airlines flies Wednesdays and Sundays from Kuala Lumpur to Buenos Aires via Cape Town and Johannesburg. South Africa Airways flies Thursdays from Johannesburg to Buenos Aires via São Paulo, and Sundays via Cape Town.

Airports

Buenos Aires' Aeropuerto Internacional Ministro Pistarini (commonly known as Ezeiza; ☎ 4480-0235) has excellent connections from North America, Europe, the UK and Australia (via New Zealand), plus routes from southern Africa across the Atlantic (some via Brazil). Most domestic flights and some flights to neighboring countries use Aeroparque Jorge Newbery

(☎ 4771-2071), a short distance from downtown Buenos Aires.

Airline Offices

Many major international airlines and all domestic carriers have offices or representatives in Buenos Aires. Most international airlines serve Ezeiza for long-distance international flights, but a few from neighboring countries use Aeroparque Jorge Newbery.

Aeroflot
(☎ 4312-5573) Av Santa Fe 822, Retiro
Aerolíneas Argentinas
(☎ 4320-2000) Perú 2, Montserrat
(☎ 4327-1941) Arroyo 807, Retiro
(☎ 4783-2507) Av Cabildo 2900, Núñez
AeroMéxico
(☎ 4315-1936) Av Santa Fe 840, Retiro
Aeroperú
(☎ 4311-6431) Av Santa Fe 840, Retiro
Air France
(☎ 4317-4700) Paraguay 610, 14th floor, Retiro
Alitalia
(☎ 4310-9999) Suipacha 1111, 28th floor, Retiro
American Airlines
(☎ 4318-1111) Av Santa Fe 881, Retiro
Andesmar
(☎ 4312-1077) Esmeralda 1063, 1st floor, Retiro
Austral Líneas Aéreas
(☎ 4317-3605) Av Leandro N Alem 1134,
Retiro
Avianca
(☎ 4394-5990) Carlos Pellegrini 1163, 4th floor,
Retiro
British Airways
(☎ 4320-6600) Av Córdoba 650, San Nicolás
Canadian Airlines
(☎ 4322-3632) Av Córdoba 656, San Nicolás
Cubana de Aviación
(☎ 4326-5291) Sarmiento 552, 11th floor, San
Nicolás
Dinar Líneas Aéreas
(☎ 4326-0135) Diagonal Roque Sáenz Peña
933, San Nicolás
Ecuatoriana
(☎ 4311-3010) Suipacha 1065, Retiro
Iberia
(☎ 4327-2739) Carlos Pellegrini 1163, 1st floor,
Retiro
Japan Airlines
(☎ 4393-1896) Av Córdoba 836, 11th floor, San
Nicolás
KLM
(☎ 4480-9470) Reconquista 559, 5th floor, San
Nicolás

Korean Air
  (☎ 4311-9237) Av Córdoba 755, Retiro
LanChile
  (☎ 4316-2200) Florida 954, Retiro
Líneas Aéreas del Estado (LADE)
  (☎ 4361-7071) Perú 714, San Telmo
Líneas Aéreas de Entre Ríos (LAER)
  (☎ 4311-5237) Maipú 935, Retiro
Líneas Aéreas Privadas Argentinas (LAPA)
  (☎ 4819-5272) Carlos Pellegrini 1075, Retiro
Lloyd Aéreo Boliviano (LAB)
  (☎ 4326-3595) Carlos Pellegrini 141, San Nicolás
Lufthansa
  (☎ 4319-0600) MT de Alvear 636, Retiro
Malaysia Airlines
  (☎ 4312-6971) Suipacha 1111, 14th floor, Retiro
Mexicana
  (☎ 4312-6152) Av Córdoba 755, 1st floor, Retiro
Pluna
  (☎ 4342-4420) Florida 1, San Nicolás
South African Airways
  (☎ 4311-8184) Av Santa Fe 794, 3rd floor, Retiro
Southern Winds
  (☎ 4312-2811, fax 4313-5883) Florida 868, 13th floor, Retiro
Swissair
  (☎ 4319-0000) Av Santa Fe 846, 1st floor, Retiro
TAP (Air Portugal)
  (☎ 4811-0984) Cerrito 1136, Retiro
Trans Brasil
  (☎ 4394-8424) Florida 780, 1st floor, San Nicolás
Transporte Aéreo Costa Atlántica (TACA)
  (☎ 4307-1956) Bernardo de Irigoyen 1370, 1st floor, Constitución
Transportes Aéreos de Mercosur (TAM)
  (☎ 4816-1000) Cerrito 1026, Retiro
United Airlines
  (☎ 4316-0777) Av Eduardo Madero 900, 9th floor, Retiro
Varig
  (☎ 4329-9204) Florida 630, San Nicolás
Vasp
  (☎ 4311-2699) Av Santa Fe 784, Retiro

BUS

Buenos Aires' massive Estación Terminal de Omnibus (☎ 4310-0700) is at Av Antártida Argentina and Ramos Mejía in Retiro, a short distance from Retiro train station (Map 11). Its Centro de Informes y Reclamos (☎ 4313-9594), Oficina 29, 2nd floor, provides general bus information. It also monitors the taxis that serve the terminal, so direct any complaints about taxi drivers to them.

Each of Retiro's hundred-plus bus companies has a desk resembling an airline ticket counter (some of them shared), where tickets are issued for national and international destinations. Discounted tickets are less common than in the past, but student identification can still sometimes yield a reduction of 20% on any fare except special promotions.

Departures are frequent to the most popular destinations. Reservations are normally not necessary except during peak summer and winter holiday seasons, but purchasing your ticket a day ahead of time is still not a bad idea. .

From Buenos Aires, General Urquiza (☎ 4313-2771) has nightly service to Montevideo (US$25, nine hours). La Internacional (☎ 4313-3167) has regular buses to Asunción, Paraguay (21 hours), via the Gran Chaco towns of Formosa and Clorinda in northern Argentina for US$56 (regular), US$78 (more comfortable *servicio diferencial*) or US$95 (*coche cama* sleepers). Nuestra Señora de la Asunción (☎ 4313-2325) and Chevallier Paraguaya (☎ 4313-2349) have comparable service and prices.

Pluma (☎ 4313-3893) goes to Brazilian destinations, including Foz do Iguaçu (US$60, 19 hours), Porto Alegre (US$71, 21 hours), Florianópolis (US$85, 26 hours), Camboriú (US$90, 27 hours), Curitiba (US$95, 35 hours), São Paulo (US$101, 42 hours) and Rio de Janeiro (US$117, 48 hours). Rápido Yguazú (☎ 4315-6981) also serves Brazilian routes.

Several companies cross the Andes to Santiago, Chile (US$60, 21 hours): TAC (☎ 4313-2627), Chevallier (☎ 4314-5555) and Fénix Pullman Norte (☎ 4313-0134), which has connections from Santiago to the Peruvian border at Arica. El Rápido Internacional (☎ 4315-0804) and Ormeño Internacional (☎ 4313-2259) have direct connections to Lima (US$190, 96 hours).

For complete bus schedules and fares, visit or telephone the terminal. Also, the sensationalist tabloid daily *La Razón* – whatever its other shortcomings – publishes a section with bus schedules and fares from Buenos Aires.

TRAIN

There are no international rail services to or from Argentina.

Private operators have assumed control of the profitable freight service on the formerly state-owned railways, but have shown no interest in providing passenger service except on commuter lines in and around Buenos Aires. The provinces of Buenos Aires, Río Negro, Chubut, Tucumán and La Pampa continue to provide reduced long-distance passenger service.

The Mitre line operates from Estación Retiro, the Roca line from Estación Constitución, and the Sarmiento line from Estación Once de Septiembre (popularly known as 'Once') in Balvanera. Administered by the province of Buenos Aires, Ferrobaires (☎ 4304-0035) operates the Ferrocarril Roca serving the Atlantic beach resorts of Mar del Plata, Pinamar and other destinations in Buenos Aires province. Operated by the province of Tucumán, Ferrocarriles Tucumán SA (Tufesa; ☎ 4313-8060) operates the Ferrocarril Mitre to Rosario, Santiago del Estero and Tucumán. The Ferrocarril Sarmiento (☎ 4861-0041), though primarily a commuter line, still links the capital to Santa Rosa, in La Pampa province.

Classes of service range from the rigid bench seats of *turista* (tourist or 2nd class) to comfortable *coche cama* or *dormitorio* sleeper compartments. During holiday periods such as Christmas and Independence Day (July 9), it is important to buy tickets as far in advance as possible. Train fares are still lower than bus fares on comparable routes, but trains are also much slower.

CAR & MOTORCYCLE

Although Argentina is self-sufficient in oil, the price of *nafta* (petrol) has risen to world levels at about US$1 per liter for 95-octane *super*, US$0.80 for 85-octane *normal*, although *gas-oil* (diesel fuel) costs only about US$0.40. Unleaded fuel is now the rule, but can still be difficult to find in some off-the-beaten-track areas. In some areas, notably Buenos Aires province, tolls on privatized highways are very high – as much as US$4 per 100km.

Although motorcycles are fashionable among some Argentines, they are expensive and the author has never seen any place that rents them in Argentina. Motorcycle helmets are legally obligatory, but not even motorcycle cops seem to bother with them.

Documents & Insurance

Formally, Argentina requires an International or Inter-American Driving Permit to supplement your national or state driver's license. In practice, police rarely examine these documents closely and generally ignore the latter. Drivers must carry their title document (*tarjeta verde* or 'green card'; for foreign vehicles, customs permission is the acceptable substitute), triangular emergency reflectors (*valizas*), and 1kg fire extinguishers. Headrests are imperative for the driver and each passenger.

Liability insurance is obligatory, and police may ask to see proof of insurance at checkpoints. Fortunately, unlike many services in Argentina, it is reasonably priced. A four-month policy with US$1 million in liability coverage costs as little as US$120 (paid in cash) and is also valid, with slightly reduced coverage, in the neighboring countries of Chile, Bolivia, Paraguay, Brazil and Uruguay. Among reputable insurers are Seguros Rivadavia, which has many offices in Buenos Aires, and the Automóvil Club Argentino (ACA).

Road Rules & Hazards

Anyone considering driving in Argentina should know that many Argentine drivers are reckless, aggressive and even willfully dangerous – they ignore speed limits, road signs and even traffic signals. Traffic accidents are the leading cause of death for Argentines below the age of 54.

Tailgating is a serious hazard; it is not unusual to see half a dozen cars a meter or less apart, waiting for their chance to overtake a truck which itself may be exceeding the speed limit. During the Pampas harvest season, pay particular attention to slow-moving farm machinery, which is not a hazard in its own right, but brings out the worst in impatient Argentine motorists. Night driving is inadvisable because of animals on the road in some regions, as well as drivers who seem to believe they can see in the dark and, consequently, disdain headlights.

Argentine police contribute almost nothing toward traffic safety. You will rarely see police patrolling the highways, where high-speed, head-on collisions are common, but you will meet them at major intersections and roadside checkpoints where they conduct meticulous document and equipment checks. If one of these policemen asks to check your turn signals (which almost no Argentine bothers to use), brake lights or handbrake, it may well be a warning of corruption in progress. The police may claim that equipment violations carry fines up to US$300, but this is really a pretext for graft. If you are uncertain about your rights, state in a very matter-of-fact manner your intention to contact your embassy or consulate. Offer a *coima* (bribe) only if you are confident that it is 'appropriate' and unavoidable.

Note that provincial police forces (most notoriously those of Buenos Aires province) are the most *coimero* (corrupt) in the country. The Policía Federal (Federal Police, who presumably control transit in the city of Buenos Aires) and the Gendarmería (Federal Border Guards, who monitor national highways) are no saints, but they're generally less openly and aggressively corrupt.

Automóvil Club Argentino

If you drive in Argentina, especially in your own car, it may be worth joining the Automóvil Club Argentino (ACA), which has nationwide offices, service stations and garages offering free road service and towing in and around major cities. ACA also recognizes members of overseas affiliates, such as the American Automobile Association (AAA), as equivalent to its own members. It often grants them the same privileges, including discounts on maps, accommodations, camping, tours and other services. Otherwise, ACA membership costs about US$32 per month, which is more expensive than most of its overseas counterparts.

ACA's head office (☎ 4802-6061) is at Av del Libertador 1850 in Palermo (Map 13). There are branch offices at Godoy Cruz and Demaría in Palermo (☎ 4773-7892) and at Av Cabildo and Virrey Arredondo in Belgrano (☎ 4783-2478; Map 14).

BICYCLE

Bicycling is an interesting, inexpensive alternative for getting to Argentina. Racing bicycles are suitable for some paved roads, but these are often narrow; a *todo terreno* (mountain bike) would be safer and more convenient, allowing you to use the unpaved shoulder and the very extensive network of graveled roads throughout the country. Bicycling is an increasingly popular recreational activity among Argentines, and though Argentine bicycles are improving in quality, they are still not equal to those made in Europe or North America.

There are two major drawbacks to cycling in Argentina: the wind, which can slow your progress to a crawl, and Argentine motorists. On many of the country's straight, narrow two-lane highways, many motorists show a total disregard for anyone but themselves and can be a real hazard to bicyclists.

HITCHHIKING

Though Argentina (along with Chile) is probably the best country to *hacer dedo* in South America, hitchhiking is never entirely safe in any country. The major drawback in Argentina is that vehicles are often stuffed with families and children, but truckers will frequently take backpackers. At *servicentros* at the outskirts of large Argentine cities, where truckers gas up their vehicles, it is often worthwhile soliciting a ride.

Travelers who decide to hitch should understand that they are taking a small but potentially serious risk. People who do choose to hitch will be safer if they travel in pairs and let someone know where they are planning to go.

BOAT

Buenos Aires has regular ferry and hydrofoil *(aliscafo)* service to Colonia, Uruguay, with bus combinations to Montevideo, as well as direct ferries to Montevideo and Piriápolis. These sail from Dársena Norte, near downtown at Madero and Viamonte (Map 11), or from Dársena Sur, Av Pedro de Mendoza 20 near La Boca (Map 10). There is now a US$10 departure tax from these terminals. (For more on these services, see Colonia and Montevideo in the Excursions chapter.)

Cacciola (☎ 4749-0329), at Lavalle 520 in the riverside suburb of Tigre, goes daily to Carmelo, Uruguay, at 8:30 am and 4:30 pm for US$11; children pay US$9.35. Movilán/Deltanave (☎ 4749-4119) also goes to Carmelo, at 8:30 am and 3:30 pm. There is also a US$5 departure tax from Tigre.

Línea Delta (☎ 4749-0537) goes from Tigre to Nueva Palmira, Uruguay, daily at 7:30 am. Fares are US$15 one way, US$26 roundtrip.

WARNING

The information in this chapter is particularly vulnerable to change: prices for international travel are volatile, routes are introduced and canceled, schedules change, special deals come and go, and rules and visa requirements are amended. Airlines and governments seem to take a perverse pleasure in making price structures and regulations as complicated as possible. You should check directly with the airline or a travel agent to make sure you understand how a fare (and ticket you may buy) works. In addition, the travel industry is highly competitive and there are many lurks and perks.

The upshot of this is that you should get opinions, quotes and advice from as many airlines and travel agents as possible before parting with your hard-earned cash. The details in this chapter should be regarded as pointers and are not a substitute for your own careful, up-to-date research.

Getting Around

TO/FROM THE AIRPORTS

Buenos Aires has two airports. Aeropuerto Internacional Ministro Pistarini (commonly known as Ezeiza; ☎ 4480-0235), the main international airport, is about 35km south of downtown (Map 1). Nearly all domestic flights and some to neighboring countries leave from Aeroparque Jorge Newbery (☎ 4771-2071), on the Costanera Av Rafael Obligado in Palermo (Map 13), only a few kilometers north of downtown.

Ezeiza

The cheapest alternative to and from Ezeiza is the No 86 bus (US$1.20). If you're going to the airport, be sure the bus says 'Ezeiza,' since not all No 86s go all the way to the airport. The bus starts in La Boca and goes along Av de Mayo past the Plaza del Congreso. The more comfortable (and slightly faster) 'Servicio Diferencial,' which costs about US$5, guarantees a seat. Both buses leave Ezeiza from the Aerolíneas Argentinas terminal, a short walk from the international terminal where all carriers except Aerolíneas arrive. Theoretically neither bus allows very bulky luggage; normal backpacks and suitcases are OK, but for a judicious tip you should be able to take almost anything. Because of heavy traffic, figure at least 1½ hours to Ezeiza.

Manuel Tienda León (☎ 4314-3636, 4314-2577), Av Santa Fe 790 in Retiro (Map 11), runs a comfortable and efficient service to and from Ezeiza (US$14 one way, about 45 minutes depending on traffic) in buses and minibuses, depending on demand, and also offers hotel pickup. Regular services start at 4 and 5 am, then continue every half-hour until 11 pm. From the airport, buses run from 6:30 am to 9:30 pm.

Recently, however, San Martín Bus (☎ 4314-4747, smbus@starnet.net.ar), Av Santa Fe 887 (Map 11), has begun to provide slightly cheaper competition (US$11 one way), departing hourly between 5:15 am and 9:15 pm. It also offers door-to-door service in the downtown area. There is a 10% discount for international student card holders.

Taxis to and from downtown cost about US$30, plus a US$2 surcharge for using the *autopista* (freeway), but they may end up being cheaper than Manuel Tienda León if you have a group of three or four. The Ministerio de Economía y Obras y Servicios Públicos issues a list of authorized taxi fares from Ezeiza.

Aeroparque Jorge Newbery

Buses for downtown leave from Av Costanera Rafael Obligado, just a short walk outside the Aeroparque Jorge Newbery terminal. The cheapest alternatives to the airport are city buses No 37C ('Ciudad Universitaria') from Plaza Italia in Palermo (Map 13); No 45 northbound from Plaza Constitución (Map 9), Plaza San Martín in Retiro (Map 11), as well as intermediate points; and No 160B from Av Las Heras or Plaza Italia in Palermo (US$0.50; Map 13).

Manuel Tienda León in Retiro (Map 11) runs buses to Aeroparque (US$5), starting at 7:10 am and continuing half-hourly to 10:10 pm. Service to the city runs half-hourly from 7:50 am and stops at 10:50 pm.

Taxis to and from downtown cost about US$6.

BUS

Buenos Aires has a large, complex bus system serving the Capital Federal and Gran Buenos Aires. The best guides to the bus system are the *Guía Peuser*, which details nearly 200 different routes and includes a foldout map, and the *Capital Federal y Gran Buenos Aires* (commonly known as the 'Guía Lumi'), which comes in a slightly larger but more convenient wire-binder format. However, not all No 60 buses, for example, go all the way to Tigre, nor do all No 86 buses go to Ezeiza. (Check the sign in the window for their final destinations.)

WAYNE BERNHARDSON

Both the Peuser and Lumi guides are for sale at most kiosks and bookstores.

Many *porteños* have memorized the system and can instantly tell you which bus to take and where to get off for a particular destination. Unlike the Subte (underground), fares depend on distance. When you board, tell the driver where you're going and he will charge you accordingly; most buses now have automatic ticket machines, which accept only Argentine coins but make small change. The minimum fare is around US$0.60 to US$0.70, depending on the route. Many bus routes (but not all) run 24 hours a day.

Drivers are usually polite enough to give warning of your stop. If not, or if you find yourself standing at the back of a crowded bus, ask other passengers for help. Anyone taller than Napoleon or Carlos Menem will have to bend over to see out the windows.

Like other porteño motorists, bus drivers are fast and ruthless, and accidents are not unusual. Hang on tight.

TRAIN

Despite reductions in long-distance train service, local rail lines continue to serve most of Gran Buenos Aires, though service improvements lag behind those on the Subte. (System maps are still tough to find, for instance.)

From Estación Retiro (Map 11), the former Belgrano Norte line Ferrovías (☎ 4314-1444) goes to the city's northern suburbs, as does Transporte Metropolitano General San Martín (TMS; ☎ 4772-5013). From Estación

Constitución (Map 9), Transportes Metropolitanos General Roca (TMR; ☎ 4304-0021) reaches the southern suburbs as far as the city of La Plata. Metrovías (formerly Ferrocarril Urquiza; ☎ 4553-9214) runs the northwestern lines from Estación Federico Lacroze, at the terminus of Línea B of the Subte, while the Ferrocarril Sarmiento (☎ 4861-0041) serves outlying southwestern districts from Estación Once (Subte: Plaza Miserere, Línea A; Map 6). The Urquiza and Belgrano lines also run some tourist excursions in Buenos Aires province.

UNDERGROUND

South America's oldest underground railway, Buenos Aires' Subte opened in 1913 and is still quick and efficient. It consists of five lines, each identified alphabetically (Líneas A, B, C, D and E). Four of these run from downtown to the capital's western and northern outskirts, while the other (Línea C) runs north-south, connecting the two major train stations of Retiro and Constitución (Map 5).

On the oldest Subte line (Línea A), starting at Plaza de Mayo, the tarnished elegance of the tiled stations and the worn vintage

Subte

Línea A runs from Plaza de Mayo, under Av Rivadavia, to Primera Junta.

Línea B runs from LN Alem, under Av Corrientes, to Federico Lacroze, the station for the Ferrocarril Urquiza.

Línea C runs between the major train stations of Retiro and Constitución, with transfer stations for all other lines.

Línea D runs from Catedral, on Plaza de Mayo, with recent extensions past Palermo to José Hernández, at the corner of Av Cabildo and Virrey del Pino, and to Juramento, at the corner of Av Cabildo and Juramento. A new station at Monroe is planned for 1999.

Línea E runs from Bolívar, on Av de Mayo, to Plaza de los Virreyes.

woodwork of the cars offer a distant reminder of the city's 'belle époque.' The Subte serves only a relatively small part of a city that has sprawled to be many times larger than when the system opened. Several stations, most notably on Línea D between Catedral and Palermo stations, have impressive murals.

The private operator Metrovías has delivered notable improvements in cleanliness, security and emergency assistance, and has expanded the system's geographical reach toward the affluent northern barrios. In 1997, usage increased nearly 12% over the previous year, for a total of more than 220 million passengers.

One of the first visible signs of progress was the introduction of comfortable new Japanese cars on Línea B, which runs under Av Corrientes. The company has also begun to restore the magnificent tile artwork in many older stations. (Note, however, that the doors on the vintage cars of Línea A, which runs under Avenida de Mayo, do not always close automatically.)

On the minus side, some stations can be stifling hot (particularly in summer), trains are often very crowded, and ubiquitous SUBTV monitors pummel commuters with blaring soft drink ads even in stations lacking other improvements.

Metrovías maintains a Centro de Atención al Pasajero (☎ 4553-9214), open 8:30 am to 6:30 pm weekdays for complaints and comments, at Andén 1 at Estación Federico Lacroze, the end of the line for Línea B.

Fichas (tokens) for the Subte cost US$0.50, though prices may go up. (City government, however, recently vetoed a US$0.05 increase). To save time and hassle, buy a pocketful, since lines get very backed up during rush hour and even at other times. Trains operate 5 am to 10 pm Monday through Saturday and 8 am to 10 pm on Sundays. Service is frequent on weekdays, but weekend waiting time can be considerable. Backpacks and suitcases are permitted, allowing for convenient connections between Constitución and Retiro stations in particular.

At a few stations, like Alberdi on Línea A, you can only go in one direction – in this case toward Primera Junta rather than Plaza de Mayo (so you may have to backtrack to reach your ultimate destination). At many stations, platforms are on opposite sides of the station, so make sure of your direction *before* passing through the turnstiles, or you may have to backtrack many stops to reach your destination – unless you prefer to leave and pay an additional fare.

CAR & MOTORCYCLE

No sane person would recommend driving in Buenos Aires but, for a price, all the standard car-rental agencies will let you take your chances. Renting a car is marginally cheaper here than elsewhere in the country, but a car is much less useful because congestion is heavy, parking is difficult and expensive, and public transportation is abundant.

WAYNE BERNHARDSON

Biker sculpture by Yöel Novoa

To rent a car, you must have a valid driver's license and be at least 21 years of age; some agencies may not rent to anyone younger than 25. It may also be necessary to present a credit card such as MasterCard or Visa.

Even at independent agencies, charges are now very high. The cheapest (and smallest) vehicles go for about US$27 per day plus US$0.27 per km. (Customers can sometimes negotiate a lower rate by paying in cash rather than by credit card.) Insurance and gasoline are extra. Although unlimited-mileage deals do exist, they usually apply to weekly or longer periods and are very expensive. It's worth trying to make a reservation with one of the major international agencies in your home country as these can sometimes guarantee lower rates.

Except as indicated, all the following agencies are in Retiro (Map 11):

AI	MT de Alvear 678	☎ 4312-9475
Budget	Av Santa Fe 869	☎ 4311-9870
Dollar	MT de Alvear 523	☎ 4315-8800
Econo	MT de Alvear 866	☎ 4315-8104
Hertz	Ricardo Rojas 451	☎ 4312-1317
Localiza	Paraguay 1122	☎ 4816-3999
	Cabildo 2669	☎ 4780-0208
National	Av Córdoba 725,	
	1st floor	☎ 4314-0705
Unirent	Paraguay 864	☎ 4315-0777

Motorists should be aware that between 7 am and 7 pm on weekdays the area in the Microcentro (Map 5) bounded by Av Leandro N Alem, Av Córdoba, Av de Mayo and Av 9 de Julio is off limits to private motor vehicles, except for buses, taxis and delivery vans. Fines are stiff.

TAXI & REMISE

Buenos Aires' numerous, reasonably priced taxis are conspicuous by their black-and-yellow paint jobs. All are now digitally metered; it costs about US$1 to drop the flag and another US$0.10 per 100m. Drivers are generally polite and honest, but there are exceptions (be sure the meter is set at zero). If you're carrying a large amount of luggage, there may be a small charge in addition to the metered amount. Drivers do not expect a big tip (even for longer trips such as to

Ezeiza from downtown), but it's customary to let them keep small change. Almost no drivers speak English.

Increasingly popular, *remises* are radio taxis without meters. They generally offer fixed fares within a given zone and are slightly cheaper than ordinary taxis. Unlike taxis, they may not cruise the city in search of fares. Most hotels and restaurants will gladly ring remises for you.

When it rains, demand is high and taxis can be hard to find, so you may have to wait out the storm in a *confitería*.

BOAT

Rowboats (US$0.50) carry passengers who don't care to walk across the high bridge over the Riachuelo, from La Boca to the industrial suburb of Avellaneda, in Buenos Aires province (Map 10).

BICYCLE

The capital's ferocious traffic is a disincentive, but plenty of cyclists still manage to get around the city more or less safely. In late 1997, the city administration inaugurated a new 7km *bicisenda* (bike path) from Palermo to downtown, along Av Presidente Figuera Alcorta and Av del Libertador, ending near Cerritos in Retiro. Southbound cyclists should not continue beyond the sign indicating *fin bicisenda* (end of bike path), where the trail apparently continues beyond the Facultad de Derecho (Law School) in Recoleta. It in fact leads to a potentially dangerous *villa miseria* (shantytown).

For places to rent bicycles, see Activities in the Things to See & Do chapter.

WALKING

Its lack of hills helps make Buenos Aires a good walker's city. In the congested downtown, foot traffic often moves faster than vehicles, though narrow sidewalks can also slow your movement. The most pleasant areas to explore on foot are San Telmo, La Boca and Barrio Norte, and the parks of Palermo and Belgrano. In the summer heat and humidity, however, walking can be exhausting, and beware the aggressive porteño drivers who *never* even think of surrendering right-of-way. (An average of 400 pedestrians per year die in traffic accidents in Buenos Aires.)

ORGANIZED TOURS

Many agencies offer half-day and full-day city tours, but unless your time is very limited, try to get around on your own. The municipal Dirección General de Turismo (☎ 4371-1496, 4476-3612), on the 5th floor of the Centro Cultural San Martín at Sarmiento 1551 in Congreso (Map 5), has suspended its free and very worthwhile (though often crowded) weekend guided tours (in Spanish only) of city barrios. It's worth contacting them, though, to see whether they have resumed their theme-oriented offerings, which meet at a given point to explore areas such as San Telmo, Palermo's parks and lakes, and Parque Lezama.

Buenos Aires Tur (☎ 4371-2304), Lavalle 1444, Oficina 16, in San Nicolás (Map 5), offers half-day bus tours (US$14) that visit locations in the Microcentro, San Telmo, La Boca, Recoleta and Palermo. These take place daily at 9:30 am and 2:30 pm (Sundays at 2 pm only). Other tours include weekday afternoon visits to Tigre and the Delta via the Tren de la Costa (US$32); the same on Sunday morning US$60 with lunch included) and a gaucho fiesta in the province of Buenos Aires (US$60).

Buenos Aires Visión (☎ 4394-2986), at Esmeralda 356, 6th floor, in the Microcentro (Map 5), has similar itineraries and also arranges excursions to La Plata.

Buenos Aires Así (☎ 4315-1460), Marcelo T de Alvear 624, 2nd floor, in Retiro (Map 11), has some more unconventional offerings, including a ground tour of the city supplemented by a 20-minute helicopter flight (US$170), and a series of cultural-historical walking tours (US$16 to US$25).

Historical Tours (☎ 4311-1019, histours@commet.com.ar), downstairs at Paraguay 647 in Retiro (Map 11), focuses on theme-oriented tours with multilingual guides on topics like immigration (visiting San Telmo, La Boca and Puerto Madero; US$35) and Evita Perón ('Argentina in the '40s'; US$30), among others. Lihué Expediciones (☎ 4311-9610), Maipú 926, 1st floor, in Retiro (Map 11), offers literary walking tours, following the footsteps of Jorge Luis Borges and other porteño authors.

Aristarain Viajes (☎/fax 4322-3790), Viamonte 611, 6th floor (Map 5), runs a series of dining and drinking tours, focusing on the capital's better restaurants and Argentine wines, but also where their goodies come from – the *frigorífico* (slaughterhouse) of Mataderos, the Bolsa Argentina de Cereales (corn exchange) and the Mercado de Hacienda de Liniers (livestock market).

Things to See & Do

Most *porteños* 'belong' to a *barrio* where they spend almost all their lives. The majority of the 48 barrios in the Capital Federal (Map 3) are of limited interest to tourists, as nearly all key attractions are situated in just a handful of neighboring barrios in the eastern part of the city. This guide is organized around these barrios, which are defined in Orientation in the Facts for the Visitor chapter. Visitors would do well to familiarize themselves with the core barrios for orientation purposes.

Note that most museums charge about US$1 admission, but are usually free of charge on Wednesdays or Thursdays. Many close in the summer months of January and February, when most porteños take their holidays in Mar del Plata. The *Buenos Aires Herald* publishes a brief English-language guide (US$4) to 84 different museums in the capital and adjacent parts of Buenos Aires province. More thorough, but much more expensive, is the bilingual *Buenos Aires: Sus Museos/Its Museums* (1998), which covers 99 different museums, all within the Capital Federal. Some are very esoteric or specialized, such as the Museo Forense de la Morgue Judicial (Forensic Museum of the Morgue). Both guides are available at most bookstores.

SAN NICOLÁS & THE MICROCENTRO (MAP 5)

In the early part of the century, Calle Florida, then closed to motor vehicles between noon and 1:30 pm only, was the capital's most fashionable shopping street – a status since lost to Av Santa Fe in Retiro and Recoleta despite a recent renaissance achieved through the renovation of buildings such as the extraordinary **Galerías Pacífico** near Florida and Av Córdoba. Military privilege has guaranteed the pristine maintenance of landmarks like Retiro's Beaux Arts **Centro Naval** (1914), across Av Córdoba from the Galerías Pacífico (Map 11).

Today both Florida and perpendicular Lavalle are *peatonales* (pedestrian malls), while demolition of older buildings has created the broad avenues of Corrientes (the main theater district), Córdoba and Santa Fe (which runs through Retiro and Recoleta). In mid-1998, a municipal government project undertook the extension of the Lavalle peatonal east from San Martín toward Av Leandro N Alem, as well as creating a new one along Reconquista between Rivadavia and Juan D Perón, and anticipated further improvements in widening narrow sidewalks, planting street trees and sprucing up the facades of many historic buildings.

Among the most distinguished buildings on Florida, the Spanish Renaissance **Banco de Boston** (1924), at the intersection with Diagonal Roque Sáenz Peña, features a stone entryway carved in the USA and shipped to Buenos Aires to be mounted on the front of the building. Sculptor Jorge Fioravanti worked five years on the statue of Sáenz Peña (the president responsible for the introduction of universal male suffrage in 1912) directly opposite the entrance.

A short distance away, at Diagonal Roque Sáenz Peña 543, the **Edificio Menéndez-Behety** (1926) was the Buenos Aires headquarters of a Patagonian wool empire that transcended the boundaries of Argentina and Chile. Ground-level remodeling has impacted the building negatively, but the upper floors retain their original style. At the end of the block, where Diagonal Roque Sáenz Peña meets Rivadavia, the **Catedral Metropolitana** overlooks the Plaza de Mayo in Montserrat (Map 7; see the Montserrat section). A block east, at Rivadavia and 25 de Mayo, is the headquarters of **Banco de la Nación** (1939).

Near the foot of Corrientes, the massive **Correo Central** (main post office; 1928) entered from Sarmiento, fills an entire block bounded also by Av Leandro N Alem and

Bouchard. It took 20 years to complete this impressive and beautifully maintained Beaux Arts structure, originally modeled on New York City's main post office. The mansard (two-tier) roof was a later addition.

A recent improvement to the area, across Av Alicia Moreau de Justo (formerly Av Dávila), is the development of waterfront access at Puerto Madero, which stretches south toward San Telmo. The project is an upscale recycling of the formerly abandoned port area into restaurants, offices and loft apartments, comparable to London's Docklands.

Even broader than Corrientes, **Av 9 de Julio** is a pedestrian's worst nightmare (fortunately, there's a tunnel underneath it). At the intersection with Corrientes, the famous **Obelisco** soars above the Plaza de la República. Dedicated in 1936, on the 400th anniversary of the first Spanish settlement on the Río de la Plata, the phallic Obelisco itself symbolizes Buenos Aires much as the Eiffel Tower represents Paris or the Washington Monument does Washington, DC.

West of Av 9 de Julio, the city's major landmark and pride is the **Teatro Colón** (1908), at Libertad 621, one of the world's finest performing arts venues and the Southern Hemisphere's largest theater until the construction of the Sydney Opera House in 1973. A block south, fronting on Plaza Lavalle, note the colorful portals of the **Conventillo de las Artes**, an artists' space at Libertad 543, only three doors away from the austere neoclassical **Escuela Presidente Roca** (1902).

On the plaza itself is a cluster of used bookstalls frequented by passing pedestrians and lunchtime browsers from the French-style **Palacio de Justicia** (1904), popularly known as the Tribunales, the federal law courts at Talcahuano 550. Here, every Monday at 9:53 am, Jewish leaders and relatives of victims of the July 18, 1994 bombing of the Asociación Mutualista Israelita Argentina (AMIA) gather to observe a moment of silence in a protest known as 'Memoria Activa' (Active Memory).

At the north end of Plaza Lavalle, at the corner of Av Córdoba and Libertad, Jewish symbols adorn the facade of the **Templo de la Congregación Israelita**, Argentina's largest synagogue. Concrete sidewalk planters, constructed after recent attacks against Jewish targets, provide security from potential car bombs, while a police canine patrol stands guard across the street. Alongside, at Libertad 769, the **Museo Judío Dr Salvador Kibrick** (☎ 4372-2474) is open 4 to 6:30 pm Tuesdays and Thursdays; admission is free.

Av Corrientes' major landmark, the **Teatro General San Martín**, is the city's only major cultural construction since WWII. Its utilitarian exterior camouflages pleasing interior spaces, including three theaters, a cinema and several galleries and exhibition spaces. Its 8th-floor **Museo de Artes Plásticas Eduardo Sívori**, a branch of the main site in Palermo's Parque 3 de Febrero (Map 13), is open noon to 8 pm daily except Monday; admission costs US$1 but is free on Wednesdays. The **Museo de Arte Moderno** (☎ 4374-9426) has a small exhibition hall on the 9th floor, which keeps identical hours; the main site of the museum is in San Telmo (Map 8). The **Centro Cultural General San Martín** is a later addition, with entry from the Sarmiento side of the building.

Galerías Pacífico

Covering an entire city block bounded by Florida, Av Córdoba, San Martín and Viamonte, this impressive Parisian-style building has finally fulfilled the commercial purpose that its designers envisioned when they built it in 1889, with the proposed name of the Bon Marché. The worldwide economic crisis of the 1890s necessitated the sale of part of the unfinished building, subdivided into quarters by two large perpendicular passageways, to the Ferrocarril del Pacífico for its administrative offices. The railroad subsequently acquired the rest of the building which became state property after Juan Perón's nationalization of the railroads.

In 1945, the completion of vaulted ceilings above those passageways and a central cupola at their junction made space for a dozen panels, covering 450 sq meters, by muralists Antonio Berni, Juan Carlos Castagnino,

Manuel Colmeiro, Lino Spilimbergo (a close friend of the famous Mexican muralist Davíd Alfaro Siqueiros) and Demetrio Urruchúa. All were adherents of the Nuevo Realismo (New Realism) school, heirs of an earlier social-activist tendency in Argentine art. For years, the building went semi-abandoned, but a joint Argentine-Mexican team later repaired and restored the murals, which became a focal point of the building's renovation as an upscale shopping center in 1992.

Museo Mitre

Bartolomé Mitre was a soldier, journalist and Argentina's first legitimate president under the Constitution of 1853 (although his term ran from 1862-68 and he spent much of his term leading the country's armies against Paraguay). After leaving office, he founded the influential daily La Nación, still a porteño institution.

At San Martín 366, the Museo Mitre (☎ 4394-8240) is a sprawling colonial edifice (plus additions) where Mitre resided with his family – a good reflection of 19th-century upper-class life. A side exit led directly to the newspaper's offices. Take a glance at the library, which holds more than 80,000 volumes. The museum is open 1 to 6:30 pm weekdays. Admission is US$1.

Archivo y Museo Histórico del Banco de la Provincia de Buenos Aires Dr Arturo Jáuretche

Making sense of Argentina's chaotic economic history is no easy task, but this well-organized facility offers a superb introduction to the subject since viceregal times. It includes outstanding displays on the country's early economic regions, the financing of political independence and establishment of public credit (including the controversial Baring Brothers loans of the early 19th century), numismatics, and paper money and counterfeiting.

In the heart of the financial district at Sarmiento 362, the museum (☎ 4331-1775, 4331-7943) is open 10 am to 6 pm weekdays, 2 to 6 pm Sundays. Admission is free, and guided tours are available by appointment.

Teatro Colón

Ever since it opened in 1908 with a presentation of Aida, this world-class facility for opera, ballet and classical music has impressed visitors. Even through times of economic hardship, the elaborate Colón remains a high national priority, in part because it's the only facility of its kind in the country. Presidential command performances take place on the winter patriotic holidays of May 25 and July 9. No events take place in the summer months of January and February.

Within the lobby is a small but popular museum with exhibits of costumes, instruments and photographs of performers and performances. Very worthwhile guided visits cost US$5 and take place hourly between 11 am and 3 pm weekdays, and 9 am and noon Saturdays. Guides are available in Spanish, English, German, French, Portuguese and even Danish. (Only Spanish and English tours are always available.) There is often a free tour at 3 pm Thursday; there are no tours in January.

On these tours, visitors see the theater from the basement workshops (which employ over 400 skilled carpenters, sculptors, wigmakers, costume designers and other técnicos) to the rehearsal rooms and the stage and seating areas. Note especially the maquetas, scale models used by the sculptors to help prepare the massive stage sets. (The enormous pillars, statues and other props consist of painted lightweight Styrofoam.)

Occupying an entire block bounded by Libertad, Viamonte, Cerrito (Av 9 de Julio) and Tucumán, the imposing seven-story Colón (☎ 4382-6632) seats 2500 spectators and has standing room for another thousand. The main entrance is on Libertad, opposite Plaza Lavalle, but tours enter from the Viamonte side.

Other San Nicolás Museums

At Tucumán 846, the Asociación Cristiana Femenina de Buenos Aires (YWCA; ☎ 4322-1550) was the **Casa Natal de Borges**, the birthplace of literary great Jorge Luis Borges. Free guided tours of the house take place at 4:30 pm on Wednesdays.

Puerto Madero

Buenos Aires' waterfront has been the object of controversy since the mid-19th century, when competing commercial interests began to fight over the location of a modernized port for Argentina's burgeoning international commerce in beef and grains. In some ways, the struggle over the port has been a kind of microcosm of the Argentine experience, reflecting arguments over what sort of country Argentina should become.

At its simplest level, the problem has a geographical basis. Buenos Aires had no natural harbor, and the muddy banks of the Río de la Plata made it necessary to transfer cargo from freighters, which had no place to dock, to lighters that floated the cargo to shore directly east of the Plaza de Mayo. According to historian James Scobie, by 1881 a 500-ton steamship needed more than three months to unload its cargo in Buenos Aires, while at most other ports it took less than two weeks.

This slow, costly and sometimes dangerous process engendered two opposing solutions. The simpler and cheaper of the two, advocated by Argentine engineer Luis Huergo in the 1870s, was to widen, deepen and straighten the channel of the Riachuelo to port facilities at La Boca and Barracas, which had long served coastal trade and the fishery. Development there, favored by provincial landowners and local merchants, would promote their interests instead of those of the new commercial elite centered around the distant Plaza de Mayo. Huergo expected that the largely vacant area between Plaza de Mayo and La Boca would fill in gradually, while the focus of development would be at the south end of town.

Eduardo Madero, a wealthy downtown exporter, had more grandiose ideas and, more importantly, stronger political and financial backing, both in the federal government and in Britain. Madero proposed transforming the mudflats into a series of modern basins and harbors consistent with the aspirations and ambitions of a cosmopolitan elite.

As arguments over the two alternatives continued, federal-provincial conflicts (including a brief civil war) eventually resulted in the city's separation from the province as a federal district. Thanks in part to this jurisdictional dispute, work on Huergo's La Boca alternative began and even continued after the Argentine Congress surprisingly accepted – without debate – Madero's vague proposals in 1882.

By the time of its final completion in 1898 (four years after Madero's death), Puerto Madero had exceeded its budget and Madero himself had come under scrutiny for his links to politicians who had acquired nearby lands likely to increase in value, and for his attempts to buy up all the landfill in the area. By 1910, the amount of cargo was already too great for the port, and poor access to the rail terminus at Plaza Once made things even worse. New facilities in a rejuvenated La Boca partly assuaged these problems, but bandaid congressional actions failed to solve the problems until 1926, when completion of Retiro's Puerto Nuevo, near the new rail terminal, superseded Madero. Even then, according to Scobie, and into the 1970s, Buenos Aires was notorious for some of the world's highest port-loading costs.

Even as it lay dormant, Puerto Madero continued to be an object of controversy. As debris from the costly, pharaonic public works projects of the military dictatorship of 1976-83 filled the river east of the old port's four *diques* (basins), the area remained off-limits to the public. What ideas the military might have had for Puerto Madero is open to conjecture – they had planned a satellite city in the landfill that became the city's Reserva Ecológica Costanera Sur – but their sudden fall from power after the 1982 Falklands war precluded that possibility.

Over the past several years, though, developers have begun to recycle the red brick warehouses around the diques into a project resembling London's Docklands – ironically appropriate for a project whose original blueprint, a century earlier, drew on London's Millwall and Royal Albert Docks. Stretching from Retiro to San Telmo, on the east side of Av Alicia Moreau de Justo (formerly Av Dávila), these handsome but utilitarian buildings now comprise a gaggle of upscale shops, restaurants and offices and surround a 450-berth yacht harbor. Despite its very small permanent population (as yet), Puerto Madero has the distinction of being the newest of the capital's 48 barrios.

Yet for all the talk of its displacing traditional entertainment and gastronomical areas like Recoleta, today's Puerto Madero is still a work-in-progress. Only a handful of yachts have rented berths here, and the planned landscaping and bike paths that would encourage visitors are far from complete. As in the 19th century, foreign companies are moving into Puerto Madero, but rather than British grain merchants, they're chain restaurants like Planet Hollywood (housed in a new building vaguely resembling the Sydney Opera House) and a Howard Johnson's hotel. Foreign businessmen make the short walk from the Sheraton to the many restaurants along the diques for power lunches, yet most of the time the area still

ROBERT FRERCK

seems strangely deserted. Modernization of the warehouses on the east side of the diques is lagging well behind the west side (believe it or not, the warehouse known as Hangar 8, on Dique 4, owes its grotesque bright-blue paint job to a one-day shoot for an automobile commercial).

By its projected completion in 2005, the 140-hectare project will have cost US$1.9 billion. Supposedly, it figures into the facilities for Buenos Aires' hoped-for future bid for the Olympic Games (a long shot until the resolution of terrorist bombings against Jewish/Israeli targets in Buenos Aires in recent years). In the meantime, as it did a century ago, Puerto Madero still represents what Buenos Aires wants to be but hasn't yet achieved.

Things to See
More than 23,000 naval cadets and officers trained aboard the **Museo Fragata Sarmiento**, permanently docked in Dique 3 (Map 5). Built in Birkenhead, England, in 1897 at a cost of £125,000, this impeccably maintained 85m vessel covered 1.1 million nautical miles sailing around the world 40 times between 1899 and 1938 but never participated in combat.

On board are detailed records of its lengthy voyages, a gallery of its commanding officers, a poster for a 1945 film based on its history, and even the stuffed carcass of the ship's pet dog Lampazo. US President Theodore Roosevelt was among the distinguished guests, but perhaps the greatest test of its seaworthiness was the visit of Roosevelt's successor William Howard Taft, who weighed more than 140kg and, no doubt, came to dine on board.

The *Sarmiento* (☎ 4334-9386) is open 9 am to 8 pm daily; admission costs US$2, but children under 5 are free.

To the south, near San Telmo, at Dique 1 (Map 8), the **Museo Corbeta Uruguay** served nearly a century as a coastal patrol vessel after its construction in 1874. The high point of its career was the rescue of shipwrecked Swedish Antarctic explorer Otto Nordenskjöld and his expedition in 1903. The *Uruguay* (☎ 4314-1090) is open to the public 10 am to 9 pm daily; admission costs US$2.

The **Museo de la Policia Federal** (☎ 4394-6857), in the heart of the financial district at San Martín 353, 7th floor, is open Tuesday to Friday, 2 to 6 pm. Children younger than age 15 are not permitted.

BALVANERA (Map 6)

Balvanera, site of the Congreso Nacional, comprises part of the area popularly known as Congreso, which includes adjacent parts of Montserrat and San Nicolás. To the west, around Plaza Miserere, Once is the historic Jewish garment district.

Except for the **Palacio del Congreso** at the west end of Av de Mayo, opposite the Plaza del Congreso in the neighboring barrio of Montserrat (Map 7; see the Montserrat section), the immediate Congreso area has fewer imposing landmarks than one might expect, but there are still occasional surprises like the now closed **Confitería del Molino** at Avs Rivadavia and Callao, a rococo structure that may yet become a cultural center.

Eight blocks north of the Palacio del Congreso, Swedish architect Karl Nystromer designed the eclectic **Palacio de las Aguas Corrientes** (city waterworks; 1894), a classic of porteño architecture fronting on Av Córdoba. Popularly known as 'Obras Sanitarias,' it occupies an entire block bounded by Ayacucho, Av Córdoba, Riobamba and Viamonte. Topped by French-style mansard roofs, the building's facade consists of 170,000 glazed tiles and 130,000 enameled bricks from England. Ground-floor offices surround a dozen massive water tanks holding a total of more than 60 million liters. (The steady leak on the Riobamba side is a palpable symbol of the capital's decaying infrastructure.) On the 1st floor, the **Museo del Patrimonio Aguas Argentinas** (☎ 4379-0105) is open 9 am to noon on weekdays. Admission is free.

Torcuato de Alvear

For better or worse, no other single person has left a greater imprint on Buenos Aires than its first mayor, Torcuato de Alvear, appointed to the post by President Julio Argentino Roca in 1882. Son of General Carlos de Alvear (a colleague of Jose de San Martín), the single-minded Torcuato immediately set out to transform the city from the cozy Gran Aldea (Great Village) to the 'Paris of the South,' a world capital to showcase Argentina's international aspirations.

Even those who agreed with Alvear's goals sometimes questioned his methods. Convinced that Buenos Aires' architecture and public spaces should embody greatness, the Francophile mayor sought to replace the congested colonial streets, comprising one-story houses and narrow sidewalks, with wide boulevards linking grandiose buildings on expansive plazas. In implementing his plans, he literally allowed nothing to stand in his way. According to one story, when the telephone company was slow to move its lines in the admittedly unsightly Recova Vieja, an arcade crossing the present-day Plaza de Mayo, he personally cut the wires to speed up the demolition work.

The rejuvenated Plaza de Mayo was a triumph, as was the Av de Mayo (begun in 1889 but not completed until 1894, four years after Alvear's death). Not everyone thought highly of his taste, however. One of the signatures of his administration was a series of immense concrete grottoes, most since demolished, in public parks throughout the city. He also drew criticism for favoring increasingly affluent northern barrios such as Recoleta and Palermo, while neglecting poorer areas such as San Telmo.

Alvear's egotism did have limits. When a municipal commission suggested renaming Recoleta's much-improved Blvd Bella Vista after him, Torcuato at least had the modesty to insist that present-day Av Alvear be named after his father.

Three blocks west, on Pasteur between Viamonte and Tucumán in Once, is the site of the **Asociación Mutualista Israelita Argentina** (AMIA). Destroyed by a terrorist bomb in 1994, the current construction site is a daily reminder of the unresolved crime linked to murky elements of the Buenos Aires provincial police and Middle Eastern extremists. The Once district was, and to some degree still is, home to the capital's largest concentration of Jewish merchants.

At Viamonte 2790 (Subte: Pueyrredón), the **Casa Museo Bernardo A Houssay** (☎ 4961-8748) was the residence of Argentina's 1947 Nobel Prize winner in physiology. It's open from 2 to 6 pm on weekdays.

Farther west, in the Abasto district, the historic **Mercado de Abasto** (1895) is being recycled by US-Hungarian financier George Soros into yet another upscale shopping center. The building (bounded by Av Corrientes, Agüero, Lavalle and Anchorena) received an architectural prize in 1937 for its Av Corrientes facade. The Abasto neighborhood was once home to tango legend Carlos Gardel and is still home to several key tango clubs. Av Corrientes in the Abasto is the focus of urban revitalization efforts.

MONTSERRAT (Map 7)

Juan de Garay refounded Buenos Aires in 1580, about 1½ km north of Pedro de Mendoza's presumed encampment in 1536 near Parque Lezama in the present-day barrio of San Telmo. In accordance with Spanish law, Garay laid out the large Plaza del Fuerte (Fortress Plaza), later called the Plaza del Mercado (Market Plaza), then the Plaza de la Victoria after victories over British invaders in 1806 and 1807. It acquired its present name Plaza de Mayo after the date Buenos Aires declared independence from Spain, May 25, 1810.

Major colonial buildings at this site included the **Cabildo** (colonial town council), now truncated from the original construction (1725-65), and the church, built on a plot now occupied by the **Catedral Metropolitana**, across Rivadavia (literally in San Nicolás). Within the cathedral is the tomb of the repatriated José de San Martín, who

The Cabildo from Plaza de Mayo

died in France. In the center of the plaza is the **Pirámide de Mayo**, a small obelisk covering an earlier monument. The Madres de la Plaza de Mayo (the Mothers of Plaza de Mayo) still march around it at 3:30 pm every Thursday, in their unrelenting campaign for a full account of Dirty War atrocities during the military dictatorship of 1976-83.

At the east end of the plaza, the **Casa Rosada** (presidential palace), begun during the presidency of Domingo F Sarmiento, occupies a site where colonial riverbank fortifications once stood. (Today, after repeated landfills, it stands more than a kilometer inland.) From the building's balcony, Juan and Eva Perón, General Leopoldo Galtieri, Raúl Alfonsín and other politicians have convened throngs of impassioned Argentines when they felt it necessary to demonstrate public support. Between the Catedral Metropolitana and the Casa Rosada, at Rivadavia and 25 de Mayo (in San Nicolás), the **Banco de la Nación** headquarters (1939) is the work of famed architect Alegandro Bustillo.

In 1955, naval aircraft strafed the Casa Rosada and other nearby buildings in the Revolución Libertadora that toppled Juan Perón. On the north side of the appropriately bureaucratic **Ministerio de Economía**, on Hipólito Irigoyen just west of Av Paseo Colón, an inconspicuous plaque commemorates the attacks:

The scars on this marble were the harvest of confrontation and intolerance. Their imprint on our memory will help the nation achieve a future of greatness.

As recently as 1990, dissident junior officers of the so-called *carapintada* movement attempted to seize control of army headquarters and overthrow President Carlos Menem.

Towering above the Casa Rosada, just south of Parque Colón, military engineers – inspired by the Beaux-Arts Correo Central (post office) in San Nicolás – built the army headquarters at the **Edificio Libertador**, the real locus of Argentine political power for many decades. A twin building planned for the navy literally never got off the ground.

A few blocks east, at the corner of Adolfo and Defensa, the **Farmacia de la Estrella** is a functioning homeopathic pharmacy with gorgeous woodwork and elaborate turn-of-the-19th-century ceiling murals depicting health-oriented themes. Upstairs is the **Museo de la Ciudad**. A block away (bounded by Adolfo Alsina, Bolívar, Moreno and Perú), the **Manzana de las Luces** (Block of Enlightenment) includes the city's oldest colonial church, Jesuitic **Iglesia San Ignacio** (1712), a late-Baroque-style building.

Most other public buildings in this area belong to the late 19th century, when the Av de Mayo first connected the Casa Rosada with the **Plaza del Congreso** and **Palacio del Congreso**, obliterating most of the historic and dignified Cabildo in the process. British diplomat James Bryce found these developments symbols of progress:

One great thoroughfare, the Av de Mayo, traverses the centre of the city from the large plaza in which the government buildings stand to the still larger and very handsome plaza which is adorned by the palace of the legislature. Fortunately it is wide, and being well planted with trees it is altogether a noble street, statelier than Piccadilly in London, or Unter den Linden in Berlin, or Pennsylvania Avenue in Washington ...

The streets are well kept; everything is fresh and bright. The most striking new buildings besides those of the new Legislative Chambers, with their tall and handsome dome, are the Opera-house, the interior of which equals any in Europe, and the Jockey Club, whose scale and elaborate appointments surpass even the club-houses of New York.

Bryce might have been surprised by modern Buenos Aires' faded elegance and failure to keep pace with European and North American capitals, but visitors to the area can still glimpse remnants of the city's 'belle epoque,' even though the locus of downtown activities has moved north to streets like Florida, Lavalle, and Avs Corrientes and Córdoba in San Nicolás, and Av Santa Fe in Retiro.

South of the Plaza de Mayo, at Defensa and Av Belgrano, the 18th-century **Iglesia y Convento de Santo Domingo** prominently marks the approach to San Telmo. At the corner of Defensa and México, the stuccoed former **Casa de la Moneda** (National Mint; 1877) now belongs to the army's Instituto de Estudios Históricos del Ejército. At the opposite corner of the block, behind an English-style brick facade at Balcarce 677, the mint's former **Anexo Casa de la Moneda** (1911) houses the **Archivo del Ejército**, the army's historical archive.

Two blocks west of the old mint, at México 564, Jorge Luis Borges worked at the former **Biblioteca Nacional** (National Library; 1901). Originally designed as headquarters of the **Lotería Nacional** (National Lottery) and then adapted by the same architect, Carlos Mora, for its later use, the classical-style building is notable for the columns and arches of its three-story facade. Since the library's move to Recoleta, it now houses the **Centro Nacional de la Música** (National Music Center). Directly south, at the corner of Perú and Chile, **Plazoleta Rodolfo Walsh** memorializes an outspoken journalist victim of the military terror of the 1970s.

Probably the city's greatest landmark, second only to the Teatro Colón as a classical performing-arts center, is the **Teatro Avenida** at Av de Mayo 1212. Nearly gutted by fire in 1979, it reopened in 1994 with a performance by Spanish tenor Plácido Domingo.

As you pass the **Mercado del Congreso**, two blocks south of the Plaza del Congreso at Moreno 1749, glance upward for a view of the *guardapolvos* (literally 'dust guards') on the upper floors. Instead of the gargoyles often found on neo-European porteño architecture, these mini-sculptures are of cattle, swine and grapes.

Museo del Cabildo

Modern construction has twice truncated the mid-18th-century Cabildo, but there remains a representative sample of the *recova* (colonnade) that once ran entirely across the Plaza de Mayo. The two-story building itself is more intriguing than the scanty exhibits, which include mementos of the early 19th-century British invasions, some modern paintings in colonial and early independence-era styles, and religious art from missions of the Jesuits and other orders. Look for a small group of fascinating early photographs of the plaza. The attractive interior patio has a modest *confitería* serving sandwiches and the like.

At Bolívar 65, the museum (☎ 4334-1782) is open 12:30 to 7 pm Tuesday to Friday, 3 to 7 pm Sunday. Admission costs US$1. Guided tours take place at 4:30 pm.

Catedral Metropolitana

Also on the Plaza de Mayo, the Catedral Metropolitana was built on the site of the original colonial church and not finished until 1827. It's an important religious and architectural landmark. Note the bas-reliefs on the triangular facade above the neoclassical columns.

The cathedral is, however, an even more important national historical site, containing the tomb of José de San Martín, Argentina's most revered hero. In the chaos following independence, San Martín chose exile in France, never returning alive to Argentina even though, in 1829, a boat on which he traveled sighted Buenos Aires on its way to Montevideo.

In 1878, under the administration of President Nicolás Avellaneda, artisans began work on the tomb, designed and executed by French sculptor Carriére Belleuse, which was completed in 1880. In 1998, the Dirección Nacional de Arquitectura spent approximately US$100,000 to rehabilitate the tomb from the ravages of humidity.

Casa Rosada

Off-limits during the military dictatorship of 1976-83, the presidential palace (formally known as the Palacio de Gobierno Nacional) is no longer a place to avoid – visitors can even approach and photograph the *Granaderos* (grenadiers) who guard the main

The Casa Rosada presidential palace

ROBERT FRERCK

entrance. On the east side of the building, between the building and Parque Colón, excavations have unearthed remains of the old fort and customs buildings that were buried during construction of new port facilities in the 1890s.

The basement **Museo de la Casa de Gobierno** (☎ 4476-9841), entered at Hipólito Yrigoyen 219 on the south side of the building, includes material on Italian architect Francesco Tamburini, whose remodeling almost seamlessly transformed the former Casa de Gobierno and Correo Central (main post office) into the present structure. The most interesting part of the museum, though, is the catacombs of the Fuerte Viejo, a colonial ruin dating from the 18th century and also visible from the pedestrian walkway on the west side of Parque Colón.

The museum also provides a chronology of Argentine presidents, but it stops at 1966 – perhaps because events since then are too painfully contemporary. For this reason, though, the museum remains as notable for what it omits as what it contains. It's open 10 am to 6 pm Monday, Tuesday, Thursday and Friday, and 2 to 6 pm Sunday. Admission costs US$1 but is free on Mondays; guided tours take place at 4 pm daily.

Guided tours of the Casa Rosada proper take place at 3 pm Tuesdays and Thursdays (US$5 for adults, US$2 for children). Make reservations at the museum at least one hour in advance, and bring identification.

Manzana de las Luces

In colonial times, this was Buenos Aires' center of learning and, to some degree, it still symbolizes high culture in the capital. The first to occupy the block were the Jesuits. On the north side of the Manzana de las Luces, fronting on Adolfo Alsina, remain two of the five original buildings of the Jesuit **Procuraduría**. Dating from 1730, these are still currently undergoing restoration which includes defensive tunnels discovered in 1912. Since independence in 1810, this site has been occupied by the Universidad de Buenos Aires, whose entrance is at Perú 222. (Note the designation 'Universidad' on the facade, which

extended across the entire block until remodeling in 1894.)

Fronting on Bolívar, the **Iglesia San Ignacio**, with its rococo interior, appeared in 1712; after demolition in 1904, there remains only a single original cloister. It shares a wall with the **Colegio Nacional de Buenos Aires** (1908), where generations of the Argentine elite have sent their children to receive secondary schooling.

Slow-paced historical tours conducted by the Instituto de Investigaciones Históricas de la Manzana de las Luces Dr Jorge E Garrido (☎ 4342-6973), Perú 272, provide the only regular public access to the block's interior, where there is a small theater-in-the-round reconstruction of Buenos Aires' first legislature, the neoclassical Sala de Representantes. Tours are given in Spanish only.

Three separate tours cost US$3 each: the Colegio Nacional, Universidad de Buenos Aires and its tunnels at 3 pm on weekends; the Sala de Representantes at 4:30 pm on weekends; and the Iglesia San Ignacio and the Procuraduría at 5 pm on Sundays only. All meet 15 minutes prior to departure.

Museo de la Ciudad

The ground floor of this turn-of-the-century building, at the corner of Defensa and Adolfo Alsina, is home to the Farmacia de la Estrella, while the former upstairs residence, reached by a spiral staircase, has permanent and temporary exhibitions on porteño life and history, as well as a research library. Some exhibits can be very innovative, like 'Doors of Buenos Aires,' which focuses on everyday artistry as seen in commonplace objects such as knockers, handles, knobs and stained glass. Unfortunately, the staff can be surly, and the air is often thick with tobacco smoke.

Upstairs at Adolfo Alsina 412, the Museo de la Ciudad (☎ 4331-9855) is open 11 am to 7 pm weekdays, 3 to 7 pm weekends. Admission costs US$1 but is free on Wednesdays.

Museo Nacional del Grabado

This historic landmark displays a collection of mostly contemporary woodcuts and engravings in the restored early-19th-century Casa de la Defensa, which may retain some elements of the original structure despite an ill-advised remodeling for a restaurant in the 1970s.

At Defensa 372, the museum (☎ 4345-5300) is open 2 to 6 pm daily, but is closed on Saturdays. Admission, which costs US$2, usually includes a sample woodcut.

Iglesia y Convento de Santo Domingo

At the corner of Defensa and Belgrano, this mid-18th-century Dominican church (also known as the Iglesia de Nuestra Señora del Rosario) has a long and colorful history. Still showing the scars of shrapnel launched against British troops who holed up here during the invasion of 1806, its **Museo de la Basílica del Rosario** displays the flags captured from the British. Secularized during the presidency of Bernardino Rivadavia (1826-27), the building became a natural history museum, its original single tower serving as an astronomical observatory, until Juan Manuel de Rosas restored it to the Dominican order. It was gutted by fire during the 1955 Revolución Libertadora which sent Juan Perón into exile.

It's open 9 am to 1 pm and 4:30 to 8:30 pm daily; guided tours take place at 3 pm Sundays. Alongside it, the **Instituto Nacional Belgraniano** lionizes Argentina's second-greatest hero, Manuel Belgrano, military hero of the independence era and designer of the Argentine flag. Belgrano lies in a granite mausoleum here, and an eternal flame burns at the gate.

Palacio del Congreso

Costing more than twice its original budget, the Congreso set a precedent for contemporary Argentine public works projects. Modeled on Washington, DC's Capitol and topped by an 85m copper dome, the palace was completed in 1906. It faces the Plaza del Congreso, where the **Monumento a los Dos Congresos** honors the congresses of 1810 in Buenos Aires and 1816 in Tucumán, both of which led to Argentine independence. The monument's enormous granite steps symbolize the high Andes, while the fountain at its base represents the Atlantic Ocean, but the hordes of pigeons that stain the monument and foul its waters are poor surrogates for the Andean condor. In the waning days of the military dictatorship in 1983, graffiti blanketed the monument, but regular sandblasting has since kept it relatively clean.

Free guided tours of the Senado (upper house; ☎ 4959-3000) are available at 11 am on Monday, Wednesday and Friday (English, French, Spanish) and 4 pm (English) and 5 pm (Spanish); go to the entrance at Hipólito Irigoyen 1849. Tours of the Cámara de Diputados (lower house; ☎ 4370-7100), in Spanish only, are available at 11 am weekdays and at 5 pm on Monday, Wednesday and Friday; use the entrance at Rivadavia 1864.

A block east of the Palacio del Congreso, the recently relocated **Biblioteca del Congreso** (☎ 4371-3643), Hipólito Irigoyen 1760, is the legislature's research library. It's open to the public 24 hours a day.

Other Montserrat Museums

Visitors interested in colonial religious art, most notably wood carvings, should visit the **Capilla San Roque** at the Basílica San Francisco, Adolfo Alsina 430. The mid-18th-century church has been remodeled several times. It's open only on the 16th of every month, from 6:30 to 11 am and 4:30 to 7 pm.

At Moreno 350, the recently opened **Museo Etnográfico Juan Ambrosetti** (☎ 4331-7788) displays archaeological and anthropological collections from throughout Argentina, with a sample of materials from elsewhere in South America. Administered by the Universidad de Buenos Aires, it's open 2:30 to 6:30 pm Wednesday through Sunday, with guided tours at 3:30 and 4:30 pm on weekends. Admission costs US$1 but is free for children under 12.

The **Museo del Traje** (Museum of Dress & Uniforms; ☎ 4343-8427), Chile 832, displays civilian and military clothing from colonial times to the present. It's open from 10 am to 6 pm on weekdays.

The **Museo y Archivo Histórico de la Dirección General Impositiva** (☎ 4381-1047) deals with the history of taxation (or perhaps, more accurately, tax evasion) in Argentina. In the former Hotel Majestic, a

Reserva Ecológica Costanera Sur

During the Proceso of 1976-83, military authorities limited access to the Buenos Aires water-front, dyking and filling the area with sediments dredged from the Río de la Plata and debris from the demolitions from the construction of the city's freeways and broad avenues. While plans for a new satellite city across from the port stalled, trees, grasses, birds and rodents spontaneously colonized the low-lying, 350-hectare area that soon mimicked the ecology of the Delta del Paraná.

In 1986, the municipal Concejo Deliberante declared the area an ecological reserve. Despite its lack of services, the Reserva Ecológica Costanera Sur has become a popular site for weekend outings. It has also become a cruising area for the capital's homosexuals.

Reached by bus No 2 from Av Belgrano, the reserve (☎ 4315-1320) is at Av Tristan Achával Rodríguez 1550 (Map 2). It's open 7 am to 8 pm daily in summer, 7 am to 6 pm the rest of the year. Guided visits (☎ 4343-3778), including some by moonlight, can be arranged at the Fundación Vida Silvestre Argentina, Defensa 245 in Montserrat (Map 7).

landmark in its own right, at Av de Mayo 1317, 5th floor, the museum is open 11 am to 5 pm weekdays; admission is free.

SAN TELMO (MAP 8)

Only six blocks south of Plaza de Mayo, San Telmo is still untransformed by the rampant gentrification of barrios like Recoleta, Retiro and Palermo. It remains an artists' quarter where bohemians find large spaces at low rents, but it's also the site of high-density slum housing in *conventillos* (tenements) once built as single-family housing for the capital's elite.

Changes are in the offing, though, as the Municipalidad continues to spruce up the area bounded by Defensa and Avs Independencia, Paseo Colón and San Juan. Improvements have included widening sidewalks for cafés and street fairs, planting trees, installing traditional street lamps and cobbling the roadways. The idea is to encourage tourist activities beyond the usual Sunday visit to Plaza Dorrego or night-time excursion to the barrio's tango bars, but there's always the chance it will produce a sanitized Santelmoland that costs the barrio its unique colonial atmosphere.

Historically, San Telmo is famous for the rugged street fighting that took place when British troops, at war with Spain, invaded the city in 1806 and occupied it until the following year, when covert porteño resistance became open counterattack. As British forces advanced up narrow Defensa, the impromptu militia, supported by women and slaves pouring cauldrons of boiling oil and water from the rooftops and firing cannons from the balconies of the house at **Defensa 372** in Montserrat, routed the British back to their ships. Victory gave porteños confidence in their ability to stand apart from Spain, even though the city's independence had to wait another three years.

Just south of Chile between Defensa and Balcarce, the cobbled **Pasaje San Lorenzo** was once a rushing arroyo that impeded transport in colonial times. Look for the **Casa Mínima** at San Lorenzo 380, an example of the narrow-lot architectural style known as *casa chorizo* (sausage house). Barely 2m wide, the lot was reportedly a manumission gift from colonial slave owners to their former chattels. On Sundays, San Lorenzo hosts an art fair. The cobbled **Pasaje Giuffra**, two blocks south, also covered a former watercourse. At Bolívar and Independencia is a noteworthy Carnaval-oriented **mural**.

To the east, on Av Paseo Colón, the oval Plazoleta Olazábal features Rogelio Yrurtia's masterful sculpture *Canto al Trabajo* (moved here from its original site on Plaza Dorrego). Across the plazoleta, the neoclassic **Facultad de Ingeniería** of the Universidad de Buenos Aires, originally built for the Fundación Eva Perón, is an oddball landmark once described by Gerald Durrell as 'a cross between the Parthenon and the Reichstag.' Two blocks south, at Carlos Calvo 257, a different sort of architectural oddity is the brick **Dansk Kirke**, a neo-Gothic Lutheran church dating from 1930. Two blocks west, at the corner of Carlos Calvo and Bolívar, the **Mercado San Telmo** (1897) is still a functioning fruit and vegetable market for barrio shoppers; its interior is more spacious than the modest corner entrance would suggest.

At Defensa and Humberto Primo, **Plaza Dorrego** hosts the famous weekend flea market, the Feria de San Telmo. It's best on Sunday when the closure of Defensa to automobiles between Avs Independencia and San Juan gives a bigger stage for street performers, which range from one-woman bands, tap dancers, Michael Jackson moonwalkers and human statues to tango performers (who themselves range from amateur buskers and three-chord rock bands to highly professional singers and dancers). Not all of them are equally good – some are truly awful – but there's almost always something worth seeing.

Half a block east, at Humberto Primo 340, is the mid-18th-century **Iglesia Nuestra Señora de Belén** (1750), part of which contains the **Museo Penitenciario Nacional** (1760), first a convent and later a women's prison. Both have undergone substantial modification.

After a yellow-fever epidemic hit the once-fashionable area in the late 19th century, the porteño elite evacuated to higher ground west and north of the present-day Microcentro. As immigrants began to pour into the city, many older houses became conventillos housing European families in cramped, divided quarters with inadequate sanitary facilities. One such conventillo was the **Pasaje de la Defensa**, now recycled as a shopping gallery, at Defensa 1179. Originally built for the Ezeiza family in 1880, the two-story, three-patio edifice once housed 32 families.

Despite the neighborhood's historic colorful buildings, cramped conditions still exist – look for crumbling older houses with laundry hanging from the balconies. A good example is the sprawling building at Balcarce 1170, at the corner of Humberto Primo. Another former conventillo, recently redeveloped as artists' workshops, is the **Galería del Viejo Hotel**, Balcarce 1053.

To the south, at Defensa and Brasil, the trees and shrubbery of **Parque Lezama** are suffering from years of municipal neglect. The presumptive site of Pedro de Mendoza's original foundation of the city in 1536, the park is appropriately home to the **Museo Histórico Nacional**. Across from the park, at Av Brasil 315, is the striking turn-of-the-century **Iglesia Apostólica Ortodoxa Rusa** (Russian Orthodox Church), the work of architect Alejandro Christopherson.

Museo Penitenciario Nacional

Containing a handful of worthwhile but poorly organized exhibits, the Iglesia Nuestra Señora de Belén was a Jesuit school until the order's expulsion in 1767, when the Bethlemite order took it over. After secularization in the early 1820s, it became a men's and then a women's prison until 1978. The best items on display are a photograph of the famous anarchist Simón Radowitzky's release from prison in Ushuaia, in southern Argentina, and a wooden desk carved by inmates at Ushuaia for president Roberto M Ortiz.

At Humberto Primo 378, the museum (☎ 4362-0099) is open 10 am to noon and 2 to 5 pm Tuesday to Friday, and noon to 6 pm Sunday. Admission costs US$1.

Museo del Cine Pablo Ducrós Hicken

Only very recently moved from the Once district in Balvanera to new quarters in San Telmo, the city's previously neglected film museum promises to improve, especially with the completion of a new project to integrate it with the Museo de Arte Moderno, around the corner on Av San Juan.

The Museo del Cine's best past exhibits have been its Sala María Luisa Bemberg, containing sets and scenery from the late director's well-known films *Camila, Yo, La Peor de Todas* and *Miss Mary* (the latter in English, starring Julie Christie), and the personal effects of actress Niní Marshall. Also interesting are models like that of the *Merrimac*, on which Domingo F Sarmiento sailed from the USA back to Argentina and learned en route that he had been elected president in absentia. There is also a good selection of historical photographs from what has been one of Latin America's most important film industries, as well as a research library with a collection of 12,000 *Sucesos Argentinos* newsreels and 8000 Argentine movies.

At Defensa 1220, the museum (☎ 4361-2462) is open 10 am to 6:30 pm weekdays. Admission is US$1, but free on Wednesdays.

Museo de Arte Moderno
Housed in a recycled tobacco warehouse, the modern art museum has become one of San Telmo's highlights for its collection of figurative art of Argentine artists, as well as special exhibitions and film and video events. At Av San Juan 350, the museum (☎ 4361-1121) is open 10 am to 8 pm Tuesday to Friday, 11 am to 8 pm weekends and holidays. Admission costs US$1, but is free on Wednesdays. The museum is closed in January.

Museo Histórico Nacional
Appropriately located in Parque Lezama, this historical museum offers a panorama of the Argentine experience from its shaky beginnings and independence to the present. Its Sala de la Conquista displays paintings depicting the Spanish domination of wealthy, civilized Peru and Columbus' triumphant return to Spain, which contrast sharply with paintings of the Mendoza expedition's struggle on the shores of the Río de la Plata. There is also a map of Garay's second founding of the city in 1580, four decades later.

In the Sala de la Independencia and other rooms are portraits of major figures of the independence and republican periods, such as Simón Bolívar, his ally and rival Jose de San Martín, both in his youth and in disillusioned old age, and Juan Manuel de Rosas and his bitter but eloquent enemy Sarmiento, the latter with his perpetual scowl.

There are also portrayals of the British invasions of 1806 and 1807, and of late-19th-century *porteño* life.

At Defensa 1600, the Museo Histórico Nacional (☎ 4307-1182) is theoretically open 2 to 6 pm daily except Monday, but seems frequently closed for repairs. Admission is free. To get there, take bus No 86 from Plaza del Congreso in Montserrat (Map 7).

Helft Collection
Stressing modern Argentine painters and sculptors such as Guillermo Kuitca, Alberto Heredia and Libero Badii, but also including works by foreign artists as diverse as Marcel Duchamps, Man Ray and Yoko Ono, this very unconventional private collection of modern art occupies a San Telmo house renovated to display its contents under optimum conditions. Arranged by appointment only, free guided tours (☎ 4307-9175) are available in Spanish, English, French, German, Italian and Hungarian.

LA BOCA (MAP 10)
Literally Buenos Aires' most colorful barrio, La Boca was settled and built up by Italian immigrants along the **Riachuelo**, a sinuous waterway lined with meat-packing plants and warehouses that separates the capital from the industrial suburb of Avellaneda in Buenos Aires province. Much of La Boca's color springs from the brightly painted houses and corrugated metal roofs of the **Caminito**, a popular pedestrian walkway and former rail terminus which takes its name from a popular tango. The rest comes from petroleum and industrial wastes that tint the waters of the Riachuelo, where rusting hulks and dredges lie offshore and rowers strain to ferry passengers who prefer not to climb the high girder bridge to Avellaneda.

It would probably be easier to refine the oily Riachuelo (where malarial mosquitoes once bred) into diesel fuel than to clean it up. Indeed, it has even been suggested that mining its sediments for their accumulated mercury, chrome and other heavy metals might be a profitable enterprise. Some optimists even fish here, but any life form that can survive these waters is more likely to resemble Godzilla than anything edible in your local market.

María Julia Alsogaray, President Menem's environment secretary, has pledged to swim in the Riachuelo at the completion of a highly publicized cleanup campaign, but by then she may well be hobbling in old age and the polluted watercourse solid enough to support her. (To be fair, some of the harbor's most hazardous eyesore rustbuckets have been removed.) When rains are heavy and tides are high, floods submerge much of the surrounding area, and people get around by rowboat. Elevated sidewalks – a meter or more above street level – usually keep pedestrians dry as the waters rise.

Areas like La Boca were once places where immigrants could find a foothold in the country, but conditions were less than idyllic. British diplomat James Bryce described the barrio as

a waste of scattered shanties . . . dirty and squalid, with corrugated iron roofs, their wooden boards gaping like rents in tattered clothes. These are inhabited by the newest and poorest of immigrants from southern Italy and southern Spain, a large and not very desirable element among whom anarchism is rife.

In fact, French Basques preceded the Italians as settlers here. Today the area is still a flourishing working-class neighborhood, but it also sustains an artists' colony, the legacy of the late local painter Benito Quinquela Martín. The symbol of the community's solidarity is the Boca Juniors soccer team, the former club of disgraced superstar Diego Maradona. The team plays at the **Estadio Dr Camilo Cichero**, more popularly known by its nickname La Bombonera, at the corner of Brandsen and Del Valle Iberlucea. (Along the Brandsen side of the stadium, look for the murals of barrio life.)

Visitors arriving from San Telmo by bus will note the **Casa de Almirante Brown** in the 400 block of its namesake avenue. This is a replica of the country house of the Irish founder of the Argentine navy. A more authentic landmark is the **Puente Nicolás Avellaneda** that crosses the Riachuelo, linking La Boca to the industrial suburb of Avellaneda;

before the bridge's completion in 1940, floods had washed away several others. A new and welcome development is the *malecón*, a landscaped riverfront walkway along Av Don Pedro de Mendoza, stretching from the bridge to the Vuelta de Rocha meander to help control floods. Though the new street lighting was long overdue, the malecón hasn't improved the Riachuelo's unmistakable aroma, and most of the recently planted street trees have already died.

Within the bridge building is a scale model of the construction. When its escalators are not working, most pedestrians prefer to avoid climbing eight flights of stairs, opting instead to pay US$0.50 to be rowed across the Riachuelo. Check out Vicente Walter's bas-relief sculptures at Av Pedro de Mendoza 1629 above the presently closed restaurant **La Barca**. Past Caminito, at the corner of Alvarado, have a look at the **Barracas Descours y Cabaud** (1902), an industrial warehouse now being recycled in part as the Teatro Espejo; it also included a block of workers' housing.

Visitors also come to La Boca to savor the atmosphere of **Necochea**, a street lined with pizzerías and garish cantinas. (Many of these places housed brothels when the tango was not the respectable, romantic middle-class phenomenon it is today.) To the east, bounded by Ministro Brin, Suárez, Caboto and Olavarría, **Plaza Solís** is another hub of barrio activity. In some ways this is a rough neighborhood, and some indications of change are for the worse; graffiti once confined to bare walls now mars the murals, and armed robberies have taken place in the area.

The No 86 bus from Plaza del Congreso is the easiest route to La Boca, although Nos 20, 25, 29, 33, 46, 53, 64 and 97 also stop in the vicinity of the Caminito.

Museo de Bellas Artes de La Boca

Once the home and studio of Benito Quinquela Martín, La Boca's fine-arts museum exhibits his works and those of other early-20th-century Argentine artists (on whom there is almost no accompanying information). In keeping with the museum's maritime theme, one of its most entertaining features is an exhibition of painted bowsprits (the poles projecting forward at the front of ships), but the most interesting feature is Quinquela Martín's studio, the only space with adequate natural light for viewing his oils of barrio life. There are outdoor sculptures on the rooftop terrace, but don't overlook the tiled 'murals' on the sidewalk at the entrance.

At Av Pedro de Mendoza 1835, the museum (☎ 4301-1080) is open 10 am to 6 pm weekdays, 11 am to 8 pm weekends. Admission is free. The street level is also home to the Escuela Pedro de Mendoza, an elementary school.

Museo de Cera

Wax-figure reconstructions of historical figures and dioramas of scenes in Argentine history are the specialty of this rather tacky private institution. Among the historical personages depicted are Juan de Solís, Guillermo Brown, Mendoza, Garay, Rosas and Gardel, but indigenous leaders such as Calfucurá, Catriel and Namuncurá are also immortalized.

In an interesting building at Del Valle Iberlucea 1261, the museum (☎ 4301-1497) is open 10 am to 6 pm weekdays, 10 am to 7 pm weekends. Admission costs US$2.50.

RETIRO (MAP 11)

North of Av Córdoba, the barrio of Retiro derives its name from its former status as a monks' retreat on the city's outskirts during early colonial times. French landscape architect Charles Thays designed the densely forested **Plaza Libertador General San Martín**, once the site of a slave market and later of a bullring. It now features the obligatory equestrian statue of the liberator. Surrounding the plaza are several landmark public buildings. The **Palacio San Martín**, an Art-Nouveau mansion, was originally built for the elite Anchorena family and later acquired by the state for its Ministerio de Relaciones Exteriores y Culto (Foreign Ministry). The **Círculo Militar**, the largest private residence in Argentina (12,000 sq meters) was built in 1909 for *La Prensa* founder Jose C Paz. Now military property, it houses the **Museo de Armas** (Weapons Museum; ☎ 4312-9774) at Maipú 1030, at the corner of Av Santa Fe. It's open 2:30 to 7 pm Tuesday through Friday, and 2:30 to 6 pm on weekends; admission costs US$2. (More interesting and worthwhile are the several modern art galleries in the vicinity. For more information on these, see the Shopping chapter.)

On an odd triangular site at the corner of Florida and Santa Fe, **Administración de Parques Nacionales** occupies a neo-Gothic house built for the Haedo family at the turn of the century. Another local landmark is the nearby apartment building at **Maipú 994**, the last residence of the late author Jorge Luis Borges.

Across Av Córdoba from Plaza Lavalle in San Nicolás, the lavishly ornamented **Teatro Cervantes** (1921) is a landmark theater, built with private funds but acquired by the state after it went broke in 1926. Its facade was designed as a replica of Spain's Universidad de Alcalá de Henares. The building underwent remodeling after a fire in 1961. It now houses the **Museo Nacional del Teatro** (National Theater Museum) and offers guided tours (US$4) at 2 pm Tuesday to Friday.

Retiro's major museum is the **Museo Municipal de Arte Hispanoamericano Isaac Fernández Blanco** on Suipacha between Arroyo and Av del Libertador.

The 76m **Torre de los Ingleses**, across Av del Libertador from Plaza San Martín, was a donation by the city's British community in 1916. The Big Ben clone testifies to the partial truth of the aphorism that 'an Argentine is an Italian who speaks Spanish, wishes he were English, and behaves as if he were French.' During the Falklands/Malvinas War of 1982, the Torre was the target of bombs; since then, the plaza in which it stands has been renamed the **Plaza Fuerza Aérea Argentina** (Air Force Plaza). Currently undergoing restoration, the Torre itself is due to reopen to the public for views of Retiro from its mirador.

Opposite the plaza is the **Estación Retiro**, built in 1915 when the British controlled the country's railroads. While much of Retiro is a chic, upper-class area, the part beyond the **Estación Terminal de Omnibus** (1982), has long been a shantytown. It only recently has begun to enjoy basic municipal services like paved streets, a safe tap-water supply and regular electricity. It's not a recommended area to explore on foot.

Museo Municipal de Arte Hispanoamericano Isaac Fernández Blanco

Dating from 1921, this appealing building is typical of a neocolonial style that developed as a reaction against French influences in turn-of-the-19th-century Argentine architecture. Its exceptional collection of colonial art includes silverwork from Alto Perú (present-day Bolivia), oils with religious themes, Jesuit statuary, costumes and antiques. Unfortunately, there's little effort to interpret its collections and place them in any historical context.

Also known as the Palacio Noel, after the designing architect, the building and its collections suffered damage, since repaired, in the bombing of the Israeli embassy in 1992. Nearby, the former house of porteño poet Oliverio Girondo is due to undergo restoration as a literary cultural center under the auspices of the museum.

At Suipacha 1422, the museum (☎ 4327-0272) sits among attractively landscaped, densely forested grounds that offer sanctuary from the bustling Microcentro. It's open 2 to 7 pm daily except Monday; it shuts down completely in January and February. Admission costs US$1 but is free on Thursdays.

Museo Nacional del Teatro

Exhibits at this agreeably low-key museum trace the history of Argentine theater from its colonial beginnings, stressing the 19th-century contributions of the Podestá family, Italian immigrants who popularized the gauchesque drama *Juan Moreira*. Collection items include a gaucho suit worn by Gardel during his Hollywood film *El Día Que Me Quieras* and the *bandoneón* belonging to Paquita Bernardo, the first Argentine musician to play the accordion-like instrument, who died of tuberculosis in 1925 at the age of 25. There is also a photo gallery of famous Argentine stage actors.

Part of the Teatro Cervantes at Av Córdoba 1199, at the corner of Av del Libertad, the museum (☎ 4815-8883, ext 195) is open noon to 7 pm weekdays. Admission is free.

RECOLETA & BARRIO NORTE (Map 12)

During the yellow-fever epidemic of the 1870s, many upper-class porteños relocated from San Telmo to Recoleta, now one of the city's most fashionable districts. It takes its name from a Franciscan convent (1716), but is best known for the **Cementerio de la Recoleta** (Recoleta Cemetery; 1822), an astonishing necropolis where, in death as in life, generations of the Argentine elite repose in ornate splendor.

Barrio Norte, not a formal barrio, is a largely residential extension of Recoleta often grouped with Retiro, but the vernacular boundaries among all these areas and Palermo are often indistinct.

Alongside the cemetery, the **Iglesia de Nuestra Señora de Pilar**, a Baroque-style colonial church consecrated in 1732, is a national historical monument. Within easy walking distance are the important **Centro Cultural Ciudad de Buenos Aires**, the **Museo Nacional de Bellas Artes** (Fine Arts Museum), the **Centro Municipal de Exposiciones**, which hosts book fairs and other cultural events, and the monolithic **Biblioteca Nacional** (National Library).

Recoleta's many attractive public gardens and open spaces include **Plaza Intendente Alvear**, **Plaza Francia** (where the capital's largest crafts fair takes place on Sundays) and other parks stretching into Palermo and Belgrano. One of the barrio's most characteristic and entertaining sights is its *paseaperros* – professional dog walkers who often stroll with a dozen or more animals on leash. (See Walking the Dog.)

Among the monumental buildings is the neo-Gothic **Facultad de Ingeniería** (Engineering School) at the corner of Av Las Heras and Azcuénaga. The work of Uruguayan architect Arturo Prins, the never-completed building intended as the Facultad de Derecho (Law School) lacks the pointed ogival towers characteristic of the style.

Life & Death in Recoleta & Chacarita

Death is the great equalizer, except in Buenos Aires. When the arteries harden after decades of dining at Au Bec Fin and finishing up with coffee and dessert at La Biela or Café de la Paix, the wealthy and powerful of Buenos Aires move ceremoniously across the street to the Cementerio de la Recoleta, joining their forefathers in a place they have visited religiously all their lives. Perhaps no other place says more about Argentina and Argentine society.

According to Argentine novelist Tomás Eloy Martínez, Argentines are 'cadaver cultists' who honor their most revered national figures not on the date of their birth but on the date of their death. Nowhere is this obsession with mortality and corruption more evident than at Recoleta, where generations of the elite repose in the grandeur of ostentatious mausoleums. It is a common saying (and only a slight exaggeration) that 'it is cheaper to live extravagantly all your life than to be buried in Recoleta.'

Traditionally, money alone is not enough: you must have a surname like Anchorena, Alvear, Aramburu, Avellaneda, Mitre, Martínez de Hoz or Sarmiento. The remains of Evita

Perón, secured in a subterranean vault, are an exception that infuriates the presumptive aristocracy. One reason for this is that the dead often play a peculiar, and more than just symbolic, role in Argentine politics. Evita rests in Recoleta only after her embalmed body's odyssey from South America to an obscure cemetery in Milan to her exiled husband's house in Madrid, finally returning to Buenos Aires in 1974. (Embalming is uncommon in Argentina.) The man responsible for her 'kidnapping' was General Pedro Aramburu, a bitter political enemy of the Peróns who reportedly sought the Vatican's help in sequestering the cadaver after Perón's overthrow in 1955.

Aramburu himself was held for 'ransom' by the left-wing Peronist Montoneros *after* his assassination in 1970. Only when the military government of General Alejandro Lanusse ensured Evita's return to Perón in Madrid did Aramburu's body reappear for entombment in Recoleta, now only a few short 'blocks' from Evita. To locate Evita's grave, ask directions to the relatively modest tomb of the 'Familia Duarte' (her maiden name).

Outside Recoleta's walls, the gourmet corridors RM Ortiz and Junín, along with a string of *albergues transitorios* (hotels that rent by the hour) on Azcuénaga, raise interesting questions about the connections between food, sex and death in Argentina.

Juan Perón himself lies across town, in the much less exclusive graveyard of Chacarita, which opened in the 1870s to accommodate the yellow-fever victims of San Telmo and La Boca.

Although more democratic in conception, Chacarita's most elaborate tombs match Recoleta's finest. One of the most visited belongs to Carlos Gardel, the famous tango singer. Plaques from around the world cover the base of his life-size statue, many thanking him for favors granted. Like Evita, Juan Perón and others, Gardel is a quasi-saint toward whom countless Argentines feel an almost religious devotion. The steady procession of pilgrims exposes the pervasiveness of spiritualism in a country that prides itself on European sophistication.

One of the best places to witness this phenomenon is the Chacarita tomb of Madre María Salomé, a disciple of the famous healer Pancho Sierra. Every day, but especially on the second day of each month (she died on October 2, 1928), adherents of her cult leave floral tributes – white carnations are the favorite – and lay their hands on her sepulcher in spellbound supplication. The anniversary of Gardel's death (June 26, 1935), when pilgrims jam the cemetery's streets, is another major occasion.

Tombs at Recoleta

ROBERT RATTNER

Organized tours regularly visit the Cementerio de la Recoleta, open 7 am to 6 pm daily, on Junín across from Plaza Alvear (Map 12), but most visitors wander about on their own. There are free guided tours (☎ 4803-1594) at 2:30 pm the last Sunday of each month.

To visit Chacarita, which attracts fewer visitors than Recoleta, take Línea B of the Subte to the end of the line at Federico Lacroze, from which it is a short walk (Map 2). Look for the family crypt of Juan Perón, a tomb marked as 'Tomás Perón' (Juan Perón's father), but do not miss the tombs of Gardel, Madre María, poet Alfonsina Storni, aviator Jorge Newbery, tango musician Aníbal 'Pichuco' Troilo and comedian Luis Sandrini. Like Recoleta, Chacarita is open 7 am to 6 pm daily.

Around the corner from Chacarita, alongside each other, Avenida Elcano, the Cementerio Alemán (German Cemetery) and the Cementerio Británico (British Cemetery) are far less extravagant than either Recoleta or Chacarita but have their own points of interest. The Cementerio Alemán contains a monument to Germany's WWII dead, though the symbolism is imperial rather than Hitlerian. The Británico is both more and less than its name suggests – there may be more Irish, Jewish, Armenian, Greek and other immigrant tombs than there are truly British surnames. Perhaps the most notable headstone is that of Tierra del Fuego pioneer Lucas Bridges, author of the classic *The Uttermost Part of the Earth*, who died on board ship from Ushuaia, in southern Argentina, to Buenos Aires in 1950.

Walking the Dog

Buenos Aires supports a legion of *paseaperros* – professional dog walkers sometimes seen with up to 30 canines on leash. Employed by busy or sedentary apartment-dwellers, who either can't or won't take the time to exercise their animals properly, paseaperros can spend 20 hours or more a week strolling through areas like Recoleta, Parque Lezama and even downtown with a variety of dogs ranging from scruffy mongrels to expensive purebreds. On their frequent outings, paseaperros often develop a better rapport with the animals than do the owners, and the capital's leashed packs are a remarkably orderly and often entertaining sight.

As in any large city, the abundance of animals is a cause for concern. Every day, 400,000 canines deposit 68 metric tons of *soretes* and 120,000 liters of urine in the streets, sidewalks and parks of the capital. For this reason, city authorities may begin to regulate the profession by limiting dog walkers to 10 animals at a time, for example, and obliging them to carry a broom and bag to clean up after their charges. Some of these requirements already exist in law, but enforcement is nil.

Dog walkers, for their part, claim they take responsibility for their charges and that it is individual dog owners who let their animals run off leash that are the biggest problem. Possibly the most overlooked animal problem, though, is the legion of feral felines that infest city parks, schoolyards and vacant lots. Breeding and feeding uncontrolled (thanks in part to misguided catlovers who leave dishes of kibble in public places), the cats create their own waste problems and, in addition, more than decimate the wild bird populations.

Centro Cultural Ciudad de Buenos Aires

Part of the original Franciscan convent alongside its namesake church and cemetery, this renovated cultural center (also known as the Centro Cultural Recoleta) houses a variety of facilities, including museums, galleries, exhibition halls and a cinema. Its **Museo Participativo de Ciencias** (☎ 4806-3456) is a hands-on science museum, open 9 am to 4 pm weekdays, and 3 to 7 pm weekends and holidays. The **Microcine** offers films most days, and there are frequent free films outdoors in summer. Recent modifications to the building include the **Plaza del Pilar**, a colonnade facing Av del Libertador. The plaza sports a variety of restaurants for different tastes and budgets, and the upscale Buenos Aires Design Recoleta shopping center.

At Junín 1930, the center (☎ 4803-1041) is open 2 to 9 pm Tuesday to Friday, 10 am to 9 pm weekends and holidays. Admission to the center is free, but the Museo Participativo charges US$5 for everyone five years or older.

Salas Nacionales de Cultura

Housed in the Palais de Glace, a onetime skating rink only a few minutes' walk from the Centro Cultural Recoleta, this worthwhile museum offers rotating cultural, artistic and historical exhibitions, plus the occasional commercial event necessitated by financial considerations.

At Posadas 1725, the unusual circular building (☎ 4804-1163) is open 1 to 8 pm weekdays, 3 to 8 pm weekends. Admission varies depending on the program.

Museo Nacional de Bellas Artes

Dating from 1933, the former pumphouse for the city waterworks was designed by architect Julio Dormala and later modified by Alejandro Bustillo (famous for his alpine-style civic center in the northern Patagonian city of Bariloche). Visitors who have seen the filthy Riachuelo in La Boca may be shocked at the blue, unpolluted waters in 'realist' painter Pío Collivadino's 1961 depiction of the waterway, but the country's most important fine-arts museum contains many other works of national and international significance, including many on porteño themes by Benito Quinquela Martín and other Argentine artists of the 19th and 20th centuries. Occasional sculptures and wood carvings add some variety, but the museum fails to reflect the vitality of the most contemporary porteño and Argentine art.

European masters on display include Renoir, Rodin, Monet, Toulouse-Lautrec and Van Gogh. At Av del Libertador 1473, just north of the cemetery, the museum (☎ 4803-0802) is open 12:30 to 7:30 pm daily except Monday; it opens at 9 am on Saturdays. Admission is free.

Biblioteca Nacional
After two decades of construction problems and delays, the national library moved from Montserrat to this modernistic facility in 1992, but the plaster is already cracking on some of the landscaped outdoor terraces. Prominent Argentine and Latin American literary figures, such as Ernesto Sábato, often lecture here. Open 10 am to 9 pm weekdays, the library (☎ 4806-4729), at Agüero 2510, overlooks Av del Libertador, offering panoramic views of the capital.

Other Recoleta Museums
The **Museo Roca** (☎ 4803-2798), at Vicente López 2220 between Azcuénaga and Av Pueyrredón, celebrates the perpetrator of the infamous 'Conquista del Desierto' that brought Patagonia under effective Argentine control by a calculated war of Indian extermination. It's open 2 to 5 pm weekdays.

At Laprida 1222, the **Museo Xul Solar** (☎ 4824-3302), whose name is the pseudonym of Jorge Luis Borges' eccentric friend Alejandro Schulz Solari, an abstract painter who produced brightly hued watercolors and oils. It's open 2 to 8 pm weekdays, but it's closed in January and February. Admission costs US$3, US$1 for children under 12 and senior citizens.

Much of Nobel Prize winner Bernardo Houssay's medical and experimental equipment is on display in the **Museo Houssay de Ciencia y Tecnología** (☎ 4963-8612), in the

Facultad de Ciencias Médicas at Paraguay 2155, 1st floor. It's open 11 am to 3 pm weekdays. Houssay's residence, also a museum, is nearby in Balvanera (see earlier in this chapter).

Opened in late 1998 is the **Fundación Internacional Jorge Luis Borges** (☎ 4822-8340), at Anchorena 1660, a project of Borges' widow María Kodama. It's open 4 to 9 pm weekdays.

PALERMO (Map 13)
Ironically, the 19th-century dictator Juan Manuel de Rosas' most positive legacy is the wide-open spaces of Palermo, straddling Av del Libertador northwest of Recoleta. Once the tyrant's private retreat, the area became public parkland after his fall from power. One measure of his disgrace is that the man who overthrew him, Entre Ríos *caudillo* and former ally Justo José de Urquiza, sits here astride his mount in a mammoth equestrian monument on the corner of Avs Sarmiento and Presidente Figueroa Alcorta. The surrounding Parque 3 de Febrero bears the date of Rosas' defeat in 1852 at the battle of Caseros in Entre Ríos province. Domingo F Sarmiento, another contemporary who detested Rosas, was president of the country when development of the park resumed.

La Costanera

Northwest of downtown, the Av Costanera Rafael Obligado, popularly known as 'La Costanera,' is a riverside strip of restaurants and discos with occasional green spaces providing the main riverside access for the inhabitants of Buenos Aires. Its major architectural landmark is the vaguely Tudor-style **Club de Pescadores** (Fishermen's Club), a private club that dates from 1937 and sits at the end of a 150m pier (Map 13). Beyond Aeroparque Jorge Newbery, the municipal airport, the road loops around the **Balneario Parque Norte** (Map 2), where many porteños take a break from the busy downtown area. The park's numerous moderately priced *parrillas* are popular on weekends.

When British diplomat James Bryce visited Buenos Aires after the turn of the century, he marveled at the opulence of the porteño elite who frequented the area, and perhaps he envisioned the capital's late-20th-century traffic congestion:

On fine afternoons, there is a wonderful turnout of carriages drawn by handsome horses, and still more of costly motor cars, in the principal avenues of the Park; they press so thick that vehicles are often jammed together for fifteen or twenty minutes, unable to move on. Nowhere in the world does one get a stronger impression of exuberant wealth and extravagance. The Park itself, called Palermo, lies on the edge of the city towards the river, and is approached by a well-designed and well-planted avenue.

Now a major recreational resource for all porteños, Palermo contains the city's **Jardín Botánico Carlos Thays** (botanical gardens; open 8 am to 6 pm daily) at the intersection of Av Las Heras and Santa Fe, now undergoing restoration with help from London's famous Kew Botanical Gardens; the nearby **Jardín Zoológico** (zoo) fronting on Av Sarmiento; the **Rosedal** (rose garden) on Av Pedro Montt; the **Planetario Galileo Galilei** at Avs Sarmiento and Figueroa Alcorta; the **Campo de Polo** (polo grounds) at Avs del Libertador and Dorrego; and the **Hipódromo Argentino** (racetrack) across the street. As you might guess, some of these were not really for the masses, but the porteño elite no longer have the park to themselves. Visitors from all over the city now stroll its shady lanes, paddle canoes and pedal *bicis-cafos* (pedal boats) on its artificial lakes.

The area of Palermo closest to Recoleta, known as Barrio Parque or Palermo Chico, is home to many foreign diplomatic missions. The boundaries between the two barrios are less distinct on the ground than they are on maps. Though nominally part of Recoleta (Map 12), the area fronting on Av Córdoba, between Avs Pueyrredón and Coronel Díaz and bounded on the northeast by Mansilla, is known as Palermo Viejo, while the section between Mansilla and Av Santa Fe is Alto Palermo.

Much of Adolfo Bioy Casares' novel *Diary of the War of the Pig* takes place in an area delineated by between Av del Liberta-dor, Av Santa Fe, Parque Las Heras and the Jardín Zoológico.

Villa Freud

So obsessively introspective is Argentine and especially porteño society that other Latin Americans joke that an Argentine can commit suicide by jumping off his own ego. More than 37,000 psychotherapists practice in Buenos Aires, many of them in Palermo's so-called Villa Freud, a polygonal area bounded by Av Santa Fe, Av Scala-brini Ortiz, Av Las Heras and Av Coronel Díaz (Map 13).

Buenos Aires' standing as a center for psychiatric therapy and research dates from the 1940s, when many Jewish refu-gees from Germany and Austria took up residence here. It flourished after WWII, with support from the universities, but suf-fered during the dictatorship of 1976-83, when military authorities, many of them overtly anti-Semitic, characterized the field and its practitioners as 'subversive.'

Since the end of the Dirty War in 1983, positive developments like the return to democracy and negative developments like the unceasing economic crisis and large-scale unemployment have helped revive interest in therapy, and not just among intellectuals. Even working people have an interest, as reflected by neighborhood clinics and a series of inexpensive paper-back books called *Freud para Todos* (Freud for Everyone).

Still, Villa Freud is the locus of the porteño psyche, perhaps exemplified by the Psicolibro Club, a discussion group sponsored by the Palermo bookseller Libre-ría Paidós (☎ 4801-2860), Av Las Heras 3471, Local 31 (Map 13). At the same location since 1957, Paidós also publishes the magazine *Psicolibro*, which always features, in some form, the image of Sigmund Freud on its cover.

Literary great Jorge Luis Borges spent much of his childhood at **Serrano 2135**, only four blocks southwest of Plaza Italia. (This area has theoretically been renamed Borges.) Another five blocks southwest, at the junction of Serrano and Honduras, one of the newest centers of porteño nightlife is the lively, even raucous **Plaza Cortázar** (formerly Plaza Racedo).

Worth a note in passing is the apartment building at **Aráoz 2180**, the famous revolutionary Ernesto 'Che' Guevara's onetime Buenos Aires address, but this building dates only from 1972 and replaced the one that Che's family lived in. Still, there are enough older buildings around to give you an idea what the neighborhood must have looked like when the Guevaras moved here in 1948.

Palacio Errázuriz

The **Museo Nacional de Arte Decorativo** (National Museum of Decorative Arts; ☎ 4806-8306) and the **Museo de Arte Oriental** (Museum of Oriental Art; ☎ 4801-5988) share facilities at the Palacio Errázuriz, a stunning Beaux-Arts building at Av del Libertador 1902. The former is open 2 to 8 pm weekdays, 11 am to 7 pm weekends, with guided tours at 5 pm weekdays, at 5 and 6 pm weekends. The latter is open 3 to 7 pm Tuesday through Sunday, with guided tours at 5 pm Wednesday though Friday. Admission costs US$5 for the former, US$3 for the latter, which was undergoing repairs at the time of writing.

Museo del Instituto Nacional Sanmartiniano

In Barrio Parque, occupying the small Plaza Grand Bourg at the junction of Aguado, Elizalde and Castilla, this temple of indiscriminate hero worship is a 1:75 scale replica of San Martín's home-in-exile at Boulogne-Sur-Mer, France. It's open 9 am to noon and 2 to 5 pm weekdays, 2 to 5 pm weekends only.

Museo de Motivos Argentinos José Hernández

Whether intentionally or not, no other Buenos Aires museum so effectively exposes Argentina's ambivalence toward its national icon, the gaucho. Brimming with the gaucho accoutrements that symbolize the country's folk culture, it showcases items such as exquisite silverwork (credited to individual artisans) from Bernardo de Irigoyen and vicuña ponchos from Catamarca. It also displays revealing historical photographs of aristocratic families like the Martínez de Hoz in their tailored gaucho drag – the Argentine counterpart to George Bush posing as a Texas buckaroo.

Other notable materials include precolonial basketry and pottery, Mapuche Indian crafts, and an excellent life-size recreation of a *pulpería*, a rural shop or 'company store' on a cattle or sheep *estancia*. Though the museum takes its name from the author of the gaucho epic poem *Martín Fierro*, its only display on Hernández himself consists of a sample of translations into such improbable languages as Chinese, Ukrainian and Slovak.

In fact, the museum (☎ 4802-7294), at Av del Libertador 2373, should really be called Museo Carlos Daws after the Anglo-Argentine who donated most of its artifacts. It's open 8 am to 7 pm weekdays and 3 to 7 pm weekends. Admission costs US$1, but it's free on Wednesdays. It's closed in February.

Jardín Japonés

Created in 1979, on the centenary of the arrival of Argentina's first Japanese immigrants, the Jardín Japonés (Japanese Garden) is one of the capital's best-kept public spaces. Because of the lack of suitable rock of any kind near Buenos Aires, granite for the landscaping came from the rivers of Córdoba province.

Part of Parque 3 de Febrero, at Avs Casares and Adolfo Berro just north of Plaza Alemania, the garden (☎ 4804-4922) is open 10 am to 6 pm daily. Admission costs US$2 for adults, US$1 for children; it's free for retired people on Tuesdays and Wednesdays. Besides the gardens proper, there's an exhibition hall with rotating exhibits of art and photography.

Jardín Zoológico

Admission to the much-improved Jardín Zoológico (☎ 4806-7412), entered on Av

Jardín Japonés

Sarmiento from either Av Las Heras or Av del Libertador, costs US$3 for adults but is free for children under age 13. In addition to the main facility, there are a *granja infanta* (children's zoo), *calesita* (merry-go-round), *trencito* (train) and *laberinto* (maze). It's open 9:30 am to 6 pm Tuesday through Sunday.

Museo de Artes Plásticas Eduardo Sívori

Named for an Italo-Argentine painter who studied in Europe, this once-unimpressive museum of Argentine art recently moved to new and more spacious quarters that allow more frequent and diverse exhibitions than its former site in Recoleta. Sívori's own Parisian works reflect European themes, but later works returned to Argentine motifs, mainly associated with rural life on the Pampas.

At Av de la Infanta Isabel 555, across from the Puente del Rosedal (Rose Garden Bridge) in Parque 3 de Febrero, the museum (☎ 4774-9452) is open 10 am to 8 pm Tuesday to Friday, 10 am to 7 pm weekends and holidays. Admission costs US$1 but is free

on Wednesdays. Its library is open 10 am to 7 pm Tuesday to Friday.

Museo Nacional del Hombre

On the border with Belgrano, at 3 de Febrero 1370, the National Museum of Man (☎ 4783-3371) displays crafts from the indigenous peoples of the Argentine provinces. It's open 10 am to 6 pm on weekdays.

BELGRANO (Map 14)

Bustling Av Cabildo, the racing heartbeat of Belgrano, is an overwhelming jumble of noise and neon reminiscent of the Las Vegas Strip – but for its lack of casinos. Though it's one huge consumer feeding frenzy with little to commend it except its numerous cinemas, less than a block on either side of the avenue, Belgrano becomes a leafy barrio of museums, plazas, parks and a decent range of restaurants.

Belgrano residents tend to subdivide the barrio into three areas. West of Av Cabildo is the mostly residential zone of Belgrano R, while east of Av Cabildo toward the

Brightly painted housing in working-class La Boca

High rise apartments downtown

A Parisian-style townhouse

Tango in San Telmo

Postcards memorializing Carlos Gardel

San Telmo is famous for its antiques boutiques and weekend flea market

Rogelio Yrurtia's *Canto al Trabajo* on San Telmo's Plazoleta Olazábal

Iglesia Nuestra Señora de Belén in San Telmo

railroad tracks is known as Barrancas del Belgrano, after its sloping parklands. Between the railroad tracks and the river is Bajo Belgrano, also known as Belgrano Chico. In general, Belgrano is pretty dead on Sundays, but that makes it an even better place for strolling and dining.

Only a block east of Av Cabildo, **Plaza General Manuel Belgrano** is the site of one of the capital's major outdoor markets, held on Sundays. It's best from late afternoon on. Facing the plaza are two important museums: the **Museo Histórico Sarmiento** (once the site of the Congreso and executive offices) honors the 19th-century president Domingo F Sarmiento, while the **Museo de Arte Español Enrique Larreta** displays the art collection of former resident novelist Enrique Larreta.

At Vuelta de Obligado 2042, near the Museo de Arte, stands the Italianate **Iglesia de la Inmaculada Concepción**, a church popularly known as 'La Redonda' because of its impressive dome. The **Museo Casa de Yrrutia**, a few blocks from Juramento at O'Higgins 2390, once belonged to sculptor Rogelio Yrurtia.

Four blocks east of Plaza Belgrano, French landscape architect Charles Thays took advantage of the contours of **Barrancas de Belgrano** to create an attractive, wooded public space on one of the few natural hillocks in the city. Retirees spend the afternoon at the chess tables beneath its *ombú* (umbra tree), while children skate around the bandshell. The nearby **Museo Libero Badii**, at 11 de Septiembre 1990, displays the unconventional creations of one of Argentina's foremost modern sculptors.

Across Juramento from the Barrancas, Belgrano's incipient **Chinatown** fills about half the 2100 block of Arribeños, with a couple other businesses in the 2200 block. At its current rate of growth, it will take a long time to acquire a definable identity, but the single modest Chinese restaurant

A Symbol of Unity – or Division?

In the barrio of Núñez, almost at the edge of the Capital Federal, the Escuela de Mecánica de la Armada (Naval Mechanics' School or ESMA) was the military government's single most notorious torture site during the Guerra Sucia (Dirty War) of the late 1970s. So powerfully controversial a symbol is the handsome neoclassical building that, in early 1998, President Carlos Menem ordered the relocation of the ESMA, and the building's demolition, so that a 'monument to national unity' could be created.

Menem's plan ignited a firestorm of protest from human rights groups concerned that the demolition might destroy evidence of disappeared persons. They simultaneously argued that the preserved building should become a museum of state terrorism, in the hope that the experience of the Dirty War would never be repeated. The Buenos Aires city government raised legal objections, arguing that the building occupies city property which, when no longer needed by the federal government, reverts to the city, and a court injunction has stalled the demolition for the foreseeable future.

At the same time, the city's Secretaría de Cultura has authorized the Dirección General de Museos to create a Museo de la Memoria (Museum of Memory) which will include film, photographs, sound materials, documents and oral histories of the events of 1976-83. The new museum is still undecided: it could be a thematic venture in a custom-built facility, or it could be a *museo de sitio* (on-site museum) – in which case it is hard to imagine a more grimly appropriate site than the ESMA. The director wants to avoid politicization of the museum, but the emotions the topic still exposes make this a difficult task indeed.

While it stands, the dubious landmark of the ESMA and its gardens are on the 8200 block at Av del Libertador near Ramallo (Map 2), reached by bus No 29 which passes through the downtown area from La Boca and Plaza de Mayo. The building is not open to the public.

reinforces its authenticity by not offering a Spanish-language menu. There are scattered Chinese businesses on nearby streets.

Museo Histórico Sarmiento

Lagging only slightly behind Palermo's Instituto Nacional Sanmartiniano in its dedication to hero worship, this aging museum contains memorabilia of Domingo F Sarmiento, one of Argentina's most famous diplomats, statesmen and educators. Despite his provincial origins and the perpetual scowl on his face, the classically educated Sarmiento was an eloquent writer who analyzed 19th-century Argentina from a cosmopolitan, clearly Eurocentric point of view, most notably in his masterful polemic *Facundo, or Civilization and Barbarism* (widely available in English).

The building itself was briefly the site of the Congreso Nacional during the presidency of Nicolás Avellaneda (1874-80), when both chambers voted to federalize the city of Buenos Aires, inciting a brief civil war with the powerful province of Buenos Aires. The once-deteriorating house has undergone some restoration.

At Cuba 2079, opposite Plaza Belgrano, the museum (☎ 4783-7555) is open 3 to 8 pm

Domingo F Sarmiento

Tuesday to Friday and Sunday. Admission is US$1, with informative guided tours at 4 pm Sunday for no additional charge. From Av Callao in San Nicolás and Balvanera, take bus No 60, disembarking at Cuba and Juramento. It's about two blocks from the new Juramento Subte station, at the corner of Av Cabildo and Juramento.

Museo de Arte Español Enrique Larreta

Hispanophile novelist Enrique Larreta (1875-1961) resided in this elegant colonial-style house, which now displays his private art collection to the public. The house itself is a study in spaciousness. (If this were a conventillo, two families would probably occupy the marble-columned bathroom alone.) The collections are derivative despite the inclusion of interesting items such as 19th-century Spanish fans with painted scenes and landscapes. Photography is permitted only without flash.

Centered around a massive ginkgo tree, the gardens are magnificent but their organization is very formal. Open-air theater performances take place here in summer; enter from the Vuelta de Obligado side of the building. At Juramento 2291 across from Plaza Belgrano, the museum (☎ 4784-4040) is open 2 to 7:45 pm Monday, Tuesday and Friday, and 3 to 7:45 pm on Sundays and holidays. Guided tours take place at 4 and 6 pm on Sundays. Admission costs US$1 but is free on Tuesdays. It is usually closed in January.

Weekly guided tours of Belgrano, conducted by art historians under the auspices of this museum, take place at 4 pm Saturdays, weather permitting, and follow a variety of itineraries. Make reservations at the museum or at the Café de la Redonda across the street. These tours, which end with tea at the café, cost US$6.

Museo Casa de Yrurtia

Reclusive Rogelio Yrurtia (1879-1950), best known for his sculpture *Canto al Trabajo* on Plazoleta Olazábal in San Telmo, designed his Mudéjar-style residence with the expectation that it would house a museum.

Cluttered with Yrurtia's work, which focuses on human torsos, and works by his wife, painter Lía Correa Morales, the house also has a small but attractive garden whose centerpiece is the larger-than-life-size *Boxers* (titled in English), first exhibited at the St Louis World's Fair of 1904. Yrurtia seems to have been ambivalent about fig leaves; only about half his figures have them. Among the non-Yrurtia items, the painting *Rue Cortot, Paris* is the only Picasso in the country.

At O'Higgins 2390, the museum (☎ 4781-0385) is open 3 to 7 pm Tuesday to Friday, 4 to 8 pm weekends. Admission costs US$1. Informative guided tours take place at 4:30 pm Saturday afternoons for no extra charge. Guides can be a bit pedantic toward visitors whom they suspect know little Spanish.

Museo Libero Badii

Jurist Valentín Alsina built this 19th-century Italian-Renaissance house on the Barrancas de Belgrano, which now displays the unconventional sculptures of one of Argentina's foremost modern artists. The private collection is open to the public at 11 de Septiembre 1990, but the Fundación Banco de Crédito Argentino (☎ 4784-8650), which owns it, keeps irregular hours and usually locks the building – try standing around looking lost at the entry.

Nevertheless, it is theoretically open 10 am to 6 pm Tuesday to Friday, 3 to 7 pm weekends. Admission is free.

CABALLITO (MAP 15)

Site of one of the Universidad de Buenos Aires campuses, toward the west end of both Línea A and Línea B of the Subte, Caballito is a mostly residential barrio dotted with parks and scattered museums. The oval **Parque del Centenario** is a large open space containing the **Museo de Ciencias Naturales Bernardino Rivadavia** (☎ 4982-5243), Av Angel Gallardo 470, open 2 to 7 pm daily. Besides the fossils in its Sala Florentino Ameghino, named after a famous 19th-century Argentine paleontologist, it also contains a four-ton meteorite from Argentina's Chaco province. Admission costs US$1 but children under 12 get in free.

Also on the north side of the park, at Av Patricias Argentinas 550, the telescopes at the **Observatorio Astronómico** (☎ 4863-3366) are open to the public from 9 to 10 pm Friday and Saturday. Admission costs US$3 for adults, US$2 for children.

Also in Caballito, the **Primer Museo Histórico Dr Ernesto Che Guevara** (☎ 4903-3285; Subte: Primera Junta), Nicasio Oroño 458, honors the famous Argentine guerrilla who played a key role in Cuba's 1959 revolution and died in Bolivia in 1967. It's open 5 to 10 pm weekends, with free guided tours.

ACTIVITIES

Visitors accustomed to easy access to public facilities for sports and exercise may find the congested downtown area frustrating, but health clubs and gyms are increasingly common in the Microcentro and inner barrios. The extensive greenery of Recoleta and Palermo provides good areas for jogging, cycling and the like, especially on weekends when certain areas are closed to automobiles.

Cycling

While Buenos Aires traffic is less than conducive to enjoyable cycling, and the monotonous topography makes it hard to get a really good workout, there are places suitable for bicycles, most notably the roads of the Palermo parks and the waterfront east of Puerto Madero, both of which are closed to automobile traffic on Sundays.

There is a new *bicisenda* (bike path) running from Palermo to Núñez via Av Casares, Av Figueroa Alcorta and Av Udaondo to Av del Libertador; when taking this route toward Palermo, do not continue along the railroad tracks, which pass through a rough neighborhood. Another bicisenda, along Avs Figuera Alcorta and del Libertador, connects Palermo with Retiro.

Rental bicycles are available at the Velódromo Municipal (bicycle track) at Av Belisario Roldán in Palermo's Parque 3 de Febrero (Map 13), at the Nuevo Circuito KDT (☎ 4802-2619) at Av Salguero 3450 near the Costanera, and at the corner of Av del Libertador and Av Infanta Isabel in Parque 3 de Febrero (weekends only).

The capital's Asociación de Ciclistas Urbanos (ACU; ☎ 4981-0578) organizes free bicycle tours.

Swimming

Most people find the sediment-laden waters of the Río de la Plata unappealing (not to mention too toxic) for swimming, but some do take advantage of the relatively unpolluted channels of the Delta del Paraná, reached by launch from the suburb of Tigre, for an occasional dip despite the usually muddy approaches. Only those landowners wealthy enough to import sand have usable beaches, and then only briefly until the next heavy rain.

A handful of *polideportivos* (sports clubs) have moderately priced pools which can get very crowded. The most accessible of these are Polideportivo Parque Chacabuco (☎ 4921-5576), Av Eva Perón 1410 in its namesake barrio (Subte: Emilio Mitre; Map 15), for only US$3 per day; and Polideportivo Martín Fierro (☎ 4941-2054), Oruro 1310 in the barrio of San Cristóbal (Subte: Urquiza) for US$2.

Otherwise, major upscale hotels have swimming pools open to their guests, but many other pools are open to members only and require a substantial membership fee and monthly dues. Try, however, the indoor pool at Ateneo Cecchina (☎ 4374-4958), Bartolomé Mitre 1625 in San Nicolás (Map 5), where vouchers valid for four sessions cost US$35; the outdoor pool at Palermo's Club de Amigos (☎ 4801-1213), Av Figueroa Alcorta 3885 (US$3 admission, US$12 pool use) near the Velódromo Municipal (Map 13); the outdoor pool at Palermo's Punta Carrasco (☎ 4807-1010), Avs Costanera and Sarmiento (US$10 to US$15; Map 13); the outdoor pool at Belgrano's Balneario Coconor (☎ 4786-4576), Av Costanera and La Pampa (US$15 to US$20; Map 13); and the artificial lake at Belgrano's Balneario Parque Norte (☎ 4787-1382), at Av Cantilo and Güiraldes (US$9 to US$13; Map 13).

Golf

Buenos Aires' most convenient golf course is the 18-hole Golf Club Lagos de Palermo (☎ 4772-7261), at Av Tornquist 1426 on the border between Palermo (Map 13) and Belgrano (Map 14). It's open 7 am to 5 pm daily except Monday; greens fees are US$30 weekdays, US$40 weekends. There are driving ranges at the Asociación Argentina de Golf (☎ 4803-4305) at Av Costanera 1835 (Map 13), and at the Costa Salguero Golf Center (☎ 4805-4732), Avs Costanera and Salguero (Map 13).

For more details and information on golf courses outside the capital, contact the Asociación Argentina de Golf (☎ 4394-2743), Av Corrientes 538, 11th floor (Map 5).

Tennis

The three lighted clay courts at the Canchas de Tenis Bakerloo are at La Pampa 1235 in Belgrano (Map 14), while the Buenos Aires Lawn Tennis Club (☎ 4772-0983) is at Olleros 1510 in Palermo (Map 13). Rates are about US$12 to US$15 hourly.

Climbing

A city whose highest elevation is only 25m might seem an unlikely place for Andeanists, but there are several climbing walls scattered throughout the city. The most convenient are Fugate (☎ 4982-0203), Gascón 238 in Almagro (Subte: Castro Barros; Map 15) and Boulder (☎ 4802-4113), Arce 730 in Palermo (Subte: Olleros; Map 13). Both are generally open evenings, and offer climbing lessons both in Buenos Aires and on field trips.

Tango Classes

Besides the clubs mentioned in the Entertainment chapter, there are several other alternatives for tango instruction. For general information, contact the Academia Nacional del Tango at Av de Mayo 831 in Montserrat (Map 7), alongside Café Tortoni. The Universidad de Buenos Aires, in the Microcentro at 25 de Mayo 217 (Map 5), teaches beginner lessons (US$7 for nonstudents) from 6:30 to 8 pm Fridays; more advanced dancers take the floor from 8 to 10 pm. El Dorado, Hipólito Yrigoyen 947 in Montserrat (Map 7), offers lessons at 8:30 pm Thursday and Friday, with full-fledged dancing starting at 10:30 pm. Gricel

(☎ 4957-7157), La Rioja 1180 in the barrio of San Cristóbal, has Sunday lessons from 7 to 9 pm and Monday lessons from 8 to 10 pm. The Teatro Suizo, on Rodríguez Peña near Sarmiento in San Nicolás, also has Sunday inexpensive tango lessons (Map 5).

Caminito Tango Club (☎ 4301-1520), Del Valle Iberlucea 1151 in La Boca (Map 10), has tango lessons 8 pm to midnight on Wednesdays. At Tucumán 846, the birthplace of Jorge Luis Borges, the Asociación Cristiana Femenina de Buenos Aires (YWCA; ☎ 4322-1550), in San Nicolás (Map 5), offers tango lessons 6:30 to 9 pm on Tuesdays and Thursdays.

LANGUAGE COURSES

Buenos Aires offers many opportunities for Spanish language instruction. Consult the Sunday classified section of the *Buenos Aires Herald*, which offers several columns' worth of possibilities, including individual tutoring and even opportunities for teaching English. The *Herald* also publishes an occasional education supplement that details a variety of learning alternatives, primarily but not exclusively oriented toward Spanish-speakers wishing to learn English.

Before signing up for a course, read the description carefully, note all fees and try to determine whether it suits your particular needs. Remember that small groups or individual tutoring often offer the best opportunities for improving language skills, but the latter is usually considerably more expensive.

The Instituto de Lengua Española para Extranjeros (ILEE; ☎/fax 4375-0730, ilee@ overnet.com.ar), Oficina C, 7th floor, Lavalle 1619, in San Nicolás (Map 5), has conversation-based courses at basic, intermediate and advanced levels. Private classes cost US$17 per hour, while group lessons (no more than four students) are US$12 an hour. Specialized instruction in areas such as Latin American literature and commercial

Spanish costs US$30 per hour. The institute can also help arrange accommodations in a private home for around US$400 to US$500 per month single, US$600 per month double.

Another alternative is the Instituto Nacional de Enseñanza Superior en Lenguas Vivas (☎ 4393-7351), Carlos Pellegrini 1515 in Retiro (Map 11), where month-long intensive courses, with four hours of daily instruction at a basic, intermediate or advanced level, cost $450. Three-month courses, with four hours of instruction weekly, cost US$50 per month.

A further alternative is the Centro de Estudio del Español (☎/fax 4315-1156, martinduh@ act.net.ar), Reconquista 719, 111/4 E (Map 5). Two hours daily instruction for four weeks costs US$320 plus US$20 in course materials, while shorter courses cost US$11 per hour plus materials. Individual tutoring costs US$17 hourly.

The Universidad de Buenos Aires (UBA; ☎ 4343-1196, fax 4343-2733), 25 de Mayo 221 in the Microcentro (Map 5), offers good instruction at its Laboratorio de Idiomas de la Facultad but only for a few hours weekly. This is suitable if you're staying for an extended period in the city, but it's not very efficient if your visit will be relatively brief.

Tradfax (☎ 4373-5581, fax 4373-6074, royal@einstein.com.ar), Av Callao 194, 2nd floor in Congreso (Map 6), offers three-hour daily classes in general Spanish for US$180 per week. Commercial Spanish classes cost about US$30 more per week, while individual classes cost US$18 per hour. The organization also arranges lodging in nearby hotels from US$210 per week single, US$245 per week double.

There are also many private tutors within the city, charging in the range of US$18 to US$22 per hour, such as English-speaking Dori Lieberman (☎/fax 4361-4843, dorotea@ gramar.filo.uba.ar).

Places to Stay

Buenos Aires offers a wide range of accommodations, from youth hostels and down-in-the-mouth *hospedajes* to simple but very fine family-oriented hotels to five-star luxury lodgings of jet-set stature. Given the service sector's elevated price levels, there are few outstanding values, but affordable, acceptable accommodations are still available.

Budget accommodations tend to be well beyond their prime, though not necessarily bad, while many mid-range hotels are either showing their age or have undergone shoddy remodeling. (This is even true of some top-end accommodations.) There are, however, good values in all categories, and a number of places still offer discounts up to 15% for payment in cash. Budget hotels generally do not include breakfast, while mid-range and upper-end hotels almost always do.

In ascending order of desirability, the main areas for budget accommodations are Constitución and Barracas near the southern train station (abundant), San Telmo (limited but increasing), the Microcentro (limited), and the Congreso area overlapping parts of Montserrat, Balvanera and parts of San Nicolás (abundant). The latter includes the theater district of Av Corrientes.

All these areas, however, have both very good and very bad places. San Telmo is the most interesting and picturesque zone, followed by Congreso for its convenient access to the nightlife of Avs Corrientes and Santa Fe. Both the Microcentro and Congreso have decent mid-range accommodations as well. Many budget hotels double as *albergues transitorios*, short-term accommodations utilized by young couples in search of privacy.

In areas such as Barrio Norte in Recoleta and Retiro, top-end accommodations are the rule rather than the exception. Budget travelers will find few alternatives, though some mid-range places exist. The Microcentro and Congreso also have additional top-end hotels. Accommodations of all kinds are very limited in the largely residential barrios of La Boca, Palermo and Belgrano.

Travelers should note that tourist offices are usually reluctant to recommend budget accommodations or even to admit that they exist. This is partly because some of the cheapest accommodations can be pretty squalid, but mostly because the staff have the idea that foreign visitors should stay in *hoteles de categoria*, the best available (and usually most expensive) lodging. Often, with gentle persistence, travelers can extract information on more economic alternatives, and the municipal tourist office is making a determined effort to gather better information on budget alternatives.

Hotel checkout times vary, but they are often as early as 10 am and rarely later than noon. While most places are flexible within reason, some will charge guests who overstay their limit for an extra day. Travelers should verify each hotel's policy and give advance notice if they need extra time. Most places are willing to provide temporary luggage storage for travelers with late afternoon or evening flights or bus trips.

Be aware that most hotels tack on very high surcharges for phone calls that guests place from their rooms.

PLACES TO STAY – BUDGET
San Nicolás & the Microcentro (Map 5)

Not to be confused with Retiro's exclusive Marriott Plaza Hotel, the ramshackle but passable *Hotel Plaza* (☎ 4371-9747), Rivadavia 1689 in Congreso, rents tiny singles with shared bath for US$12/15 and charges only slightly more, US$15/20, with private bath.

Some English is spoken at *Hotel Bahía* (☎ 4382-1780), Av Corrientes 1212, where rates are US$20 double; they may give a 10% discount with student card. There's at least one credible report of theft from guest rooms, so watch your belongings.

Central, friendly *Hotel Maipú* (☎ 4322-5142), in an interesting but deteriorating building at Maipú 735, has simple but clean pleasant rooms, some with balconies, for US$19/24 single/double with shared bath, US$22/29 with private bath. Some internal rooms are dark, and in damp winter weather they can be musty.

Hotel O'Rei (☎ 4393-7186), at Lavalle 733 in the Microcentro just a block from Florida, is one of the best located budget hotels, but rooms fronting directly onto the Lavalle *peatonal* can be noisy. Several readers have griped about grumpy management, but others seem to find it just fine. Rooms with shared bath cost US$19/25, with private bath US$22/30. Laundry facilities are no longer available. Ask for discounts on longer-term stays.

Hotel Sportsman (☎ 4381-8021), in a pleasant older building in decent repair at Rivadavia 1425, between Paraná and Uruguay in Congreso, is popular despite its indifferent staff and some sagging mattresses. Rooms with shared bath (US$12/20) are better value than rooms with private bath (US$20/30). Students get a 10% discount. Under the same management, the rather better *Hotel Europa* (☎ 4381-9629), Bartolomé Mitre 1294 in Congreso, has rooms with private bath for US$26/35 (10% less with student discount).

The remodeled *Hotel Orense* (☎ 4476-3173), Bartolomé Mitre 1359 in Congreso, charges US$23/40 with private bath, heat and air-con, but it's worth haggling a bit here.

Balvanera (Map 6)

Greatly improved *Gran Hotel Oriental* (☎ 4952-3371), at Bartolomé Mitre 1840, charges US$18/20 for singles/doubles with shared bath, US$24/28 with private bath, both with breakfast. Some rooms have balconies but get street noise, while interior rooms are quieter.

Still a decent value is friendly *Gran Hotel Sarmiento* (☎ 4374-8069), on a quiet block at Sarmiento 1892, where simple but tidy rooms (some a bit cramped) with private bath cost US$25/35.

Montserrat (Map 7)

Hotel Central (☎ 4304-3783), Adolfo Alsina 1693, has singles/doubles with shared bath for US$12/20, with private bath for US$20/25.

Some rooms are small at *Hotel Cevallos* (☎ 4372-7636), Virrey Cevallos 261, but it's congenial, clean and well maintained for US$20/28 (US$5 extra for TV). Reader-recommended *Hotel La Argentina* (☎ 4342-0078), well-located at Av de Mayo 860, has flexible, friendly staff and free luggage storage, but it's also close to one of Buenos Aires' most popular all-night dance clubs. Rooms are US$20/30.

Some travelers have enjoyed the once-elegant *Hotel Reina* (☎ 4383-2264) at Av de Mayo 1120, where rooms with shared bath and breakfast cost US$20/30 (20% less with student discount), but some singles have been created with improvised partitions and are very small. Rates with private bath are US$25/37.

Just off Av de Mayo at Tacuarí 80, *Gran Hotel España* (☎ 4343-5541) is less magnificent than its name would suggest, but does have clean and reasonably spacious rooms, all with private bath, for US$26/34. Rooms go for US$27/33 at *Hotel Roma* (☎ 4381-4921), Av de Mayo 1413, which gets only a tepid endorsement.

San Telmo (Map 8)

Hostels Once the site of Buenos Aires' only hostel, San Telmo now has two, making the barrio a logical place for shoestring travelers to stay.

In a rambling old building with considerable charm, the official *Albergue Juvenil* (☎ 4394-9112) at Brasil 675 near Constitución station and easily reached by Subte, has 90 beds, a TV lounge and a pleasant outdoor patio, but can be noisy when groups from the provinces visit the capital – avoid winter holidays in particular. Prices are US$10 per person including breakfast but without kitchen privileges. It's helpful and friendly, but sometimes closes between noon and 6 pm; HI/AYH membership is obligatory.

Not affiliated with Hostelling International, *El Hostal de San Telmo* (☎ 4300-6899, fax 4300-9028, elhostal@satlink.com), superbly located at Carlos Calvo 614, is an outstanding facility for US$10 per person in three and four-bed rooms. Those near and directly above the common areas, though, can be a bit noisy. Kitchen access, laundry service, cable TV and email are all available.

Hotels Close to colorful Plaza Dorrego, dilapidated but passable *Residencial Carly* (☎ 4361-7710), Humberto Primo 464, has singles for US$10 with shared bath, US$12/14 for singles/doubles with private bath, both with kitchen access. The staff is lackadaisical and there are also noisy kids, but at these prices you can't expect too much.

At amiable, well-kept *Hotel Zavalia* (☎ 4362-1990), Juan de Garay 474 near Parque Lezama, rooms with shared bath cost only US$10/15, while those with private bath cost US$15/20. Rooms vary in quality (some have large balconies), but the main drawback is that families with children can make it noisy at times.

Hotel Bolívar (☎ 4361-5105), Bolívar 886, is San Telmo's budget favorite; several rooms have sunny balconies for US$15/22 with private bath. There are slightly cheaper singles with shared bath. *Hotel Victoria* (☎ 4361-2135), Chacabuco 726, has very good ground-floor rooms, though some are a bit musty, for US$15/25 with private bath, kitchen access, laundry facilities and an attractive patio. Across the street at Chacabuco 747, *Hotel Embajador* (☎ 4362-6617) has similar facilities for about the same price. Union-run *Hotel Oxford* (☎ 4361-8581), Chacabuco 719, offers rooms for US$24/38 including breakfast.

Constitución & Barracas (Map 9)

Not affiliated with Hostelling International, the new *Che Lagarto* (☎ 4331-0726, 4304-7618, diego@fsoc.uba.ar), Combate de los Pozos 1151 in San Cristóbal on the border of Constitución, charges US$7 per person.

A few blocks north of the Autopista 25 de Mayo, at Carlos Calvo 1463 in Constitución, *Hotel Carlos I* (☎/fax 4305-3700) offers singles/doubles for around US$15/25.

Near Estación Constitución, *Hotel Brasil* (☎ 4304-5441), Av Brasil 1340, charges US$30 double, while *Hotel Central* (☎ 4373-8785), across the street at Av Brasil 1327 costs US$30/40. (Note that this area has many albergues transitorios, which rent rooms on an hourly basis.)

Retiro (Map 11)

Budget accommodations are hard to find in this area, but the new *Recoleta Youth Hostel* (☎ 4812-4419, fax 4815-6622, mpa@interserver.com.ar), not yet officially affiliated with Hostelling International, occupies a recycled mansion at Libertad 1218 (despite its name, it lies within the boundaries of Retiro). Unquestionably the best located hostel in town, it charges US$10 per person.

Friendly but ramshackle *Hotel Versailles* (☎ 4811-5214), Arenales 1364, has spacious rooms and an excellent Barrio Norte location, but it's worn and past its peak with singles/doubles for US$25/35 without breakfast.

Recoleta & Barrio Norte (Map 12)

Residencial Hotel Lion D'Or (☎ 4803-8992), Pacheco de Melo 2019, is very cheap by barrio standards with singles/doubles for US$15/25, but it's often full. For reasonable accommodations in a lively university area, try *Hotel Rich* (☎ 4961-7942), at Paraguay 2080 near the Facultad de Medicina of the Universidad de Buenos Aires. Rates are US$20/25 with private bath.

Outer Barrios

Two university hostels, under the same management, may be worth a look for US$10 with breakfast: *Residencia Universitaria Encuentro* (☎ 4865-5684) at Sarmiento 4470 (Subte: Angel Gallardo) in the barrio of Almagro (Map 15) and *Residencia Universitaria Los Amigos* (☎ 4306-6021), Av Entre Ríos 2165, in the barrio of Parque Patricios, on the border of Constitución (Map 9). Both are oriented toward monthly accommodation, but accept short-term visitors. Discounts are possible for longer stays.

The *Metropolitán Hotel I* (☎ 4862-3366, ☎/fax 807-9039), Av Corrientes 3973, in

Almagro (Subte: Medrano), has singles/doubles for US$14/16 with shared bath, US$20/24 with private bath. Breakfast is included, and English is spoken. Under the same management, with the same prices, is *Hotel Metropolitán II* (☎ 4932-7457, ☎/fax 4807-9039), Av Boedo 449, in the barrio of Boedo (Subte: Castro Barros or Boedo). It also offers reduced rates for longer stays.

PLACES TO STAY – MID-RANGE
San Nicolás & the Microcentro (Map 5)

Across from the budget favorite Hotel O'Rei, reader-recommended *Hotel El Cabildo* (☎/fax 4322-6695), Lavalle 748 in the Microcentro, is slightly dearer with singles/doubles at US$35/45. Another reader recommendation, *Hotel Lisboa* (☎ 4381-2152), Bartolomé Mitre 1281, costs US$30/50 with cable TV and breakfast.

The family-style *Cardton Hotel* (☎/fax 4382-1697), an older mansion in good repair at Juan D Perón 1559 in Congreso, is another excellent value. Rooms with cable TV start at US$30/35. Under the same management, though slightly more expensive at US$40/50, is the remodeled and recommended *Hotel Americano* (☎ 4382-4223, fax 4382-4229), nearby at Rodríguez Peña 265 in Congreso.

Near Plaza del Congreso, the remodeled *Hotel de los Dos Congresos* (formerly Hotel Mar del Plata; ☎ 4372-0466), Rivadavia 1777, charges US$40/52 with private bath, air-con, cable TV and other amenities, but without breakfast. Further renovations may increase rates.

Once a leading budget hotel, well-kept *Petit Hotel Goya* (☎ 4322-9311), Suipacha 748, is no longer cheap at US$40/50 (including breakfast if the hotel bill is paid in cash), but it's friendly, spotless, central, quiet and comfortable.

Rates also start around US$40/50 at the *Tucumán Palace Hotel* (☎ 4311-2298, fax 4311-2296), Tucumán 384, which has drawn some criticism for 'deferred maintenance.' Competitively priced but criticized as 'shabby' by some visitors, *King's Hotel* (☎ 4322-8461, fax 4393-4452), Av Corrientes 623,

costs US$40/60. There's been at least one complaint of theft from rooms.

The spotlessly clean *Hotel Parlamento* (☎ 4374-1410, fax 4371-3789), Rodríguez Peña 61 in Congreso, is friendly but a bit worn for US$50/60. For about the same price, about US$55/70, rooms at the *Normandie Hotel* (☎/fax 4371-7001), Rodríguez Peña 320, are more threadbare than its attractive lobby would suggest.

The Art Nouveau *Gran Hotel Argentino* (☎/fax 4334-4001), Carlos Pellegrini 37 in the Microcentro, is reasonable value for US$50/60 with a good breakfast, English-speaking personnel. More spacious and comfortable rooms cost US$70/80. At *Hotel Plaza Roma* (☎ 4314-0666, fax 4312-0839), Lavalle 110 near Puerto Madero, rooms with private bath and breakfast cost US$50/80.

For US$55/65 with breakfast, about half the price of other four-star accommodations, *Hotel Regidor* (☎ 4314-9516), Tucumán 451, the relatively spartan rooms with cable TV are an excellent value, but the staff can be snooty toward casually dressed visitors. *Hotel Regis* (☎ 4327-2605, fax 4327-2612), in the cinema district at Lavalle 813, costs US$58/68 without breakfast.

Some visitors consider the four-star *Hotel Italia Romanelli* (☎/fax 4312-6361), Reconquista 647, greatly overrated for US$68/80, citing high telephone charges (almost universal in Argentina, however) and very overpriced drinks. Rates include access to a nearby pool and sauna. In the heart of the theater district, the *Columbia Palace Hotel* (☎/fax 4373-2123), Av Corrientes 1533, charges US$60/72. Clean but worn, the *Liberty Hotel* (☎ 4325-0261, fax 4325-0265), Av Corrientes 632, charges US$69/88.

Owners of the convenient *Hotel Phoenix* (☎ 4312-4845, fax 4311-2846), an architectural gem at San Martín 780, have made substantial investments in an attempt to restore the splendor of the days when it hosted the Prince of Wales. Its 60 rooms now sport modern conveniences without diminishing the appeal of the original antiques, but improvements have come at a price – what was once a relatively inexpensive hotel now costs US$69/80 (including a varied, abundant breakfast). There's a 10% cash discount.

Hotel Concorde (☎ 4313-2018, fax 4313-2818), 25 de Mayo 630, has drawn some favorable comment despite faded elegance. Rates are US$72/85.

Balvanera (Map 6)

In a quiet building on a noisy street, the very clean and recommended ***Hotel Ayamitre*** (☎/fax 4953-1655), Ayacucho 106, has rooms with TV, phone and air-con, for US$40/50 with breakfast.

Hotel Molino (☎/fax 4374-9112), Av Callao 164, charges US$48/60 with air-con, private bath and telephone, but some rooms are small and front on this very busy, noisy street.

The three-star ***Sarmiento Palace Hotel*** (☎ 4953-3404, fax 4953-6247), Sarmiento 1953, with cable TV and 24-hour room service, is clean, friendly and reasonably quiet for prices starting at US$52/72; better rooms are only slightly more expensive.

Charming, friendly ***Hotel Lyon*** (☎ 4372-0100, fax 4814-4252), Riobamba 251, has spacious, well-maintained suites with private bath, cable TV, telephone and other conveniences for US$68/80. Even larger ones cost only a little more, making it an outstanding value for a family or group. Rates are comparable at ***Hotel Lourdes*** (☎ 4951-7467), Av Callao 44.

Montserrat (Map 7)

Many of the abundant mid-range hotels on and around Av de Mayo, are either tattered (though usually not dirty) or cheaply remodeled.

With singles/doubles for about US$35/45 without breakfast (10% less with student discount), the ***Turista Hotel*** (☎ 4331-2281), Av de Mayo 686, has some adherents but has also drawn negative commentary. It gets hot in summer, and the air-con is balky.

Among the best values in the barrio is the ***Chile Hotel*** (☎/fax 4383-7112), an Art-Nouveau landmark at Av de Mayo 1297, where rooms with private bath and a good breakfast cost US$35/50. Although the street noise is considerable, corner rooms

have huge balconies with choice views of the Congreso Nacional and the Casa Rosada. The so-so ***Novel Hotel*** (☎/fax 4345-0504), Av de Mayo 915, charges US$36/46.

Correspondents offer mixed reviews of ***Hotel Avenida*** (☎ 4331-4341), Av de Mayo 623, two blocks west of Plaza de Mayo, where rooms with private bath and breakfast cost US$38/48. Several visitors consider its bright, spacious and air-conditioned rooms a lesser value than other cheaper places – perhaps because the staff are less cheerful than the rooms – but recent reports suggest improvement. For US$35/50 (10% less with student discount), ***Hotel Palace Solís*** (☎/fax 4371-6266), Solís 352, three blocks south of Plaza del Congreso, also gets mixed reviews.

Several other hotels are in the US$40/50 range, including friendly ***Hotel Madrid*** (☎/fax 4381-9021), Av de Mayo 1135, with cable TV and breakfast, and ***Hotel Callao*** (☎ 4372-3534), in an interesting building at Av Callao 292. For US$40/52, ***Hotel Marbella*** (☎ 4383-8566), Av de Mayo 1261, gets high marks from readers.

Gran Hotel Hispano (☎ 4342-4431, fax 4322-7114), at Av de Mayo 861, charges US$45/52 without breakfast. The clean, friendly ***Astoria Hotel*** (☎ 4334-9061), Av de Mayo 916, costs US$50/60.

Nuevo Hotel Mundial (☎ 4383-0011, fax 4383-6318), Av de Mayo 1298, across from Chile Hotel, has standard rooms, with cable TV and breakfast for US$54/63; better rooms cost US$65/75. The rest of the hotel doesn't quite match the attractive lobby, but it has a restaurant, hairdresser, boutique and other services. There's a 10% discount for cash payment and additional discounts for extended stays.

At ***Hotel Napoleón*** (☎/fax 4383-2031, napoleon@hotelnet.com.ar), Rivadavia 1364, clean but cheesily remodeled rooms with private bath, breakfast and TV are no great bargain for US$60/75 and up.

Retiro (Map 11)

Modest ***Hotel Central Córdoba*** (☎ 4311-1175, fax 4315-6860), San Martín 1021, is friendly, pleasant, quiet, clean and central, but also well-worn; some rooms are small, though charitable visitors might call them cozy. Singles/doubles are US$35/45 with private bath, phone and TV, but without breakfast. Comfortably old-fashioned **Hotel San Antonio** (☎ 4312-5381), Paraguay 372, charges US$45/55 with breakfast.

One correspondent praises the superbly located **Promenade Hotel** (☎ 4312-5681, fax 4311-5761), Marcelo T de Alvear 444, which charges US$55/65 without breakfast, but another found its attractive lobby a misleading approach to 'grubby, grimy and noisy' rooms above.

Gran Hotel Orly (☎/fax 4312-5344, orly@ compudata.com.ar), Paraguay 474, is a good mid-range value with spacious rooms for US$60/70 (guests making reservations by email get a 20% discount).

A few doors down at Paraguay 450, the somewhat rundown **Hotel Waldorf** (☎ 4312-2071, fax 4312-2079) charges US$62/66, while **Hotel Diplomat** (☎ 4311-9370, fax 4311-2708), San Martín 918, is a bit dearer for US$60/70.

Recoleta & Barrio Norte (Map 12)

Mid-range accommodations in Recoleta are higher than in some barrios, but the **Prince Hotel** (☎ 4811-8004), Arenales 1627, between Rodríguez Peña and Montevideo, goes for US$40/50 for singles/doubles. Well-located, in an older building at Marcelo T de Alvear 1893, **Hotel El Castillo** (☎ 4813-2048), charges US$45/55 without breakfast. Location is also the best feature at the cordial **Alfa Hotel** (☎ 4812-3719, fax 4814-3775), Riobamba 1064, where simple but well-kept, sunny rooms cost US$50/60 with breakfast.

The otherwise dignified **Guido Palace Hotel** (☎ 4812-0341, fax 4812-0674), Guido 1780, has an attractive 5th floor patio, but the walls are scuffed and comforts few considering the price of US$60/70 without breakfast. Prices have risen to US$64/81 at the **Ayacucho Palace** (☎ 4806-0611, fax 4806-1815), a stylish French building at Ayacucho 1408, but there's a US$5 per room cash discount.

Palermo (Map 13)

Accommodations of any kind are relatively scarce in Palermo, but family-style **Key's Hotel** (☎/fax 4772-8371), on a shady block at Zapata 315, has singles/doubles for US$24/36; it's near the Ministro Carranza Subte station.

There are a few mid-range choices on and around Av Santa Fe, near the Palermo Subte station on Línea D. **Hotel Panamé** (☎ 4772-1058), Godoy Cruz 2774, offers decent value at US$38/46 with private bath, breakfast and TV, though some downstairs rooms can be dark. Across the street at Godoy Cruz 2725, the remodeled **Palermo Hotel** (☎/fax 4773-7951), Godoy Cruz 2725, is spotlessly clean but lacks personality and sits almost on the noisy corner of Av Santa Fe; some interior rooms are a bit small. Rates are US$42/60.

Hotel Pacífico (☎/fax 4771-4071), Santa María de Oro 2554, is plain and a bit worn for US$40/45 with breakfast; there's a US$5 cash discount.

Belgrano (Map 14)

Since Belgrano is primarily residential and commercial, accommodations of any kind are few. The only really moderately priced choice, half a block from the Belgrano border and a block off Av Cabildo, is **Hotel Mórdomo** (formerly Hotel Majale; ☎ 4544-2711, fax 4545-1263), Ciudad de la Paz 2942, in a quiet, residential area in the barrio of Núñez. Singles/doubles are US$37/45.

PLACES TO STAY – TOP END

Top-end hotels almost invariably quote prices in US dollars, but do accept Argentine currency. All take credit cards. The very expensive luxury hotels often do not include the whopping 21% IVA in their rates, so verify before committing. Prices indicated below for these hotels are generally the *precio mostrador* (rack rate), but nearly all of them have substantial discounts, depending on such factors as the night of the week (weekdays are usually cheaper), season of the year (January, for example, when most people leave the capital's steamy environs for the Atlantic beaches), and advance booking and purchase.

San Nicolás & the Microcentro (Map 5)

Hotel Carsson (☎/fax 4322-3551, carsson@ datamarkets.com.ar), Viamonte 650 in the Microcentro, is central, clean and pleasant, with English-speaking staff. Singles/doubles with breakfast cost US$70/83 plus IVA. Rooms fronting on Viamonte tend to be noisy, however.

Best Western now manages the *Comfort Hotel* (☎ 4814-4917), Viamonte 1501 in Congreso, but standards are not yet up to the chain's level. It's understaffed, dark and cramped, but still a good value with the extraordinary 50% discount with student card. Otherwise, rates are US$100 double.

For aging charm in the Microcentro, try the very central *Hotel Continental* (☎ 4326-1700, fax 4322-1421), Diagonal Roque Sáenz Peña 725, where rates are US$109/121. Four-star *Hotel Lafayette* (☎/fax 4393-9081, lafayette@hotelnet.com.ar), Reconquista 546 between Tucumán and Lavalle, costs US$130/140 with buffet breakfast.

The always crowded *Savoy Hotel* (☎ 4370-8000, fax 4370-8000, savoy@redinf .com.ar), Av Callao 181 in Congreso, has doubles for US$150, suites for US$180, both including a buffet breakfast, cable TV, voicemail and electronic security locks.

Gran Hotel Colón (☎ 4320-3500, fax 4320-3507), Carlos Pellegrini 507 in the Microcentro, charges US$160/185 for comfortable rooms with verdant balconies (thanks to large potted plants) overlooking the Obelisco near one of the capital's most famous (and noisiest!) intersections, Avs 9 de Julio and Corrientes.

There are several luxury hotels in the downtown area. The *Crowne Plaza Panamericano* (☎ 4348-5000, fax 4348-5251), Carlos Pellegrini 525 between Tucumán and Lavalle, charges US$260/270 plus IVA, while the *Hotel Libertador Buenos Aires* (☎ 4322-2095), Av Córdoba 680, costs US$275 double plus IVA. The latter has two bars, a restaurant, a pool and a gym. Conveniently central at Tucumán 535, with attentive staff, the venerable *Claridge Hotel* (☎ 4314-7700, fax 4314-8022) is the best in San Nicolás. Rates are US$290 for very comfortable rooms with cable TV and other amenities.

Balvanera (Map 6)

The prestigious *Bauen Hotel* (☎ 4372-1600, fax 4322-9703), Av Callao 360 near Av Corrientes, charges US$142 for a double, with facilities that include restaurants, a nightclub and even a theater.

Montserrat (Map 7)

Congreso is more a mid-range than an upscale area, but the four-star *Castelar Hotel* (☎ 4383-5000, fax 4383-8388, castelar@ hotelnet.com.ar), in a magnificent building at Av de Mayo 1152, is one of the best top-end values with singles/doubles for US$89/95 – only slightly dearer than some truly mediocre mid-range places.

Hotel Nogaró (☎ 4331-0091, fax 4331-6791), Diagonal Presidente Julio A Roca 562, is a bit tattered by four-star standards, but a 15% cash discount makes rooms starting at US$124/145 a little more palatable. Among its more appealing features is the good natural light in most rooms, not always common in the densely built downtown area.

Retiro (Map 11)

The four-star *Hotel Lancaster* (☎ 4312-4061, fax 4311-3021), a handsome brick building, is at Av Córdoba 405, at the corner of Reconquista. Rates are US$95 single or double with breakfast. For business visitors in particular, the comparably priced *Aspen Suites Hotel* (☎ 4313-9011, fax 4313-8059), Esmeralda 933, draws praise for its central location and outstanding service.

The modern highrise *Hotel Conquistador* (☎ 4328-3012, fax 4328-3252, conqhot@ microstar.com.ar), Suipacha 948, features pleasant personnel, an attractive lobby, mezzanine bar and rooftop restaurant. Rates for singles/doubles are US$114/125 plus IVA, including a buffet breakfast and access to a gym and sauna. At Paraguay 1207, opposite Plaza Libertad, *Hotel Bisonte* (☎ 4816-5770, fax 4816-5775) costs US$139/169 with IVA.

At Parera 183, between Av Alvear and Quintana, the tasteful *Hotel Park Plaza Recoleta* (☎ 4815-5028, fax 4815-4522) charges US$153 single or double plus IVA. The clean, comfortable *Crillón Hotel* (☎ 4312-8181, fax 4312-9955), Av Santa Fe 796, charges US$150/170 plus IVA, with a good buffet breakfast included.

The renovated Barrio Norte highrise *Hotel Presidente* (☎ 4816-2222, fax 4816-5985), Cerrito 850, costs US$190 to US$211 single or double, IVA included, with buffet breakfast, and sauna and gym access.

Opposite Plaza San Martín at Florida 1005, the Marriott corporation now manages the elegant German Baroque *Marriott Plaza Hotel* (☎ 4318-3000, fax 4318-3008), which dates from 1909 and has two restaurants, a bar and modern amenities like a gym. Rates are US$300 double plus IVA.

Opposite the Plaza Fuerza Aérea, the soaring towers of the modern *Sheraton Buenos Aires Hotel* (☎ 4318-9000, fax 4318-9353), San Martín 1225, are less central and convenient, and much less personable. Rates are US$275/295 plus IVA.

One of the area's newest luxury lodgings, frequented by visiting entertainers, is the *Caesar Park Hotel* (☎ 4819-1296, fax 4819-1299, hotel@caesar.com.ar), a soaring brick construction at Posadas 1232. 'Superior' singles or doubles cost US$270 plus IVA, while 'deluxe' rooms go for US$310, both including a buffet breakfast. (The Caesar Park also has nonsmoking rooms, an unusual hotel practice in Argentina.) For US$330 plus IVA, the business-oriented *Park Hyatt Buenos Aires* (☎ 4326-1234, fax 4321-1235), Posadas 1086, also has a health club with gym and pool.

Recoleta & Barrio Norte (Map 12)

Probably Barrio Norte's best top-end value has been the three-star *Wilton Palace Hotel* (☎/fax 4811-1818, info@hotelwilton.com.ar), Av Callao 1162, recommended for its cleanliness and good service. Rooms, though, are a bit small, and there's been a substantial price increase to US$138 single or double.

Few places match the Old World charm of *Hotel Plaza Francia* (☎/fax 4804-9631), Eduardo Schiaffino 2189 at the corner of Av del Libertador, where singles/doubles cost US$140/152. It's close to the Cementerio de la Recoleta, restaurants and numerous museums. Rates at the *Hotel Recoleta Plaza* (☎ 4804-3471, fax 4806-3476), Posadas 1557 between Ayacucho and Av Callao, are US$135/145 plus IVA.

If you plan to eat so much that walking back to the hotel might be an effort, consider the five-star *Etoile Hotel* (☎ 4805-2626, fax 4805-3613, hotel@etoile.com.ar), RM Ortiz 1835, a highrise located right on Recoleta's restaurant row. Standard suites start at US$200 per night plus IVA, and reach US$290 per night plus IVA for the diplomatic suite, but there's a 10% discount for reservations by email.

At the elegant *Alvear Palace Hotel* (☎ 4808-2100, fax 4804-0034), Av Alvear 1891, doubles can reach US$350 upward. Another US$50 gets you a suite (most of which have spas). Since opening in 1928, it has been one of few places to maintain its standards through all the country's hard times. It has a particularly noteworthy rooftop garden.

WAYNE BERNHARDSON

Recoleta's Alvear Palace Hotel

Palermo (Map 13)

Torre Cristóforo Colombo (☎ 4777-9633, fax 4775-9911), Santa María de Oro 2747 between Juncal and Cerviño, is a luxury highrise 'aparthotel' starting at US$110 for a one-bedroom 'junior' suite with a kitchenette and up to US$220 for a two-bedroom suite with living room and a spacious outdoor terrace. Rates do not include IVA.

Places to Eat

Food in Buenos Aires ranges from cheap and simple to costly and sophisticated. In some places, decent fixed-price meals are available for US$5 or less, but side orders such as french fries and soft drinks can drive à-la-carte prices up rapidly. Chinese *tenedor libre* restaurants provide the most food for the least money – all you can eat for as little as US$4 – but quality varies considerably. Most also offer a wide variety of Argentine standards.

In run-of-the-mill restaurants, which are often very good, the standard fare is basic pasta like ravioli and gnocchi, short orders such as *milanesa* (breaded steak usually fried but sometimes baked), and the more economical cuts of beef. Count on fried potatoes, green salads and desserts as well. By spending just a little more, you can find the same sort of food with better-quality ingredients. More cosmopolitan meals are available at the capital's innumerable high-class restaurants, but these can be very costly indeed. One good place to catch up on the latest in *haute cuisine* is the Good Living section in the Sunday *Buenos Aires Herald*, where Dereck Foster also offers the latest on Argentine wines. Be aware, however, that by his criteria, 'inexpensive' meals can easily cost US$15.

Travelers on a very limited budget should try the *rotiserías* (delis), which sell dairy products, roast chicken, pies, turnovers and *fiambres* (processed meats). Such places often have restaurant-quality food for a fraction of the price. Many supermarkets also have lunch counters with surprisingly good food at equally surprisingly low prices.

Burger-oriented fast-food imports like McDonald's and Wendy's are fast displacing their indigenous clones such as *Pumper Nic* – a fact that says nothing positive about the quality of the latter, but a great deal about the economic clout of the former. All such fast-food places are shockingly expensive compared to standard restaurants serving much better food; in quality, they fall just short of *vomitivo*, a word which needs no translation. For better-quality fast food, try bus or train terminal cafeterias or the ordinary *comedor*, which usually has a limited menu often including simple but filling fixed-price meals. Comedores also often serve *minutas* (short orders) such as steak, eggs, milanesa, salad and french fries.

Confiterías mostly serve sandwiches, including *lomito* (steak), *panchos* (hot dogs) and hamburgers. *Restaurantes* offer much larger menus (including pasta, *parrillada* and fish), professional waiters and often more elaborate decor. There is, though, a great difference between the most humble and the most extravagant.

Restaurant meals are generally relaxed affairs. Breakfasts are negligible, but other meals can last for hours. Lunch starts around midday, but dinner starts much later than in English-speaking countries. Almost nobody eats before 9 pm, and it is not unusual to dine after midnight even during the week. (Reservations are rarely necessary, except at the most elaborate restaurants.)

If a snack or drink is in order, consider stopping in at a café. Everything from marriage proposals to business transactions to revolutions originate in Buenos Aires cafés, where many Argentines spend hours on end over a single cup of coffee, although simple food orders are also available. Cafés also serve beer, wine and hard liquor.

Bars are establishments where people go to drink alcohol. Gentrified bars may be called pubs (pronounced as in English). Additional cafés and bars appear in the Entertainment chapter.

FOOD

Ever since European livestock transformed the Pampas into enormous cattle ranches, the Argentine diet has relied on beef. When Charles Darwin rode across the province of Buenos Aires in the 1830s, he could not contain his astonishment at the gauchos' diet, which he himself followed of necessity:

I had now been several days without tasting any thing besides meat: I did not at all dislike this new regimen; but I felt as if it would only have agreed with me with hard exercise. I have heard that patients in England, when desired to confine themselves exclusively to an animal diet, even with the hope of life before their eyes, have scarce been able to endure it. Yet the Gaucho in the Pampas, for months together, touches nothing but beef ... It is, perhaps, from their meat regimen that the Gauchos, like other carnivorous animals, can abstain long from food. I was told that at Tandeel, some troops voluntarily pursued a party of Indians for three days, without eating or drinking.

After scientists discovered fossil remains of the world's largest meat-eating dinosaur in Patagonia, an Argentine on the Internet joked that 'it figures that the world's greatest carnivore would be an Argentine.' Many Argentines recognize that a diet so reliant on beef is unhealthy, but sedentary *porteños* continue to ingest it in large quantities at the capital's countless *parrillas*. As long as you don't make it a lifestyle, you can probably indulge yourself on the succulent grilled meat, often stretched on a vertical spit over red-hot coals in the picture windows of the city's most prestigious restaurants.

To Argentines, the Spanish word *carne* (meat) is synonymous with beef – lamb, venison and poultry all fall under other categories. The most popular form is the *parrillada*, a mixed grill of steak and other cuts that no visiting carnivore should miss. A traditional parrillada will include offal such as *chinchulines* (small intestines), *tripa gorda* (large intestine), *ubre* (udder), *riñones* (kidneys) and *morcilla* (blood sausage), but don't let that put you off unless you're a vegetarian.

Despite the obsession with beef, Argentina offers more ethnic and regional variety than most visitors expect. Everyone quickly recognizes the Italian influence in such pasta dishes as spaghetti, lasagna, cannelloni and ravioli. Less obvious is the tasty *ñoquis* (gnocchi in Italian), an inexpensive staple when the budget runs low at the end of the month. Ñoquis are a traditional restaurant special on the 29th of each month, but in times of economic crisis people may joke that 'this month we'll have ñoquis on the 15th.'

Some regions of Argentina have very distinctive dishes, which are also available in the capital. The Andean Northwest is notable for spicy dishes, more closely resembling the food of the central Andean highlands than the blander fare of the Pampas. From Mendoza north, it is common to find Middle Eastern food. Argentine seafood, while less varied than Chilean, deserves attention; per capita fish consumption is rising notably. Freshwater fish are outstanding but relatively unusual in the capital.

Since the early 1980s, health food and vegetarian fare have acquired a niche in the diets of some Argentines, but outside Buenos Aires and a few other large cities, vegetarian restaurants are less common. International

Meatless Meals in Cattle Country

Argentine cuisine is known for red-meat dishes, but vegetarians no longer have much trouble making do except, perhaps, in the most out of the way places. Since the 1980s, vegetarian restaurants have become commonplace in Buenos Aires, and nearly all of them have the additional appeal of being tobacco-free.

Even standard parrillas serve items acceptable to most vegetarians – such as green salads (often large enough for two people) and pasta dishes such as ravioli, cannelloni and *ñoquis* – but before ordering pasta, be certain it doesn't come with a meat sauce. If you have trouble being served a meatless dish, try pleading allergies. Remember that meat *(carne)* is beef – chicken, pork and the like are considered in a different category, though they are sometimes referred to as *carne blanca* (white meat). Vegans will find far fewer menu options.

Entering the Subte

Downtown traffic

By motorcycle or bus?

Tugboat on the Río de la Plata

Laid-back La Boca is known for its bright colors, Italian restaurants, music and art

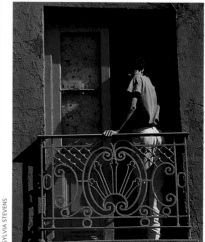

La Boca snapshots

La Boca's pedestrian walkway, the Caminito

cuisine of a high quality is readily available, especially if money is no object.

One of our most memorable bilingual menus came from a Chinese restaurant where an unusually creative mistranslation turned Spanish *camarones a la plancha* (grilled shrimp) into English 'ironed shrimp.' Despite this vivid image, most Asian food in Argentina is unremarkable Cantonese, but a boom in tenedor-libre restaurants, where all-you-can-eat meals still cost as little as US$4, has been a boon for budget travelers. Most also have salad bars with excellent ingredients, but they also tack on a US$1 surcharge if you don't order anything to drink. Prices for mineral water, soft drinks and beer are usually not outrageous, compared to upscale restaurants, but these restaurants make their profit on beverages.

Traditional fare at a parrilla

Breakfast

Argentines eat little or no breakfast. Most common is coffee, tea or *yerba mate* with *tostadas* (toast), *manteca* (butter) and *mermelada* (jam). In cafés, *medialunas* (small croissants), either *dulces* (glazed) or *saladas* (plain), accompany your *café con leche* (coffee with milk). For about US$5, a midmorning breakfast may consist of coffee plus a *tostado*, a thin-crust toasted sandwich with ham and cheese, and a glass of fresh-squeezed orange juice.

Lunch & Dinner

Argentines compensate for skimpy breakfasts with enormous lunches, starting about noon or 1 pm, and dinners, never earlier than 9 pm and often much later.

Beef, in a variety of cuts and styles, is the most common main course. Most Argentines prefer beef *cocido* (well done), but restaurants will prepare it *jugoso* (rare) or *a punto* (medium) on request. French fries or green salad usually accompany beef dishes.

An *asado* or parrillada is the standard, ideally prepared over charcoal or a wood fire and accompanied by *chimichurri*, a tasty marinade. Serious carnivores should not miss *bife de chorizo*, a thick, tender, juicy steak. *Bife de lomo* is short loin, *bife de costilla* or *chuleta* is T-bone, and *asado de tira* is a narrow strip of roast rib. *Vacío* is sirloin. *Matambre relleno* is stuffed and rolled flank steak, baked or eaten cold as an appetizer. Thinly sliced, this rotisería standby makes excellent sandwiches. *Bife a caballo* comes topped with two eggs and french fries.

Carbonada is a beef stew with rice, potatoes, sweet potatoes, maize, squash, chopped apples and peaches. *Puchero* is a slow-cooked casserole of beef, chicken, bacon, sausage, morcilla, maize, peppers, tomatoes, onions, cabbage, sweet potatoes and squash; the cook may add garbanzos or other beans. Rice cooked in the broth is a common accompaniment.

Milanesa is one of the cheapest and commonest short-order items on the menu. This author is tired of ordinary milanesa, but tastier and more elaborate versions are available – try *milanesa napolitana* with tomato sauce and mozzarella, and *milanesa maryland*, made with chicken and accompanied by fried bananas and creamed corn.

Pollo (chicken) is sometimes part of the standard parrillada, but it also comes separately with french fries or salad. The standard fish is *merluza* (hake), most commonly fried in batter and served with mashed potatoes. Spanish restaurants are the best bets for well-prepared seafood.

Snacks

One of the world's finest snacks is the *empanada*, a tasty turnover filled with vegetables, hard-boiled egg, olives, beef, chicken, ham and cheese or other fillings. These are cheap and available almost everywhere; buy them by the dozen in a rotisería before a long bus or train trip. Empanadas *al horno* (baked) are lighter than empanadas *fritas* (fried).

Pizza, a common market and restaurant snack, is one of the cheapest items on the menu when purchased by the slice. In many pizzerías, it is cheaper to eat standing up at the counter than seated at a table. Toppings are standardized – not customized as in North America – but there are more options when buying an entire pizza rather than slices. For slices, be sure to try *fugazza*, a cheap and delicious cheeseless variety with sweet onions, or *fugazzeta*, which comes with mozzarella cheese. Many Argentines eat their pizza accompanied by *fainá*, a dense chickpea (garbanzo) dough baked and sliced to match.

For Argentines at home or on the road, a common afternoon snack is *mate con facturas* (mate with sweet pastries). If you visit an Argentine family in the afternoon, stop by a bakery to bring some along.

Desserts

Fresh fruit is the most common *postre* (dessert) in Argentine homes. Peeling fruit by hand seems uncouth to cultured Argentines who surgically peel all fruit (except grapes) with a table knife. In restaurants, *ensalada de fruta* (fruit salad), *flan* (egg custard) or *queso y dulce* (cheese with preserved fruit, sometimes known as *postre vigilante)* are frequent choices. The 'dulce' can consist of *batata* (sweet potato) or *membrillo* (quince). Flan is topped with *crema* (whipped cream) or *dulce de leche*, a sweet caramelized milk which is an Argentine obsession. *Almendrado*, vanilla ice cream rolled with almonds, is also common.

Stemming from the Italian tradition, Argentine helado (ice cream) is world-class. It first appeared in Buenos Aires in the mid-19th century when, in the absence of freezers, blocks of ice were shipped from Europe and the United States.

DRINKS

Argentines consume a great variety of liquids, both nonalcoholic and alcoholic. The most Argentine among them is *mate*, a cultural bellwether described in the Facts about Buenos Aires chapter.

There are few drinking restrictions, although 18 is the legal age for alcohol consumption in public.

Soft Drinks

Argentines drink prodigious amounts of soft drinks, from the ubiquitous Coca-Cola and 7-Up to the local tonic water, Paso de los Toros. Mineral water, both *con gas* (carbonated) and *sin gas* (plain) is widely available, but tap water is potable despite the city's aging infrastructure. If no carbonated mineral water is available, *soda*, which often comes in large siphon bottles, is usually the cheapest thirst-quencher.

In many restaurants, soft drinks can be quite expensive. It's not unheard of for a US$5 tenedor libre to charge US$3 for a Coca-Cola.

Breaking Your Diet

Coming from the Italian tradition, Argentine *helado* (ice cream) is the continent's best and comparable to the best anywhere in the world. Chains like Massera, located throughout the country, are not bad, but the best Argentine ice cream comes from smaller *heladerías*, which make their own in small batches on the premises or nearby; look for the words *elaboración propia* or *elaboración artesanal*. Such places often have dozens of flavors, from variations on conventional vanilla and chocolate to common and exotic fruits and unexpected mixtures. During winter, when Argentines rarely eat ice cream, the best heladerías often close.

Rarely will Argentine ice cream disappoint you, but only truly special shops are mentioned in the text. When restaurant desserts seem a bit expensive, a quarter kilo of helado is a relatively economical alternative, especially when shared.

Fruit Juices & Licuados

Jugos are not so varied as in tropical South America. For fresh-squeezed orange juice, ask for *jugo de naranja exprimido* – otherwise you may get tinned juice. (Oranges are very cheap in Argentina, but transforming them into fresh juice miraculously increases their value tenfold.) *Pomelo* (grapefruit), *limón* (lemon) and *ananá* (pineapple) are also common. *Jugo de manzana* (apple juice), a specialty of Patagonia's Río Negro valley, is available everywhere.

Licuados are milk-blended fruit drinks, but on request they can be made with water. Common flavors include banana, *durazno* (peach) and *pera* (pear).

Coffee, Tea & Chocolate

Serious coffee drinkers will be delighted to find that coffee will always be espresso (accompanied by enough packets of sugar to fuel a Brazilian Volkswagen). *Café chico* is a thick, dark coffee served in a very small cup. *Cortado* is a small coffee with a touch of milk, usually served in a glass – for a larger portion ask for *cortado doble*. Similar but containing more milk, café con leche (latte) is served for breakfast only – avoid the faux pas of ordering it after lunch or dinner, when you should request a cortado.

Tea, produced domestically in the provinces of Corrientes and Misiones, is also a common drink. Usually it comes with lemon slices, but if you drink it with milk, do not order *té con leche*, which means a tea bag immersed in warm milk. Rather, ask the waiter for *un poquito de leche* after being served your tea.

Argentine chocolate can be delicious. For breakfast, try a *submarino*, a semisweet chocolate bar dissolved in steamed milk, but note that prices vary greatly. Ordinary *chocolate*, made with powdered cocoa, can be surprisingly good if submarinos are not available.

Alcohol

Beer, wine, whiskey and gin should satisfy most visitors' alcoholic thirst, but don't overlook *ginebra bols* (which differs from gin) and *caña* (cane alcohol), which are national specialties.

Quilmes, brewed in the namesake Buenos Aires suburb but available everywhere, is an excellent beer. Bieckert is another popular brand. In bars or cafés, ask for the excellent *chopp* (draft or lager).

Argentine wines receive less publicity abroad than Chilean ones, but *tintos* (reds) and *blancos* (whites) are both excellent and inexpensive. (When prices on almost everything else skyrocket, wines miraculously remain reasonable, and a bottle of good wine may be cheaper than a liter of Coca-Cola.) Especially at home, where jug wines are present at almost all meals, Argentines often dilute their wine with soda water or ice (yes, even reds!).

The major wine growing areas are near Mendoza, San Juan, La Rioja and Salta. Among the best known brands are Orfila, Suter, San Felipe, Santa Ana and Etchart. Try to avoid cheap boxed wines such as Termidor.

PLACES TO EAT – BUDGET
San Nicolás & the Microcentro (Map 5)

For around US$3 or even less, the express cafeteria at supermarket *Coto*, Viamonte 1571 in Congreso, offers a wide variety of surprisingly good meals despite zero atmosphere (or maybe lots of it from another point of view – the entire main floor is blissfully tobacco-free).

Cabaña Blanca, Florida 243 in the Microcentro, is an antiseptically pleasant milk bar with good sandwiches, fruit salads and the like. Upgraded from a former budget cafeteria, but still reasonably priced, *La Bancaria*, Reconquista 335, is now popular with power lunchers from the financial district. *Baraka* (☎ 4322-0937), Tucumán 874, offers a variety of weekday lunch specials, including the usual minutas, for about US$6.

The Patio de Comidas, a food mall on the lower level of the Galerías Pacífico, on the Florida *peatonal* between Viamonte and Av Córdoba, has a number of moderately priced fast-food versions of some very good restaurants for about US$5 to US$7 or so, including *Romanaccio* for pizza and pasta, and *Freddo* for ice cream (no cheaper than

Freddo's anywhere else, however). Since all have common seating, it's a good choice for diners unable to agree on a single place to eat.

Despite Argentina's abundance of Italian surnames, most 'Italian' food is actually hybrid Italo-Argentine. Exceptions to this rule tend to be pricey, but *La Casona del Nonno* (☎ 4322-9352), Lavalle 827, has good US$4 lunch specials, and the dining areas include a separate, well-ventilated nonsmoking section upstairs.

Another Italian alternative is *El Sótano* (☎ 4372-7750), in the basement of the Sociedad Benevolenza di Italia at Juan D Perón 1372 in Congreso. Its lunch-time US$7 *menú ejecutivo* (set menu) is a real bargain because they seem willing to substitute just about anything on the list.

The Microcentro's best tenedor libre is *Xin Dong Fang*, Maipú 512, but *La Casa China* (☎ 4371-1352), Viamonte 1476, is a step above its competitors for Asian food; the US$8 lunch menu is good value. Of the other Chinese tenedor libre restaurants, try *Restaurante Chino* (☎ 4393-5407) at Suipacha 477, *China Doll* at Suipacha 544, *La Fronda* at Paraná 342 and *Los Amigos* at Rodríguez Peña 384 in Congreso. All charge around US$5, with drinks extra.

Although it's part of a chain, *Bar La Robla* (☎ 4811-4484), Viamonte 1615, prepares excellent seafood and standard Argentine dishes that are far from monotonous, in a pleasant environment at moderate prices. Its US$3.50 lunch specials, including an appetizer and a small glass of *clericó* (aperitif mixture of white wine and fruit), are excellent value. Service is superb, and there's a small but clearly designated and effectively segregated tobacco-free area. Another convenient branch (☎ 4381-3435) is at Montevideo 194 in Congreso.

Traditionally, one of the capital's most popular and economical parrillas is Congreso's *Pippo* (☎ 4374-6365), at Paraná 356 with another entrance on Montevideo. Another traditional Congreso parrilla is *Chiquilín* (☎ 4373-5163), Montevideo 321, which can get very crowded and noisy, but the food is good and it has a reasonably effective nonsmoking area. *Don Pipón*

(☎ 4381-9561), Esmeralda 521 in the Microcentro, is another inexpensive parrilla, but possibly the best value at present is *La Posada de 1820*, San Martín 606.

The consistently best pizzería is the unsung *Pizzería Güerrín* (☎ 4371-8141), Av Corrientes 1372, which sells very inexpensive individual slices of superb fugazza, fugazzeta and other specialties, plus excellent empanadas, cold lager beer to wash it all down, and many appealing desserts. It's cheaper to buy at the counter and eat standing up, but there is a much greater variety of toppings if you decide to be seated and served, or order an entire pizza to take out.

The traditionally excellent *Pizzería Serafín* (☎ 4371-2666), nearby at Av Corrientes 1328, is well worth a visit – their chicken empanadas are always good. In the same site at Av Callao 83 since 1936, *La Americana* (☎ 4371-0202) also has very fine pizza and exceptional empanadas.

Reader endorsements for vegetarian restaurants include *La Huerta* at Lavalle 893 in the Microcentro; *Valle Esmeralda* (☎ 4394-9266) at Esmeralda 370 (tenedor libre for US$6); and *Granix* at Florida 126.

For ice cream addicts, Buenos Aires is paradise. The author's favorite, distinguished by the outline map of Italy above its unpretentious storefront, is *Heladería Cadore* (☎ 4374-3688), Av Corrientes 1695, at Rodríguez Peña in Congreso. Chocoholics could overdose on their exquisite *chocolate amargo* (semisweet chocolate) or *chocolate blanco* (white chocolate), while the *mousse de limón* (lemon mousse) also merits special mention. *Vía Flaminia*, Florida 121 in the Microcentro, is also a good choice.

Culture-bound fast-food junkies will find countless *McDonald's* in Buenos Aires, the most central of which are at Lavalle 964 and Florida 570. Under siege from McDonald's, the indigenous *Pumper Nic* has its main locale at Suipacha 435.

Balvanera (Map 6)

Cervantes II (☎ 4372-8869), Juan D Perón 1883 in Congreso, has enormous servings of standard Argentine fare at reasonable prices, but it is often so crowded that patrons may wish to take their food away instead of eating in; alternatively, go late for lunch or early for dinner. They enforce the non-smoking section only if someone complains, however. Mobbed at lunch, *El Toboso* (☎ 4476-0519), Av Corrientes 1838, is a decent, moderately priced parrilla with other kinds of daily specials, but very expensive drinks (US$2.50 for mineral water) drive up the prices. The paté spread is a nice touch not found at other similar places.

Buenos Aires Herald restaurant critic Dereck Foster notes that non-Argentine Latin American restaurants tend to start with good intentions and varied menus, but often retreat to more conventional local offerings. One exception is *La Casa de Orihuela* (☎ 4951-6930), Adolfo Alsina 2163, which serves exceptionally well-prepared Peruvian and regional dishes. Its US$6 fixed-price lunch is one of the city's best values, well worth a detour from other parts of town. The decor is pleasing, the service cheerful and efficient.

The best chicken empanadas (usually breast meat) are at *La Continental*, Av Callao 202 at Juan D Perón. *Schlotzky's Deli*, Av Corrientes 1872, is the local branch of a New York-style chain now widely franchised in Latin America. The self-service, tenedor-libre *La Ciboulette* (☎ 4373-2178), Sarmiento 1802, offers decent vegetarian fare for US$8.

The traditional *La Viña del Abasto*, Jean Jaurés 3007, has been a local institution since 1943. On the Almagro side of the Abasto, just beyond the western edge of Balvanera, *Los Sabios* (☎ 4864-4407), Av Corrientes 3733 (Map 15), serves vegetarian food.

Montserrat (Map 7)

Reader-recommended, inexpensive *Plaza España* (☎ 4383-3271), Av de Mayo 1299, features abundant portions and perks like free aperitifs. For equally cheap or even cheaper local fare, try the hole-in-the-wall *Restaurant San Francisco*, Defensa 177 near Plaza de Mayo, or *Café Bar Alexa* at Defensa 435. *Almafuerte* (☎ 4342-1729), Defensa 598, offers a varied Spanish-Argentine menu with cheap lunch specials.

A hangout for the city's Peruvian community, *Status* (☎ 4382-8531), Virrey Cevallos 178 in Congreso, is a modest but friendly place with large portions and reasonable prices, deserving a stop if you're nearby.

San Telmo (Map 8)

On balance, San Telmo probably offers the best combination of high-quality, low-priced dining in the city, though some of the most expensive restaurants are also here. One good, inexpensive choice is *Jerónimo* (☎ 4300-2624), Estados Unidos 407, where most entrées cost between US$3 and US$5, and desserts are about US$1.50. *La Vieja Rotisería*, on Defensa between Carlos Calvo and Estados Unidos, also prepares good budget food. Diners form long lines outside *DesNivel*, Defensa 855, for their reasonably priced home-style pasta and parrillada.

Surrounding Plaza Dorrego are several café-restaurants, including *Bar Plaza Dorrego* at the corner of Defensa and Humberto Primo, and *Café del Arbol* at Humberto Primo 422. All the places on the plaza will serve their patrons outdoors under the trees (except, of course, when vendors jam the plaza for the Sunday flea market). Down the block at Humberto Primo 489, *Mitos Argentinos* (☎ 4362-7810) has lunch specials in the US$8 to US$10 range.

It's stretching it a bit to call *Nicole de Marseille* (☎ 4362-2340), Defensa 714, a French restaurant or even Franco-Argentine, but its three-course weekday lunches with a wide choice of entrées and desserts are good value for US$6. *Ming Li*, Defensa 1154, is a US$6.50 Chinese tenedor libre; drinks cost an additional US$2.

Reader-endorsed *Las Marías II*, at Bolívar 964-966, is an unpretentious but outstanding pizzería with friendly and efficient staff; try the *veneciana de pollo*. On the fringes of San Telmo, spicy cuisine from the northwestern Andean province of Jujuy is the specialty at friendly *La Carretería*, Brasil 656, across from the Albergue Juvenil hostel.

At the corner of Defensa and Brasil, across from Parque Lezama, *Heladería Florencia* serves very fine ice cream.

La Boca (Map 10)

For the most part, food in La Boca is fairly routine but also inexpensive by current Argentine standards. Especially on weekend afternoons, the sidewalk seating and colorful decor at *La Barbería* (☎ 4301-8770), Av Don Pedro de Mendoza 1965, make it a good place to stop for a cold beer or cider on tap, but the empanadas are a little expensive (though very good). Next door at Pedro de Mendoza 1981, the ambient *El Corsario* has similar fare, including pizza and pasta. *Puerto Viejo* is a decent parrilla, two blocks south on the corner of Pedro de Mendoza and Benito Quinquela Martín.

El Viejo Puente de Mario (☎ 4301-2170), Almirante Brown 1499, at the corner of Pedro de Mendoza, has cheap minutas but much more expensive seafood. *Campo e Mare* (☎ 4302-0785), Aráoz de Lamadrid 701, has moderately priced pasta and salads in an attractive setting.

Across the street from Boca Juniors' 'Bombonera' stadium, *La Cancha* (☎ 4362-2975), Brandsen 697, is a popular hangout for soccer fans. *El Samovar de Rasputín*, on Del Valle Iberlucea 1251 near Pedro de Mendoza, is cheap and very informal, as is *Los Angeles de Caminito*, almost next door at Del Valle Iberlucea 1243. (Both have live music as well.)

Like the other gaudy cantinas on its street, *Spadavecchia*, Necochea 1180, is more notable as a place to party than to eat, but the food is passable. It's only open evenings, but other nearby eateries are also open for lunch: *Gennarino* (☎ 4301-6617) at Necochea 1210, and *Tres Amigos* (☎ 4301-2441) and *Il Piccolo Vapore* (☎ 4301-4455), on opposite corners of Necochea and Suárez. This area has seen some violent robberies, so be cautious.

Helados Sorrento, Olavarría 658, serves the barrio's best ice cream.

Retiro (Map 11)

Supermercado Disco, a supermarket at Montevideo 1037, has an inexpensive cafeteria. *Lo de Alvarado* (☎ 4812-3462), Marcelo T del Alvear 1521, serves spicy salteña empanadas.

Crowded *Alimentari* (☎ 4313-9382), San Martín 899 at Paraguay, has outstanding medialunas for breakfast, but try also *Yinyang* (☎ 4311-3788), a macrobiotic restaurant at Paraguay 858.

La Querencia (☎ 4393-3205), Esmeralda 1392, specializes in spicy Tucumán-style empanadas. Travelers who won't be crossing the Andes will find passable Chilean seafood and other typical dishes at *Los Chilenos* (☎ 4328-3123), Suipacha 1042.

Ice creamery *Freddo* has a branch at Av Santa Fe and Montevideo.

Recoleta & Barrio Norte (Map 12)

Cocina y Cía (☎ 4823-4431), a tenedor libre at Av Santa Fe 2461, has varied food of excellent quality, including parrillada and vegetarian fare, for US$6. Drinks, however, are pretty expensive.

Another of Recoleta's cheaper eateries is the simple but attractive *Salomona* (☎ 4801-1844), Guido 1936, which has a variety of relatively inexpensive lunch specials (beware the costly drinks and desserts). Reasonably priced *Henry J Bean's* (☎ 4801-8477), a US import at Junín 1749, offers 10% student discounts. Nearby *Tenorio*, Junín 1793, is also reasonably priced and sometimes has live music.

Porteño diners jam *Río Rhin Norte* (☎ 4802-0197), Tagle 2521, for a wide variety of four-course lunch or dinner specials for US$7 or even less.

A step up from most Chinese all-you-can-eats is *Gran Fu Ia* (☎ 4803-5522), Av Las Heras 2379. The US$10 price tag for dinner reflects its higher-quality fare, including items such as prawns not normally found in such places, but lunches cost only US$6. It also prepares spicy à-la-carte dishes that most Argentines shun.

Part of a respectable pizza-and-pasta chain, *Romanaccio* (☎ 4811-4071), Av Callao 1021, has a well-arranged nonsmoking section. At the corner of Azcuénaga and Peña, *Kugenhaus* has a good selection of takeout food and continental pastries.

For ice cream, try any of several branches of *Freddo*, the most convenient of which are at Ayacucho and Quintana, and at Junín and Guido. Despite expansion, the company has maintained its traditional high quality.

Al Queso, Queso (☎ 4806-9480), Av Pueyrredón 2078, has a wide variety of cheeses.

Palermo (Map 13)

Palermo's best cheap eats are at the cafeteria at the supermarket *Coto*, Av Cabildo 545 between Maure and Gorostiag (Subte: Olleros). The menu is identical to that at the Viamonte branch near Av Corrientes in Microcentro (see the Budget entry for San Nicolás).

La Querencia, Lazo 3110, across from Plaza Alférez Sobral, is part of a small chain specializing in spicy Tucumán-style empanadas. *Fortín Salteño* (☎ 4777-8139), Soldado de la Independencia 990, also serves spicy northern dishes, including empanadas, *locro* (a type of stew) and humitas.

El Caballito Blanco (☎ 4806-4550), Las Heras 2999, is a classic, reasonably priced porteño pizzería.

Ice cream aficionados will find Palermo branches of *Freddo* at the corner of Av del Libertador and Teodoro García, and at the corner of Av Coronel Díaz and Cerviño. *El Piave* (☎ 4778-0940), Maure 1598, is an exceptional ice creamery as well.

There's a branch of *Al Queso, Queso* at the corner of Cerviño and Scalabrini Ortiz.

Belgrano (Map 14)

Across the tracks from Barrancas de Belgrano, the very economical *Contigo Perú* (☎ 4780-3960), Echeverría 1627, is a hangout for the local Peruvian community. For tangy northern empanadas, try *La Paceña* (☎ 4788-2282), Echeverría 2570.

Cloé (☎ 4784-8436), Cuba 2208 at Mendoza, is a popular neighborhood confitería with decent light meals. *Confitería Zurich*, at the corner of Cuba and Echeverría, is also a barrio hangout.

There's a branch of the macrobiotic restaurant *Yinyang* (☎ 4783-1546) at Echeverría 2444. *Cantina Chinatown* (☎ 4783-4173), Mendoza 1700, has US$5 lunch specials.

Express Allegro (☎ 4783-3439), on the Belgrano border at Virrey del Pino 2448 in Colegiales, has a varied, inexpensive menu including a fixed-price lunch for US$6 and a tenedor-libre parrillada for US$9, both including a free drink. Three blocks down at Virrey del Pino 2732, *Don Agustín* (☎ 4789-0834) has a US$7 tenedor libre, while *Buffet Libre* (☎ 4784-2900), Juramento 1650, has all-you-can-eat for US$8.

Among the numerous pizzerías, *Don Miranda*, Olazábal 2352, has tenedor-libre pizza and pasta for US$6 at lunch, slightly more at dinner. *Pepe's Pizza* (☎ 4788-8673), Mendoza 1909, is exclusively a takeout. *Genoa* (☎ 4784-7784), Av Cabildo 2492, at Monroe, is probably the best choice, but try also *La Farola de Núñez*, just over the northern Belgrano line at Av Cabildo 2899. *La Siembra* (☎ 4784-4274), at Monroe and Vuelta de Obligado, serves pizza and pasta in pleasant surroundings.

Belgrano has a remarkable selection of ice cream parlors, all deserving of a visit. The local branch of *Freddo* is at the corner of Juramento and Arcos, but *Heladería Chungo*, Virrey del Pino 2500 in Colegiales, is worth a detour in itself. *Furchi*, Av Cabildo 1506, serves Italian-style gelato, while *Heladería Gruta* (☎ 4784-8417), Antonio José de Sucre 2356, is also outstanding.

PLACES TO EAT – MID-RANGE
San Nicolás & the Microcentro (Map 5)

If you visit only one parrilla in Buenos Aires, focus on the excellent food at *La Estancia* (☎ 4326-0330), Lavalle 941 in the Microcentro, and ignore the bogus rent-a-gauchos. Highly regarded, but pricier, Microcentro parrillas include *La Rural* (☎ 4322-2654) at Suipacha 453 and *Los Troncos* (☎ 4322-1295) at Suipacha 732, where the daily menú ejecutivo costs US$12.

Readers' and author's opinions are unanimous that *Broccolino* (☎ 4322-7652), Esmeralda 776, is one of Buenos Aires' best Italian values. Offering a bewildering variety of sauces for the pasta, along with friendly and highly professional English-speaking staff, it also has a nonsmoking section.

Since 1929, *ABC* (☎ 4393-3992), Lavalle 545, has been a lunch-time classic for Middle

European specialties like goulash. Across the street from each other in the financial district, *Clinton Plaza* (☎ 4314-6780), Reconquista 545, and *Daddy's Bar* (☎ 4393-9081), Reconquista 546, are also both popular lunch spots. In the Paseo La Plaza complex at Montevideo 350 in Congreso, *Las Cañas* (☎ 4372-7162) has excellent midday lunch specials for US$10. For Greek food, with live entertainment, try *Oniro* at Juan D Perón 924.

One of the Microcentro's classics, *El Palacio de la Papa Frita* is a good, popular and reasonably priced chain offering a standard Argentine menu. There are branches at Lavalle 735 (☎ 4393-5849), at Lavalle 954 (☎ 4322-1559) and another at Corrientes 1612 (☎ 4374-8063) in Congreso.

At the original branch of *Los Inmortales* (☎ 4326-5303), at Av Corrientes 1369 beneath the huge billboard of Carlos Gardel, try their very reliable pizzas as you peruse the historic photographs of Gardel and his contemporaries on the walls; the popular pizzería has another branch (☎ 4322-5493) at Lavalle 748 in the Microcentro. Another classic pizzería, *Los Idolos* at Suipacha 436, has better atmosphere and service than food.

At Puerto Madero, *Puerto Sorrento* (☎ 4319-8731), Av Alicia Moreau de Justo 410, is a very good seafood restaurant whose menú ejecutivo, for about US$13, is an excellent value, but the cost of drinks can drive up the price dramatically.

Balvanera (Map 6) & Montserrat (Map 7)

Spanish and Basque restaurants are usually the best alternatives for seafood, such as *El Hispano* (☎ 4382-7543) at Salta 20 (Map 7). For Basque meals including a wide variety of seafood, try the traditional *Laurak Bat* (☎ 4381-0682), part of the Centro Cultural Vasco at Av Belgrano 1174 (Map 7) – in the same place since 1877. For dessert, try the *natillas*, a tasty custard. The *Taberna Baska* (☎ 4383-0903), Chile 980 (Map 7), also serves Basque food.

Complaints that the Argentine legislature never accomplishes anything for lack of attendance may be true, at least when the

Quorum (☎ 4951-0855), directly behind the Congreso Nacional at Combate de los Pozos 61 (Map 6), offers its US$12 'menú legislativo.' Reader's choice *Campo dei Fiori* (☎ 4381-1800), San José 491, at the corner of Venezuela (Map 7), has Montserrat's best Italian food.

Molière (☎ 4343-2623), on the border of San Telmo at Chile 299, corner of Balcarce (Map 7), features an international menu and live entertainment with no cover charge. Open late, it attracts a mixed-age crowd.

San Telmo (Map 8) & Constitución (Map 9)

In a restored colonial house at Defensa 1000 a block north of Plaza Dorrego (Map 8), *La Casa de Estéban de Luca* (☎ 4361-4338) has very fine food at moderate prices. *El Virrey de San Telmo* (☎ 4361-0331), Humberto Primo 499 (Map 8), offers an international menu. *La Scala de San Telmo* (☎ 4362-1187), Pasaje Giuffra 371 (Map 8), serves a mid-range to upscale international menu to the accompaniment of live classical music.

French cuisine is the focus at attractive *La Carbonera* (☎ 4361-6201), Carlos Calvo 375 (Map 8). For Swiss food, try *La Petit*, Salta 2158 in Constitución (Map 9).

Part of the Casal de Catalunya cultural center at Chacabuco 863 (Map 8), *Hostal del Canigó* (☎ 4304-5250, 4300-5252) serves Catalonian specialties like *pollo a la punxa* (chicken with calamari) along with Spanish and Argentine dishes. Prices are moderate, the large lunch portions include a complimentary glass of sherry, and the dining room's woodwork and tilework lend it great atmosphere. One block south, at Chacabuco 947 (Map 8), the *Federación de Sociedades Gallegos* also serves Spanish seafood.

Across the street from its namesake tanguería, at the corner of Balcarce and Av Independencia (Map 8), *El Viejo Almacén* is an increasingly popular eatery. *Candombe de Buenos Aires* (☎ 4361-9733), Balcarce 869 (Map 8), features Middle Eastern specialties like lamb. *Calle de Angeles* (☎ 4361-3633), Chile 318 (Map 8), serves a US$20 menu weekdays for lunch and daily for dinner except Sunday.

Retiro (Map 11)

Particularly popular for lunch, moderately priced *Payanca* (☎ 4312-5209), Suipacha 1015, features spicy northern Argentine cuisine from the province of Salta. It's one of the best values in the barrio. *La Mosca Blanca* (☎ 4313-4890), Av Ramos Mejía 1430, has a good reputation and reasonable prices.

Dora (☎ 4311-2891), Av Leandro N Alem 1016, serves massive portions. Menu prices appear steep, but most dishes suffice for two people; the imposing half portion of bife de chorizo (US$9), for instance, weighs nearly half a kilo. LP correspondents continue to praise its seafood and pasta, as well as 'incredible' desserts (which *are* expensive).

Nearby *El Salmón* (☎ 4313-1731), at Reconquista 968 near Paraguay, with a similar and slightly cheaper menu, gets mixed reviews. Another branch (☎ 4315-3362) is less than a block north at Reconquista 1014.

Two parrillas, *La Chacra* (☎ 4322-1409) at Av Córdoba 941 and *Las Nazarenas* (☎ 4312-5559) at Reconquista 1132, are among the capital's most prestigious.

Filo (☎ 4311-0312), San Martín 975, is a lively pizza-and-pasta place where the menu changes frequently. It has friendly service and great decor, but prices are not for the financially challenged. The classic pizzería *Los Inmortales* has a branch at Marcelo T de Alvear 1234 (☎ 4393-6124).

One of the capital's most enduring vegetarian alternatives, *La Esquina de las Flores* (☎ 4813-3630), has moved its restaurant from the nearby corner of Montevideo to the upstairs of its health-food store at Av Córdoba 1587. Daily fixed-price specials cost US$10 (US$6 for children), but there are less expensive à-la-carte choices as well. The Esquina is also something of a cultural center, offering lectures and workshops on food, diet, health and similar topics, and producing radio and TV programs. Another nearby vegetarian alternative is *Lotos*, Av Córdoba 1577.

At Tres Sargentos 427, *Lotus Downtown* (☎ 4312-5706) is the central branch of Palermo's well-known, highly regarded Thai restaurant. It's open for lunch only on weekdays, for dinner on Saturdays, and closed Sundays.

Recoleta & Barrio Norte (Map 12)

At the Buenos Aires Design Recoleta/ Terrazas de Plaza del Pilar complex (☎ 4806-1111, ask for the individual restaurant extension unless otherwise indicated below), a food mall alongside the Centro Cultural Ciudad de Buenos Aires, choices range from relatively cheap fast-food offerings to elaborate and sophisticated fare. The official address is at Av Pueyrredón 2501, but it's more easily accessible from the Junín entrance to the center. All locales have both indoor and outdoor seating.

One of the best values here is *Munich del Pilar* (☎ 4806-0149), where a US$10 weekday menú ejecutivo offers a choice of meat, chicken or pasta entrées and includes drinks. *Molière*, closest to the Centro Cultural, serves an excellent grilled salmon with appetizer and a large glass of house wine for US$15; service is well-intentioned but erratic.

Several others in the complex are worth checking out: *Café Champs Elysée* (more a confitería; ☎ 4806-0098), known for tantalizing desserts; *Caruso* (☎ 4806-3299), a pricey trattoría; *Campos del Pilar* (☎ 4806-1111, ext 1276), a parrilla; *Café Rex* with its cinematic décor; *Mumy's*, serving pricey hamburgers but also some reasonable combinations; and *Romanaccio*, good for pizza and pasta.

Across from the cemetery, on Recoleta's restaurant row, seafood specials range from US$14 to US$17 at *El Figón de Bonilla* (☎ 4804-7771), Junín 1721. One block south, at Vicente López 1900, *Bar Rodi* (☎ 4801-5230) is a good value for beef and pasta.

Café de las Flores, at the corner of Posadas and Ayacucho, is a moderately priced confitería with an adequate smoke-free section. At the corner of Schiaffino and Av del Libertador, in the highly regarded Hotel Plaza Francia, *Restaurant Schiaffino* costs around US$10 for lunch and US$15 for dinner. *José Luis*, Av Quintana 456, is a mid-range seafood spot.

Restaurant Ruso (☎ 4805-7079), Azcuénaga 1562 in Barrio Norte, specializes in Russian food at reasonable prices (at least by Barrio Norte standards) of around US$8 to US$10 for lunch, US$15 for dinner. The downtown porteño classic *El Palacio de la Papa Frita* has its Barrio Norte locale at Laprida 1339 (☎ 4826-3151). *A Mamma Liberata*, José Uriburu 1755, serves a US$12 Italian menú ejecutivo.

Renowned as an outstanding value, the *Restaurant del Club Sirio* (☎ 4806-5764), Pacheco de Melo 1902, serves a US$18 Middle Eastern tenedor libre Monday to Saturday evenings. *Viejo Horizonte* (☎ 4806-0553), part of the Club Libanés at Junín 1460, also serves Middle Eastern food.

The classic pizzería *Los Inmortales* has branches at Av Callao 1165 (☎ 4813-7551) and at Junín 1727 (☎ 4803-3331). Otherwise, try informal *Pizza Banana* (☎ 4812-6321), Ayacucho 1425 at Pacheco de Melo, or *Pizza Cero* at Av Alvear and Schiaffino.

Palermo (Map 13)

West of Av Santa Fe, Jorge Luis Borges' old haunts of Palermo Viejo have a cluster of good restaurants, especially in and around the thriving nightlife area of Plaza Cortázar (formerly Plaza Racedo), with more varied ethnic food than in most other parts of the city. Attractive *Fiori y Canto* (☎ 4963-3250), on the edge of Palermo Viejo at Av Córdoba 3547, offers a varied menu of pizza, pasta and parrilla, with particularly delicious homemade bread. *Sarkis* (☎ 4772-4911), Thames 1101, south of Av Córdoba in the barrio of Villa Crespo, serves Middle Eastern food. *Cielito Lindo* (☎ 4832-0054), El Salvador 4499, is one of the capital's handful of Mexican restaurants.

Montoya, Gascón 1701, serves seafood, fish and crepes in attractive surroundings. The vegetarian institution *La Esquina de las Flores* (☎ 4832-8528) has a Palermo branch at Gurruchaga 1632.

For pizza, there's *El Angel Azul*, at the corner of Güemes and Scalabrini Ortiz, and *Pizzería Doña Flor* (☎ 4831-2223), Malabia 2497, which also serves large portions of standard minutas at reasonable prices.

East of Av Santa Fe, *La Cátedra* (☎ 4774-9859), Cerviño 4699 (Subte: Palermo), serves an excellent three-course lunch (including a small bottle of wine and coffee) for

US$12 weekdays. Its US$7 salad bar is even more economical, but à-la-carte prices are notably higher. *Pizza Cero* (☎ 4803-3449), Cerviño 3701, has better decor than food.

Indochine (☎ 4772-4159), Báez 165 in Barrio Las Cañitas near the Campo Argentino de Polo, has a rather incoherent but interesting menu of various Asian dishes, ranging from Japanese to Thai, Vietnamese and Indonesian. Also near the polo grounds, *Lotus Neo Thai* (☎ 4771-4449), J Ortega y Gasset 1782, is no longer the only eatery of its kind in the city, but it's probably still the best. *Mykonos*, Olleros 1752, is a new Greek restaurant that may be worth a try.

Belgrano Plaza (☎ 4774-3100), at the corner of Av Federico Lacroze and 11 de Septiembre, serves a variety of pizza, pasta, parrilla and sandwiches. It has sidewalk seating.

Belgrano (Map 14)

El Ceibal (☎ 4784-2444), Av Cabildo 1421, one of the capital's better parrillas and pizzerías, traditionally has fine food and service, but there's less atmosphere than in its former Palermo location and, since a recent shutdown for tax evasion, its future is in question. Still, on weekends they offer a dozen different fixed-price meals for US$8 or US$9 – try northwestern Argentine specialties such as locro, *cazuela de humita* (a maize stew) and *tamales tucumanos*.

L'Altro Cesare (☎ 4781-7365), Monroe 2248, is a very fine Italian restaurant with outstanding service and some innovative dishes – try the *canelones con humita* (maize) for US$8 and the very light chocolate mousse (US$5) for dessert. Most pasta dishes are reasonable, but some of the more unusual sauces cost extra, making it expensive for diners who are not selective – though there's also a US$5 tenedor libre special. The small nonsmoking area is not really adequate.

Munich Belgrano (☎ 4784-1989), Monroe 2444, is no relation to its near-namesake in Recoleta but serves an Argentine-continental menu. The tiny (only nine tables) *Casita Suiza* (☎ 4781-9961), opposite Plaza Noruega at Mendoza 2587, specializes in moderately priced Swiss dishes like crepes and fondues, but also serves a variety of empanadas and pastries. *Antiguo Belgrano*, at the corner of Cuba and Blanco Encalada, is an agreeable beer-and-pizza kind of place. *Marcovaldo* (☎ 4786-0088), down the block at Cuba 2220, is a more elite Italian choice.

Garbis (☎ 4788-2360), Monroe 1799, is a spacious Middle Eastern restaurant specializing in reasonably priced items like hummus and shishkebab, among others. Opposite Plaza Belgrano, at the corner of Juramento and the peatonal Sagasta Isla, alongside Iglesia La Redonda, *La Recova* and *Marco Polo* (☎ 4788-4400) are popular mid-range international restaurants. The appealing *La Broqueta de Belgrano* (☎ 4786-3349), Cuba 2290, has tenedor libre from about US$11.

Reservations are essential for either lunch or dinner at *Mis Raíces* (☎ 4786-6633), Arribeños 2148, which specializes in Jewish food. In Colegiales, on the Belgrano border, the vegetarian institution *La Esquina de las Flores* (☎ 4783-9992) is at Ciudad de La Paz 1571.

North of Aeroparque, *Los Años Locos* (☎ 4785-4995) is a popular parrilla on Av Costanera Rafael Obligado at La Pampa. Several similar restaurants dot the Costanera, which loops through the area here.

Outer Barrios

Despite its out-of-the-way location in the barrio of Barracas, south of Constitución and San Telmo, *Buenos Aires Sur* (☎ 4301-6758), Villarino 2359, is a very popular and highly recommended bar-restaurant among both locals and visitors. Bus No 12 goes there from Plaza Italia and Plaza del Congreso, while Nos 20 and 45 go there from Retiro and Plaza de Mayo.

PLACES TO EAT – TOP END
San Nicolás & the Microcentro (Map 5)

Cicerón, Reconquista 647 in the Microcentro, is an upscale Italian restaurant in the Hotel Italia Romanelli (☎ 4312-6361). The very Victorian *Clark's* (☎ 4325-3624), Sarmiento 645, is one of the capital's classics, and is very expensive.

In the Puerto Madero complex at Alicia Moreau de Justo 516, *Cabaña Las Lilas* (☎ 4313-1336) has fine beef, wine and service but prices are high at about US$80 for two. Reader-recommended *La Caballeriza* (☎ 4314-2648), Alicia Moreau de Justo 560, is also for carnivores.

Balvanera (Map 6) & Montserrat (Map 7)

An open secret is the popular smorgasbord at the *Swedish Club* (☎ 4334-1703), 5th floor, Tacuarí 143 (Map 7). Theoretically open to members only, it now takes place every Wednesday, but visitors can 'request' an invitation by phone. The US$26 price tag makes it a special occasion for most people.

Ichisou (☎ 4942-5853), Venezuela 2145 (Map 6), is an expensive but highly regarded Japanese restaurant, open for dinner only. At Moreno 1370 (Map 7), the *Club Vasco Francés* (☎ 4382-0244) serves fresh seafood (from Spain) and delicacies like frogs legs at premium, but not outrageous, prices.

Beef is the standard at *Rodizio* (☎ 4334-3638), Av Alicia Moreau de Justo 838 (Map 7). The varied menu at *Cholila* (☎ 4315-6200), Alicia Moreau de Justo 102 in Puerto Madero (Map 7), draws a less conventional crowd than the nearby restaurants that are strictly for carnivores.

San Telmo (Map 8)

San Telmo lacks top-end accommodations, but upscale and even formal dining is another matter. Jacket and tie are pretty much obligatory at places like *El Repecho de San Telmo* (☎ 4362-5473), housed in a landmark late-colonial building at Carlos Calvo 242.

Retiro (Map 11)

Diana (☎ 4327-2134), at the corner of Av del Libertador and Esmeralda, serves a Mediterranean menu, with meals in the US$30-plus range. For French cuisine, try *Catalinas* (☎ 4313-0182) at Reconquista 875, where the prix-fixe dinner costs US$45. *Súbito* (☎ 4815-1725), at Posadas 1245 in the Patio Bullrich shopping center, is an upscale Italian place. For Japanese cuisine, the choice is the expensive *Midori* (☎ 4814-5151), in the

Caesar Park Hotel at Posadas 1232. Across the street at Posadas 1229, **Harry Cipriani** (☎ 4813-4291) is a high-society hangout where dinner and drinks run about US$80 for two.

Recoleta & Barrio Norte (Map 12)

If price is no object, check out Recoleta's restaurant row on Junín and RM Ortiz, opposite the Cementerio de la Recoleta and the Centro Cultural. Fixed-price lunches or dinners are in the US$20 to US$30 range, but à-la-carte meals can be much dearer. Recently there has been a big turnover here as some local institutions have moved to Puerto Madero.

Among the traditional favorites are **Harper's** (☎ 4801-7155) at Junín 1763; **Clark's** (☎ 4801-9502) at Junín 1777, whose US$22 lunch menu and US$25 dinner menu are good values; and **Hippopotamus** (☎ 4804-8310) at Junín 1787, which offers a reader-endorsed US$18 menú ejecutivo. The latter's premises contain a popular but very formal disco/nightclub.

The **Shorthorn Grill** (☎ 4804-9464), RM Ortiz 1805, but with another entrance around the corner at Guido 1965, serves dinner and tango for US$35; tango only costs US$25, including two drinks. **Lola** (☎ 4804-3410), RM Ortiz 1809, features an expensive French menu; the desserts include a US$7 flan. **Munich Recoleta** (☎ 4804-4469), RM Ortiz 1871, serves a German and international menu.

Barrio Norte's appealing **French Bistro** (☎ 4806-9331) is a pricey continental restaurant at French 2301 at the corner of Azcuénaga, but selective diners can probably eat at mid-range prices. Long acknowledged as one of Buenos Aires' prestige restaurants, **Au Bec Fin** (☎ 4801-6894), Vicente López 1825, has prices to match.

Palermo (Map 13)

Franco-Argentine **Dolli** (☎ 4806-3366), at the corner of Av Figueroa Alcorta 3004 and Tagle, is one of Buenos Aires' landmark restaurants; prices are high but not outrageous.

On the fringes of Recoleta and Palermo Chico, **Bar del Museo**, on the grounds of the Museo Nacional de Arte Decorativo at Av del Libertador 1902, is an upscale café where lunch specials cost around US$25. **Traiano** (☎ 4772-4104), Jorge Newbery 1638, is an expensive Italian eatery but portions are large and shareable.

Río Alba (☎ 4773-5748), Cerviño 4499, is an elegant parrilla in the heart of the barrio. **Llers** (☎ 4773-9303), Demaría 4711 at Sinclair, is another of the capital's elite Argentine-style restaurants. At the corner of Gorostiaga and Soldado de la Independencia, **La Esquinita** (☎ 4777-4141) is comparable.

Belgrano (Map 14)

The **2020 Restaurant** (☎ 4783-6152), Arcos 1984, is an expensive Italian locale where fixed-price meals cost well upwards of US$20; parrillada is also available. **La Fornarina** (☎ 4783-4904), Arcos 1805, is an equally expensive Italian place.

Chinatown (☎ 4763-3456), Juramento 1656, around the corner from barrio's actual (and rather small) Chinatown, is generally regarded as the city's best Chinese restaurant. **Tomasso** (☎ 4788-8056), Av del Libertador 5932, is one of the city's landmark pizza and pasta venues.

Entertainment

Visitors should note that for many entertainment events, including movies, live theater and tango shows, *carteleras* along Av Corrientes sell a limited number of heavily discounted tickets. Most tango shows aren't worth US$40, but for half that they're worth considering. Buy tickets as far in advance as possible, but if you want to see a show or movie on short notice, especially at midweek, just phone or drop by to see what's available. Discount tickets for the newest shows or most recently released hit films are rare.

Cartelera Vea Más (☎ 4372-7285, 4372-7314, ext 219), Local 19 in the Paseo La Plaza complex at Corrientes 1660 (Map 5), is open 10 am to 11 pm daily. Although the street address is on Corrientes, this cubbyhole office is more easily accessible from Sarmiento, one block south. Three blocks east, Cartelera Baires (☎ 4372-5058), at Local 25 in the Galería Teatro L'Orange at Corrientes 1372 (Map 5), is open 10 am to 10:30 pm Monday through Thursday, 10 am to midnight Friday and Saturday, and 2 to 10:30 pm Sunday. Cartelera Espectáculos is at Lavalle 742 (Map 5), in the midst of the downtown movie district.

Many *porteño* dailies have detailed entertainment supplements, including *La Nación* (Thursday), *Ambito Financiero*, the *Buenos Aires Herald*'s expanded *getOut!* and *Clarín* (all on Friday), *Argentinisches Tageblatt* (Saturday) and *Página 12* (Sunday). Another good source for entertainment listings is the monthly freebie *Magazine Plus*, widely available around town.

CAFÉS & BARS

Café society is a major force in the life of Argentines in general and porteños in particular. They spend hours debating – if rarely solving – their own problems, as well as the country's and the world's, over a chessboard

Florencio Molina Campos' painting of a gaucho bar scene

and a cheap *cortado*. Many cafés double as bars, serving alcohol as well as caffeine, and their ambiance can range from bare bones to true luxury.

Av Corrientes is a favorite hangout for porteño intellectuals. Traditionally famous for nonconformist atmosphere is the once-spartan *Café La Paz*, Av Corrientes 1599 (Map 5). After briefly closing in 1997, it reopened as a brighter and superficially more inviting place, with a more expensive and extensive food menu, but whether it can preserve its bohemian legacy is open to question. Nearby *Café Pernambuco*, Av Corrientes 1680, still has a good atmosphere for a cup of coffee or glass of wine.

Some hybrid cafés double as bookstores, offering live music, poetry readings, occasional films and other cultural events. *Foro Gandhi* (☎ 4374-7501), Av Corrientes 1551 (Map 5), is an arts-oriented coffee house offering live tango music and foreign film cycles at bargain prices.

It's been at the same Barrio Norte location since 1938, but only in the last decade has *Clásica y Moderna* (☎ 4812-8707), Av Callao 892 (Map 12), become the intimate, sophisticated bookstore-café it is today. Besides offering live performances of folk, jazz and popular music, it serves mid-range to upscale meals and even keeps the day's newspapers for patrons' convenience. Among those who have performed at this intimate venue are Mercedes Sosa, Susana Rinaldi and even Liza Minelli.

A favorite Microcentro hangout is the *Young Men's Bar* (☎ 4322-9543), Av Córdoba 800 (Map 5). If you're looking for a chess match, or following the literary footsteps of Jorge Luis Borges, try the very traditional *Richmond* (☎ 4322-1341), at Florida 468 in the Microcentro since 1917 (Map 5).

At 25 de Mayo 774, the *Seddon Bar* (☎ 4313-0669) is a popular nightspot featuring jazz, tango and salsa at night, when there's a US$5 cover (one drink included; Map 5). On Tuesdays and Wednesdays there are tango lessons from 8 to 10 pm. The classic *Confitería Ideal* (☎ 4601-8234), Suipacha 384 (Map 5), now 88 years old and counting, also has tango shows.

The always-crowded *Florida Garden* (☎ 4312-7902), Florida 899 in Retiro (Map 11), is popular with politicians, journalists and other influential sorts. Particularly crowded during its late afternoon happy hour, the *Shamrock* (☎ 4812-3584), Rodríguez Peña 1220 in Barrio Norte (Map 12), has become a popular Irish-style pub, but the traditional pick is still the *Druid In* (☎ 4312-3688), Reconquista 1040 in Retiro (Map 11), which has Celtic music on weekends.

For freshly brewed tea and delectable pastries, the swank *London City*, Av de Mayo 599 in Montserrat (Map 7), is the place to go. A bit farther south, *Viejos Tiempos*, Defensa 333 (Map 7), has good ambiance even if it lacks the patina of age. *Bar del Museo*, opposite the Museo de la Ciudad at Adolfo Alsina and Defensa, just south of Plaza de Mayo (Map 7), also draws a bohemian crowd.

Before or after dining, and on Sunday mornings in particular, some of the porteño elite while away the hours on caffeine at *La Biela* (☎ 4804-0432), Av Quintana 598 in Recoleta (Map 12). The rest exercise their purebred dogs nearby, so watch your step while crossing the street to *Café de la Paix* (☎ 4804-6820), Av Quintana 595. Another elegant Recoleta café is the Alvear Palace Hotel's *Winter Garden*.

A recent development, of course, is the multi-screen TV sports bar, such as the *World Sports Café* (☎ 4807-5444), Junín 1745 in Recoleta (Map 12).

US-owned *Mundo Bizarro*, at Guatemala 4802 in the newly popular Plaza Cortázar area of Palermo Viejo (Map 13), is pretty much what it sounds like – expect the unexpected, especially during the 'gin and sin' happy hour.

Many cafés are also good places for meals. For more café listings, see the Places to Eat chapter.

TANGO

Tango is experiencing a major boom at both the amateur and professional levels, and among all ages and classes. One of the best sources on local trends is the free bimonthly newsletter *Buenos Aires Tango*, widely distributed around town, which is full of ads for both shows and lessons. Another source is the trilingual (Spanish, English, German) pocket-sized guidebook *El Compadrito Editorial El Holandés*, priced at US$3.50 but often available as a freebie.

Finding spontaneous tango is not easy, but you'll have the best luck at San Telmo's Sunday flea market on Plaza Dorrego (Map 8), where very professional dancers entertain tourists without pandering to them. Other than that, plenty of clubs in San Telmo, Barracas and La Boca portray Argentina's most famous cultural export for prices up to US$40 per show or more, depending whether dinner is included.

At the lower end of the scale, the cover for shows at *Bar Sur* (☎ 4362-6086), Estados Unidos 299 in San Telmo (Map 8), are US$15, which includes unlimited pizza but not the fairly expensive drinks. It's open 9 pm to 4 am daily except Sunday. *Claroscuro* (☎ 4300-1598), Balcarce 971 (Map 8), is another moderately priced, recommended tango place, with prices around US$20 and good food on top of it. The more central *La Casa de Luis Cardei* (☎ 4373-8781), in the Paseo La Plaza complex at Av Corrientes 1660 in Congreso (Map 5), has Friday and Saturday night shows for US$22.

Café Homero (☎ 4773-1979), a popular neighborhood tanguería at Cabrera 4946 in Palermo Viejo (Map 13), has no cover charge but does enforce a US$30 minimum-consumption rule; shows take place at 11 pm Thursday to Saturday. Nearby at Cabrera 4737, *Club del Vino* (☎ 4833-0050) has a US$15 cover at 10 pm Friday nights and a US$30 cover at 9:30 pm Saturday nights.

Several nightspots in the neighborhood of Abasto, Carlos Gardel's old haunts, are also good choices. *Club Almagro* (☎ 4774-7454), Medrano 522 in Almagro (Map 15), has very reasonably priced tango shows that, unlike the big budget extravaganzas, invite audience participation. Showtimes are from 11 pm Tuesdays, Fridays and Saturdays, and from 9 pm Sundays. It also offers early evening tango classes daily, starting between 6 and 9:30 pm depending on the day. Other Abasto tango venues include *Babilonia* (☎ 4862-0683), just west of the Mercado de Abasto at Guardia Vieja 3360 in Balvanera

(Map 6), a cultural center which also offers alternative theater and a tapas bar, and *Fernandezes* (☎ 4866-4129), at Guardia Vieja and Billinghurst in Almagro (Map 15).

The restaurant *Mitos Argentinos* (☎ 4362-7810), at Humberto Primo 489 near Plaza Dorrego in San Telmo (Map 8), offers Sunday tango shows (from 12:30 pm) and classes as well (from 6 pm). The classic tanguería *Caño 14* (☎ 4803-3660) has moved from its old San Telmo venue to Vicente López 2134 in Recoleta (Map 12). The classic *La Cumparsita* (☎ 4361-6880), Chile 302 in San Telmo (Map 8), costs US$30 with two drinks and a *picada* (snack plate); the show starts at 10:30 pm.

Yet another neighborhood tango option is the *Centro Cultural Torquato Tasso* (☎ 4307-6506), Defensa 1575 (Map 8), which offers classes as well as shows. (It also features alternative rock bands.) *El Chino* (no phone), a former warehouse at Beazley 3565 near Av Amancio Alcorta in the barrio of Nueva Pompeya (Map 2), has become one of the capital's 'in' tango places, open from 11:30 pm Fridays and Saturdays. It's not the easiest place to reach by bus, but No 188 from Plaza Italia or Plaza Miserere (Once) will go there, as will No 46 from Plaza Constitución.

Its publicity brochure demonstrates the pitfalls of employing a translator with no qualifications beyond ownership of a bilingual dictionary, but *Casa Blanca* (☎ 4331-4621), Balcarce 668 in (Map 7), really appears to glory in hosting disgraced heads of state (Brazil's Fernando Collor de Mello and Mexico's Carlos Salinas de Gortari) and dropping the names of show-biz patrons (Omar Sharif, Oliver Stone, Mick Jagger, Eric Clapton). It does present some of the biggest names in tango, though; regular shows take place at 10 pm weekdays, and at 9 and 11 pm Saturday. Ask about 30% student discounts.

Open daily at 10 pm, *El Viejo Almacén* (☎ 4307-7388), at the corner of Balcarce and Independencia (Map 8; note the mural on the wall across the street), has drawn some criticism for being more oriented toward singing than dancing, but the two-hour show (US$40) remains highly professional. *Señor Tango* (☎ 4303-0231), Vieytes 1665 in

Tango at El Querandí

Barracas, has tango shows at 10:15 pm daily (US$40 with two drinks); with dinner, which starts at 8:30 pm, the price is US$55.

At *La Ventana* (☎ 4331-0127), Balcarce 425 in Montserrat (Map 7), dinner and show costs US$60, with hotel pickup included (ask for 20% student discounts). Showtime is 10 pm. Next door, *Michelangelo* (☎ 4328-2646), Balcarce 433, is a recycled colonial building with professional tango performances for US$65 per person with dinner and unlimited drinks.

La Convención (☎ 4781-9796), Carlos Calvo 375 in San Telmo (Map 8), has expensive meals and tango classes from 6 to 8 pm Tuesday and Sunday, shows at 10:30 pm Fridays and Saturdays.

At the same site since 1920, but remodeled in 1992, *El Querandí* (☎ 4345-0331), Perú 302 in Montserrat (Map 7), has dinner and show at 8:30 pm daily except Sunday for US$55 (the show starts at 10:30 pm).

FLAMENCO
Despite national pride in the tango, the dance from the mother country retains a foothold in Buenos Aires, both as show (in the US$30 to US$40 range, though some are cheaper and even free) and as lessons. Among the city's flamenco venues are *Avila*

Bar (☎ 4383-6974), Av de Mayo 1384 in Montserrat (Map 7), with shows at 11 pm Tuesday through Saturday, at 10 pm Sunday; *Bonfacio* (☎ 4805-2636), Guido 1930 in Recoleta (Map 12), at 11:30 pm Friday and Saturday; and *Dominguín* (☎ 4342-9863) at Alicia Moreau de Justo 1130 in Puerto Madero (Map 7), at 11:30 pm Fridays and Saturdays. *El Balcón de San Telmo* (☎ 4362-2354), Humberto Primo 461 (Map 8), has Saturday lessons at 9 pm, followed by a no-cover show at 10:30 pm.

CLASSICAL MUSIC
Teatro Colón (☎ 4382-0554), Libertad 621 (Map 5), is Buenos Aires' landmark classical music venue, having hosted figures as prominent as Enrico Caruso, Plácido Domingo, Luciano Pavarotti and Arturo Toscanini. The season for opera and classical music runs from March through November, but really hits its stride in the winter months of June through August. The Orquesta Filarmónica de Buenos Aires, often featuring guest conductors from throughout Latin America, normally plays at 9 pm Mondays.

From May to September, the Mozarteum Argentina (☎ 4811-3448) presents free weekly chamber music concerts at midday; also contact the *Teatro Opera* (☎ 4326-1225), Av Corrientes 860 in the Microcentro (Map 5), for details. The Orquesta de Cámara Mayo plays regularly at various venues throughout the city, including the *Auditorio de Belgrano* (☎ 4783-1783), Av Cabildo and Virrey Loreto, in Belgrano.

Other classical music venues include *Teatro Avenida* (☎ 4381-0662) at Av de Mayo 1212 in Montserrat (Map 7), which specializes in ballet, and the *Teatro Coliseo* (☎ 4807-1277) at Marcelo T del Alvear 1125 in Retiro (Map 11). Tickets for classical performances range from about US$20 to US$70, but some venues offer series discounts.

THEATER
Av Corrientes, between Avs 9 de Julio and Callao, is the capital's Broadway or West End, but there are dozens of venues throughout the city, where live theater enjoys widespread popularity; during the peak winter

season, upwards of a hundred different scheduled events may take place. Tickets at the most prestigious theaters, like the Cervantes and the Avenida, can cost anywhere from US$20 up to US$100 for prime attractions, but check carteleras for bargain seats. The *Buenos Aires Herald* and other newspapers carry thorough listings of major productions, but some deserving theater companies receive relatively little attention from the mainstream media.

The capital's main formal theater facility is the *Teatro General San Martín* (☎ 4374-8611), Av Corrientes 1530 in Congreso (Map 5), where more than a quarter million people attended shows in its three main theaters during 1997. In addition to major productions, it also has several smaller auditoriums that occasionally host more unconventional (and sometimes free) events. Holders of international student cards get 50% discounts at paying events.

Other major theater venues, all located in the Microcentro and San Nicolás area (Map 5) unless otherwise indicated, include *Teatro Nacional Cervantes* (☎ 4816-4224) at Libertad 815 in Retiro (Map 11) near Plaza Lavalle; *Teatro Maipo* (☎ 4322-4882) at Suipacha 443; *Teatro Presidente Alvear* (☎ 4374-6076) at Av Corrientes 1659; *Teatro Blanca Podestá* (☎ 4382-2592) at Av Corrientes 1283; *Teatro del Pueblo* (☎ 4326-3606) at Diagonal Roque Saénz Peña 943; the uniquely designed *Teatro Complejo La Plaza* (☎ 4370-5350) at Av Corrientes 1660; *Teatro Avenida* (☎ 4383-4964) at Av de Mayo 1212 in Montserrat (Map 7); and *Teatro del Sur* (☎ 4383-5702) at Venezuela 1286, five blocks southeast of Plaza del Congreso in Montserrat (Map 7).

Teatro Fundación Banco Patricios (☎ 4373-3776) underwrites unconventional theater in remodeled facilities at Av Callao 312, one block south of Av Corrientes, in Balvanera (Map 6). The intimate *Teatro El Vitral* (☎ 4371-0948), Rodríguez Peña 344 also one block south of Corrientes (Map 5), has three small venues seating about 40 people each. Another intimate theater venue/company is the *Equipo Teatro Payró* (☎ 4312-5922), San Martín 766 (Map 5).

Teatro de la Ribera (☎ 4302-8866), Av Don Pedro de Mendoza 1821 in La Boca (Map 10), is a community-oriented theater company presently suffering financial difficulties; the building itself was a donation of artist and booster Benito Quinquela Martín, who almost single-handedly put the barrio on the tourist map. In Montserrat at Av Paseo Colón 413 (Map 7), *Teatro Colonial* (☎ 4342-7958) offers classics like Hamlet. *Teatro La Otra Orilla* (☎ 4862-7718) is at Tucumán 3527 in the Abasto area of Almagro (Map 15). *Teatro de la Comedia* (☎ 4812-4228), Rodríguez Peña 1062 in Barrio Norte (Map 12), recently reopened as a theater venue.

Free theater presentations take place at many different sites, including *Teatro Margarita Xirgu* (☎ 4300-2448) alongside the Casal de Catalunya (☎ 4300-5252) at Chacabuco 863/875 in San Telmo (Map 8; performances are in Spanish rather than Catalan). Less conventional companies to watch for, most of which have no regular venue but appear sporadically around town, include *Teatro Casita de la Selva* (☎ 4672-5700) at La Selva 4022 in the outlying barrio of Vélez Sarsfield (Map 2), Catalinas Sur, La Runfla, Diablo Mundo and Las Calandracas. The Grupo Teatral Escena Subterránea performs in the capital's subway stations.

CINEMAS

Buenos Aires is famous for its cinemas, which play first-run films from around the world, but there is also an audience for unconventional and classic films. The main cinema districts are along the Lavalle *peatonal*, west of Florida, on Avs Corrientes and Santa Fe, all easy walking distance from downtown, and in the shopping centers of Retiro and Palermo. The barrio of Belgrano also has a concentration of cinemas, along with some outer barrios, but as the number of cinemas has grown, the number of films offered has dropped; essentially, commercial blockbusters are playing on more screens, while less ambitious films struggle to find outlets.

Ticket prices have risen to about US$7 for first-run showings, but most cinemas offer half-price discounts Wednesdays and sometimes for the first afternoon showing daily. Wednesday showings can be mobbed, so go early. There is usually a midnight (or later) *trasnoche* scheduled for Friday and Saturday nights.

The *Sala Leopoldo Lugones* (☎ 4374-8611) at the Teatro General San Martín, Av Corrientes 1530 in Congreso (Map 5), regularly offers thematic foreign film cycles as well as reprises of outstanding commercial films. In addition to current releases, the *Auditorio Maxi* (☎ 4326-1822), Carlos Pellegrini 657 in the Microcentro (Map 5), also does retrospectives and less commercial films. *Cine Cosmos* (☎ 4953-5405), Av Corrientes 2046 (Map 6), carries similar fare.

Since Spanish translations of English-language film titles are often misleading, check the *Buenos Aires Herald* to be certain what's playing. Except for children's films and cartoon features, which are invariably dubbed, foreign films almost always appear in the original language with Spanish subtitles.

Buenos Aires' cinemas include:

Alto Palermo 1&2
 (☎ 4827-8362) Av Santa Fe 3251
Ambassador
 (☎ 4322-9700) Lavalle 777, San Nicolás
América
 (☎ 4811-3818) Av Callao 1057, Recoleta
Atlas Belgrano 1&2
 (☎ 4781-7200) Av Cabildo 2165
Atlas Lavalle
 (☎ 4322-1936) Lavalle 869, San Nicolás
Atlas Recoleta
 (☎ 4803-3313) Guido 1952
Atlas Santa Fe 1&2
 Av Santa Fe 2015
Belgrano Multiplex 1-6
 (☎ 4781-8183) Obligado & Mendoza
Capitol
 (☎ 4812-2379) Av Santa Fe 1848, Recoleta
Cinemark Puerto Madero 1-8
 (☎ 4315-3008) Av Alicia Moreau de Justo 1960
Cineplex Lavalle 1, 2, 3
 (☎ 4393-8610) Lavalle 727, San Nicolás
Galerías Pacífico 1&2
 (☎ 4319-5357) Florida 753, San Nicolás
Gaumont 1, 2, 3
 (☎ 4371-3050) Rivadavia 1635, San Nicolás

General Paz 1-4
 (☎ 4781-7200) Av Cabildo 2702, Belgrano
Grand Splendid
 (☎ 4812-7204) Av Santa Fe 1880, Recoleta
L'Orange
 (☎ 4373-2411) Av Corrientes 1372, San Nicolás
Lorca 1&2
 (☎ 4371-5017) Av Corrientes 1428, San Nicolás
Los Angeles 1, 2, 3
 (☎ 4372-2405) Av Corrientes 1770, San Nicolás
Losuar 1&2
 (☎ 4371-6100) Av Corrientes 1743, San Nicolás
Maxi 1&2
 (☎ 4326-1822) Carlos Pellegrini 657, San Nicolás
Metro 1, 2, 3
 (☎ 4382-4219) Cerrito 570, San Nicolás
Monumental 1-4
 (☎ 4393-8865) Lavalle 780, San Nicolás
Normandie 1-4
 (☎ 4322-1000) Lavalle 855, San Nicolás
Ocean 1&2
 (☎ 4322-1515) Lavalle 739, San Nicolás
Paseo Alcorta 1-4
 (☎ 4806-5665) Figueroa Alcorta & Salguero, Palermo
Patio Bullrich 1-6
 (☎ 4815-8328) Av del Libertador 750, Retiro
Premier 1, 2, 3
 (☎ 4374-2113) Av Corrientes 1565, San Nicolás
Santa Fe 1&2
 (☎ 4812-8980) Av Santa Fe 1947, Recoleta
Savoy 1-4
 (☎ 4781-9400) Av Cabildo 2829, Núñez
Solar de la Abadia 1&2
 (☎ 4778-5181) Luis María Campos & Maure, Palermo
Trocadero 1-6
 (☎ 4393-8321) Lavalle 820, San Nicolás

DANCE CLUBS

Recoleta and Palermo are the main areas for the capital's dance clubs, which tend to be exclusive and expensive; cover charges are often US$20 and upwards, and drinks are also pricey. There are plenty of others scattered around the city, however. Remember that very few open before midnight and there's not usually much action until after 1 or 2 am.

Obsesión (☎ 4327-3532), Esmeralda 565 (Map 5), is a new Microcentro dance club featuring salsa and rock, but also offering tango lessons from 6 to 8 pm Sundays. *Ozono*, another new club at Uruguay 142 in Congreso (Map 5), is difficult to characterize because music ranges from free form jazz to rock to techno on any given night. Saturday is consistently the biggest dance night.

Morocco (☎ 4342-6046), Hipólito Yrigoyen 851 in Montserrat (Map 7), is a favorite haunt of Argentine and other Spanish-speaking pop stars, but some porteños argue it's not what it used to be. Cover charges range from US$15 to US$30. If you still have some energy when it closes its doors, the nearby *Pantheon*, Av de Mayo 948, *opens* at 6 am Sunday morning.

In Recoleta near the Retiro boundary is *Shampoo* (☎ 4813-4427), Av Quintana 362 (Map 12). *Hippopotamus* (☎ 4802-0500), part of its namesake restaurant at Junín 1787, is a Recoleta institution (Map 12). Palermo clubs include the well-established *Trump's* (☎ 4801-9866), Bulnes 2772, and *Metrópolis*, Av Santa Fe 4389 (Map 13). Recent readers' recommendations include the dressy *Buenos Aires News* (☎ 4778-1500) complex at Avs del Libertador and Infanta Isabel (where the doormen can get picky about whom they condescend to admit; Map 13). The US$15 cover includes one beer or soft drink.

Visitors to *New York City* (☎ 4555-4139), Av Alvarez Thomas 1391 in the barrio of Villa Ortúzar, near the boundary with Chacarita and Colegiales (Map 2), should know that this has been a favored hangout of Dirty War torturer Alfredo Astiz. (Astiz, who can't leave the country because of Interpol warrants against him, is increasingly persona non grata just about everywhere else.)

Gay Nightspots

Gay visitors will find a cluster congenial bars and dance clubs in the Barrio Norte area in Recoleta, plus others scattered throughout town, mostly but not exclusively in Retiro and Palermo. The main public cruising area is around Av Santa Fe and Pueyrredón in Barrio Norte, where it's often possible to get free or discount admission tickets.

Contramano (men only, US$8 cover with one drink), Rodríguez Peña 1082 in Recoleta (Map 12), is one of the city's oldest gay venues, with a slightly older clientele as well. Also in Barrio Norte, open Wednesday through Sunday at TM de Anchorena 1170, the gigantic *Bunker* (mixed clientele, including heterosexuals) is a techno-style club with a hefty cover charge. Nearby reader recommended clubs include *Gasoil*, Anchorena 1179, for a well-choreographed male strip show (US$12, one drink included); *Abaco*, Anchorena 1347, for its drag show (US$10, one drink included); *In Vitro*, Azcuénaga 1006; and *Area*, Junín 1081. Closer to the center of Recoleta, try *Teleny* (US$10 cover with one drink) at Juncal 2479.

In Retiro (Map 11), there's the popular but claustrophobically small *Enigma* (mostly pop music, Fridays and Saturdays only) at Suipacha 927, and *Experiment* (☎ 4328-1019) at Carlos Pellegrini 1085. *Bach Bar*, José Antonion Cabrera 4390 in Palermo Viejo (Map 13), is a smaller, quieter and more intimate venue. It's closed Mondays.

The Montserrat and Balvanera area also has several clubs, though they're not so close together as those in Barrio Norte. *Tercer Milenio* (salsa and other Latin styles) recently moved to new quarters at Adolfo Alsina 934 in Montserrat (Map 7); it's open Fridays only. *Vaivén* (men only), a new and well-designed club at Juan D Perón 1871 between Av Callao and Riobamba in Congreso (Map 6), hasn't really developed an identity yet, but it bears watching. *Angel's*, close to Barrio Norte at Viamonte 2168 (Map 6), is open Thursday through Sunday and usually offers free admission, but is nothing special. Also near Barrio Norte, *Boicot*, Pasaje Dellepiane 657 in San Nicolás (Map 5), is a lesbian club.

ROCK & BLUES

Buenos Aires has a thriving rock and blues scene. For the most up-to-date information, consult *Clarín*'s Friday Suplemento Jóven, which also lists free events, and the weekend editions of *Página 12*.

El Samovar de Rasputín (☎ 4302-3190), Del Valle Iberlucea 1251 in La Boca (Map

10), presents blues and rock bands on weekends, from 11:30 pm. Admission is US$5. Another possibility is the **Blues Special Club**, Almirante Brown 102, opposite Parque Lezama in La Boca, near the San Telmo boundary.

In San Telmo proper, **La Casa del Pueblo**, Defensa 740 (Map 8), also features rock 'n' roll bands. **Arpegios**, downstairs at Cochabamba 415, is open only erratically. **Coco Bahiano**, Balcarce 958 (Map 8), is a reggae club. In nearby Constitución, try **Cemento**, Estados Unidos 1200 (Map 9).

Though not strictly rock and blues, **La Trastienda** (☎ 4342-7650) at Balcarce 460 in Montserrat (Map 7), is a good place for salsa and meringue, with a younger crowd up to about 25 years old. There are Wednesday lessons from 9 pm to midnight.

The Recoleta branch of the **Hard Rock Café** (☎ 4807-7625), directly above the Buenos Aires Design Recoleta complex, at the junction of Pueyrredón and Azcuénaga (Map 12), has live music, mostly but not exclusively cover bands, on weekends; it's open noon to 3 am daily and offers 15% student discounts.

Oh My God (☎ 4775-5238), Migueletes 1241 in Palermo (Map 13), has live rock with a cover charge of US$5 Friday and Saturday nights. **La Casona del Conde** (☎ 4862-5215), Honduras 3852 in Palermo Viejo (Map 13), features groups like the female a-cappella unit Las Blacanblus.

Dr Jekyll (☎ 4788-2411), Monroe 2315 in Belgrano (Map 14), features porteño bands like ska specialists Los Cafres, but depending on the night the music varies – there are even tango classes.

JAZZ

Founded in 1858, the legendary **Café Tortoni** (☎ 4342-4328), Av de Mayo 829 in Montserrat (Map 7), has occupied its present site since 1893. Oozing 19th-century atmosphere from the woodwork and billiard tables, it presents a greater variety of live entertainment than it once did, including both tango and traditional jazz in a number of rooms. La Porteña jazz band plays at 8:30 pm Thursdays, the Creole jazz band at

11:30 pm Fridays, and the Fénix jazz band at 11:15 pm Saturdays. Cover charge for live acts is around US$9, plus a minimum consumption of US$6. Patrons with student cards can get a substantial discount.

Informal enough that patrons discard their peanut shells on the floor, **Bárbaro** (☎ 4311-6856), Tres Sargentos 415 in Retiro (Map 11), employs some of the same groups on other nights. For contemporary jazz, try the Congreso venues of **Girondo** (☎ 4371-8838), at Paraná 328 just off Av Corrientes (Map 5), or **Evenos** (☎ 4381-7776) at Bartolomé Mitre 1552 (Map 5), which also attracts popular artists of the stature of Charly García.

Oliverio Allways (☎ 4372-6906), in the Hotel Bauen at Av Callao 360 in Balvanera (Map 6), has live jazz and blues. **Remember** (☎ 4953-0638), Av Corrientes 1983 (Map 6), is an informal Balvanera pub that showcases jazz, plus occasional blues and live theater.

Teatro La Carbonera (☎ 4362-2651), Balcarce 868 at Carlos Calvo in San Telmo (Map 8), features both live jazz and theater presentations.

SPECTATOR SPORTS

Spectator sports in Buenos Aires are limited primarily to soccer, horse racing, polo and boxing, though tennis, rugby, cricket and Formula One automobile racing have their adherents (visiting pedestrians and drivers may conclude that most porteño drivers consider themselves Formula One competitors). Among the best known Argentine athletes and sports figures are soccer legend Diego Maradona, tennis stars Guillermo Vilas and Gabriela Sabatini, the late boxers Oscar Bonavena and Carlos Monzón, and ex-Formula One standout Carlos Reutemann, now a Peronist politician in the province of Santa Fe.

Soccer

By any standard, Argentine soccer is world-class: the national team won the World Cup in 1978 (at home) and 1986. Buenos Aires has the highest density of first-division soccer teams in the world – eight of the country's

20 are based in the capital, with another five in the suburbs of Gran Buenos Aires.

Argentine fans are no less rabid than those in Europe and violence has become an unfortunate byproduct in a country whose *barras bravas* are the equivalent of British 'football hooligans.' Then again, it may just be the frustration of having paid extortionate prices to watch 90 minutes of apparently vigorous exercise that always seems to end in a scoreless tie.

Club officials themselves apparently contribute to the problem by giving their barras free tickets and transport, encouraging confrontations between fans of arch rivals. (Visitors should take special caution *not* to wear colors of the opposing teams, and neutral single colors like black or tan would be best.) In early 1998, a Buenos Aires judge briefly suspended all matches because of the clubs' failure to control fan disorder.

The soccer season extends from March to December. For information on tickets and schedules, contact the clubs listed below; where two addresses and telephones appear, the first is club offices, while the second is the stadium, where tickets are normally purchased. *Entradas populares* (standing-room admissions) cost about US$10, while *plateas* (fixed seats) cost US$20 and upward, depending on their location and the significance of the match.

Argentinos Juniors
  (☎ 4582-8949) Boyacá 2152
  (☎ 4551-6887) Punta Arenas 1271

Boca Juniors
  (☎ 4362-2260) Brandsen 805

Club Atlético Vélez Sarsfield
  (☎ 4641-5663) Av Juan B Justo 9200

Deportivo Español
  (☎ 4613-0968) Fernández 2100
  (☎ 4612-9648) Santiago de Compostela 3801

Ferrocarril Oeste
  (☎ 4431-9203) Cucha Cucha 350
  (☎ 4432-3989) Martín de Gainza 244

Huracán
  (☎ 4942-1965) Av Almancio Alcorta 2570

River Plate
  (☎ 4788-1200) Av Presidente Figueroa Alcorta 7597

San Lorenzo de Almagro
  (☎ 4923-9212) Av Fernández de la Cruz 2403
  (☎ 4918-3455) Av Perito Moreno between Av Fernández de la Cruz and Varela

Horse Racing

Buenos Aires' *Hipódromo Argentino* (☎ 4777-9009), at the intersection of Av del Libertador 4101 and Av Dorrego in Palermo (Map 13), is the site of horse races on Mondays, Fridays and Sundays. Admission costs upwards of US$10; betting starts at US$2.

Polo

Given Argentina's history of horses, and the past century's British influence, polo is a high-profile sport – if not exactly for the masses. In style, however, Argentine polo is rougher and more competitive than in Europe.

The *Campo Argentino de Polo* (☎ 4774-4517), at the intersection of Avs del Libertador and Dorrego in Palermo, just across from the Hipódromo Argentino (Map 13), is the site of the most important events, but the northern suburb of Pilar has the highest density of polo clubs.

Most polo matches take place in October and November, culminating in December's annual Campeonato Abierto Argentino de Polo (Argentine Open Polo Championship), which celebrated its centenary in 1993. Most events are open to the public free of charge. For current information, contact the Asociación Argentina de Polo (☎ 4331-4646), Hipólito Yrigoyen 636 in Montserrat (Map 7), which keeps a schedule of activities throughout the country.

For a list of stores selling polo equipment, see the entry in the Shopping chapter.

Pato

Of gaucho origins, the polo-like game of *pato* takes its name from the original game ball, which was literally a duck encased in a leather bag (since replaced by a ball with handles). In what passes for an animal rights victory in Argentina, the live duck is no longer ripped to shreds. Likewise, the players no longer face death or dismemberment in what was once a very violent sport.

For information on pato matches and tournaments, which usually take place at the polo grounds in Palermo, contact the Asociación Argentina de Pato (☎ 4311-0222), Av Belgrano 530, 5th floor, in Montserrat (Map 7).

Boxing

The main venue for boxing matches is **_Luna Park_** (☎ 4311-8005), an enclosed stadium at Bouchard 465, at the foot of Av Corrientes (Map 5). Luna Park also serves as a venue for second-tier international rock acts.

Shopping

Compulsive shoppers will adore Buenos Aires. The main shopping zones are downtown (along the Florida *peatonal*) and the more fashionable and expensive Av Santa Fe. Retiro (around Plaza San Martín at the north end of Florida) and Recoleta also offer plentiful options. Popular street markets take place in San Telmo, Recoleta and Belgrano. Buenos Aires' best buys are antiques, jewels, leather goods, shoes and souvenirs such as *mate* paraphernalia.

It's worth reiterating that many places add a 10% surcharge to credit-card purchases – ask before you pay.

WHAT TO BUY
Antiques & Collectibles
San Telmo is the main zone for antiques, though La Boca also merits some exploration. In addition to Sunday's outdoor Feria de San Telmo on Plaza Dorrego (Map 8), the stretch of Defensa from Pasaje Giuffra south past Plaza Dorrego is lined with antique shops, most of them excellent. Many are within small *galerías*, including Galería Cecil at Defensa 845, Galería French at Defensa 1070, opposite Plaza Dorrego, and Galería de la Defensa at Defensa 1179, a block south of Plaza Dorrego. Other San Telmo shops worth a visit are Churriche Antigüedades (☎ 4362-7612) at Defensa 1031, Arte Antica Antigüedades (☎ 4362-0861) at Defensa 1133 and Loreto Antigüedades (☎ 4361-5071) in the Galería French.

In Palermo, with premium prices, is Susan Borghi (☎ 4777-8184), Av Federico Lacroze 2307 (Map 13).

Vía Caminito, Aráoz de Lamadrid 774 in La Boca (Map 10), is a low-key shop specializing in local art and collectors' items such as sheet music and movie posters. Nearby Siglo XX Cambalache, Aráoz 802 (Map 10), is a good antique and second-hand store. Cambalache Artesanías is on Del Valle Iberlucea between Olavarría and Aráoz, next to the Caminito Tango Club.

Leather Goods & Shoes
Among the city's many leather shops, try Kerguelen (☎ 4922-2907) at Santander 747 in the barrio of Parque Chacabuco (Subte: José M Moreno; Map 15); Rossi y Carusso (☎ 4811-5357) at Av Santa Fe 1601 in Barrio Norte (Map 12); Chiche Farrace in the Galerías Pacífico (Map 5); Dalla Fontana (☎ 4311-1229) at Reconquista 735 (Map 5); and El Sol at Av del Libertador 1096 in Recoleta (Map 12). For general leather goods, Welcome Marroquinería (☎ 4312-8911), Marcelo T de Alvear 500 in Retiro (Map 11), has been a Buenos Aires institution since 1930. Casa López (☎ 4311-3044) is nearby at Marcelo T de Alvear 640/658 (Map 11), with an additional branch at Galerías Pacífico (Map 5).

For shoes, you can look just about anywhere along Av Corrientes or Florida. For women's footwear, try Perugia (☎ 4804-6340) at Av Alvear 1862 in Recoleta (Map 12). Guido Mocasines, Rodríguez Peña 1290 in Barrio Norte (Map 12), is widely acknowledged as the city's best traditional shoemaker; there's a branch (☎ 4811-4567) four blocks northeast, at Av Quintana 333 between Av Callao and Rodríguez Peña. López Taibo, Av Alvear 1902 in Recoleta (Map 12), sells men's shoes. Flabella (☎ 4322-6036), Suipacha 263 (Map 5), specializes in shoes for tango dancers.

For an only-in-Buenos-Aires experience, visit the Congreso outlet of Pierre Cardin (☎ 4372-0560), which shares a building with the capital's chapter of the not-yet-defunct Communist Party, Av Callao 220 between Juan D Perón and Sarmiento (Map 6). Pierre Cardin also has a Recoleta store at Ayacucho 1895 (Map 12).

Crafts & Souvenirs
Several provincial tourist offices, especially those along Avs Santa Fe and Callao, have small but worthwhile selections of regional crafts. Look especially at the Casa de

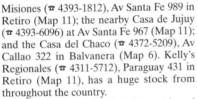

Filete & Its Future

Buenos Aires has a thriving modern art scene, but visitors should not shortchange *filete*, the finest manifestation of *porteño* folk art. Introduced by Sicilian immigrants, who embellished cartwheels and side-boards with curlicues and other flourishes, these elaborate line drawings replicate the moldings and wrought iron ornamentation of early-20th-century architecture. Not taking themselves too seriously, the skilled *fileteadores* (signpainters) add *piropos*, self-deprecating aphorisms such as 'the tent is small and we are too many clowns.'

Porteño fileteador Domingo Andanese calls filete 'a painted tango' that expresses the soul of the city. During the dark days of the Proceso from 1976-83, though, the soulless military government actually prohibited filete on buses and trucks, on the grounds that the elaborate artwork made it difficult to read numbers and routes. Astonishingly, this decree is still in force, though fileteadores are lobbying the city legislature for its repeal.

Still found in some bus interiors, filete also survives in souvenir plaques in markets like San Telmo's Plaza Dorrego. It also appears in contemporary contexts like Martiniano Arce's cover for the Grammy-winning Fabulosos Cadillacs' CD *Fabulosos Calavera* – work that would not be out of place on a Grateful Dead album.

Misiones (☎ 4393-1812), Av Santa Fe 989 in Retiro (Map 11); the nearby Casa de Jujuy (☎ 4393-6096) at Av Santa Fe 967 (Map 11); and the Casa del Chaco (☎ 4372-5209), Av Callao 322 in Balvanera (Map 6). Kelly's Regionales (☎ 4311-5712), Paraguay 431 in Retiro (Map 11), has a huge stock from throughout the country.

For typical items such as silverwork and mate paraphernalia, check out places like Artesanías Argentinas (☎ 4812-2650) at Montevideo 1386 in Barrio Norte (Map 12; look for the expensive but excellent polished wooden boxes, with silver latches, from

Salta) and Lionel Frenkel (☎ 4312-9806) at San Martín 1088 in Retiro (Map 11). Che Bandoneón (☎ 4312-7193), Paraguay 697 in Retiro (Map 11), specializes in tango souvenirs, as do Che Papusa (☎ 4312-7181) at Florida 844 in Retiro (Map 11) and Compañía del Lejano Sur (☎ 4319-5296) in the Galerías Pacífico at Florida 753 (Map 5).

Rancho Grande (☎ 4311-7603), Av Córdoba 543, Local 63, in Retiro (Map 11), sells gaucho souvenirs.

Several San Telmo craftsworkers sell filete, the colorful line paintings so typical of the capital since the early 1900s. These dealers include Adrián Clara (☎ 4381-2676); Jorge Muscia (☎ 4361-5942) at Carlos Calvo 370; Martiniano Arce at Perú 1089, 1st floor; and Mabel Matto at Estados Unidos 510, 1st floor (all on Map 8).

In La Boca, at the corner of Aráoz and Caminito (Map 10), opposite Vía Caminito, the enclosed Centro de Exposiciones Caminito is a new and very tourist-oriented souvenir and crafts market.

Jewelry

Try Arrighi (☎ 4814-0981), Arenales 1388 in Barrio Norte (Map 11), or Susana Cruz, with locations at Galerías Pacífico (☎ 4813-1949; Map 5), Av Callao 1751 in Recoleta (☎ 4813-2887; Map 12), in the Buenos Aires Design Recoleta complex (☎ 4806-1111) at Av Pueyrredón 2501 in Recoleta (Map 12), and at Av Santa Fe 1210 (☎ 4319-5280) in Retiro (Map 11).

Wine

Savoy (☎ 4371-1995, fax 4371-1532) carries a large selection of Argentine wines. With outlets at Florida 872 in Retiro (Map 11), Av Callao 35 in Congreso (Map 5), Av Callao 1201 in Barrio Norte (Map 12) and Pueyrredón 2180 in Recoleta (Map 12), it also takes phone orders and offers free delivery.

Videos

For sale or rental of video versions of Argentine films (in Spanish only), check Lavalle Producciones (☎ 4372-1118), Lavalle 1999, at the corner of Ayacucho (Map 6). Another alternative is El Ciudadano (☎ 4325-5731),

Esmeralda 461 in the Microcentro (Map 5), which has exceptionally knowledgeable staff.

Note that Argentine videos use the PAL system which is incompatible with North American video technology unless converted.

Music

Free Blues (☎ 4373-2999), Rodríguez Peña 438 in Congreso (Map 5), buys, sells and trades used CDs, cassettes and LPs. Buenos Aires' biggest music retailer is Musimundo (☎ 4394-7203) at Florida 259 (Map 5), with another convenient branch in Barrio Norte (☎ 4823-7144) at Av Santa Fe 2055 (Map 12).

Stamps

Correo Argentino, the privatized postal service, also has a philatelic service for stamp collectors in the Correo Central, Sarmiento 189, Oficina 51 (Map 5). Collectors might also contact the Federación Argentina de Entidades Filatélicas, Juan D Perón 1479, 4th floor, in Congreso.

Polo Equipment

La Picaza, at Guido 1923 in Recoleta (☎ 4804-8267; Map 12) and at Av Callao 1423 in Barrio Norte (☎ 4801-1887; Map 12), carries what is probably the best selection of polo equipment and souvenirs in town. Another polo outfitter, Alberto Vannucci (☎ 4811-3112), Av Callao 1773 in Recoleta (Map 12), is particularly good for saddles and blankets, while Logi Polo House (☎ 4801-9631), Cabello 3374 in Palermo (Map 13), is the best place for polo sticks.

Jorge Cánaves (☎ 4785-3982, canaves@ feedback.com.ar), Av Libertador 6000 at Juramento in Belgrano (Map 14) also focuses on horsegear and polo outfitting, as does La Polera (☎ 4806-0586) at José Uriburu 1710 in Barrio Norte (Map 12).

In addition to selling polo equipment, La Martina (☎ 4478-9366) at Paraguay 661 in Retiro (Map 11) organizes full-day polo lessons, with afternoon matches, on the outskirts of the capital, but these have drawn criticism for their cost and attitude. Try contacting La Picaza or Alberto Vannucci for polo excursions in Pilar.

WHERE TO SHOP
Galerías & Department Stores

Ritzy one-stop shopping centers, some of them recycled landmarks, have begun to take business away from the Microcentro's traditional commercial center. The most appealing of these is the restored Galerías Pacífico (☎ 4319-5118), which occupies an entire block bounded by Florida, Córdoba, San Martín and Viamonte (Map 5). It has an outstanding selection of shops and restaurants on three levels. Visit the information booth near the street-level entrance on Florida for a copy of the monthly guide which includes a diagram of shops as well as listings by specialty.

The famous Harrods (☎ 4312-4411) at Florida 821 in Retiro (Map 11) once rivaled its London namesake. However, it has become an ill-stocked, dark and depressing venue that looks ready to hold a going-out-of-business sale. Somehow, though, it

Galerías Pacífico

continues to hang on – possibly because of efforts to franchise the name throughout South America despite furious but ineffective legal objections from Britain.

The 24,000-sq-meter Patio Bullrich (☎ 4815-3501) at Av del Libertador 750 (Map 11) once hosted livestock auctions, but an elegant remodeling job has transformed it into a more aristocratic meat market that suffers from an oppressive atmosphere of heavy-handed security almost reminiscent of the Proceso. On the other hand, if you need Persian rugs, US$800 suits and the like, it's worth a visit. There's another entrance at Posadas 1245, opposite the Caesar Park Hotel, near the Retiro-Recoleta border.

More casual, though almost equally extravagant, is the Buenos Aires Design Recoleta (☎ 4806-1111), Av Pueyrredón 2501 (Map 12), which also includes a number of restaurants and nightspots in its Plaza del Pilar.

The Alto Palermo Shopping Center (☎ 4821-6030), Av Coronel Díaz 2098 at Arenales (Subte: Bulnes; Map 13), is a modern mall-type facility with nearly 200 shops. The airy Paseo Alcorta (☎ 4801-8035), at Jerónimo Salguero 3172 in Palermo (Map 13), covers 100,000 sq meters.

Opened in November 1998, the remodeled Mercado de Abasto encloses 120,000 sq meters at the corner of Av Corrientes and Anchorena (Subte: Carlos Gardel; Map 6). More than 200 shops, a dozen cinemas, a covered plaza and a children's museum are among the facilities.

Markets & Ferias

One of the capital's most interesting shopping districts, San Telmo (Map 8) is known for its fascinating flea market, the Feria de San Telmo, which takes place from 10 am to about 5 pm weekends on Plaza Dorrego (vendors prefer that customers refrain from touching items on display). Prices have risen considerably at the nearby gentrified antique shops, but there are good restaurants, and buskers, mimes and tango dancers frequently perform unannounced.

Only a short walk from Plaza Dorrego, there is now a Sunday market in spacious

Tren de la Costa

Inaugurated in 1891 as recreational transport, but closed for more than three decades until its resuscitation in 1995, the former 'Tren del Bajo' connected the capital with its northern riverside suburbs. This flagrantly touristic version runs from Retiro to Tigre (changing trains at Estación Mitre/Maipú in Olivos) with stops at a number of recycled stations, plus a few newer ones, whose main attractions are their modern shopping centers. The largest are at Estación Libertador and San Isidro, while Estación Barrancas, in the suburb of Acassuso, has an antiques market from 11 am to 7 pm weekends and holidays.

The fare to Tigre is US$1.50 weekdays, US$2 weekends, and allows you to make as many stops as you wish. For more details, contact Tren de la Costa (☎ 4732-6132).

Parque Lezama, at the corner of Brasil and Av Paseo Colón (Map 8), which also gets a fair number of street performers. In La Boca, at the Riachuelo end of the Caminito (Map 10), the Feria Artesanal Plazoleta Vuelta de Rocha takes place from 10 am to 6 pm weekends and holidays. There is also an artists' market on the Caminito itself, open 10 am to 6 pm daily.

Another popular artisans' market takes place Sundays in Recoleta's Plaza Intendente Alvear at Av Pueyrredón and Av del Libertador (Map 12). The Feria Artesanal Plaza General Manuel Belgrano, at Juramento and Cuba in Belgrano (Map 14), takes place from 10 am to 8 pm weekends and holidays, but it gets better as the day goes on – not until 4 or 5 pm do legitimate craftsworkers finally outnumber peddlers of kitsch.

In the southwestern barrio of Mataderos, at the corner of Av Lisandro de la Torre and Bragado (Map 2), the Feria de Mataderos is a lively market with 200 merchants selling practical goods in a 'general store' atmosphere. It is frequented by gauchos, folksingers and other performers and is open

11 am to 7 pm weekends. From downtown, take bus No 155 westbound on Tucumán.

Buenos Aires' most unusual and least touristic market is the Feria Urkupiña, where nearly 3000 vendors, mostly Bolivian, sell just about everything under the sun. The market operates on Mondays from 8 am until dark and is on Av General Paz in the suburban partido of Lomas de Zamora.

Art Galleries

Most of Buenos Aires' dozens of art galleries offer fairly conventional works, either European or consciously derivative of European traditions, but a handful of venues promote more locally based, innovative works. For an up-to-date listing of events and current exhibits, consult the monthly tabloid newsletter *Arte al Día* (☎ 4805-7672), available at galleries and museums throughout the city.

For modern Argentine art, the best gallery is Galería Ruth Benzacar (☎ 4313-8945), downstairs at Florida 1000 in Retiro (Map 11), but other worthwhile places (all in Retiro) include Galería Federico Klem (☎ 4312-2058) downstairs at Marcelo T de Alvear 636, Galería Rubbers (☎ 4393-6010) at Suipacha 1175, Galería Vermeer (☎ 4394-3462) across the street at Suipacha 1168, Galería Aguilar (☎ 4394-6900) nearby at Suipacha 1178, and Galería Zurbarán (☎ 4815-1556) at Cerrito 1522. Under the railroad bridge in Palermo, Galería der Brücke (☎ 4775-2175), Av del Libertador 3883 (Map 13), also displays interesting work.

At Del Valle Iberlucea 1271 in La Boca (Map 10), La Vuelta de los Tachos is a small gallery whose business depends on the barrio's reputation as an artists' colony.

Bookstores

Buenos Aires' landmark bookseller El Ateneo (☎ 4325-6801), Florida 340 in the Microcentro (Map 5), has a large selection of travel books in the basement, including Lonely Planet guides. In addition to its emphasis on Argentine history and literature, it also stocks foreign-language books, which are, unfortunately, expensive. There's a branch at Vuelta de Obligado 2108 in Belgrano (Map 14).

Librería ABC at Av Córdoba 685 in Retiro (Map 11) has similar stock. Atlántida (☎ 4311-6323), in the Galerías Pacífico at Florida and Córdoba (Map 5), also offers a good selection of current books.

For the most complete selection of guidebooks in town, including nearly every Lonely Planet title in print, visit the specialty shop Librerías Turísticas (☎ 4963-2866, fax 4962-5547) at Paraguay 2457 in Barrio Norte (Subte: Pueyrredón; Map 12). Its prices are also the most reasonable for foreign-language guidebooks.

Av Corrientes, between Avs 9 de Julio and Callao, is a popular area for book browsing. LiberArte (☎ 4371-7098), Corrientes 1555 (Map 5), contains a superb selection of books on cultural and political topics. Next door, at Av Corrientes 1551, Foro Gandhi (☎ 4374-7501) is a hybrid bookstore/coffeehouse similar to Barrio Norte's Clásica y Moderna (☎ 4812-8707), Av Callao 892 (Map 12). For more details on these last two, see Cafés & Bars in the Entertainment chapter.

Book-lovers should explore the basement stacks at Librería Platero (☎ 4382-2215), Talcahuano 485, just off Corrientes (Map 5). Perhaps the capital's best bookstore, it has an inventory that includes a remarkable selection of new and out-of-print books about Argentina and Latin America. The staff is knowledgeable in almost every field, and trustworthy and efficient in packaging and sending books overseas. Another good shop with similar stock is Aquilanti (☎ 4952-4546), Rincón 79 in Balvanera (Map 6). Librería Lola (☎ 4322-3920), Viamonte 976, 2nd floor, Local D (Map 5), has a good selection of new and used books on biology, earth sciences, anthropology and history.

French speakers can find a wide selection of reading material at Oficina del Libro Francés, with locations at Esmeralda 861 in Retiro (☎ 4311-0363; Map 11) and Talcahuano 342, 2nd floor, in San Nicolás (☎ 4374-4747; Map 5). The former is open 9 am to 12:30 pm daily except Sunday and 3 to 6:30 pm weekdays; the latter is open 9:30 am to 7:30 pm weekdays, 10 am to 12:30 pm Saturdays.

Several street markets have good selections of used books (mostly in Spanish).

Check out Plaza Lavalle (Map 5), 10 am to 6 pm weekdays; Plazoleta Santa Fe outside the Palermo Subte station (Map 13); and Plaza Primera Junta (end of the line for Línea A) in the barrio of Caballito (Map 15).

Other possibilities include Librería Alberto Casares (☎ 4322-0794) at Suipacha 521 (Map 5), Librería El Túnel (large selection) at Av de Mayo 767 (Map 7), Librería Huemul (☎ 4825-2290; strong on history) at Av Santa Fe 2237 in Barrio Norte (Map 12), and Librería L'Amateur (collectibles) at Esmeralda 882 in Retiro (Map 11).

For a listing of books about Buenos Aires, see Books in the Facts for the Visitor chapter.

Excursions

Just beyond the Capital Federal, Buenos Aires province offers several interesting and worthwhile destinations: the riverside suburb of Tigre and the spreading Delta del Paraná (including Isla Martín García), the provincial capital of La Plata, the devotional center of Luján, and the province's gaucho capital, San Antonio de Areco.

Just as economic decline forced the owners of Britain's stately homes to open their properties to the public, so hard times in the ranching sector have nudged owners of the Pampas' expansive *estancias* to open their gates and houses to tourists, both for day trips and extended stays. Provided visitors understand their limitations, these can be ideal for a country weekend, but some are very expensive.

Among estancia tour operators are José de Santis (☎ 4342-8417, fax 4343-9568,

desantis@argentinae.com), Diagonal Roque Sáenz Peña 616, 5th floor in the Microcentro (Map 5); Abriendo Tranqueras (☎ 4783-5720) at La Pampa 2900 in Belgrano (Map 14); Comarcas (☎ 4826-1130) at Laprida 1380 in Recoleta (Map 12), and Turar (☎ 4342-2971, fax 343-1868), Bartolomé Mitre 559, 4th floor, in the Microcentro (Map 5).

Other excursions take travelers across the Río Paraná to the Uruguayan capital of Montevideo and the colonial gem of Colonia del Sacramento, commonly known simply as Colonia.

TIGRE & THE DELTA DEL PARANÁ

Within commuting range of the capital, this riverside suburb (population 290,000) is a popular weekend retreat and the best point

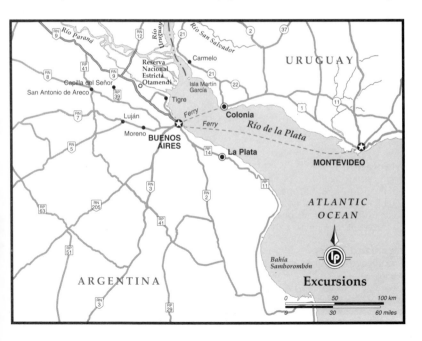

of departure for exploring the Delta del Paraná and visiting historic Isla Martín García. At the Estación Fluvial is the local Dirección de Turismo (☎ 4512-4497).

One of Tigre's best attractions is the **Puerto de Frutos**, in the 1200 block of Av Cazón, where a major crafts fair takes place each weekend (though it's open 11 am to 7 pm every day). Its restaurant also serves up tasty dishes. Another attraction is the **Museo Naval de la Nación** (☎ 4749-0608), Paseo Victorica 602, which traces the history of the Argentine navy since its founding by Irishman Guillermo Brown. It's open 8 am to 12:30 pm Monday through Thursday, until 5:30 pm Fridays; weekend hours are 10 am to 6:30 pm.

The **Museo de la Reconquista** (☎ 4749-0090), Liniers 818, was the house where Viceroy Liniers coordinated resistance to the British invasions of the early 19th century; it also deals with Delta del Paraná history.

Tigre's counterpart to Disneyworld, but even tackier, is the **Parque de la Costa** (☎ 4732-6300) on Pereyra, open 11 am to midnight Wednesday through Sunday. Admission, including unlimited rides and games, costs US$19 for adults, US$15 for children ages 9 to 12.

Farther upstream on the Río Paraná de las Palmas, the estuaries and gallery forests of the **Reserva Nacional Estricta Otamendi** comprise the closest unit of Argentina's national park system to Buenos Aires (see Reserva section).

Orientation

Tigre is at the confluence of the Río Luján and the Río Tigre, beyond which is the 2000km maze of waterways that constitutes the delta. The delta's major channel is the Río Paraná de las Palmas.

Organized Tours

In addition to its tours of Isla Martín García, Cacciola (☎ 4749-0329), Lavalle 520, offers daily excursions around the Paraná de las Palmas (US$7 to US$12) on the *Motonave Santa Fe*, and weekend and holiday tours (US$30, lunch included, 3 1/2 hours) on the *Humberto M*.

Places to Stay & Eat

Hotels are relatively few and far between in the delta, but try *Hotel Laura* (☎ 4749-3898) on Canal Honda off the Paraná de las Palmas; it has doubles with private bath for US$60 on weekdays, US$80 on weekends. Though it has drawn some complaints for high prices and poor service, it also offers a US$15 delta excursion. *Hotel I'Marangatu* (☎ 4749-7350), on the Río San Antonio, charges US$80 during the week, US$100 on weekends, while *La Manuelita* (☎ 4749-0987), on the Río Carapachay, charges US$45 during the week, US$50 on weekends. *Hotel Astor* is strictly an *albergue transitorio*.

In Tigre proper, at Lavalle 557, the riverfront *B&B Escauriza* (☎ 4749-2499, fax 4744-0938) offers exactly what it says – homestyle lodging for US$35 per person with breakfast.

On the Río Tres Bocas, about 20 minutes from Tigre by launch, *La Riviera* (☎ 4749-6177, 4749-5960) is a popular restaurant offering good food and live music. It's frequented by gay clientele (but by no means exclusively). On weekends during Carnaval, the celebrants are at their most outrageous.

Getting There & Away

Bus No 60 from Av Callao in Buenos Aires goes all the way to Tigre (US$1.70, 75 to 90 minutes, depending on traffic), but the train is probably quicker when traffic is heavy – and it's also a bit cheaper (US$1.30). The Ferrocarril Mitres leaves from Plataforma 1 or 2 at Estacíon Retiro (Map 12).

Getting Around

Catamaranes Interisleña (☎ 4731-0264) runs a series of *lanchas colectivas* (collective launches) from Tigre's Estación Fluvial, Lavalle 419, to various destinations in the delta for $5 per person roundtrip (children under age 8 go free). These will drop you off or pick you up at any riverside dock – just flag them down as you would a bus. Other companies with similar services, also at the Estación Fluvial, are Delta Argentino (☎ 4749-0537) and Lanchas Marsili (☎ 4413-4123).

ISLA MARTÍN GARCÍA

Navigating among the densely forested multiple channels of the Tigre and Paraná rivers, en route to historic Isla Martín García, travelers can easily imagine what ideal hideaways these waterways were for colonial smugglers. Just off the Uruguayan coastal region, directly south of the city of Carmelo, the Isla Martín García is most famous – or infamous – as a prison camp. Four Argentine presidents have been held in custody here, and the Servicio Penitenciario of Buenos Aires province still uses it as a halfway house for prisoners near the end of their terms. At present, though, the island is more a combination of historical monument, tranquil nature reserve and recreational retreat from the bustle of the Capital Federal.

History

In colonial times, Spain and Portugal contested possession of the island. Unlike the sedimentary islands of the flood-prone delta, 180-hectare Martín García rises 27m above sea level; this high ground made it suitable for a fortress to guard the approach to the Uruguay and Paraná rivers. Irish Admiral Guillermo Brown gave the Provincias

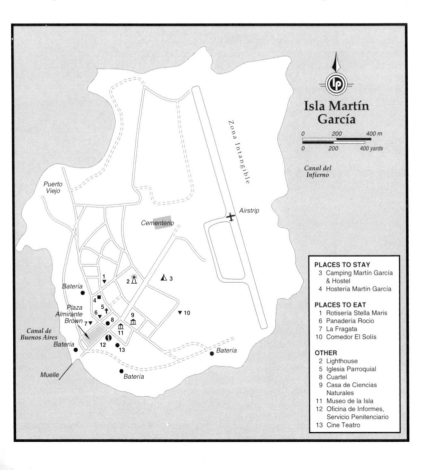

Isla Martín García

Canal del Infierno

PLACES TO STAY
3 Camping Martín García & Hostel
4 Hostería Martín García

PLACES TO EAT
1 Rotisería Stella Maris
6 Panadería Rocio
7 La Fragata
10 Comedor El Solís

OTHER
2 Lighthouse
5 Iglesia Parroquial
8 Cuartel
9 Casa de Ciencias Naturales
11 Museo de la Isla
12 Oficina de Informes, Servicio Penitenciario
13 Cine Teatro

Unidas del Río de la Plata (United Provinces of the River Plate) their first major naval victory here in 1814, when a commando raid dislodged royalist troops who escaped to Montevideo. Both England and France took advantage of Argentine conflicts with Brazil to occupy the island in the early 19th century.

For most of the 20th century, the Argentine navy has controlled the island. At the turn of the century, Nicaraguan poet Rubén Darío lived in what is now the natural history center while serving as Colombian consul in Buenos Aires. During WWII authorities briefly detained the crew of the German destroyer *Graf Spee*, sunk off Montevideo.

The Argentine military regularly confined political prisoners here, including Presidents Hipólito Yrigoyen (twice in the early 20th century), Marcelo T de Alvear (around the same time), Juan Perón (briefly in 1945) and Arturo Frondizi (1962-63). Many speculate that the military dictatorship of 1976-83 used the island as a detention center and that sealed subterranean tunnels may contain evidence of such activity.

Things to See & Do

Martín García's main points of interest are its historic buildings. The **Oficina de Informes**, uphill from the *muelle* (passenger pier), is also the headquarters of the Servicio Penitenciario, which manages the island's halfway-house prisoners. Other buildings of interest include the ruins of the former **Cuartel** (naval barracks), the **Panadería Rocio** (a still-operating bakery dating from 1913), the rococo **Cine Teatro**, the **Museo de la Isla** and the **Casa de Ciencias Naturales**. At the northwestern end of the island, beyond a block of badly deteriorating and overgrown houses, the **Puerto Viejo** (old port) has fallen into disuse due to sediments that have clogged the anchorage. The **cementerio** contains the headstones of many conscripts who died in an epidemic in the early 20th century.

The densely forested northern part of the island offers quiet, pleasant walks if you don't mind fending off the mosquitoes. South of the airstrip, the **Zona Intangible** is closed to casual hikers because of its botanical value and the hazard of fire.

The restaurant Comedor El Solís has a **swimming pool** open to the public.

Organized Tours

Guided tours depart from Cacciola's Terminal Internacional (☎ 4749-0329) at Lavalle 520 in Tigre. Tickets are also available at their downtown Buenos Aires office (☎ 4394-5520) at Florida 520, 1st floor, Oficina 113 (Map 5). On Tuesdays, Thursdays, weekends and holidays, the enclosed catamaran leaves Tigre at 8 am, returning from Martín García at 4 pm (be at dockside early for the return trip). The roundtrip fare is US$28; for US$39, the tour includes lunch at Cacciola's La Fragata restaurant, but there are cheaper and better meal alternatives.

On arrival at the island, provincial authorities collect a US$2 per person entrance fee to support the maintenance of its Reserva Natural y Cultural Isla Martín García. Passengers then split into two groups – those who opt for the full excursion receive a free aperitif, while the rest follow a well-informed guide to the island's many historic buildings. Very worthwhile if you understand Spanish, the 1½-hour tours leave plenty of time for exploring the island on your own.

Places to Stay & Eat

Pleasant, shady *Camping Martín García* (☎ 4728-1808; reservations are essential) charges US$3.50 per person. It also offers simple hostel accommodations for US$7 per person with shared bath (US$10 with private bath), but bring your own sheets and towels. The facility tends to be very crowded in summer and on weekends, so the best time for an overnight stay is probably on weekdays or just before or after the peak summer season.

Tour company Cacciola offers full-board overnight packages, including transportation, for US$89 per person at its *Hostería Martín García*; additional nights cost US$50 per person. *Comedor El Solís*, with a US$10 *tenedor libre* including tasty *boga* and dessert, is a better value than the expensive lunch at Cacciola's *La Fragata*, which is included in the full excursion. Drinks at Solís are extra but not outrageous. *Rotisería Stella Maris* also has decent, simple meals and drinks, while the *Panadería Rocio* is renowned for its fruitcakes.

Shopping

Artisanal goods available at shops on the island include *mate* gourds and wooden ships, along with the usual T-shirts and mugs manufactured elsewhere.

Getting There & Away

Without your own boat, the only practical way to the island is a guided tour that departs from Tigre (from US$28; see Organized Tours). To get to Tigre from downtown Buenos Aires, take city bus No 60 northbound from Av Callao (US$1.70). Leave early, since it takes around 1½ hours.

Visitors camping on the island who do not wish to take the guided tour pay only US$23 roundtrip.

RESERVA NACIONAL ESTRICTA OTAMENDI

About 80km northwest of Buenos Aires, the Reserva Nacional Estricta Otamendi comprises a variety of distinct but narrowly differentiated environments depending on subtle differences in elevations and soils. The main divisions, however, are the floodprone, river-deposited sediments of the *bajíos ribereños* and the better-drained *pampas onduladas*. In addition to the riverside gallery forests and the pampas grasslands, there are numerous birds, amphibians, fish and even mammals like the *carpincho* (capybara), swamp deer and the rarely seen river otter.

Getting There & Away

Otamendi is an easy day trip from the capital by the Ferrocarril Mitre from Estación Retiro (Map 11); take the train toward José León Suárez and, at Villa Ballester, change to the train toward Zárate. Disembark at Estación Otamendi, where the reserve is only a 400m walk.

Many buses from Retiro and Once also pass by Otamendi en route to the city of Campana, but leave passengers at the junction of RN9, about 2km from the reserve.

LA PLATA

After the city of Buenos Aires became Argentina's federal capital, Governor Dardo Rocha founded La Plata in 1882 to give the province its own new capital. After detailed study, Rocha selected Pedro Benoit's elaborate plan, closely resembling that of Washington, DC, with major avenues and broad diagonals connecting the city's public buildings and numerous plazas.

La Plata's grandiose public buildings reflect Benoit's blueprint for an important administrative, commercial and cultural center, but the city does not overwhelm the human dimension. Some buildings, like the famous Museo de Historia Natural, are undergoing badly needed repairs. Adolfo Bioy Casares' novella *The Adventures of a Photographer in La Plata* (1989) gives readers a good sense of life in the city.

La Plata, 56km southeast of Buenos Aires via RP 14, is a city of about 225,000, with a total population of roughly 560,000 including the surrounding area. Its basic design is a conventional grid, but the superposition of diagonals has created a distinctive diamond pattern, connecting the plazas and permitting traffic to flow smoothly between them. While most public buildings are on or around Plaza Moreno, the commercial center is near Plaza San Martín.

Information

Conveniently located but almost hostile toward all but the most routine requests for information, the Entidad Municipal de Turismo (☎ 482-9656), in the Pasaje Dardo Rocha at the corner of Calles 6 and 50, is open 9 am to 6 pm daily except Sunday, when hours are 9 am to 1 pm. It distributes a sketchy city map and a few brochures.

On the 13th floor of the Torre Municipal at Calle 12 and Av 53, the provincial Subsecretaría de Turismo (☎ 429-5553) is more helpful but keeps limited hours, 9 am to 3 pm weekdays. If you can persuade them to let you on the roof, there are magnificent views of the city.

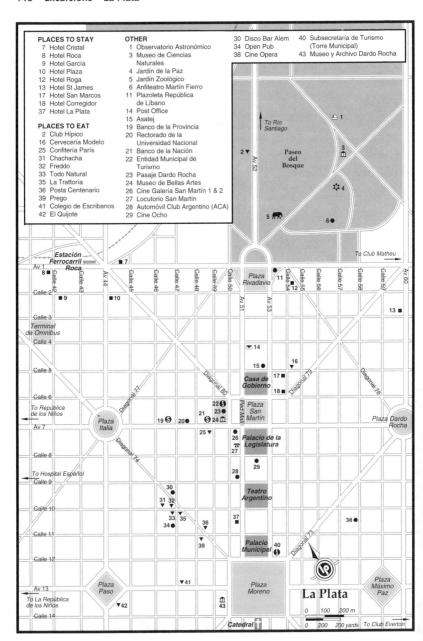

PLACES TO STAY
7 Hotel Cristal
8 Hotel Roca
9 Hotel García
10 Hotel Plaza
12 Hotel Roga
13 Hotel St James
17 Hotel San Marcos
18 Hotel Corregidor
37 Hotel La Plata

PLACES TO EAT
2 Club Hípico
16 Cervecería Modelo
25 Confitería París
31 Chachacha
32 Freddo
33 Todo Natural
35 La Trattoría
36 Posta Centenario
39 Prego
41 Colegio de Escribanos
42 El Quijote

OTHER
1 Observatorio Astronómico
3 Museo de Ciencias
Naturales
4 Jardín de la Paz
5 Jardín Zoológico
6 Anfiteatro Martín Fierro
11 Plazoleta República
de Líbano
14 Post Office
15 Asatej
19 Banco de la Provincia
20 Rectorado de la
Universidad Nacional
21 Banco de la Nación
22 Entidad Municipal de
Turismo
23 Pasaje Dardo Rocha
24 Museo de Bellas Artes
26 Cine Galería San Martín 1 & 2
27 Locutorio San Martín
28 Automóvil Club Argentino (ACA)
29 Cine Ocho

30 Disco Bar Alem
34 Open Pub
38 Cine Opera

40 Subsecretaría de Turismo
(Torre Municipal)
43 Museo y Archivo Dardo Rocha

La Plata's area code is ☎ 221; the postal code is 1900. The post office is at the corner of Av 51 and Calle 4. In addition to serving as a telephone office, Locutorio San Martín, on Av 51 between Av 7 and Calle 8, is also a *cartelera* offering discount tickets to local entertainment events.

Argentina's nonprofit student travel agency Asatej (☎ 483-8673) has a local branch at Calle 5 No 990, at the corner of Calle 53.

Walking Tour

In the middle of **Plaza Moreno**, which occupies four sq blocks between Calles 12 and 14 and Avs 50 and 54, La Plata's **Piedra Fundacional** (Founding Stone) of 1882 marks the city's precise geographical center. Across from the plaza, on Calle 14 between Avs 51 and 53, visit the neo-Gothic **Catedral** (begun 1885, but not inaugurated until 1932). Inspired by medieval antecedents in Cologne and Amiens, it has fine stained glass and polished granite floors. The tower, whose construction was suspended for many years, is finally being completed. The building's museum (☎ 424-0112 for guided tours) is open 8 am to noon and 2 to 7 pm daily.

On the opposite side of Plaza Moreno is the **Palacio Municipal** (1886; ☎ 427-1535 for guided tours), designed in German Renaissance style by Hanoverian architect Hubert Stiers. Note, on either side, the modern towers housing most of the provincial government offices. On the west side of the Plaza, between Av 13 and Calle 14, the **Museo y Archivo Dardo Rocha** was the residence of the city's creator and contains many of his personal effects.

Three blocks northeast, on Calle 10 between Avs 51 and 53, the unfinished and slowly progressing **Teatro Argentino**, also known as the Centro de Artes y Espectáculos, replaces an earlier, much more distinguished building destroyed by fire.

Three blocks farther northeast, on Av 7 opposite Plaza San Martín, is the ornate provincial **Palacio de la Legislatura** (☎ 422-0081 for guided tours), also in German Renaissance style. To the west, on Calle 50 between Calle 6 and Av 7, once La Plata's main railroad station, the French Classic

Pasaje Dardo Rocha is the city's major cultural center; at its south end is the municipal **Museo de Bellas Artes**, the fine arts museum. Detour a couple blocks northwest, to Av 7 between Calles 47 and 48, to view the original buildings of the **Rectorado de la Universidad Nacional** (1905; once a bank, now university administrative offices). If it's a weekend or holiday, have a look at the **Feria Artesanal** (crafts fair) on Plaza Italia, at the junction of Av 7 and Diagonal 77.

Return via Calle 6 to the Flemish Renaissance **Casa de Gobierno**, housing the provincial governor and his retinue, on the north side of Plaza San Martín. If it's a hot day, stroll up Calle 54 to the landmark **Cervecería Modelo** for a cold lager beer.

Paseo del Bosque

Plantations of eucalyptus, gingko, palm and subtropical hardwoods cover this 60-hectare park, expropriated from an estancia at the time of the city's founding, at the northeastern edge of town. Its facilities include the **Anfiteatro Martín Fierro**, an open-air facility that hosts summer drama festivals, the **Museo de Ciencias Naturales** (see entry), the **Observatorio Astronómico** (open at 9:30 pm Fridays for tours), the symbolic United Nations of the **Jardín de la Paz** (Garden of Peace), a modest **Jardín Zoológico** (dating from 1907; open 9 am to 7 pm daily except Monday; guided tours between 10:30 am and 4 pm) along Av 52, and several university departments.

Cervecería Modelo

The quintessential La Plata experience is drinking and eating at this 85-year-old tavern, known simply as *La Modelo* (☎ 21-1321), at the corner of Calles 54 and 5. On a warm summer night, you can pass hours at their sidewalk tables, savoring excellent *cerveza tirada* (lager beer) and complimentary peanuts. For something more substantial, try *lomito* (steak sandwich) with french fries.

Night of the Pencils

With its leafy streets and attractive parks, it's hard to imagine that the cheerful university town of La Plata suffered more than almost any other city in the military's 1976-83 reign of terror. La Plata was, in fact, the site of the infamous Noche de las Lápizes (Night of the Pencils). On September 14, 1976, the Buenos Aires provincial police kidnapped and tortured seven students 16 to 18 years old – most of them still unaccounted for – who had protested a rise in transportation fares. Featured in a film by Héctor Olivera in 1986, the Night of the Pencils surfaced again in 1996 when local human rights organizations demanded the firing of a teacher linked to the right-wing terrorist Alianza Anti-Comunista Argentina (Argentine Anticommunist Alliance).

Museo de Ciencias Naturales

When Buenos Aires became the federal capital, provincial authorities built this museum, in the spacious park known as Paseo del Bosque, to house the paleontological, archaeological and anthropological collections of lifetime director Francisco P Moreno, the famous Patagonian explorer.

Finished in 1889, the building consists of an attractive oval with four stories and a mezzanine with showrooms, classrooms, workshops, laboratories, offices, libraries and storage. Its exterior mixes Corinthian columns, Ionic posterior walls and Hellenic windows, with Aztec and Inca-style embellishments. Since 1906, the university's school of natural sciences has functioned here.

Unfortunately, for all its resources, the museum is a major disappointment. The impressive fossil collection, for instance, suffers from a routine chronology that doesn't do justice to the subject, and the ethnographic exhibits betray a stereotypical Darwinism that's more than a century out of date. Besides its exterior repairs, the museum needs a truly professional makeover of both the interior and its display materials.

At Paseo del Bosque 1900, the museum (☎ 425-7744) is open from 10 am to 6 pm daily (except for January 1, May 1 and December 25). Admission is US$3. Free guided tours are available from 2 to 4 pm.

La República de los Niños

Evita Perón herself sponsored this scale-model city, completed shortly before her death in 1952, for the education and enjoyment of children. From its Plaza de la Amistad (Friendship Plaza), a steam train circles this architectural hodgepodge of medieval European and Islamic styles, with motifs from Grimms' and Andersen's fairy tales. Like most public works projects of its era, it's showing its age, but is worth a visit if you have crabby kids to appease; otherwise it's sort of a bargain-basement Disneyland.

República de los Niños (☎ 484-0194) is on Camino General Belgrano Km 7 and Calle 501, north of La Plata in the suburb of Manuel Gonnet. From Av 7 in La Plata, take bus No 518 or 273; not all No 273 buses go all the way. From Av 13, take bus No 338.

Admission is US$3 per person, which includes the aquarium and *granja* (farm), but the train ride and doll museum are extra. Children under 7 are free. It's open 10 am to 6 pm daily except Monday.

Places to Stay

Since visitors to La Plata are often government officials on per diem, hotels price their rooms accordingly. One of few budget hotels, *Hotel St James* (☎ 421-8089), Calle 60 No 377, charges US$20/30 for singles/doubles without breakfast. *Hotel García*, Calle 2 No 525, is the only other real budget choice.

The friendly, remodeled *Hotel Roca* (☎ 421-4916), Calle 42 No 309, charges US$25/30 with shared bath, US$31/38 with private bath. *Hotel Plaza* (☎ 421-0325), near the train station at Av 44 No 358, charges US$30/40 without breakfast but has a 3rd-floor budget double for US$30. Similar in price and standard but better located is one-star *Hotel Roga* (☎ 421-9553), on a woodsy block at Calle 54 No 334, where clean, comfortable rooms with private bath cost US$38/52.

At the top end are three-star lodgings like *Hotel La Plata* (☎/fax 422-9090), at Av 51 No 783 near Plaza Moreno; the US$47/64 rate includes half-board, with a 10% discount for those who settle for breakfast only. *Hotel Cristal* (☎ 424-1489), Av 1 No 620, charges US$47/62, while *Hotel San Marcos* (☎ 422-2249) at Calle 54 No 523 has rooms for US$54/73 and is conveniently close to the Cervecería Modelo. Four-star *Hotel Corregidor* (☎ 425-6800, fax 256-805), Calle 6 No 1026, offers some luxuries for US$88/100.

Places to Eat

Among La Plata's traditional favorites are *Club Everton*, on Calle 14 between Calles 63 and 64, and *Club Matheu*, Calle 63 No 317 between Av 1 and Calle 2, both with limited but good menus at affordable prices. Pricier but very pleasant is the *Club Hípico* (☎ 423-0937), in the Paseo del Bosque on Av 52.

For a good *parrillada*, try *El Chaparral*, Av 60 and Calle 118 in the Paseo del Bosque, which has excellent *mollejas* (sweetbreads). On Plaza Paso, at the junction of Avs 13 and 44, *El Quijote* (☎ 483-3653) occupies a commonplace building but has delicious food, particularly the *ensalada de frutos de mar* (seafood salad). Local barristers advocate the *Colegio de Escribanos*, Av 13 between Calles 47 and 48.

Chachacha (☎ 422-5294), Calle 10 No 370 between Calles 46 and 47, features an extensive choice of meat, chicken and seafood crepes, plus draft beer, at moderate prices. A popular Italian place, at Calle 47 and Diagonal 74, is *La Trattoría*. Similar but more expensive is *Prego*, Calle 11 No 805. *Posta Centenario*, on Diagonal 74 between Calles 48 and 49, specializes in pork.

Todo Natural, on Calle 47 between Calles 10 and 11, is a good natural foods market. The popular ice creamery *Freddo* has an outlet at Calles 47 and 10. For an espresso and a breath of fresh air, try the totally smoke-free *Confitería París* at the corner of Av 7 and Calle 49.

Entertainment

Cine Ocho (☎ 482-5554) has three screens at Calle 8 No 981, between Avs 51 and 53. *Cine San Martín* (☎ 483-9947), Calle 7 No 923, has two screens, while *Cine Opera* (☎ 422-6502), Calle 58 No 770, has only one.

The *Open Pub*, Calle 47 No 787, is a live rock venue. Try also *Disco Bar Alem*, Calle 47 No 717.

Getting There & Away

Bus Río de la Plata (☎ 4313-3580 in Buenos Aires) has buses every half hour from Once, Constitución and Retiro stations in Buenos Aires (US$2). The Terminal de Omnibus in La Plata (☎ 421-0992) is at Calles 4 and 42.

Train From Estación Constitución (Map 9), Transportes Metropolitana SA General Roca (TMR; ☎ 4304-0021) has 37 weekday trains to La Plata (1½ hours, US$1.50), slightly fewer on Saturdays, Sundays and holidays. The last train returns around 11 pm, but they start up again between 3 and 4 am.

Featuring a striking Art Nouveau dome and wrought-iron awning, La Plata's turn-of-the-century Estación Ferrocarril General Roca (☎ 421-9377, 421-2575), at Av 1 and Calle 44 has undergone a much needed modernization and repainting.

MORENO

About 40km west of Buenos Aires by RN7 (the road to Luján), Moreno is most notable as the site of the **Museo Florencio Molina Campos**, honoring the artist responsible for the humorously distinctive *gauchesco* paintings and illustrations that adorned calendars for so many years (and now provide chapter endings for this book). At Molina Campos (formerly Güemes) 348, the museum (☎ 462-6904) unfortunately keeps very limited hours (4 to 7 pm weekends only).

From Estación Once in Balvanera (Map 6), the Ferrocarril Sarmiento offers commuter rail service to and from Moreno. Bus No 52B from Plaza Miserere (Once) and bus No 57A from Plaza Italia in Palermo (Map 13) both pass near the museum.

Moreno's area code is ☎ 237.

LUJÁN

According to legend, in 1630 oxen pulling a cart that contained a small terra-cotta statue of the Virgin Mary en route from Pernambuco to a Portuguese farmer in Santiago del Estero would not budge until the gauchos removed the image. The devoted owner cleared the site and built a chapel where the Virgin had chosen to stay, about 5km from present-day Luján.

La Virgen de Luján soon became Argentina's patron saint, and she has since moved up to the French Gothic basilica, one of the city's two main tourist attractions. The other is a colonial historical-museum complex. On the east bank of its namesake river, Luján (population 39,000) is only 65km west of Buenos Aires via RN7.

Information

There's an information kiosk at the corner of Lavalle and 9 de Julio, but it's open erratically. Luján's Comisión de Promoción Turística (☎ 420-453, 433-500) in the Edificio La Cúpula, at the west end of Lavalle, is more reliably open and better supplied with information and brochures. Hours are 8 am to 2 pm weekdays.

Luján's area code is ☎ 2323.

The Rise & Romance of the Gaucho

No one could have predicted the rise to respectability of that accidental icon, the Argentine gaucho. Dressed in baggy *bombacha* (trousers), the modern gaucho, with a leather *rastra* (belt) round his waist and a sharp *facón* (knife) in his rastra, is the idealized version of a complex historical figure. Directly or indirectly, to most Argentines and foreigners, he is a latter-day version of the romantic characters portrayed in José Hernández' epic poem *Martín Fierro* and Ricardo Güiraldes' novel *Don Segundo Sombra*. Like his counterpart, the North American cowboy, he has received elaborate cinematic treatment. Ironically, only when he became a sanitized anachronism did he achieve celebrity.

Without the rich pastures of the Pampas and the cattle and horses that multiplied on them, the gaucho could never have flourished. In a sense, he replaced the Pampas Indian; usually a *mestizo*, the gaucho hunted burgeoning herds of cattle just as the Querandí Indians did the guanaco and rhea. As long as cattle were many, people few, and beef, hides and tallow of limited commercial value, his subsistence and independence were assured. This achieved, he could amuse himself gambling and drinking in the saloon or *pulpería*. In the 19th century, observers like Domingo F Sarmiento thought the gaucho indolent but grudgingly acknowledged that he led a good life:

> Country life, then, has developed all the physical but none of the intellectual powers of the gaucho. His moral character is of the quality to be expected from his habit of triumphing over the forces of nature; it is strong, haughty and energetic. Without instruction, and indeed without need of any, without means of support as without wants, he is happy in the midst of his poverty and privations, which are not such to one who never knew nor wished for greater pleasures than are his already.

Even as Sarmiento wrote, the gaucho's independent, self-sufficient way of life was in decline. Just as the gauchos had replaced the Pampas Indians, large landowners squeezed out the gauchos. The primitive livestock economy gave way to *saladeros* (salting plants), which made a wider variety of products – processed hides, tallow and salted or jerked beef.

For their saladeros, landowners needed labor. The gaucho, with his horseback skills, was a desirable if unwilling source of manpower, and landowners were not reluctant to use their influence to coerce him. Classifying the gaucho as a 'lawless' element, discriminatory laws soon required internal passports, and men without jobs could no longer travel freely over the Pampas.

Basílica Nuestra Señora de Luján

Every year four million pilgrims from throughout Argentina visit Luján to honor the Virgin for her intercession in affairs of peace, health, forgiveness and consolation. The terminus of their journeys is this imposing basilica, where the 'Virgencita' (she is known by the affectionate diminutive) occupies a *camarín* (chamber) behind the main altar. Devotees have covered the stairs with plaques acknowledging her favors.

Every October since the Dirty War, a massive Peregrinación de la Juventud (youth pilgrimage) originates in Buenos Aires' Once Station, 62km away. In the days of the military dictatorship, when any mass demonstration was forbidden, this 18-hour walk had tremendous symbolic importance, but since the restoration of democracy it has become more exclusively devotional. The other large gathering of believers takes place May 8, the Virgin's day.

Within the basilica, Irish visitors, in particular, will be interested to find Gaelic inscriptions, Irish surnames and a window dedicated to St Patrick. Near the basilica,

---

Punishment for 'vagrancy' was often military conscription. As sheep replaced cattle on the Pampas, land was fenced and marked, forcing the gaucho to the fringes or onto the estancias.

Unlike the frontier, the estancia was not a democracy, and the gaucho was no longer his own master, even though his livestock skills were still in seasonal demand. He became instead a hired hand for an institution whose physical aspects bespoke hierarchy. As European immigrants came to occupy many saladero jobs, which were often detested by real gauchos, friction arose between gaucho 'natives' and Italian 'gringos.' Despite resistance, the day of the free-roaming gaucho was over by the late 19th century.

Ironically, about this time, Argentina discovered the gaucho's virtues in what has become known as *literatura gauchesca* ('gauchesque' literature, or literature *about*, as opposed to *by*, the usually illiterate gauchos). *Martín Fierro* romanticized the life of the independent gaucho at the point at which he was disappearing, much like the open-range cowboy of the American West.

Hernández deplored both opportunistic strongmen like Juan Manuel de Rosas, who claimed to speak for the gaucho, and 'civilizers' like Sarmiento, who had no scruples about discarding the people of the countryside. The gaucho's fierce independence, so often depicted as lawlessness, became admirable, and Hernández almost single-handedly rehabilitated the

image of the gaucho as Argentines sought an identity in a country rapidly being transformed by immigration and economic modernization. Having fought alongside the gaucho, Hernández eloquently championed him in the public forums of his country and pleaded for his integration into the country's future, noting the positive gaucho values that even Sarmiento admitted: courtesy, independence and generosity. By the time the gaucho's fate was decided, urban Argentines had elevated him to a mythical status, incorporating these values into their own belief system.

LIBRARY OF CONGRESS

whose towers rise 106m above the Pampas, the **Museo Devocional** houses *ex-votos* (gifts) to the Virgin, including objects of silver, wood and wax, musical instruments and icons from all over the world. It's open 1 to 6 pm Tuesday to Friday, 10 am to 6 pm weekends.

Complejo Museográfico Enrique Udaondo

Occupying three full hectares bounded by Calles Lezica y Torrezuri, Lavalle, San Martín and Parque Ameghino, this museum complex includes the 30 rooms of the **Museo Colonial e Histórico**, housed in colonial buildings like the **Cabildo** and the so-called **Casa del Virrey** (no viceroy ever lived there). Exhibits cover the area's history from pre-Columbian times but stop abruptly in the mid-20th century. The **Museo de Transporte** has four showrooms with a remarkable collection of colonial and later horsecarts, the first steam locomotive to serve the city from Buenos Aires, and a patio with a windmill and a horse-powered mill. The most offbeat exhibit is the stuffed remains of the Argentine *criollo* horses ridden by adventurer AF Tschiffely from Buenos Aires to Washington, DC in the 1930s.

The museum complex (☎ 420-245) is open 12:15 to 5:30 pm Wednesday to Sunday; admission costs US$1. The combined library/archive is open 9:30 am to 6 pm weekdays but closes in January.

Places to Stay

Camping For about US$4 per person per day, *Camping El Triángulo* (☎ 430-116) on RN 7 (Av Carlos Pellegrini) across the Río Luján is basic and less than perfectly maintained, but has plenty of shade and is OK for a night. There is another pricier campground along the river near the Dirección Municipal de Turismo at Edificio La Cúpula. Informally, pilgrims camp just about anywhere they like.

Hospedajes & Hotels Several budget hotels cater to the pilgrims who come throughout the year. Opposite the bus terminal, *Hospedaje Royal* (☎ 421-295), 9 de Julio 696, has small singles/doubles at US$20/28. *Hotel Victoria* (☎ 420-582), Lavalle 136, has doubles for US$30, but without breakfast. On the north side of the basilica at Lavalle 114, friendly *Hotel Carena* (☎ 423-828) charges US$30 for a single or double with private bath.

Also nearby is dark and threadbare but clean and friendly *Hotel Venecia*, Almirante Brown 100, which has small rooms with private baths and fans for US$20/25.

South of the basilica, the once-elegant *Hotel de la Paz* (☎ 424-034), 9 de Julio 1054, has friendly owners and acceptable rooms for US$35/40 with breakfast. The unlikeliest hotel name in this major devotional center belongs to *Hotel Eros* (☎ 420-797), San Martín 129. Very clean, small rooms, but without exterior windows, cost US$42/50 with private bath.

Probably the best place to stay is the new *Hotel Hoxón* (☎ 429-970), 9 de Julio 769, where rates start at US$58 for a double, including breakfast and pool access.

Places to Eat

There's a cluster of cheap, fixed-menu restaurants near the basilica along Av Nuestra Señora de Luján, where very aggressive waiters nearly yank tourists off the sidewalk. These places are pretty much interchangeable, but most of them are pretty good values.

Half a block off the avenue at San Martín 135, *Berlín* serves Germanic specialties. Off the central Plaza Colón, the quiet *Restaurant Don Chiquito*, Colón 964, has excellent but pricey Argentine food. Along the river, north of the basilica, *El Colonial* (☎ 425-226) is a step above most other restaurants in town.

The best in town, though, is *L'Eau Vive*, Constitución 2112, between Entre Ríos and Doctor Luppi, an outstanding French restaurant run by Carmelite nuns from around the world. The US$11 midday menu is superb value, but potential diners should be aware of the limited hours: noon to 2:15 pm for lunch, 8 to 10 pm for dinner (a very early closing hour for Argentines). The service is friendly and attentive, and the restaurant is entirely nonsmoking.

Entertainment

The *Cine Nuevo Numancia 1* (☎ 430-860) is at San Martín 398, while the *Cine Nuevo Numancia 2* (☎ 430-860) is nearby at Italia 967.

The *Old Swan Pub* (☎ 433-346), San Martín 546, features salsa and merengue Wednesday nights, tango Thursday nights.

Getting There & Away

Bus Luján's Estación Terminal de Omnibus (☎ 420-032, 420-040) is on Av de Nuestra Señora del Rosario between Almirante Brown and Dr Reat, three blocks north of the basilica. Transporte Luján (Línea 52) leaves from Plaza Miserere (near Estación Once) in Buenos Aires (Map 6); Transportes Atlántida (Línea 57) connects Luján with Plaza Italia in Palermo. Talsa leaves frequently from Once for US$3.

Train The Ferrocarril Sarmiento (☎ 420-439), at Av España and Belgrano in Luján, still runs trains daily to and from Estación Once (Subte: Plaza Miserere; Map 6) in Buenos Aires.

CAPILLA DEL SEÑOR

This small town, 85km northwest of Buenos Aires via RN8 and RP39, is best known as the Sunday destination of the **Tren Histórico**, a steam locomotive pulling antique cars from the capital's Estación Federico Lacroze (end of the line for Subte Línea D; Map 4). The basic cost for the excursion is US$30, but it can be considerably higher if you indulge yourself in 1st-class comfort and eat and drink heartily in the diner. For more details, contact the Ferroclub Argentino (☎ 4373-7020) or go to Leiza Tur (☎ 4322-3091), San Martín 543, 2nd floor (Map 5).

SAN ANTONIO DE ARECO

Dating from the early-18th-century construction of a chapel in honor of San Antonio de Padua, this serene village is the symbolic center of Argentina's vestigial gaucho culture and host to the country's biggest gaucho celebration, Día de la Tradición, in November. Nestled in the verdant Pampas of northern Buenos Aires province, it was the setting for Ricardo Güiraldes'

famous coming-of-age-on-the-Pampas novel *Don Segundo Sombra* (1927). Güiraldes' nephew Adolfo played the role of Don Segundo in the 1969 film version, in which many locals served as extras.

Unlike nearly every other Argentine city, San Antonio's street life centers not around the plaza but on the main commercial street of Alsina, where there's a wealth of quality artisanal goods for sale. This is one of the best places in the country for typical souvenirs. On the south bank of the Río Areco, 113km west of Buenos Aires, San Antonio is an exceptionally popular weekend destination for *porteños*. June 13 is the Día del Santo Patrono (Patron Saint's Day).

Information

Friendly but sometimes patronizing to foreigners, San Antonio's Dirección de Turismo (☎ 453-165) is on Castex between Ruiz de Arellano and Zapiola. It's open 8:30 am to 5:30 pm weekdays, 9:30 am to 5:30 pm weekends (when it serves up to 800 visitors daily), and distributes a useful pocket-size guide, updated monthly, with a map and other useful information. It also distributes *Pregón Turismo*, a tabloid-size publication that provides more detailed material on San Antonio's attractions. There's another small information kiosk, open only sporadically, on Calle de los Martínez near the junction with RN8.

San Antonio's area code is ☎ 2326.

Walking Tour

San Antonio's compact center lends itself to walking. At the beginning of the 18th century, **Plaza Ruiz de Arellano** was the site of the corrals of the town's founding *estanciero*. In its center, the **Monumento a Vieytes** honors locally born Juan Hipólito Vieytes, a figure in the early independence movement. Around the plaza are several historic buildings, including the **Iglesia Parroquial** (Parish Church) and the **Casa de los Martínez** (site of the main house of the original Ruiz de Arellano estancia). The **Centro Cultural Usina Vieja**, half a block north of the plaza, is well worth a visit.

At the corner of E Zerboni and M Moreno, the **Parque de Flora y Fauna Autóctona**

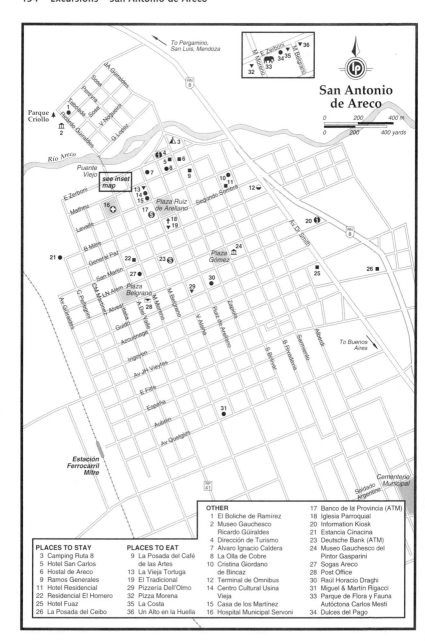

To Pergamino,
San Luis, Mendoza

RN 8

Parque
Criollo
2

Río Areco

Puente
Viejo

see inset
map

E Zerboni

Matheu

Lavalle

B Mitre

21

General Paz

San Martín

Plaza
Belgrano

27

San Antonio
de Areco

0   200   400 m
0   200   400 yards

3

1
4
5   6
7   8
9
10
11
12
13
14
15   Plaza Ruiz
17   de Arellano
16
18
19

Segundo Sombra

20

24
Plaza
Gómez

22   23
25   26

30
29
28

To Buenos
Aires

31

Estación
Ferrocarril
Mitre

RP 41

Cementerio
Municipal

Soldado
Argentino

E Zerboni
M Moreno   M Belgrano
34 35
32   33   36

OTHER
1 El Boliche de Ramírez
2 Museo Gauchesco
   Ricardo Güiraldes
4 Dirección de Turismo
7 Alvaro Ignacio Caldera
8 La Olla de Cobre
10 Cristina Giordano
   de Bincaz
12 Terminal de Omnibus
14 Centro Cultural Usina
   Vieja
15 Casa de los Martínez
16 Hospital Municipal Servoni

17 Banco de la Provincia (ATM)
18 Iglesia Parroquial
20 Information Kiosk
21 Estancia Cinacina
23 Deutsche Bank (ATM)
24 Museo Gauchesco del
   Pintor Gasparini
27 Sogas Areco
28 Post Office
30 Raúl Horacio Draghi
31 Miguel & Martín Rigacci
33 Parque de Flora y Fauna
   Autóctona Carlos Mesti
34 Dulces del Pago

PLACES TO STAY
3 Camping Ruta 8
5 Hotel San Carlos
6 Hostal de Areco
9 Ramos Generales
11 Hotel Residencial
22 Residencial El Hornero
25 Hotel Fuaz
26 La Posada del Ceibo

PLACES TO EAT
9 La Posada del Café
   de las Artes
13 La Vieja Tortuga
19 El Tradicional
29 Pizzería Dell'Olmo
32 Pizza Morena
35 La Costa
36 Un Alto en la Huella

Carlos Mesti is San Antonio's modest zoo, open 9 am to noon and 2 to 7 pm daily; admission costs US$1. Just to the north, conspicuously featured in the film version of *Don Segundo Sombra*, the **Puente Viejo** (1857) across the Río Areco follows the original cart road to northern Argentina. Once a toll crossing, it's now a pedestrian bridge leading to the **Parque Criollo y Museo Gauchesco Ricardo Güiraldes**, San Antonio's major attraction.

The elderly painter Osvaldo Gasparini and his son Luis operate the **Museo Gauchesco del Pintor Gasparini** (☎ 453-930), at the corner of Alvear and S Bolívar. Containing personal effects of Güiraldes as well as the owners' gauchesco artwork, it's open 8 am to 8 pm daily. Admission is free.

Ricardo Güiraldes and Segundo Ramírez, the real-life role model for the character Don Segundo Sombra, both lie in the **Cementerio Municipal** at the south end of town, at the junction of RN 8 and Soldado Argentino.

Centro Cultural Usina Vieja

On V Alsina between Matheu and Lavalle, dating from 1901, the Centro Cultural Usina Vieja is a recycled power plant whose exhibits and presentations have improved greatly in the past several years. Copies of Florencio Molina Campos' amusing caricatures of gaucho life, for instance, are now professionally mounted, and there are excellent metal sculptures by the local artist Perera, most notably *La Cautiva*. Work by local artisans is also on display. Admission is free. It's open 8 am to 1 pm weekdays, 10 am to 5 pm weekends.

Parque Criollo y Museo Gauchesco Ricardo Güiraldes

Inaugurated by the provincial government in 1938, a decade after Güiraldes' death, this elaborate museum is, on one level, a spurious Gaucholand of restored or fabricated buildings idealizing and fossilizing the history of the Pampas. On the other hand, the contents are genuine and the complex's 90 hectares also provide an unalloyed introduction to the gaucho as a modern cultural phenomenon, allowing visitors to sense the degree to which his consciousness has permeated contemporary Argentine society.

The centerpiece of the complex is the **Casa del Museo**, a 20th-century reproduction of an 18th-century *casco* (ranch house), which includes the Sala de los Escritores on gaucho literature (including the desk and chair of Walter Owen, who translated the gauchesco classic *Martín Fierro* into English); the Sala

Historic Estancias

Surrounding San Antonio de Areco are a number of *estancias* offering overnight accommodations for around US$125 per person, plus IVA, with full board; activities like horseback riding and polo usually cost extra. Film director María Luisa Bemberg shot part of her historical drama *Camila* at **Estancia La Bamba**. (Visit San Antonio's Dirección de Turismo for details on accommodations and tours.)

For a day in the country, countless porteños choose **Estancia La Cinacina**, where US$30 buys an all-you-can-eat *asado*, entertainment in the form of folkloric music and dance, a tour of the estancia's museum, and horseback riding. Estancia La Cinacina (☎ 42045), at B Mitre 9 only six blocks from Plaza Ruiz de Arellano, is less crowded and more comfortable on weekdays. Its Buenos Aires representative is Empresa Que La Opera (☎ 4342-1986, 4342-2841), Bartolomé Mitre 734, 10th floor; tours from the capital cost US$60 including transportation.

Unquestionably the most historic of nearby estancias is the Güiraldes family's **Estancia La Porteña** (☎ 4322-6023/5694 in Buenos Aires), which dates from 1850 and has a garden designed by the renowned French architect Charles Thays, responsible for major public parks including Buenos Aires' Jardín Botánico. **Estancia El Ombú** (☎ 92080; 4793-2454 in Buenos Aires) belonged to General Pablo Ricchieri, who first inflicted universal military conscription on the country.

Pieza de Estanciero with a wooden bed belonging to Juan Manuel de Rosas (perhaps the ultimate rural landowner); and the Sala del Gaucho with horsegear and various works of gauchesque art. Two rooms are dedicated to Güiraldes himself, another to his wife Adelina del Carril de Güiraldes, and yet another to his painter cousin Alberto.

More authentic, or at least more venerable, than the Casa del Museo is the **Pulpería La Blanqueada**, a mid-19th-century building with a credible re-creation of a rural tavern. Alongside the pulpería are **La Tahona**, an 1848 flour mill brought here from the town of Mercedes, and the **Galpón y Cuarto de Sogas**, where the estancia might have stored its carriages. Nearby is **La Ermita de San Antonio**, a colonial-style chapel with some colonial artifacts.

North of the river on Camino Ricardo Güiraldes, reached via the Puente Viejo, the grounds and buildings of the Museo Gauchesco (☎ 452-583) are open 11 am to 5 pm daily except Tuesday. Admission is US$2 for adults, US$1 for retired people, for free for children under age 12.

Special Events

Lasting a week in November, the 90-year-old Fiesta de la Tradición celebrates San Antonio's gaucho past; by presidential decree, San Antonio is the 'sede provincial de la tradición' (provincial site of tradition). The actual Día de la Tradición is November 10, but celebrations are moved to the following Sunday for convenience. Attractions include lectures, artisanal exhibits, guided tours of historic sites, displays of horsemanship, folk dancing and the like. If you're visiting San Antonio at this time, make reservations far in advance for the limited accommodations.

Places to Stay & Eat

San Antonio has decent but very limited accommodations. Prices for lodging may rise on weekends, when reservations are advisable. (All rates given here are weekend rates.) Reservations are absolutely essential during the Fiesta de la Tradición in November. At peak times, check the tourist office for B&B accommodations.

For US$5 per person, the spacious, shady riverside **Camping Ruta 8** has clean toilets and hot showers, but is prone to flooding when rains are heavy. The cheapest regular accommodations (by no means bad) are at the conveniently located **Hotel San Carlos** (☎ 453-106), at Zapiola and Zerboni, which charges US$30 double without breakfast. **Hotel Residencial** (☎ 452-166), Segundo Sombra and B Rivadavia, is comparably priced but also offers 15% student discounts.

Residencial El Hornero (☎ 452-733), at Moreno 250 and San Martín, charges US$45 without breakfast, while **Hotel Fuaz** (☎ 452-487) at Av Dr Smith 488 has rooms for US$60 with breakfast. Another good value is **La Posada del Ceibo** (☎ 454-614) on Irigoyen between RN 8 and Av Dr Smith, which charges US$55 for a double with breakfast. San Antonio's most attractive accommodations are at **Hostal de Areco** (☎ 454-063), Zapiola 25, which charges US$70 with breakfast.

San Antonio has fewer places to eat than one might expect, though the situation is improving. For homemade meals, try **El Tradicional**, Alsina 173. Otherwise, the only halfway appealing place downtown is **Pizzería Dell'Olmo** (☎ 452-506), Alsina 365.

Un Alto en la Huella (☎ 455-595), a parrilla at Belgrano and Zerboni, has a decent tenedor libre for about US$7, while nearby **La Costa**, across the street, is slightly more expensive. Two good new choices are **Pizza Morena** (☎ 456-391) at the corner of Zerboni and Moreno (good sidewalk seating as well) and **La Vieja Tortuga** (☎ 456-080) at Alsina 60, alongside the Centro Cultural Usina Vieja. The latter has live folkloric music at 10 pm Saturdays.

Decorated as an early-20th-century general store almost to the point of self-parody, **La Posada del Café de las Artes** (☎ 456-376), part of the Ramos Generales complex at Bolívar 66, nevertheless has good homemade pasta and the like at reasonable prices (hold the salt, though). They also offer excellent accommodations for US$50 a double.

Shopping

San Antonio's artisans are known throughout the country, with many of their disciples practicing their trades in other cities and provinces. Mate paraphernalia, rastras (silver-studded belts) and facones (long-bladed knives), produced by skilled silversmiths, are among the most typical. Internationally known Raúl Horacio Draghi (☎ 454-207), Guido 391, also works in leather; other top silversmiths include Miguel and Martín Rigacci (☎ 454-016), Av Quetgles 333, and Alvaro Ignacio Caldera (☎ 452-599), Alsina 17.

For horse gear and gaucho clothing, check out Sogas Areco (☎ 453-797), Moreno 280. Cristina Giordano de Bincaz (☎ 452-829), Sarmiento 112, sells weavings. El Boliche de Ramírez, on Ricardo Güiraldes opposite the Museo Gauchesco, carries a bit of everything.

For artisanal chocolates, try La Olla de Cobre (☎ 453-105), on Matheu between Zapiola and Ruiz de Arellano. In addition to its restaurant, Ramos Generales, Bolívar 66, also produces homemade sweets, cheeses and salami. Dulces del Pago (☎ 454-751), Zerboni 136, makes a variety of fruit preserves.

Getting There & Away

Frequent buses from Buenos Aires take 1½ hours (US$3.50). San Antonio's Terminal de Omnibus (☎ 456-387) is at Av Dr Smith and General Paz. TAC and Sierras de Córdoba provide long-distance services between Buenos Aires and the provinces of Cuyo (San Luis, Mendoza and San Juan) and Córdoba.

URUGUAY

Uruguay requires visas of all foreigners, except those from neighboring countries (who need only national identification cards) and nationals of Western Europe, Israel, Japan and the USA. All visitors need a tourist card; valid for 90 days, it is renewable for another 90.

Responding to new Canadian visa requirements for Uruguayans, Uruguay has reciprocally imposed visa requirements on Canadians. These include a return ticket, a photograph and a payment of US$42 to a Uruguayan consulate (plus another US$56 for same-day service). Canadians (and others such as Australians and New Zealanders) may well question whether a day trip from Buenos Aires is worth the cost and hassle.

Uruguay's unit of currency is the peso. At press time, one US dollar or one Argentine peso equaled 10.6 Uruguayan pesos. However, US dollar and Argentine pesos are widely accepted for tourist services.

Uruguay's country code is ☎ 598.

(For a listing of websites on Uruguay, see Internet Resources in the Facts for the Visitor chapter.)

COLONIA

Only an hour or two from Buenos Aires across the Río de la Plata, Colonia (full name Colonia del Sacramento) is one of the Southern Cone's underappreciated gems, attracting many thousands of Argentines but only a handful of the foreign tourists who visit the Argentine capital.

Founded in 1680 by the Portuguese Manoel Lobo, the town occupied a strategic position almost exactly opposite Buenos Aires across the Río de la Plata, but it was more important as a source of contraband, which undercut Spain's jealously defended mercantile trade monopoly. British goods made their way from Colonia into Buenos Aires and the interior through surreptitious exchange with the Portuguese in the Delta del Paraná. For this reason, Spanish forces intermittently besieged Portugal's riverside outpost for decades.

Although the two powers agreed over the cession of Colonia to Spain around 1750, the agreement failed when Jesuit missionaries on the upper Paraná refused to comply with the proposed exchange of territory in their area. Spain finally captured the city in 1762 but failed to hold it until 1777, when authorities created the Virreinato del Río de la Plata (Viceroyalty of the River Plate). From this time, Colonia's commercial importance declined, as foreign goods could proceed directly to Buenos Aires.

The capital of its department, the streets of its historic colonial core shaded by sycamores in the summer heat, Colonia is a pleasant town of about 30,000. In the course of the day, the town discloses its many aspects as sunlight strikes whitewashed colonial buildings and the river; the latter, living up to its name, is silvery in the morning but turns brownish by midday.

Big changes may be in store for Colonia if, as proposed, a massive bridge crosses the Río de la Plata from Punta Colorada, midway between Buenos Aires and the city of La Plata. The bridge project, which has attracted criticism on economic, environmental and social grounds, is still in the early planning stages.

Information

The office of the municipal Dirección de Turismo (☎ 26141) is at General Flores 499. Both helpful and increasingly well informed (though not always able to speak English), the staff has numerous brochures difficult to obtain elsewhere. It's open 7 am to 8 pm weekdays, 10 am to 7 pm weekends. The national Ministerio de Turismo (☎ 24897) maintains a ferry port branch, open 9 am to 3 pm daily.

Arriving at the port from Buenos Aires, you can change money at Banco República, which charges US$1 commission for traveler's checks. Downtown, try Cambio Colonia at General Flores and Alberto Méndez or Cambio Viaggio at General Flores 350.

Colonia's area code is ☎ 52.

Walking Tour

Also known as La Colonia Portuguesa (the Portuguese Colony), Colonia's Barrio Histórico begins at the **Puerta de Campo**, the restored entrance to the old city on Calle Manoel Lobo, which dates from the governorship of Vasconcellos in 1745. A thick fortified wall runs south along the Paseo de San Miguel to the river. A short distance west is the **Plaza Mayor 25 de Mayo**, off which leads the narrow, cobbled **Calle de los Suspiros** (Street of Whispers), lined with tile-and-stucco colonial houses. Just beyond this street, the **Museo Portugués** has good exhibits on the Portuguese period, including Lusitanian and colonial dress. Colonia's museums are generally open 11:30 am to 6 pm,

but closed Tuesdays and Wednesdays. A US$1 admission charge is valid for all the museums for one day.

At the southwest corner of the Plaza Mayor are the **Casa de Lavalleja**, once the residence of General Lavalleja, and the ruins of the 17th-century **Convento de San Francisco** and the 19th-century **faro** (lighthouse). Open 10:30 am to noon weekends, the lighthouse provides an excellent view of the old town for free. At the west end of the Plaza Mayor, on Calle del Comercio, is the **Museo Municipal**; next door is the so-called **Casa del Virrey**, the Viceroy's House, although no viceroy ever lived in Colonia (maybe one slept here). At the northwest corner of the plaza, on Calle de las Misiones de los Tapes, the **Archivo Regional** contains a small museum and bookshop.

At the west end of Misiones de los Tapes, the **Museo de los Azulejos** (Museum of Tiles) is a 17th-century house with a sampling of colonial tilework. (The museum was closed at last pass.) From there, the riverfront **Paseo de San Gabriel** leads to the north to Calle del Colegio, where a right to Calle del Comercio leads to the **Capilla Jesuítica**, the ruined Jesuit chapel. Going east along Av General Flores and then turning south on Calle Vasconcellos, you reach the landmark **Iglesia Matriz** on the Plaza de Armas, also known as Plaza Manoel Lobo.

Across General Flores, at España and San José, the **Museo Español** has exhibitions of replica colonial pottery, clothing and maps. At the north end of the street is the **Puerto Viejo**, the old port. One block east, at Calle del Virrey Cevallos and Rivadavia, the **Teatro Bastión del Carmen** is a theater building that incorporates part of the city's ancient fortifications.

Real de San Carlos

At the turn of the century, naturalized Argentine entrepreneur Nicolás Mihanovich spent US$1.5 million to build an immense tourist complex at the Real de San Carlos, 5km west of Colonia, at a spot where Spanish troops once camped before attacking the Portuguese outpost. Among the attractions erected by Mihanovich, a Dalmatian

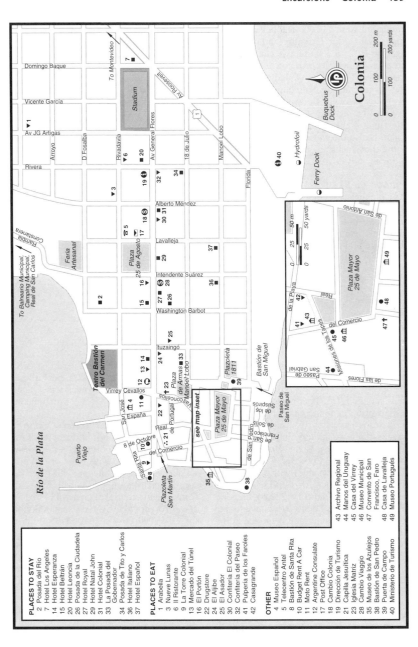

Colonia

Río de la Plata

PLACES TO STAY
2   Posada del Río
7   Hotel Los Angeles
14 Hotel Esperanza
15 Hotel Beltrán
20 Hotel Leoncia
26 Posada de la Ciudadela
27 Hotel Royal
29 Hotel Natal John
31 Hotel Colonial
33 La Posada del Gobernador
34 Posada de Tito y Carlos
36 Hotel Italiano
37 Hotel Español

PLACES TO EAT
1   Arabella
3   Nueve Lunas
6   Il Ristorante
9   La Torre Colonial
13 Mercado del Túnel
16 El Portón
22 Drugstore
24 El Aljibe
25 El Asador
30 Confitería El Colonial
32 Confitería del Paseo
41 Pulpería de los Faroles
42 Casagrande

OTHER
4   Museo Español
5   Telecentro Antel
8   Bastión de Santa Rita
10 Budget Rent A Car
11 Moto Rent
12 Argentine Consulate
17 Post Office
18 Cambio Colonia
19 Dirección de Turismo
21 Capilla Jesuítica
23 Iglesia Matriz
28 Cambio Viaggio
35 Museo de los Azulejos
38 Bastión de San Pedro
39 Puerta de Campo
40 Ministerio de Turismo
43 Archivo Regional
44 Manos del Uruguay
45 Casa del Virrey
46 Museo Municipal
47 Convento de San Francisco, Faro
48 Casa de Lavalleja
49 Museo Portugués

immigrant, were a 10,000-seat bullring (made superfluous after Uruguay outlawed bullfights in 1912), a 3000-seat *jai alai frontón*, a hotel-casino with its own power plant and a racecourse. (The casino failed in 1917 when the Argentine government began to tax every boat crossing the river.)

Only the racecourse functions today, but the ruins make an interesting excursion. There is also the **Museo Municipal Real de San Carlos**, focusing on paleontology, which unfortunately keeps no fixed hours.

Places to Stay

As Colonia has become a more popular destination for Argentine and international travelers, hotel keepers have upgraded accommodations and prices have risen, but there are still reasonable alternatives. The municipal tourist office on General Flores may help find B&B lodgings when things are full. Some hotels charge higher rates on weekends (Friday through Sunday) than weekdays (Monday through Thursday).

Budget The *Camping Municipal de Colonia* (☎ 24444) sits in a eucalyptus grove at Real de San Carlos, 5km from the Barrio Histórico. Close to the Balneario Municipal, its excellent facilities are open all year and are easily accessible by public transport. Fees are about US$4 per person.

Except for camping, really cheap accommodations have nearly disappeared. The cheapest in town, undergoing renovation at the time of writing, is the *Hotel Español* (☎ 22314), Manoel Lobo 377, with large but dark singles (if available) with shared bath for US$10, doubles for US$15. The very central *Hotel Colonial* (☎ 22906), General Flores 440, charges US$13/20 a single/double without breakfast. German is spoken at the newly popular *Posada de Tito y Carlos* (☎ 24438), 18 de Julio 491, which charges US$25/35 for clean rooms with hot water and TV. Another good choice is *Posada de la Ciudadela* (☎ 22683), Washington Barbot 164, where rates are US$20 per person.

Mid-Range The *Hotel Los Angeles* (☎ 22335), Av Roosevelt 203, is a modern,

impersonal building on a busy street some distance from the Barrio Histórico, but the service is good. Its singles/doubles are US$28/40 on weekdays, US$36/58 on weekends (breakfast included). The upgraded *Hotel Italiano* (☎ 22103), Manoel Lobo 341, charges US$35 for doubles with shared bath, US$55 with private bath and TV, breakfast included. Some rooms have balconies.

One of Colonia's best values is the serene *Posada del Río* (☎ 23002), on tree-lined Washington Barbot 258 near a pleasant sandy beach, which charges US$40/55 with private bath. Friendly, usually quiet (despite occasional noise from a nearby bar on weekends) and very clean, with all rooms facing onto a central patio, *Hotel Beltrán* (☎ 22955), General Flores 311, is one of Colonia's oldest hotels. Since remodeling, rates (including breakfast) are US$36 a double with shared bath, or US$45 with private bath, but prices rise to US$70 double on weekends. It has also opened an upscale restaurant.

Downtown *Hotel Natal John* (☎ 22081), General Flores 394, is good value for US$25 per person with TV and breakfast; the 6th floor restaurant has outstanding views. Rates at *Hotel Leoncia* (☎ 22369), Rivera 214, are US$45/60 with breakfast, while *Hotel Esperanza* (☎ 22922), near the entrance to the Barrio Histórico at General Flores 237, charges US$55/75 with breakfast.

Top End The *Gran Hotel Casino El Mirador* (☎ 22004), distant from the Barrio Histórico on Av Roosevelt, is a luxurious but sterile highrise with none of Colonia's unique personality. Rates are US$70 per person with half-board, US$80 with full board. Conveniently central at General Flores 340, *Hotel Royal* (☎ 23139) has singles/doubles for US$60/90 on weekdays, US$80/120 on weekends. Probably the most distinctive accommodations are at *La Posada del Gobernador* (☎ 23018), 18 de Julio 205 in the Barrio Histórico, but rooms are arguably overpriced at US$105 a double.

Places to Eat

Confitería El Colonial (☎ 22906), General Flores 432, is a reasonably priced breakfast

Tilework at Palermo's Plaza Italia

A residential street in Palermo Viejo

Relax or row at Parque 3 de Febrero

BRIAN McGILLOWAY

Taxis outside the Retiro train station

WAYNE BERNHARDSON

Recoleta street performer

ROBERT FRERCK

Recoleta's Plaza Intendente Alvear

Twelve tails follow one *paseaperro* through a Recoleta park

Cementerio de la Recoleta

Retiro's Torre de los Ingleses

Boats on the Delta del Paraná

Colonia, Uruguay

A *conventillo* in Montevideo, Uruguay

spot, but recent reports suggest their once enormous hot croissants have shrunk and it's not the value it once was. *Confitería del Paseo*, at the corner of Rivera and Av General Flores, may now be a better choice for breakfast or light meals.

One of Colonia's best values is *El Asador*, Ituzaingó 168, an inexpensive parrilla often jammed with locals. *El Portón* (☎ 25318), General Flores 333, is a more upscale but appealing parrilla.

El Aljibe (☎ 25342), another parrilla at General Flores and Ituzaingó, appears to charge more because of its attractive colonial setting. Down the block at General Flores 229, the extensive menu at **Mercado del Túnel** (☎ 24666) varies in quality; there are some very good dishes, but choose selectively (try eyeing the dishes of neighboring patrons). At the corner of Rivera and Rivadavia, *Il Ristorante* is a very good Italian choice.

Pulpería de los Faroles (☎ 25399), at Del Comercio and Misiones de los Tapes in the Barrio Histórico, has an upscale ambiance but is not outrageously expensive for a good meal. **Casagrande**, two doors away, is a good *confitería* that doubles as a handicrafts market.

At the tip of the Barrio Histórico, *La Torre Colonial* (☎ 24639) is a good pizzería in a remodeled tower. Readers' recommendations include the pizza at **Nueve Lunas**, at Rivadavia 413 just off Plaza 25 de Agosto, and **Arabella**, Av Artigas 384.

Entertainment

Colonia's liveliest nightspot, also a good place to eat, is **Drugstore**, Vasconcellos 179.

Shopping

Colonia's Feria Artesanal (Crafts Fair) has moved from its former site on the Plaza Mayor, in the Ciudad Vieja, to a new permanent spot at the corner of Suárez and Fosalba; it's open 9:30 am to 7:30 pm daily. Manos del Uruguay has an outlet at the corner of San Gabriel and Misiones de los Tapes, in the Ciudad Vieja.

Getting There & Away

Buenos Aires has regular ferry and *aliscafo* (hydrofoil) services to Colonia from Dársena

Norte, near downtown at the foot of Viamonte (Map 11), or from Dársena Sur, Av Pedro de Mendoza 20 in La Boca (Map 10). There is a US$10 departure tax from these terminals, which is now normally included in the fare, but ask to be sure. In Colonia, ferries land at the port at the foot of Av Roosevelt.

Ferrytur (☎ 4315-6800, 4300-1366 at Dársena Sur), Av Córdoba 699, makes two crossings to Colonia (2½ hours) every weekday, and one every Saturday and Sunday, with the ferry *Ciudad de Buenos Aires*. These depart weekdays at 8 am and 4:29 pm, weekends at 8:15 am only; return times from Colonia are noon and 8 pm weekdays, 6:59 pm Saturdays and 7 pm Sundays. Regular fares are US$23 one-way, US$17 for children ages three to nine. One-way fares for automobiles start at US$48. Day trips are available for US$31, including lunch and a city tour; there are also senior citizens' discounts.

Ferrytur's hydrofoil *Sea Cat* goes to Colonia (45 minutes) four times weekdays, three times daily on weekends for US$32 one-way; children ages three to nine pay US$24. Fares may be higher on selected peak days and in summer. There are also US$50 day trips including lunch and a city tour.

Buquebus (☎ 4313-4444, ☎ 22975 in Colonia), Av Córdoba 867, has two daily ferry sailings to Colonia on the *Eladia Isabel*, at 12:30 am daily except Sunday and at 8:15 am daily; return times from Colonia are 4 am and 7 pm. Passenger fares are the same as Ferrytur's, but slightly more expensive 1st-class service is also available. Cars weighing up to 1200kg pay US$48 exclusive of passenger fares, while those over 1200kg pay US$57. A Buquebus *colectivo* (bus or minibus) leaves the Av Córdoba office for Dársena Sur 1½ hours prior to every departure.

Buquebus also runs high-speed 'Buqueaviones' to Colonia seven times daily from Dársena Norte. Fares are identical to Ferrytur's, but more expensive 1st-class service is also available. Cars weighing in under 1200kg pay US$70, while those weighing over 1200kg pay US$80.

Passengers leaving from Colonia's ferry terminal pay a US$3 departure tax.

Getting Around

Motor scooters are an inexpensive, popular means of getting around town. Check Moto Rent on Virrey Cevallos near Av General Flores, or Budget Rent A Car (☎ 22939) at Av General Flores 91.

MONTEVIDEO

Uruguay's capital dominates the country's political, economic and cultural life even more than Buenos Aires does Argentina's. Nearly half the country's 3.2 million citizens live here, but there is a certain logic to this: Montevideo's superb natural port links the country to overseas commerce, and the almost exclusively rural economy hardly requires a competing metropolis for trade and administration.

In many ways, economic stagnation has left modern Montevideo a worn-out city where key public buildings are undistinguished, utilitarian constructions that would not be out of place in Eastern Europe. According to one *graffito*, it's 'un necrópolis de sueños rotos' (a necropolis of broken dreams). Still, the municipal administration is sprucing up public spaces like Plaza Cagancha and promoting restoration of the Ciudad Vieja (Old City), the colonial core and the city's most appealing feature.

Even more important, if Montevideo is to experience a significant renaissance, may be the emergence and growth of Mercosur, the nascent common market of Brazil, Argentina, Paraguay and Uruguay. As Mercosur's administrative headquarters, Montevideo figures to benefit more directly than any other location in the four-country customs union – even if it just takes the city's traditional bureaucratic functions to another level.

History

Spain founded Montevideo in 1726 as a response to concern over Portugal's growing influence in the Río de la Plata area. It was in turn a fortress against the Portuguese as well as British, French and Danish privateers who came in search of hides on the Banda Oriental, the 'Eastern Shore' of the Río de la Plata.

The city's port, superior to Buenos Aires in every respect except its access to the Humid Pampa, quickly made it a focal point for overseas shipping. An early-19th-century construction boom resulted in a new Iglesia Matriz, Cabildo (town hall) and other neoclassical monuments, but after independence Uruguayan authorities demolished many of these buildings and planned a new center east of the Ciudad Vieja and its port.

During the mid-19th century, the city endured an almost constant state of siege by Argentine dictator Juan Manuel de Rosas, who was determined to create a small client state to Buenos Aires. After Rosas' fall in 1851, normal commerce resumed and, between 1860 and 1911, the British-built railroad network assisted the capital's growth.

Like Buenos Aires, Montevideo absorbed numerous European immigrants in the early 20th century, when construction of the city's first locally financed meat-freezer plant was followed by two similar foreign-backed enterprises, closely linked to the export trade. Growth has continued to stimulate agricultural intensification near Montevideo to feed the rapidly increasing urban population. Much of this population consists of refugees from rural poverty who live in *conventillos*, large older houses converted into multi-family slum dwellings. Many of these are in the Ciudad Vieja, but even this population is being displaced as urban redevelopment usurps the city's picturesque but valuable central core.

Orientation

Montevideo lies on the east bank of the Río de la Plata, almost directly east of Buenos Aires on the west bank. Most visitors from Buenos Aires will arrive by ferry or hydrofoil at the Ciudad Vieja, the colonial grid on a small peninsula near the port and harbor, an area once surrounded by protective walls. To the east, the city's commercial core runs from Plaza Independencia along Av 18 de Julio to Plaza Cagancha and beyond. Across the harbor to the west, the 132m Cerro de Montevideo, the city's highest point, was a landmark for early navigators and still offers outstanding views of the city. To the east, the

Rambla, or riverfront road, leads past woodsy residential suburbs with numerous public parks and sandy beaches.

Information

The Ministerio de Turismo (☎ 409-7399) has a cubbyhole information office on the ground floor at Av Libertador General Lavalleja 1409; it's open 9 am to 6:30 pm weekdays. Look, however, for a new office due to open in the former Pluna headquarters, on the ground floor at the corner of Colonia and Lavalleja.

The Oficina de Informes (☎ 601-1757) at Terminal Tres Cruces, in the new bus station at Bulevar Artigas and Av Italia, is open 9 am to 9 pm daily and is well-prepared to deal with visitor inquiries. The very useful weekly *Guía del Ocio*, which lists cultural events, cinemas, theaters and restaurants, comes with the Friday edition of the daily *El País*.

There are many exchange houses around Plaza Cagancha and on Av 18 de Julio. Argentina's nonprofit student travel agency Asatej, an affiliate of STA Travel, has a Montevideo branch (☎ 908-0509, fax 908-4895) at Río Negro 1354, 2nd floor.

The Correo Central (main post office) is at Buenos Aires 451, corner of Misiones, in the Ciudad Vieja. Antel, the national telephone company, has convenient Telecentros at Rincón 501 in the Ciudad Vieja, at San José 1102, and at the Tres Cruces bus terminal.

Montevideo's area code is ☎ 02.

Walking Tour

To orient yourself in downtown Montevideo, take a walk from **Plaza Independencia** through the Ciudad Vieja to the port. On the plaza, an honor guard keeps 24-hour vigil over the **Mausoleo de Artigas**, topped by a 17m, 30-ton statue of the country's independence hero. The 18th-century **Palacio Estévez**, on the south side, was Government House until 1985. On the east side, the Baroque, 26-story **Palacio Salvo**, was the continent's tallest building when it opened in 1927 and is still the tallest in the city. From here, in 1939, British agents spied on the German destroyer *Graf Spee*, then at anchor in Montevideo harbor but later scuttled by

its captain. Just off the plaza is the **Teatro Solís**.

At the west end of the plaza is **La Puerta de la Ciudadela**, a modified remnant of the colonial citadel that dominated the area before its demolition in 1833. Calle Sarandí, part of which is now a *peatonal*, leads to **Plaza Constitución**, also known as Plaza Matriz, where a central sculpture, by the Italian Juan Ferrari, commemorates the establishment of Montevideo's first waterworks. On the east side of Plaza Constitución, a historical museum occupies the Cabildo (finished in 1812), a neoclassical stone structure designed by Spanish architect Tomás Toribio. Begun in 1784 and completed in 1799, the **Iglesia Matriz**, at the corner of Sarandí and Ituzaingó, is Montevideo's oldest public building, the work of Portuguese architect José de Sáa y Faría.

Detour one block northwest of Plaza Constitución to see Edmundo Prati's remarkable bas-reliefs on the **Banco La Caja Obrera** (1941), 25 de Mayo at Treinta y Tres. Returning to Calle Rincón, continue west to the Casa Rivera at Rincón and Zabala, the Museo Romántico at 25 de Mayo 428, and the Casa Lavalleja at Zabala and 25 de Mayo, all part of the **Museo Histórico Nacional**. See also the **Palacio Taranco** (1910), at 25 de Mayo and Primero de Mayo, built in an 18th-century European style by French architects commissioned by a wealthy merchant; it houses the **Museo de Arte Decorativo**, open 2 to 6 pm weekdays.

From there, visit **Plaza Zabala**, site of the colonial governor's house until its demolition in 1878; there is a statue of Montevideo's founder Bruno Mauricio de Zabala, by Spanish sculptor Lorenzo Coullant Valera. From the plaza, continue west along Washington and north to Colón and 25 de Mayo, where the **Casa Garibaldi** once sheltered the Italian hero, and then a couple blocks northwest to the **Mercado del Puerto**.

Museo Histórico Nacional

The national history museum consists of four different houses, most of them former residences of Uruguayan national heroes in the Ciudad Vieja. Built in the late 18th

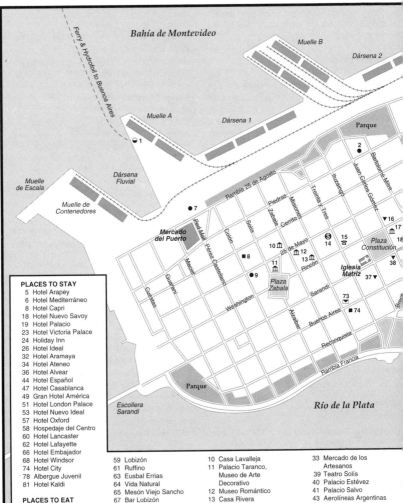

PLACES TO STAY
5 Hotel Arapey
6 Hotel Mediterráneo
8 Hotel Capri
18 Hotel Nuevo Savoy
19 Hotel Palacio
23 Hotel Victoria Palace
24 Holiday Inn
26 Hotel Ideal
32 Hotel Aramaya
34 Hotel Ateneo
36 Hotel Alvear
44 Hotel Español
47 Hotel Casablanca
49 Gran Hotel América
51 Hotel London Palace
53 Hotel Nuevo Ideal
57 Hotel Oxford
58 Hospedaje del Centro
60 Hotel Lancaster
62 Hotel Lafayette
66 Hotel Embajador
68 Hotel Windsor
74 Hotel City
78 Albergue Juvenil
81 Hotel Kaldi

PLACES TO EAT
3 Club Libanés
4 Club Alemán
16 Olivier
25 Oro del Rhin
35 Pizza Bros
37 Confitería de la Corte
38 Confitería La Pasiva
42 Oriente
45 Las Brasas
48 Emporio de la Pizza
50 La Vegetariana
52 El Fogón

59 Lobizón
61 Ruffino
63 Eusbal Errias
64 Vida Natural
65 Mesón Viejo Sancho
67 Bar Lobizón
69 La Genovesa
70 La Vegetariana
72 Mesón del Club Español
76 Mercado Central,
   Restaurant Morini
79 El Sarao

OTHER
1 Ferry Port
2 Casa Mario
7 Buquebus
9 Casa Garibaldi

10 Casa Lavalleja
11 Palacio Taranco,
   Museo de Arte
   Decorativo
12 Museo Romántico
13 Casa Rivera
14 Banco La Caja Obrera
15 Telecentro Antel
17 Cabildo, Museo y Archivo
   Histórico Municipal
20 Museo Torres García
21 Puerta de la Ciudadela
22 Mausoleo de Artigas
27 Ferrytur
28 Free Way Viajes
29 Pluna
30 Ministerio de Turismo
31 Asatej

33 Mercado de los
   Artesanos
39 Teatro Solís
40 Palacio Estévez
41 Palacio Salvo
43 Aerolíneas Argentinas
46 Sala Zitarrosa
54 LAPA
55 Manos del Uruguay
56 Telecentro Antel
71 Joventango, Mercado
   de la Abundancia
73 Correo Central
   (Main Post Office)
75 Manos del Uruguay
76 Fun Fun
77 La Bodeguita del Sur
80 Mil Años

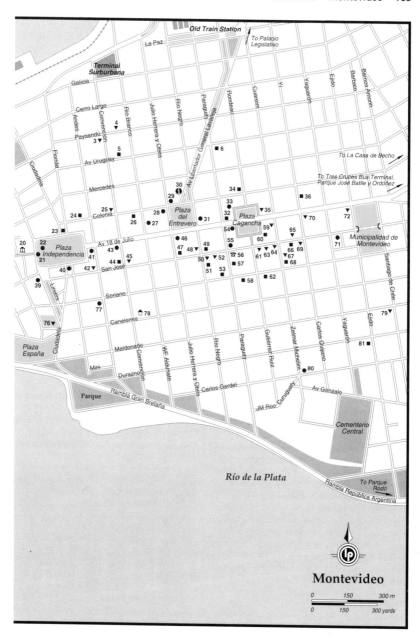

Montevideo

century, the **Casa Lavalleja**, Zabala 1469, was the home of General Lavalleja from 1830 until his death in 1853; in 1940, his heirs donated it to the state. The **Casa Rivera**, a 19th-century building at Rincón 437, belonged to General Fructuoso Rivera, Uruguay's first president and founder of the Colorado Party. The **Casa Garibaldi**, at 25 de Mayo 314, belonged to the Italian patriot who commanded the Uruguayan navy from 1843-51; it now contains many of his personal effects. All the houses are open from 12:30 to 6:30 pm Tuesday through Friday, from 2 to 6 pm Sundays and holidays.

The 18th-century **Museo Romántico**, 25 de Mayo 428, is full of paintings and antique furniture, but its exterior has been modified from the original colonial style. It keeps the same hours as the rest of the museum.

Museo Torres García

On the peatonal Sarandí 683 in the Ciudad Vieja, this museum displays the paintings of Uruguayan artist Joaquín Torres García (1874-1949), who spent much of his career in France producing abstract and even cubist work like that of Picasso, as well as idiosyncratic portraits – almost caricatures – of historical figures such as Columbus, Mozart, Beethoven, Bach and Rabelais. Open 3 to 7 pm weekdays and 11 am to 1 pm Saturdays, it also has a small gift shop and bookshop. Admission is free.

Palacio Legislativo

Dating from 1908, the neoclassical legislature was the work of Victor Meano, who won an international competition, and several other Italian architects who modified his plan over the next several years.

At the north end of Av Libertador General Lavalleja, brilliantly lighted at night, the three-story building is one of the city's most impressive landmarks. Available in English as well as Spanish, guided tours (☎ 200-1334) take place hourly between 8:30 am and 6:30 pm weekdays only.

Teatro Solís

Named for the first Spaniard to set foot in what is now Uruguayan territory, Monte-

video's leading theater opened in 1856, delayed by Rosas' siege of Montevideo (construction actually began in 1842). Performers who have appeared here include Caruso, Toscanini, Pavlova, Nijinski, Sarah Bernhardt, Rostropovich and Twyla Tharpe. See the Entertainment entry for more details.

Mercado del Puerto

At its opening in 1868, Montevideo's port was the continent's finest, but its market survives on personality and atmosphere. About 40 years ago, local entrepreneurs began to add more sophisticated restaurants to the grills that even then fed the people who brought their produce to the market, and the market gradually became a local phenomenon.

No visitor should miss the old port market building at the foot of Calle Pérez Castellano, whose impressive wrought-iron superstructure still shelters a gaggle of reasonably priced parrillas (choose your cut off the grill) and some more upmarket restaurants with outstanding seafood. Especially on Saturday afternoons, it's a lively, colorful place where the city's artists, craftsworkers and street musicians hang out. Café Roldos, at the same site since 1886, serves the popular *medio y medio*, a mixture of white and sparkling wines.

The market's restaurants are open into the late afternoon only; this is not a place for dinner. Note that there have been armed robberies near this area, even during daylight hours, so take the usual precautions.

Montevideo's leading theater

Organized Tours

Free Way Viajes (☎ 900-8931), Colonia 994, runs a recommended city tour (US$13) and another by night for US$24 (US$35 with dinner included). It organizes additional tours throughout the country and has guides available in several languages.

Special Events

Much livelier than that of Buenos Aires, Montevideo's late summer Carnaval is well worth the trip for those who can't make it to Rio de Janeiro. In secular Uruguay, Semana Santa (Holy Week) becomes the more nationalistic Semana Criolla; festivities take place at Parque Prado, north of downtown.

Places to Stay

Prices for accommodations have risen faster than inflation at large in recent years, so that many former budget hotels are now mid-range. Budget hotels are often dark and rundown, but there are exceptions.

Budget For budget travelers, one of the most reasonable and central lodgings is the *Albergue Juvenil* (☎ 908-1324), the official Hostelling International facility at Canelones 935. It charges about US$11 per night, including breakfast, with the obligatory hostel card, and has kitchen facilities, a lounge and tourist information. Its 11 pm curfew could restrict your nightlife, though it's not impossible to arrange a later arrival with the caretaker. It's closed noon to 7:30 pm daily.

Hotel Nuevo Savoy (☎ 915-7233), Bartolomé Mitre 1371, offers brightly painted doubles for as little as US$13 (shared bath) and US$18 (private bath). Some rooms are windowless and the presence of children means occasional noise, but it's friendly and well run. Recommended *Hotel Windsor* (☎ 901-5080), Zelmar Michelini 1260, charges US$11/14 for singles/doubles with shared bath, US$14/19 with private bath.

Hotel Capri (☎ 915-5970), in the Ciudad Vieja's red-light district at Colón 1460, charges US$16 for singles or doubles with private bath and color TV. Recommended

Hotel City (☎ 908-2913), Buenos Aires 462, is comparably priced.

Hotel Nuevo Ideal (☎ 908-2913), Soriano 1073, has mildewed rooms with private bath for US$15/20, but its central location and shady patio are strong points. *Hospedaje del Centro* (☎ 900-1419), at Soriano 1126 next to the Peruvian Consulate, charges US$15/18 for rooms with shared bath (few of these are available), US$18/20 with private bath. Once a luxurious single family residence, it's clean but crumbling, and some rooms are very dark.

Some rooms are also a bit dark at *Hotel Ateneo* (☎ 901-2630), Colonia 1147, where rates are US$18/20 with private bath and television; on Saturday nights, rates rise to US$29. *Hotel Ideal* (☎ 901-6389), Colonia 914, is clean and friendly with good bathrooms; rooms with shared bath are US$18/25, with private bath US$25/30. Clean, reader-recommended *Hotel Kaldi* (☎ 903-0365), Ejido 1083, charges US$20 per double on weekdays, US$30 on weekends, for rooms with color TV and phone.

Mid-Range A good choice is *Hotel Arapey* (☎ 900-7032) at Av Uruguay 925; it has singles/doubles for US$25/30. *Hotel Casablanca* (☎ 901-0918), conveniently central at San José 1039, charges US$25/30 with private bath. At a noisier location, at Av 18 de Julio 1103, the otherwise pleasant *Hotel Aramaya* (☎ 908-6192) charges US$25/35 with breakfast; some rooms have double balconies, and the service is excellent.

One of Montevideo's best budget accommodations has been *Hotel Palacio* (☎ 916-3612) at Bartolomé Mitre 1364, but it seems to be living on its reputation after unwarranted price increases. Singles and doubles with brass beds (some of them sagging), antique furniture and balconies cost US$31 with shared bath – though the water pressure can be erratic. Ask for 6th-floor accommodations, where the balconies are nearly as large as the rooms themselves and provide exceptional views of the Ciudad Vieja. Still a good place, it's not the value it once was.

Probably the best mid-range value is *Hotel Mediterráneo* (☎ 900-5090), Paraguay

1486, which charges US$30/40 for well-kept rooms with breakfast and excellent service. Enjoying literary cachet as the site of Julio Cortázar's short story 'La Puerta Condenada,' **Hotel Español** (☎ 900-3816), Convención 1317, charges US$35/45 for interior rooms, US$40/55 for those facing the street.

The central **Hotel Lancaster** (☎ 902-0029), Plaza Cagancha 1334, has good service and rooms starting at US$45/65 with breakfast. The accommodating **Gran Hotel América** (☎ 902-0392), Río Negro 1330, charges US$55/68, while **Hotel Alvear** (☎ 902-0244), Yí 1372, charges about the same. Reader-recommended **Hotel Tres Cruces** (☎ 402-3474), an eight-story, three-star highrise near the bus terminal at Migueletes 2356, charges US$55/75 with breakfast and satellite TV.

Top End Montevideo's top-end hotels lack the luxury of those in Buenos Aires, but there are some decent values; all include breakfast in their rates. Rates at the **Hotel London Palace** (☎ 902-0024), Río Negro 1278, run US$64/85 for singles/doubles with a buffet breakfast. Rooms at the **Hotel Embajador** (☎ 902-0009), San José 1212, start at US$60/80 but rise to US$80/100. Refurbished **Hotel Oxford** (☎ 902-0046), Paraguay 1286, charges US$72/87, which includes an outstanding breakfast.

The relatively new **Hotel Lafayette** (☎ 902-2351), Soriano 1170, is Montevideo's only real luxury hotel, charging US$111/129 to US$129/137, though the Moonie-operated **Hotel Victoria Palace** (☎ 902-0111), Plaza Independencia 759, makes an effort to be one; its rates are US$143/165. The recently established **Holiday Inn** (in fact, the upgraded ex-Hotel Internacional; ☎ 900-5794), Colonia 823, costs US$140 single or double.

Places to Eat

Montevideo falls short of Buenos Aires' sophistication and variety, but its numerous restaurants are unpretentious and offer excellent values. Reasonably priced, worthwhile downtown restaurants include **Restaurant Morini** (☎ 915-9733), Ciudadela 1229, and **Mesón Viejo Sancho** (☎ 900-4063), San José 1229. **La Genovesa** (☎ 900-8729), San José 1242, has good seafood with abundant portions, but note that IVA may not be included in the listed prices, nor the *cubierto* (service charge).

Lobizón, on Zelmar Michelini between Av 18 de Julio and San José, has inexpensive lunch specials and great informal atmosphere. There's even better bar atmosphere at its namesake **Bar Lobizón** (☎ 901-1334), a block south at Zelmar Michelini 1264, but on the opposite side of the street, which is open only at night, with both food and entertainment.

Uruguayans eat even more meat than Argentines, so parrillada is always a popular choice. Central parrillas include **El Fogón** (☎ 900-0900) at San José 1080, **Las Brasas** (☎ 900-2285) at San José 909, and the many stalls at the Mercado del Puerto. If you've OD'd on meat, there are several vegetarian alternatives: **La Vegetariana** at Yí 1334 (☎ 900-7661) and San José 1056 (☎ 901-0558), and **Vida Natural** at San José 1184.

Seafood is another possibility. **La Posada del Puerto** (☎ 915-4279) has two stalls in the Mercado del Puerto, while **La Tasca del Puerto** is outside on the peatonal Pérez Castellano. **La Proa** (☎ 916-2578), a sidewalk café on Pérez Castellano, has entrees for about US$8; with drinks, dinner for two should cost about US$20. It serves as many as 800 people per day, but the service is still friendly and attentive. Another popular place in the mercado is **El Palenque** (☎ 915-4704). Reader-recommended **Martín Pescador** (☎ 707-2941), Obligado 1392 near Rivera, a few blocks south of Tres Cruces, has also drawn praise for its seafood.

As in Argentina, Italian immigration has left its mark on the country's cuisine. For pizza, try **Emporio de la Pizza** (☎ 901-4681), Río Negro 1311; less traditional is **Pizza Bros**, Plaza Cagancha 1364, a lively place with good pizza and bright but not overpowering decor. For more elaborate dishes in addition to tasty pizzas, visit **Ruffino** (☎ 908-3384), San José 1166, which offers a 10% discount for cash.

Olivier (☎ 915-0617), at JC Gómez 1420 just off Plaza Constitución, is a very highly regarded but expensive French restaurant. Spanish food is available at *Mesón del Club Español* (☎ 901-5145), Av 18 de Julio 1332, and *El Sarao* (☎ 901-7688), Santiago de Chile 1137, which has flamenco shows on Fridays. For Basque food, visit *Eusbal Errias* (☎ 902-3519) at San José 1168.

For German cuisine, try the *Club Alemán* (☎ 902-3982) at Paysandú 935, 4th floor. There's Middle Eastern food at the *Club Libanés* (☎ 900-1801), Paysandú 898. *Oriente*, Andes 1311, has a good Chinese menu with tenedor libre, but some à-la-carte dishes are expensive.

Confitería La Pasiva, on Plaza Constitución at JC Gómez and Sarandí in the Ciudad Vieja, has excellent, reasonably priced *minutas* and superb *flan casero* in a very traditional atmosphere (except for the digital readout menu on one wall). The 'pasiva entrecote' has been highly recommended as sufficient for two.

Other decent confiterías include *Oro del Rhin* (☎ 902-2833), at Convención 1403 (the oldest in the city), and *Confitería de la Corte*, at Ituzaingó 1325 just off Plaza Constitución, which has fine, moderately priced lunch specials.

Entertainment

Carlos Gardel spent time in Montevideo, where the tango is no less popular than in Buenos Aires. The very informal *Fun Fun* (☎ 915-8005), Ciudadela 1229 in the Mercado Central offers a good mix of young and old. *Mil Años* (☎ 901-1373), Zelmar Michelini 1054, features tango and *candombe* (Afro-Uruguayan) dancing; show and dinner run about US$20 per person. There's also *La Casa de Becho* (☎ 924-4757), Nueva York 1415 north of Terminal Tres Cruces, in the former home of Gerardo Matos Rodríguez, composer of the tango 'La Cumparsita.' Visitors interested in lessons can try *Joventango* (☎ 901-5561), in the Mercado de la Abundancia, at the corner of San José and Yaguarón.

At the southwest corner of Plaza Independencia, at Buenos Aires 678, *Teatro Solís*

(☎ 915-1968) has superb acoustics and offers concerts, ballet, opera and plays throughout the year. It is also home to the Comedia Nacional, the municipal theater company. Get tickets at least a few days before events.

For live folkloric music, Cuban salsa and the like, the best place to go is *La Bodeguita del Sur* (☎ 902-8649), Soriano 840. For rock music and occasional live theater, try the *Sala Zitarrosa* (☎ 901-7303), at the corner of Av 18 de Julio and Julio Herrera y Obes, opposite Plaza del Entrevero.

Soccer, an Uruguayan passion, inspires large and enthusiastic crowds. The main stadium, the *Estadio Centenario* in Parque José Batlle y Ordóñez off Av Italia, opened in 1930 for the first World Cup, in which Uruguay defeated Argentina 4-2 in the title game. Later declared a historic monument, it also contains the Museo del Fútbol (Soccer Museum).

Shopping

For attractive artisanal items, at reasonable prices in an informal atmosphere, visit the Mercado de los Artesanos on Plaza Cagancha, which is also a hangout for younger Uruguayans. Another outlet is the recycled Mercado de la Abundancia, at the corner of San José and Yaguarón, with upstairs groceries and downstairs crafts.

Montevideo's biggest street fair is the Feria de Tristán Narvaja, at the corner of Av 18 de Julio and Tristán Narvaja, where more than 3000 sellers congregate from 9 am to 3 pm Sundays. Although antiques and collectibles are in stock, it's also a source of food and other practical items for the city's inhabitants.

Manos del Uruguay, at San José 1111 (☎ 900-4910) and Reconquista 602 (☎ 915-9522), is famous for its quality goods. For leather, visit Casa Mario (☎ 916-2356), Piedras 641 in the Ciudad Vieja.

Getting There & Away

Air Many international airlines serve Montevideo from Buenos Aires' Ezeiza, usually as continuations of transcontinental flights. Commuter airlines also provide international services between the two countries.

Pluna (☎ 902-3906), Colonia 1001, and Aerolíneas Argentinas (☎ 902-4171), Convención 1343, 4th floor, offer a 'Puente Aéreo' (Air Bridge) with a US$52 one-way fare between Buenos Aires' Aeroparque Jorge Newbery and Montevideo. LAPA (☎ 900-8765), Plaza Cagancha 1339, flies from Aeroparque to Montevideo. For details from Buenos Aires, see the Getting There & Away chapter.

Bus There is regular service from Buenos Aires' main bus station in Retiro (Map 11). One company to try is General Urquiza (☎ 4313-2771), which has nightly service to Montevideo (US$25, nine hours). See the Bus section of the Getting There & Away chapter for more details.

Still reasonably close to downtown, Montevideo's modern Terminal Tres Cruces (☎ 401-8998), at Bulevar Artigas and Av Italia, is a big improvement on the individual bus terminals that once cluttered Plaza Cagancha and nearby side streets. It has tourist information, decent restaurants, clean toilets, luggage check, public telephones, a *casa de cambio* and many other services.

Boat Most services across the Río de la Plata from Buenos Aires are bus-boat combinations via Colonia, but the so-called 'Buqueaviones' are high-speed ferries (upwards of 100km per hour) that arrive at the port at the foot of Pérez Castellano in the Ciudad Vieja. Users of the Buenos Aires hydrofoil port at Dársena Norte pay US$10 to travel to Montevideo, but this should be included in the fare.

Ferrytur (☎ 4315-6800) at Av Córdoba 699 in Retiro or at the Terminal Sea Cat (☎ 4314-2300) at Dársena Norte (both Map 11), does bus-hydrofoil combinations to Montevideo (US$40, four hours). Their *Sea Cat* hydrofoil has four departures weekdays and three on weekends. Their Montevideo office (☎ 900-6617) is at Río Branco 1368, but there's also a representative at Tres Cruces (☎ 409-8198).

Buquebus (☎ 4313-4444), Av Córdoba 867 in Retiro (Map 11), runs the 'Buqueaviones' (high-speed ferries) to Montevideo (2½ hours) four times daily. Fares are US$52 in

turista, US$67 in *primera*; children ages two to nine pay US$17. A Buquebus colectivo leaves the Av Córdoba offices for Dársena Norte 1½ hours prior to every departure. Vehicles up to 1200kg pay US$110, while those over 1200kg pay US$125. Buquebus's Montevideo office has moved to the entrance to Dársena 1 on the Rambla 25 de Agosto, at the foot of Pérez Castellano.

Cacciola runs a bus-launch service from Buenos Aires to Montevideo (US$25 one-way, US$45 roundtrip, eight hours; ask about off-season promotions) at 8:30 am and 4:30 pm daily via the riverside suburb of Tigre and the Uruguayan terminal at Carmelo. Tickets are available at their downtown Buenos Aires office (☎ 4394-5520) at Florida 520, 1st floor, Oficina 113; in Tigre they're at the Terminal Internacional, Lavalle 520 (☎ 4749-0329).

In Montevideo, Cacciola (☎ 401-9350) is at Terminal Tres Cruces. Return services from Montevideo leave at 12:40 am Monday through Saturday, 4 pm Sunday, and at 8:30 am daily.

Getting Around

To/From the Airport Ibat (☎ 601-0207) runs a special airport bus (US$4) from Pluna's downtown offices at the corner of Colonia and Av del Libertador; see the schedule posted there.

From the Terminal Suburbana at the corner of Rambla 25 de Agosto and Río Branco, the No 209 Cutesa and Copsa buses go the airport every 15 minutes (US$1.20).

Bus Montevideo's improving fleet of buses less frequently leaves you gasping for breath with noxious diesel fumes, and still goes everywhere for about US$0.65. The *Guía de Montevideo Eureka*, available at bookshops or kiosks, lists routes and schedules, as do the yellow pages of the Montevideo phone book. As in Argentina, the driver or conductor will ask your destination. Retain your ticket, which may be inspected at any time. This is not Buenos Aires, however – most routes cease service by 10:30 or 11 pm. For information, contact Cutcsa (☎ 200-9021, 200-7527).

Taxi Montevideo's black and yellow taxis are all metered; it costs about US$1 to drop the flag and US$0.60 per 600m. Between 10 pm and 6 am, and on weekends and holidays, fares are 20% higher. There is a small additional charge for luggage, and riders generally round off the fare to the next higher peso.

Glossary

ACA – Automóvil Club Argentino; an automobile club that provides maps, road service and insurance, and operates hotels, motels and campgrounds throughout the country

albergue transitorio – not to be mistaken for an albergue juvenil (youth hostel), this is very short-term accommodation normally used by young couples in search of privacy; an alternative euphemism, used in Uruguay, is hotel de alta rotatividad

aliscafo – hydrofoil; travels from Buenos Aires across the Río de la Plata to Colonia and Montevideo, Uruguay

argentinidad – rather nebulous concept of Argentine national identity, often associated with extreme nationalistic feelings

asado – barbecue, often a family outing in summer

autopista – freeway or motorway

banda negativa – low-cost air tickets, for which limited seats on particular domestic flights are available at discounts of up to 40% off the usual price

bandoneón – accordion-like instrument used in tango music

barras bravas – violent soccer fans; the Argentine equivalent of Britain's 'football hooligans'

barrio – neighborhood or borough of the city

boliche – nightclub, but the word usually implies informality and even rowdiness

cabildo – colonial town council

cachila – in Uruguay, an antique automobile, often beautifully maintained

cajero automático – automatic teller machine (ATM)

calle – street

cambio – see casa de cambio

característica – telephone area code

carapintada – the extreme right-wing, ultra-nationalist movement of disaffected junior officers in the Argentine military; responsible for several attempted coups during the Alfonsín and Menem administrations

carne – while this word generally means 'meat,' in Argentina it specifically means 'beef'; chicken, pork and the like may be referred to as carne blanca (white meat)

cartelera – discount ticket agency offering great bargains on tickets to cinemas, tango shows and other performances

casa de cambio – foreign exchange house, often simply called a 'cambio'

casco – 'big house' on a livestock estancia

caudillo – in 19th-century Argentine politics, a provincial strongman whose power rested more on personal loyalty than political ideals or party organization

certificado – registered mail

coima – a bribe; one who solicits a bribe is a coimero

confitería – serves mostly sandwiches, including lomito (steak), panchos (hot dogs) and hamburgers

conventillo – tenements that housed immigrants in older neighborhoods of Buenos Aires and Montevideo; on a reduced scale, these still exist in the San Telmo barrio of Buenos Aires and the Ciudad Vieja of Montevideo

cospel – token used in Argentine public telephones in lieu of coins; there are different types of cospeles for local and long-distance phones

costanera – seaside, riverside or lakeside road

criollo – in colonial period, an American-born Spaniard, but the term now commonly describes any Argentine of European descent; also describes the feral cattle of the Pampas

DDI – Discado Directo Internacional (International Direct Dialing), which provides direct access to home-country operators for long-distance collect and credit-card calls; a much cheaper alternative to the rates of the Argentine companies Telecom and Telefónica

démedos – literally 'give me two,' a pejorative nickname for Argentines who travel to cities like Miami, where many consumer items are so relatively cheap that they buy things they don't need

Dirty War – in the 1970s, the violent repression by the Argentine military, police and paramilitaries of left-wing revolutionaries and anyone suspected of sympathizing with them

estancia – historically speaking, an extensive grazing estate, either for cattle or sheep, under a dominating owner (estanciero) or manager with a dependent resident labor force of gauchos; many Argentine estancias, often very luxurious, have opened themselves to tourists for recreational activities such as riding, tennis and swimming, either for weekend escapes or extended stays

facturas – pastries
ficha – token used in the Buenos Aires underground (Subte) in lieu of coins

Gardeliano – fan of the late tango singer Carlos Gardel
gas-oil – diesel fuel
gasolero – motor vehicle that uses diesel fuel, which is much cheaper than *nafta* in Argentina
Gran Aldea – the 'Great Village'; Buenos Aires prior to the massive European immigration of the late 19th and early 20th centuries
guita – money, in *lunfardo* slang

hacer dedo – to hitchhike, literally 'to make thumb'
hoteles de categoria – top-end hotels, usually recommended by tourist offices and travel agencies to foreign visitors no matter what their economic status

ida – one-way
ida y vuelta – roundtrip
iglesia – church
interno – extension off a central telephone number or switchboard, often abbreviated 'int'
IVA – impuesto de valor agregado or value-added tax; often added to restaurant or hotel bills in Argentina and Uruguay

literatura gauchesca – 'gauchesque' literature; romantic literature about, as opposed to by, the usually illiterate gauchos of the Pampas
locutorio – private long-distance telephone office, which usually offers fax services as well
lunfardo – street slang of Buenos Aires, with origins in immigrant neighborhoods at the turn of the century

maqueta – stage set model used in theater productions
mercado paralelo – 'parallel market'; a euphemism for the black market in foreign currency, which does not exist at present
mate – see *yerba mate*
minuta – in a restaurant or confitería, a short order such as spaghetti or milanesa
museo – museum

nafta – gasoline or petrol
ñoqui – a public employee whose primary interest is collecting a monthly paycheck; So-called because potato pasta, or ñoquis (from the Italian gnocchi), are traditionally served in financially strapped Argentine households on the 29th of each month, the implication being that the employee makes his or her appearance at work only around that time
novela – television soap opera

pampero – South Atlantic cold front that brings dramatic temperature changes to northern Argentina
parada – bus stop
parrillada, parrilla – respectively, a mixed grill of steak and other beef cuts, and a restaurant specializing in such dishes
paseaperros – professional dog walker in Buenos Aires
peatonal – pedestrian mall, usually in the downtown area
peña – club that hosts informal folk music gatherings
piropo – sexist remark, ranging in tone from complimentary and relatively innocuous to rude and offensive; alternatively, an aphorism or proverb on filete, the traditional sign painting of Buenos Aires

porteño – inhabitant of Buenos Aires, a 'resident of the port'

primera – 1st-class on a train

Proceso – in full, 'El Proceso de Reorganización Nacional,' the military's euphemism for its brutal attempt to remake Argentina's political and economic culture between 1976 and 1983

propina – a tip

puchero – soup combining vegetables and meats, served with rice

pucho – in lunfardo, a cigarette or cigarette butt

puerta a puerta – express mail, literally 'door to door'

puesto – 'outside house' on a livestock estancia

pulpería – rural shop (often serving as a saloon) or 'company store' on a cattle or sheep *estancia*

quilombo – in lunfardo, a mess; originally a Brazilian term describing a settlement of runaway slaves, it came to mean a house of prostitution in Argentina

recargo – the additional charge, usually 10%, which many Argentine businesses add to credit-card transactions because of high inflation and delays in payment

recova – colonnade; very common in colonial and neocolonial Argentine architecture

río – river

RN – Ruta Nacional; a national highway

RP – Ruta Provincial; a provincial highway

ruta – highway

SIDA – AIDS

sobremesa – after-dinner conversation; an integral part of any Argentine meal

Subte – the Buenos Aires underground railway

sudestada – southeasterly storm out of the South Atlantic that often combines high tides and heavy runoff to flood low-lying barrios like La Boca

tarjeta telefónica – magnetic telephone card; a convenient substitute for cospeles

técnico – specialist in theater skills such as scenery or makeup

tenedor libre – literally 'free fork,' an 'all-you-can-eat' restaurant; also known as diente libre ('free tooth')

tercera edad – 'third age;' a Spanish-language euphemism equivalent to 'senior citizen' in English

trasnochador – one who stays up very late or all night, as do many Argentines

trasnoche – midnight (or later) cinema showing on weekends

trucho – bogus; widely used by Argentines to describe things that are not what they appear to be

turista – 2nd-class on a train

tuteo – use of the pronoun tú in Spanish and its corresponding verb forms

valizas – triangular emergency reflectors, obligatory in all Argentine motor vehicles

villas miserias – shantytowns on the outskirts of Buenos Aires and other Argentine cities

voseo – use of the pronoun vos and its corresponding verb forms in Argentina, Uruguay and Paraguay

vuelos de cabotaje – domestic flights

yerba mate – 'Paraguayan tea' (Ilex paraguariensis), which Argentines and Uruguayans consume in very large amounts

Language

Spanish in Argentina, and the rest of the Río de la Plata region, has characteristics that readily distinguish it from the rest of Latin America. Probably the most prominent differences are the usage of the pronoun *vos* in place of *tú* for 'you,' and the trait of pronouncing the letters 'll' and 'y' as 'zh' (as in 'azure') rather than 'y' (like English 'you') as in the rest of the Americas. Note that in American Spanish, the plural of the familiar 'tú' or 'vos' is *ustedes*, not *vosotros*, as in Spain. Argentines understand continental Spanish but may find it quaint or pretentious.

There are many vocabulary differences between European and American Spanish, and among Spanish-speaking countries in the Americas. The speech of Buenos Aires, in particular, abounds with words and phrases from the colorful slang known as *lunfardo*. Although you shouldn't use lunfardo words unless you are supremely confident that you know their *every* implication (especially in formal situations), you should be aware of some of the more common everyday usages. (See Lunfardo.) Argentines normally refer to the Spanish language as *castellano* rather than *español*.

Every visitor should make an effort to speak Spanish, whose basic elements are easily acquired. If possible, take a brief night course at your local university or community college before departure. Even if you can't speak very well, Argentines are gracious hosts and will encourage your use of Spanish, so there is no need to feel self-conscious about vocabulary or pronunciation. There are many common cognates, so if you're stuck, try Hispanicizing an English word – it is unlikely you'll make a truly embarrassing error. Do not, however, admit to being *embarazada* unless you are in fact pregnant. (See Cognates & Condoms for other usages to be avoided.)

Phrasebooks & Dictionaries

Lonely Planet's *Latin American Spanish phrasebook* is a worthwhile addition to your backpack. Another exceptionally useful resource is the *University of Chicago Spanish-English, English-Spanish Dictionary*. Its

Cognates & Condoms

False cognates are words that appear to be very similar but have different meanings in different languages. In some instances, these differences can lead to serious misunderstandings. The following is a list of some of these words in English with their Spanish cousins and their meaning in Spanish. Note that this list deals primarily with the Río de la Plata region, and usages may differ in other areas.

English	Spanish	Meaning in Spanish
actual	*actual*	current (at present)
carpet	*carpeta*	looseleaf notebook
embarrassed	*embarazada*	pregnant
to introduce	*introducir*	to introduce (as an innovation)
notorious	*notorio*	well known, evident
to present	*presentar*	to introduce (a person)
precise	*preciso*	necessary
preservative	*preservativo*	condom
violation	*violación*	rape

¡POR FAVORO, NO PRESERVATIVO, PLEASE!

small size, light weight and thorough entries make it perfect for travel.

Pronunciation

Spanish pronunciation is, in general, consistently phonetic. Until you become confident of your ability, speak slowly to avoid getting tongue-tied.

Vowels Vowels are very consistent and have easy English equivalents.

a is like 'a' in 'father'
e is like 'ai' in 'sail'
i is like 'ee' in 'feet'
o is like 'o' in 'for'
u is like 'oo' in 'food'; after consonants other than 'q,' it is more like English 'w'; when the vowel sound is modified by an umlaut, as in 'Güemes,' it is also pronounced 'w'
y is a consonant except when it stands alone or appears at the end of a word, in which case its pronunciation is identical to the Spanish 'i'

Consonants Spanish consonants resemble their English equivalents, with some major exceptions. Pronunciation of the letters **f, k, l, m, n, p, q, s** and **t** is virtually identical to English. Although **y** is identical in most Latin American countries when used as a consonant, most Argentines say 'zh' for it and for **ll**, which is a separate letter. **Ch** and **ñ** are also separate letters, with separate dictionary entries.

b is generally a much softer 'b' than the English one: somewhere between an English 'b' and 'v' – try saying this with your lips slightly closed (the English 'b' is pronounced with closed lips), and your top teeth on your bottom lip (the English 'v' is pronounced this way, though with open lips); when initial, or preceded by a nasal sound, the sound is as the 'b' in 'book'; for clarity between the Spanish letters 'b' and 'v,' refer to 'b' as 'b larga' and 'v' as 'b corta' (the word for the letter itself is pronounced like 'bay' in English)
c is like the 's' in 'see' before 'e' and 'i,' otherwise like English 'k'
d closely resembles 'th' in 'feather'

g is like a guttural English 'h' before Spanish 'e' and 'i,' otherwise like 'g' in 'go'
h is invariably silent; if your name begins with this letter, listen carefully when immigration officials summon you to pick up your passport
j most closely resembles the English 'h' but is slightly more guttural
ñ is like 'ni' in 'onion'
r is nearly identical to English except at the beginning of a word, when it is often rolled
rr is very strongly rolled
v is the same sound as the Spanish 'b'
x is like 'x' in 'taxi' except for very few words for which it follows Spanish or Mexican usage as 'j'
z is like 's' in 'sun'

Diphthongs Diphthongs are vowel combinations forming a single syllable. In Spanish, the formation of a diphthong depends on combinations of 'weak' vowels ('i' and 'u') or strong ones ('a,' 'e,' and 'o'). Two weak vowels or a strong and a weak vowel make a diphthong, but two strong ones are pronounced as separate syllables.

A good example of two weak vowels forming a diphthong is the word *diurno* (during the day). The final syllable of *obligatorio*

Lunfardo

Below are a few of the more common, and innocuous, lunfardo usages that you may hear on the streets. Visitors interested in more detail can look for Tino Rodríguez's *Primer Diccionario de Sinónimos del Lunfardo* (1987) or contact the Academia Porteña del Lunfardo (☎ 4383-2393), Estados Unidos 1379 in Constitución (Map 9).

guita	money
laburo	work
macanudo	terrific
morfar	to eat
palo	ten pesos
pibe	guy, dude
piola	cool
pucho	cigarette

(obligatory) is a combination of weak and strong vowels.

Stress Stress, often indicated by visible accents, is very important, since it can change the meaning of words. In general, words ending in vowels or the letters **n** or **s** have stress on the next-to-last syllable, while those with other endings have stress on the last syllable. Thus *vaca* (cow) and *caballos* (horses) both have accents on their penultimate syllables.

Visible accents, which can occur anywhere in a word, dictate stress over these general rules. Thus *sótano* (basement), *América* and *porción* (portion) all have stress on different syllables. When words appear in capitals, the written accent is generally omitted but still pronounced.

Greetings & Civilities

In their public behavior, Argentines are very conscious of civilities, sometimes to the point of ceremoniousness. Never, for example, approach a stranger for information without extending a greeting like *buenos días* or *buenas tardes*.

Yes.	*Sí.*
No.	*No.*
Please.	*Por favor.*
Thank you.	*Gracias.*
You're welcome.	*De nada.*
Hello.	*¡Hola!*
Good morning.	*Buenos días.*
Good afternoon.	*Buenas tardes.*
Good evening.	*Buenas noches.*
Good night.	*Buenas noches.*
Goodbye.	*Adiós/chau* (informal).

I understand.	*Entiendo.*
I don't understand.	*No entiendo.*

I don't speak much Spanish.
  Hablo poco castellano.

Useful Words & Phrases

and	*y*
to/at	*a*
for	*por, para*
of/from	*de, desde*
in	*en*
with	*con*
without	*sin*
before	*antes*
after	*después*
soon	*pronto*
already	*ya*
now	*ahora*
right away	*en seguida*
here	*aquí*
there	*allí*
Where?	*¿Dónde?*
Where is/are ...?	*¿Dónde está/están ...?*
When?	*¿Cuando?*
How?	*¿Cómo?*

I would like ...	*Me gustaría ...*
coffee	*café*
tea	*té*
beer	*cerveza*
wine	*vino*

How much?	*¿Cuanto?*
How many?	*¿Cuantos?*
Is/Are there ...?	*¿Hay ...?*

Do you speak English?
  ¿Habla Usted inglés?
Speak slowly, please.
  Despacio, por favor.

Getting Around

airplane	*avión*
train	*tren*
bus	*colectivo,*
	micro, omnibus
ship	*barco, buque*
ferry	*barca de pasaje*
hydrofoil	*aliscafo*
car	*auto*
taxi	*taxi*
truck	*camión*
pick-up	*camioneta*
bicycle	*bicicleta*
motorcycle	*motocicleta*
hitchhike	*hacer dedo*

I would like a ticket to ...
  Quiero un boleto/pasaje a ...
What's the fare to ...?
  ¿Cuanto cuesta el pasaje a ...?

When does the next bus leave for ... ?
¿Cuando sale el próximo omnibus para ... ?
Is there a student/university discount?
¿Hay descuento estudiantil/universitario?
Do you accept credit cards?
¿Trabajan con tarjetas de crédito?

first/last/next	
	primero/último/próximo
first/second class	
	primera/segunda clase
single/roundtrip	
	ida/ida y vuelta
sleeper	
	camarote
left luggage	
	guardería, equipaje

Accommodations

Below you will find English phrases with useful Spanish equivalents for Argentina, most of which will be understood in other Spanish-speaking countries.

hotel	*hotel, pensión, residencial*
single room	*habitación para una persona*
double room	*habitación doble, matrimonio*

How much does it cost?
¿Cuanto cuesta?
May I see it?
¿Puedo verla?
I don't like it.
No me gusta.

per night	*por noche*
full board	*pensión completa*
shared bath	*baño compartido*
private bath	*baño privado*
too expensive	*demasiado caro*
discount	*descuento*
cheaper	*mas económico*
the bill	*la cuenta*

Around Town

tourist information	*oficina de turismo*
airport	*aeropuerto*
train station	*estación de ferrocarril*

bus terminal	*terminal de omnibus*
bathing resort	*balneario*
post office	*correo*
letter	*carta*
parcel	*paquete*
postcard	*postal*
airmail	*correo aéreo*
registered mail	*certificado*
express mail	*puerta a puerta*
stamps	*estampillas*
person to person	*persona a persona*
collect call	*cobro revertido*

Toilets

The most common word for toilet is *baño*, but *servicios sanitarios* (services) is a frequent alternative. Men's toilets usually bear a descriptive term like *hombres*, *caballeros* or *varones*. Women's restrooms have a *señoras* or *damas* sign.

Countries

The list below contains only countries whose spelling differs significantly in English and Spanish.

Denmark	*Dinamarca*
England	*Inglaterra*
France	*Francia*
Germany	*Alemania*
Great Britain	*Gran Bretaña*
Ireland	*Irlanda*
Italy	*Italia*
Japan	*Japón*
Netherlands	*Holanda*
New Zealand	*Nueva Zelandia*
Peru	*Perú*
Scotland	*Escocia*
Spain	*España*
Sweden	*Suecia*
Switzerland	*Suiza*
United States	*Estados Unidos*
Wales	*Gales*

Numbers

Should hyperinflation return, you may have to learn to count in very large numbers.

0	*cero*
1	*uno*
2	*dos*

3	*tres*	22	*veintidós*
4	*cuatro*	30	*treinta*
5	*cinco*	31	*treinta y uno*
6	*seis*	32	*treinta y dos*
7	*siete*	40	*cuarenta*
8	*ocho*	50	*cincuenta*
9	*nueve*	60	*sesenta*
10	*diez*	70	*setenta*
11	*once*	80	*ochenta*
12	*doce*	90	*noventa*
13	*trece*	100	*cien*
14	*catorce*	101	*ciento uno*
15	*quince*	110	*ciento diez*
16	*dieciséis*	120	*ciento veinte*
17	*diecisiete*	200	*doscientos*
18	*dieciocho*	300	*trescientos*
19	*diecinueve*	400	*cuatrocientos*
20	*veinte*	500	*quinientos*
21	*veintiuno*	600	*seiscientos*

El Voseo

Spanish in the Río de la Plata region differs from that of Spain and the rest of the Americas, most notably in the familiar form of the second person singular pronoun. Instead of the tuteo used everywhere else, Argentines, Uruguayans and Paraguayans commonly use the voseo, a relict 16th-century form requiring slightly different endings. Regular and most irregular verbs differ from tú forms; regular verbs change their stress and add an accent, while irregular verbs do not change internal consonants, but add a terminal accent. This is true for -ar, -er and -ir verbs, examples of which are given below, with the tú forms included for contrast. Imperative forms also differ, but negative imperatives are identical in both the tuteo and the voseo.

In the list below, the first verb of each ending is regular, while the second is irregular; the pronoun is included for clarity, though most Spanish-speakers normally omit it.

Verb	Tuteo/Imperative	Voseo/Imperative
hablar (to speak)	*tú hablas/habla*	*vos hablás/hablá*
soñar (to dream)	*tú sueñas/sueña*	*vos soñás/soñá*
comer (to eat)	*tú comes/come*	*vos comés/comé*
poner (to put)	*tú pones/pon*	*vos ponés/poné*
admitir (to admit)	*tú admites/admite*	*vos admitís/admití*
venir (to come)	*tú vienes/ven*	*vos venís/vení*

Note that some of the most common verbs, like *ir* (to go), *estar* (to be) and *ser* (to be) are identically irregular in both the tuteo and the voseo, and that Argentines continue to use the possessive article *tu* (*Vos tenés tu lápiz?*) and the reflexive or conjunctive object pronoun *te* (*Vos te das cuenta?*).

An Argentine inviting a foreigner to address him or her informally will say *Me podés tutear* (you can call me 'tú') rather than *Me podés vosear* (you can call me 'vos'), even though the expectation is that both will use 'vos' forms in subsequent conversation.

700	*setecientos*
800	*ochocientos*
900	*novecientos*
1000	*mil*
1100	*mil cien*
2000	*dos mil*
5000	*cinco mil*
10,000	*diez mil*
50,000	*cincuenta mil*
100,000	*cien mil*
1,000,000	*un millón*

Days of the Week

Monday	*lunes*
Tuesday	*martes*
Wednesday	*miércoles*
Thursday	*jueves*
Friday	*viernes*
Saturday	*sábado*
Sunday	*domingo*

Time

Telling time is fairly straightforward. Eight o'clock is *las ocho*, while 8:30 is *las ocho y treinta* (literally, eight and thirty) or *las ocho y media* (eight and a half). However, 7:45 is *las ocho menos quince* (literally, eight minus fifteen) or *las ocho menos cuarto* (eight minus one quarter). Times are modified by *de la manaña* (morning) or *de la tarde* (afternoon) instead of am or pm. Transportation schedules commonly use the 24-hour clock.

LONELY PLANET

Phrasebooks

L onely Planet phrasebooks are packed with essential words and phrases to help travellers communicate with the locals. With colour tabs for quick reference, an extensive vocabulary and use of script, these handy pocket-sized language guides cover day-to-day travel situations.

- handy pocket-sized books
- easy to understand Pronunciation chapter
- clear & comprehensive Grammar chapter
- romanisation alongside script to allow ease of pronunciation
- script throughout so users can point to phrases for every situation
- full of cultural information and tips for the traveller

'... vital for a real DIY spirit and attitude in language learning'
— Backpacker

'the phrasebooks have good cultural backgrounders and offer solid advice for challenging situations in remote locations'
— San Francisco Examiner

Arabic (Egyptian) ● Arabic (Moroccan) ● Australian *(Australian English, Aboriginal and Torres Strait languages)* ● Baltic States *(Estonian, Latvian, Lithuanian)* ● Bengali ● Brazilian ● British ● Burmese ● Cantonese ● Central Asia (Uyghur, Uzbek, Kyrghiz, Kazak, Pashto, Tadjik ● Central Europe *(Czech, French, German, Hungarian, Italian, Slovak)* ● Eastern Europe *(Bulgarian, Czech, Hungarian, Polish, Romanian, Slovak)* ● Ethiopian (Amharic) ● Fijian ● French ● German ● Greek ● Hebrew ● Hill Tribes ● Hindi & Urdu ● Indonesian ● Italian ● Japanese ● Korean ● Lao ● Latin American Spanish ● Malay ● Mandarin ● Mediterranean Europe *(Albanian, Croatian, Greek, Italian, Macedonian, Maltese, Serbian, Slovene)* ● Mongolian ● Nepali ● Pidgin ● Pilipino (Tagalog) ● Portugese ● Quechua ● Russian ● Scandinavian Europe *(Danish, Finnish, Icelandic, Norwegian, Swedish)* ● South-East Asia *(Burmese, Indonesian, Khmer, Lao, Malay, Tagalog Pilipino, Thai, Vietnamese)* ● South Pacific Languages ● Spanish (Castilian) *(also includes Catalan, Galician and Basque)* ● Sri Lanka ● Swahili ● Thai ● Tibetan ● Turkish ● Ukrainian ● USA *(US English, Vernacular, Native American languages, Hawaiian)* ● Vietnamese ● Western Europe *(Basque, Catalan, Dutch, French, German, Greek, Irish, Italian, Portuguese, Scottish Gaelic, Spanish (Castilian), Welsh)*

LONELY PLANET

Guides by Region

Lonely Planet is known worldwide for publishing practical, reliable and no-nonsense travel information in our guides and on our Web site. The Lonely Planet list covers just about every accessible part of the world. Currently there are thirteen series: travel guides, shoestring guides, walking guides, city guides, phrasebooks, audio packs, city maps, travel atlases, diving & snorkeling guides, restaurant guides, first-time travel guides, healthy travel and travel literature.

AFRICA Africa on a shoestring • Africa – the South • Arabic (Egyptian) phrasebook • Arabic (Moroccan) phrasebook • Cairo • Cape Town • Cape Town city map • Central Africa • East Africa • Egypt • Egypt travel atlas • Ethiopian (Amharic) phrasebook • The Gambia & Senegal • Healthy Travel Africa • Kenya • Kenya travel atlas • Malawi, Mozambique & Zambia • Morocco • North Africa • Read This First Africa • South Africa, Lesotho & Swaziland • South Africa, Lesotho & Swaziland travel atlas • Swahili phrasebook • Tanzania, Zanzibar & Pemba • Trekking in East Africa • Tunisia • West Africa • Zimbabwe, Botswana & Namibia • Zimbabwe, Botswana & Nambia Travel Atlas • World Food Morocco
Travel Literature: The Rainbird: A Central African Journey • Songs to an African Sunset: A Zimbabwean Story • Mali Blues: Traveling to an African Beat

AUSTRALIA & THE PACIFIC Auckland • Australia • Australian phrasebook • Bushwalking in Australia • Bushwalking in Papua New Guinea • Fiji • Fijian phrasebook • Healthy Travel Australia, NZ and the Pacific • Islands of Australia's Great Barrier Reef • Melbourne • Melbourne city map • Micronesia • New Caledonia • New South Wales & the ACT • New Zealand • Northern Territory • Outback Australia • Out To Eat – Melbourne • Out to Eat – Sydney • Papua New Guinea • Pidgin phrasebook • Queensland • Rarotonga & the Cook Islands • Samoa • Solomon Islands • South Australia • South Pacific • South Pacific Languages phrasebook • Sydney • Sydney city map • Sydney Condensed • Tahiti & French Polynesia • Tasmania • Tonga • Tramping in New Zealand • Vanuatu • Victoria • Western Australia
Travel Literature: Islands in the Clouds • Kiwi Tracks: A New Zealand Journey • Sean & David's Long Drive

CENTRAL AMERICA & THE CARIBBEAN Bahamas, Turks & Caicos • Bermuda • Central America on a shoestring • Costa Rica • Cuba • Dominican Republic & Haiti • Eastern Caribbean • Guatemala, Belize & Yucatán: La Ruta Maya • Jamaica • Mexico • Mexico City • Panama • Puerto Rico • Read This First Central & South America • World Food Mexico
Travel Literature: Green Dreams: Travels in Central America

EUROPE Amsterdam • Amsterdam city map • Andalucía • Austria • Baltic States phrasebook • Barcelona • Berlin • Berlin city map • Britain • British phrasebook • Brussels, Bruges & Antwerp • Budapest city map • Canary Islands • Central Europe • Central Europe phrasebook • Corfu & Ionians • Corsica • Crete • Crete Condensed • Croatia • Cyprus • Czech & Slovak Republics • Denmark • Dublin • Eastern Europe • Eastern Europe phrasebook • Edinburgh • Estonia, Latvia & Lithuania • Europe on a shoestring • Finland • Florence • France • French phrasebook • Germany • German phrasebook • Greece • Greek Islands • Greek phrasebook • Hungary • Iceland, Greenland & the Faroe Islands • Istanbul City Map • Ireland • Italian phrasebook • Italy • Krakow •Lisbon • London • London city map • London Condensed • Mediterranean Europe • Mediterranean Europe phrasebook • Munich • Norway • Paris • Paris city map • Paris Condensed • Poland • Portugal • Portugese phrasebook • Portugal travel atlas • Prague • Prague city map • Provence & the Côte d'Azur • Read This First Europe • Romania & Moldova • Rome • Russia, Ukraine & Belarus • Russian phrasebook • Scandinavian & Baltic Europe • Scandinavian Europe phrasebook • Scotland • Slovenia • Spain • Spanish phrasebook • St Petersburg • Switzerland • Trekking in Spain • Ukrainian phrasebook • Venice • Vienna • Walking in Britain • Walking in Ireland • Walking in Italy • Walking in Spain • Walking in Switzerland • Western Europe • Western Europe phrasebook • World Food Italy • World Food Spain
Travel Literature: The Olive Grove: Travels in Greece

INDIAN SUBCONTINENT Bangladesh • Bengali phrasebook • Bhutan • Delhi • Goa • Hindi & Urdu phrasebook • India • India & Bangladesh travel atlas • Indian Himalaya • Karakoram Highway • Kerala • Mumbai (Bombay) • Nepal • Nepali phrasebook • Pakistan • Rajasthan • Read This First: Asia & India • South India • Sri Lanka • Sri Lanka phrasebook • Trekking in the Indian Himalaya • Trekking in the Karakoram & Hindukush • Trekking in the Nepal Himalaya
Travel Literature: In Rajasthan • Shopping for Buddhas • The Age Of Kali

LONELY PLANET

Mail Order

Lonely Planet products are distributed worldwide. They are also available by mail order from Lonely Planet, so if you have difficulty finding a title please write to us. North and South American residents should write to 150 Linden St, Oakland, CA 94607, USA; European and African residents should write to 10a Spring Place, London NW5 3BH, UK; and residents of other countries to PO Box 617, Hawthorn, Victoria 3122, Australia.

ISLANDS OF THE INDIAN OCEAN Madagascar & Comoros • Maldives • Mauritius, Réunion & Seychelles

MIDDLE EAST & CENTRAL ASIA Bahrain, Kuwait & Qatar • Central Asia • Central Asia phrasebook • Dubai • Hebrew phrasebook • Iran • Israel & the Palestinian Territories • Israel & the Palestinian Territories travel atlas • Istanbul • Istanbul to Cairo on a shoestring • Jerusalem • Jerusalem City Map • Jordan • Jordan, Syria & Lebanon travel atlas • Lebanon • Middle East • Oman & the United Arab Emirates • Syria • Turkey • Turkey travel atlas • Turkish phrasebook • Yemen
Travel Literature: The Gates of Damascus • Kingdom of the Film Stars: Journey into Jordan • Black on Black: Iran Revisited

NORTH AMERICA Alaska • Backpacking in Alaska • Baja California • California & Nevada • California Condensed • Canada • Chicago • Chicago city map • Deep South • Florida • Hawaii • Honolulu • Las Vegas • Los Angeles • Miami • New England • New Orleans • New York City • New York city map • New York Condensed • New York, New Jersey & Pennsylvania • Oahu • Pacific Northwest USA • Puerto Rico • Rocky Mountain • San Francisco • San Francisco city map • Seattle • Southwest USA • Texas • USA • USA phrasebook • Vancouver • Washington, DC & the Capital Region • Washington DC city map
Travel Literature: Drive Thru America

NORTH-EAST ASIA Beijing • Cantonese phrasebook • China • Hong Kong • Hong Kong city map • Hong Kong, Macau & Guangzhou • Japan • Japanese phrasebook • Japanese audio pack • Korea • Korean phrasebook • Kyoto • Mandarin phrasebook • Mongolia • Mongolian phrasebook • North-East Asia on a shoestring • Seoul • South-West China • Taiwan • Tibet • Tibetan phrasebook • Tokyo
Travel Literature: Lost Japan • In Xanadu

SOUTH AMERICA Argentina, Uruguay & Paraguay • Bolivia • Brazil • Brazilian phrasebook • Buenos Aires • Chile & Easter Island • Chile & Easter Island travel atlas • Colombia • Ecuador & the Galapagos Islands • Healthy Travel Central & South America • Latin American Spanish phrasebook • Peru • Quechua phrasebook • Rio de Janeiro • Rio de Janeiro city map • South America on a shoestring • Trekking in the Patagonian Andes • Venezuela
Travel Literature: Full Circle: A South American Journey

SOUTH-EAST ASIA Bali & Lombok • Bangkok • Bangkok city map • Burmese phrasebook • Cambodia • Hanoi • Healthy Travel Asia & India • Hill Tribes phrasebook • Ho Chi Minh City • Indonesia • Indonesia's Eastern Islands • Indonesian phrasebook • Indonesian audio pack • Jakarta • Java • Laos • Lao phrasebook • Laos travel atlas • Malay phrasebook • Malaysia, Singapore & Brunei • Myanmar (Burma) • Philippines • Pilipino (Tagalog) phrasebook • Read This First Asia & India • Singapore • South-East Asia on a shoestring • South-East Asia phrasebook • Thailand • Thailand's Islands & Beaches • Thailand travel atlas • Thai phrasebook • Thai audio pack • Vietnam • Vietnamese phrasebook • Vietnam travel atlas • World Food Thailand • World Food Vietnam

ALSO AVAILABLE: Antarctica • The Arctic • Brief Encounters: Stories of Love, Sex & Travel • Chasing Rickshaws • Lonely Planet Unpacked • Not the Only Planet: Travel Stories from Science Fiction • Sacred India • Travel with Children • Traveller's Tales

FREE Lonely Planet Newsletters

We love hearing from you and think you'd like to hear from us.

Planet Talk

Our FREE quarterly printed newsletter is full of tips from travellers and anecdotes from Lonely Planet guidebook authors. Every issue is packed with up-to-date travel news and advice, and includes:

- a postcard from Lonely Planet co-founder Tony Wheeler
- a swag of mail from travellers
- a look at life on the road through the eyes of a Lonely Planet author
- topical health advice
- prizes for the best travel yarn
- news about forthcoming Lonely Planet events
- a complete list of Lonely Planet books and other titles

To join our mailing list, residents of the UK, Europe and Africa can email us at go@lonelyplanet.co.uk; residents of North and South America can email us at info@lonelyplanet.com; the rest of the world can email us at talk2us@lonelyplanet.com.au, or contact any Lonely Planet office.

Comet

Our FREE monthly email newsletter brings you all the latest travel news, features, interviews, competitions, destination ideas, travellers' tips & tales, Q&As, raging debates and related links. Find out what's new on the Lonely Planet Web site and which books are about to hit the shelves.

Subscribe from your desktop: www.lonelyplanet.com/comet

Lonely Planet Journeys

JOURNEYS is a unique collection of travel writing – published by the company that understands travel better than anyone else. It is a series for anyone who has ever experienced – or dreamed of – the magical moment when they encountered a strange culture or saw a place for the first time. They are tales to read while you're planning a trip, while you're on the road or while you're in an armchair in front of a fire.

These outstanding titles explore our planet through the eyes of a diverse group of international writers. JOURNEYS books catch the spirit of a place, illuminate a culture, recount a crazy adventure or introduce a fascinating way of life. They always entertain, and always enrich the experience of travel.

FULL CIRCLE
A South American Journey
Luis Sepúlveda (translated by Chris Andrews)

'A journey without a fixed itinerary' with Chilean writer Luis Sepúlveda. Extravagant characters and extraordinary situations are memorably evoked: gauchos organising a tournament of lies, a scheming heiress on the lookout for a husband, a pilot with a corpse on board his plane ... *Full Circle* brings us the distinctive voice of one of South America's most compelling writers.

WINNER 1996 Astrolabe – Etonnants Voyageurs award for the best work of travel literature published in France.

GREEN DREAMS
Travels in Central America
Stephen Benz

On the Amazon, in Costa Rica, Honduras and on the Mayan trail from Guatemala to Mexico, Stephen Benz describes his encounters with water, mud, insects and other wildlife – and not least with the ecotourists themselves. With witty insights into modern travel, *Green Dreams* discusses the paradox of cultural and 'green' tourism.

DRIVE THRU AMERICA
Sean Condon

If you've ever wanted to drive across the USA but couldn't find the time (or afford the gas), *Drive Thru America* is perfect for you.

In his search for American myths and realities – along with comfort, cable TV and good, reasonably priced coffee – Sean Condon paints a hilarious road-portrait of the USA.

'entertaining and laugh-out-loud funny'– *Alex Wilber, Travel editor, Amazon.com*

SEAN & DAVID'S LONG DRIVE
Sean Condon

Sean and David are young townies who have rarely strayed beyond city limits. One day, for no good reason, they set out to discover their homeland, and what follows is a wildly entertaining adventure that covers half of Australia.

'a hilariously detailed log of two burned out friends' – *Rolling Stone*

Index

Text

Bold indicates maps.

Boxed Text

Bold indicates maps.

Buenos Aires' *porteños*

The port of Buenos Aires

A dance club in Palermo Viejo

Microcentro's pedestrian mall, Calle Florida

Buenos Aires Map Section

ROBERT FRERCK

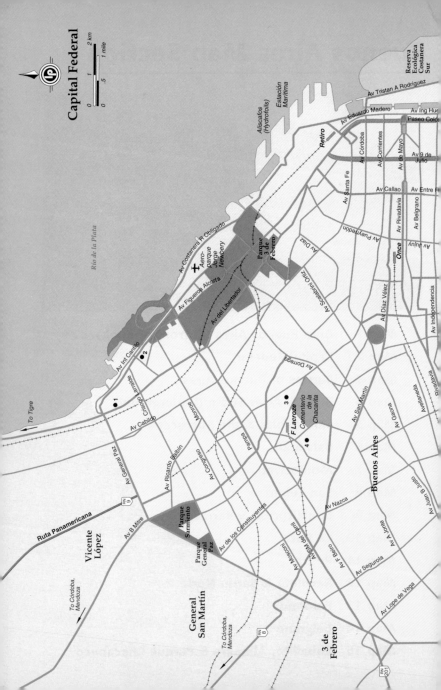

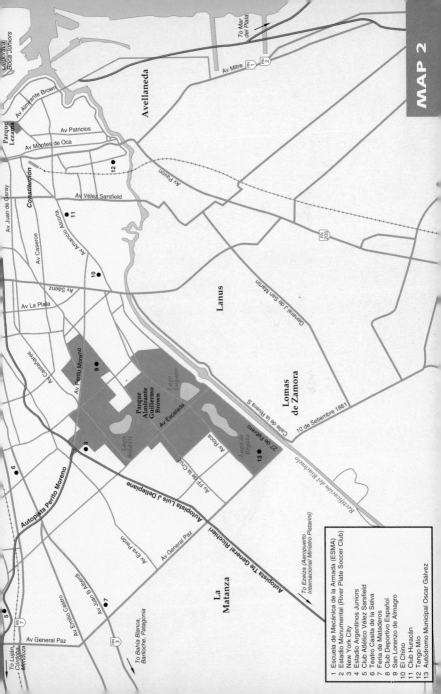

MAP 2

1 Escuela de Mecánica de la Armada (ESMA)
2 Estadio Monumental (River Plate Soccer Club)
3 New York City
4 Estadio Argentinos Juniors
5 Club Atlético Vélez Sarsfield
6 Teatro Casita de la Selva
7 Feria de Mataderos
8 Club Deportivo Español
9 San Lorenzo de Almagro
10 El Chino
11 Club Huracán
12 Tango Mío
13 Autódromo Municipal Oscar Gálvez

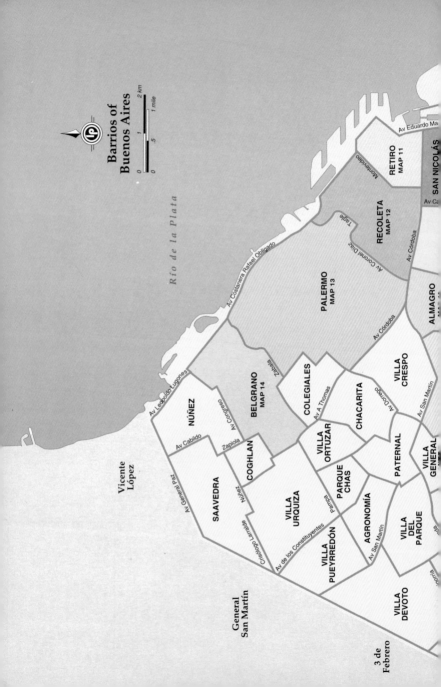

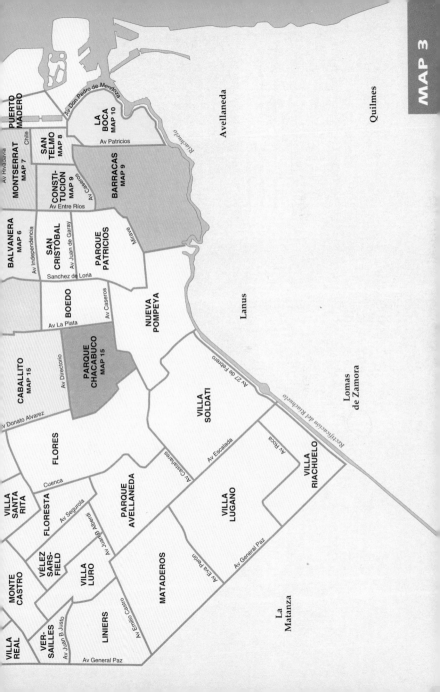

MAP 3

PUERTO MADERO

Av Don Pedro de Mendoza

LA BOCA
MAP 10

Chile

SAN TELMO
MAP 8

Av Patricios

Av Huddavia

MONTSERRAT
MAP 7

CONSTI-TUCIÓN
MAP 9

Av Entre Ríos

BARRACAS
MAP 9

Riachuelo

Av Caseros

Avellaneda

Quilmes

BALVANERA
MAP 6

Av Independencia

SAN CRISTÓBAL

Av Juan de Garay

PARQUE PATRICIOS

Mirave

Sanchez de Loria

BOEDO

Av Caseros

NUEVA POMPEYA

Av La Plata

Lanus

CABALLITO
MAP 15

Av Directorio

PARQUE CHACABUCO
MAP 15

Av 27 de Febrero

Rectificación del Riachuelo

Lomas de Zamora

Av Donato Alvarez

VILLA SOLDATI

FLORES

Av Castañares

Av Escalada

Av Roca

VILLA RIACHUELO

Cuenca

VILLA SANTA RITA

FLORESTA

Av Segurola

PARQUE AVELLANEDA

VILLA LUGANO

Av Juan B Alberdi

Av General Paz

MONTE CASTRO

VÉLEZ SARS-FIELD

VILLA LURO

MATADEROS

Av Eva Perón

La Matanza

VILLA REAL

VER-SAILLES

LINIERS

Av Emilio Castro

Av Juan B Justo

Av General Paz

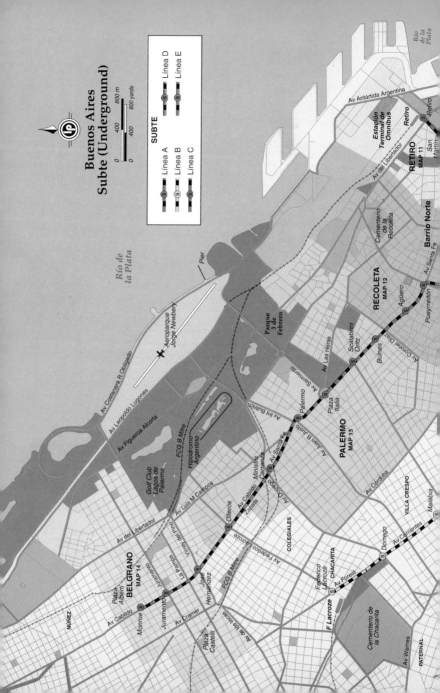

MAP 4

Reserva Ecológica Costanera Sur

Av TA Rodríguez

PUERTO MADERO

Av Ing Huergo

Av Don Pedro de Mendoza

LA BOCA
MAP 10

Avellaneda

Av Paseo Colón

Plaza de Mayo

Av Córdoba

LN Alem

Florida

Pellegrini

Lavalle

Microcentro

Diagonal Norte

Catedral

Piedras

Bolívar

Av Perú

Av de Mayo

Belgrano

SAN TELMO
MAP 8

Parque Lezama

Independencia

BARRACAS
MAP 9

Av Manuel Montes de Oca

Av 9 de Julio

9 de Julio

Av 9 de Julio

San Juan

Tribunales

Uruguay

Callao

SAN NICOLÁS
MAP 5

Moreno

Lima

MONTSERRAT
MAP 7

Sáenz Peña

San José

CONSTITUCIÓN
MAP 9

Constitución

Av Velez Sarsfield

Av Amancio Alcorta

Brandsen

Callao

Pasteur

Congreso

Av Entre Ríos

Independencia

Entre Ríos

Facultad de Medicina

Av Pueyrredón

Alberti

Pasco

Plaza Miserere

BALVANERA
MAP 6

SAN CRISTÓBAL

Jujuy

Pichincha

PARQUE PATRICIOS

Parque Patricios

Av Irala

Carlos Gardel

Medrano

Av Corrientes

Once

Loria

Castro Barros

Av H Yrigoyen

Av Belgrano

Av Jujuy

Urquiza

Boedo

Av Caseros

BOEDO

Av Sáenz

ALMAGRO
MAP 15

Plaza Almagro

Av Díaz Velez

Parque Rivadavia

Av Independencia

Boedo

Av La Plata

Av Juan de Garay

Av Juan de Garay

NUEVA POMPEYA

Av Chiclana

Angel Gallardo

Río de Janeiro

Jose M Moreno

Autopista 25 de Mayo

PARQUE CHACABUCO
MAP 15

BOEDO

Parque del Centenario

Av Acoyte

José M Moreno

Av Cobo

Av Directorio

Parque Almirante Guillermo Brown

Av Angel Gallardo

Acoyte

Primera Junta

Av L Plata

Emilio Mitre

Parque Chacabuco

Av Asamblea

Av Cobo

VILLA SOLDATI

CABALLITO
MAP 15

Jr Honorio Pueyrredón

Av San Martín

Av Gaona

Avellaneda

Av Rivadavia

Av Juan B Alberdi

Av Pedro Goyena

Av Curapaligüe

Av Directorio

Medalla Milagrosa

Av Carabobo

Av Riestra

Av Perito Moreno

VILLA GENERAL MITRE

Plaza Irlanda

Av Donato Alvarez

Av Juan B Justo

Plaza de los Virreyes

Cementerio de San José de Flores

FLORES

Varela

Av Varela

Lago Soldati

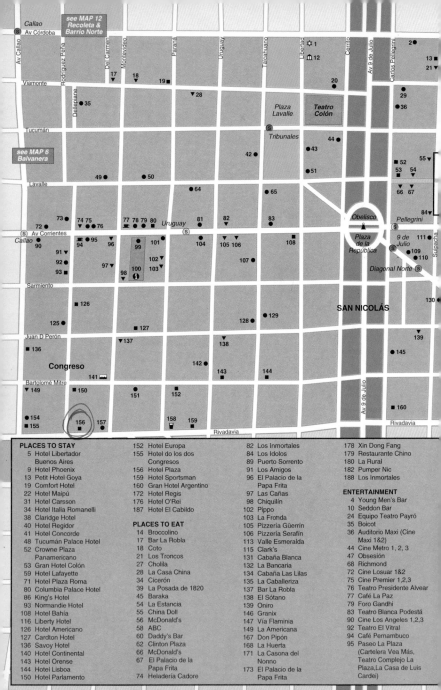

To Ferries &
Hydrofoils
to Uruguay

San Nicolás &
the Microcentro

PUERTO MADERO

Av Córdoba

Galerías Pacífico

Viamonte

Tucumán

Lavalle

Ped Mall

Plaza Roma

Luna Park

Florida

LN Alem

Av Corrientes

Microcentro

San Martín

Reconquista

25 de Mayo

Sarmiento

Av Leandro N Alem

Bouchard

Av Eduardo Madero

Dique No 4

Diagonal Roque Sáenz Peña

Gal Goemes

Juan D Perón

Ped Mall

Bartolomé Mitre

Catedral Metropolitana

Catedral

Rivadavia
Plaza de Mayo

see MAP 7
Montserrat

Lavalle

Esmeralda

Maipú

Esmeralda

Maipú

Suipacha

Av Rosales

9	Teatro General San Martín, Museo de Arte Moderno, Museo de Artes Plásticas Eduardo Sívori,
1	Girondo
5	Galería Teatro L'Orange (Cartelera Baires, Cine L'Orange)
9	Teatro del Pueblo
1	Confitería Ideal
2	Ozono
7	Cine Gaumont 1,2,3
3	Leru Bar
5	Cine Atlas Lavalle
0	Cine Normandie 1-4
4	Cine Ocean 1&2
5	Cine Ambassador
7	Cineplex Lavalle 1, 2, 3
1	Teatro Maipo
3	Cine Trocadero 1-6
6	Cine Monumental 1-4
8	Cartelera Espectáculos

SHOPPING

6	Dalla Fontana
9	Librería Lola
5	Librería Platero
3	Free Blues

78	LiberArte
107	Oficina del Libro Francés
117	El Ateneo
122	Musimundo
130	Flabella
154	Savoy
166	Librería Alberto Casares
185	El Ciudadano

OTHER

1	Templo de la Congregación Israelita
2	Alianza Francesa
3	Japan Airlines
4	Canadian Airlines
6	British Airways
7	Trans Brasil
11	Asociación Ornitológica del Plata
17	Museo Judío Dr Salvador Kibrick
15	Federal Express
20	Cámara de Comercio de los Estados Unidos en Argentina (US Chamber of Commerce)
23	Aristarain Viajes, Comunidad Homosexual Argentina
25	Centro Cultural Borges
26	Centro de Estudio del Español

30	Instituto Cultural Argentino-Norteamericano, Biblioteca Lincoln
32	Le Lab
33	OCA (private postal service)
37	Varig
42	Palacio de Justicia (Tribunales)
43	Escuela Presidente Roca
46	Casa Natal de Borges, Asociación Cristiana Femenina de Buenos Aires (YWCA)
49	Instituto de Lengua Española para Extranjeros (ILEE)
50	José Norres (Camera Repair)
51	Conventillo de las Artes
57	AB Travel/TIJE
61	KLM
63	Japanese Consulate
64	Bueno Aires Tur
69	Sociedad Rural Argentina (Argentine Agricultural Association)
70	Chilean Consulate
81	Visa
85	Telefónica, Encotel
87	Austral Líneas Aéreas
88	Instituto Goethe
100	Centro Cultural San Martín, Dirección General de Turismo de la Municipalidad de Buenos Aires

110	Dinar Líneas Aéreas
112	Teatro Opera
114	Buenos Aires Visión
118	Museo Mitre
119	Museo de la Policía Federal
120	Bolsa de Comercio de Buenos Aires (Stock Exchange)
121	Correo Central (Main Post Office)
123	Cubana de Aviación
124	Archivo y Museo Histórico del Banco de la Provincia de Buenos Aires Dr Arturo Jáuretche
125	Teatro Suizo
128	Asociación Argentina de Albergues de la Juventud (AAAJ)
129	Kinefot
133	Laboratorio de Idiomas de la Facultad, Universidad de Buenos Aires
141	Ateneo Cecchina (Swimming Pool)
145	Lloyd Aéreo Boliviano (LAB)
148	Museo Fragata Sarmiento
153	Banco de Boston
161	Municipal Tourist Kiosk
162	Pluna
163	Edificio Menéndez-Behety
164	Banco de la Nación
165	Cámara Argentina de Comercio (Chamber of Commerce)
184	Laboclick

MAP 6

MONT-
SERRAT

see MAP 7
Montserrat

see MAP 9
Constitución
& Barracas

CONSTI-
TUCIÓN

Autopista 25 de Mayo

Entre
Ríos

Combate de los Pozos

Sarandi

Venezuela

Pasco

Pichincha

Matheu

Av Independencia

Estados Unidos

Venezuela

México

Chile

Adolfo Alsina

Moreno

Av Belgrano

Déan Funes

Chile

Agrelo

SAN CRISTÓBAL

Av San Juan

To Polideportivo
Martín Fierro

Agrelo

Balvanera

Loria

Sánchez de Loria

PLACES TO STAY
14 Sarmiento Palace Hotel
17 Bauen Hotel
20 Gran Hotel Sarmiento
22 Hotel Callao
23 Hotel Lyon
29 Hotel Molino
30 Hotel Ayamitre
31 Gran Hotel Oriental
32 Hotel Lourdes

PLACES TO EAT
1   La Viña del Abasto
15 Schlotzky's Deli
16 El Toboso
21 La Ciboulette
25 Cervantes II

27 La Continental
35 Quorum
36 La Casa de Orihuela
37 Ichisou

OTHER
2   Casa Museo Bernardo
    A Houssay
3   Asociación Mutualista
    Israelita Argentina (AMIA)
4   Angel's
5   Paraguayan Consulate
6   Babilonia
7   Mercado de Abasto
8   Asociación Criadores de
    Caballos Criollos
9   Lavalle Producciones

10 Remember
11 Cine Cosmos
12 Complejo Cultural
    Ricardo Rojas
13 Turismo Unión Buenos
    Amigos (TUBA)
17 Oliverio Allways
18 Casa del Chaco
19 Teatro Fundación Banco
    Patricios
24 Pierre Cardin
26 Vaivén
28 Tradiax
33 Ex-Confitería del
    Molino
34 Aquilani
38 Gricel

300 m

300 yards

150

150

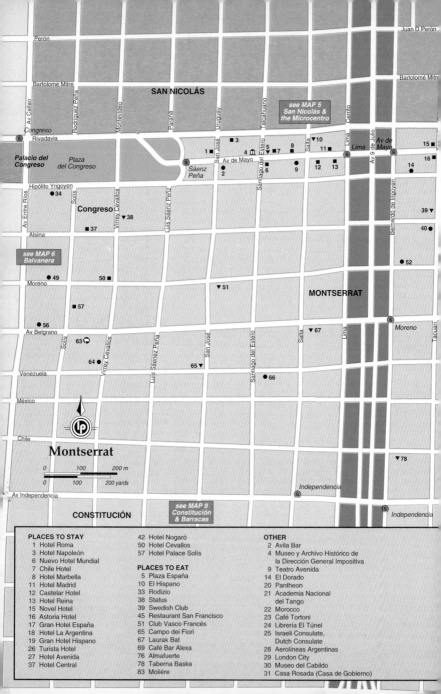

SAN NICOLÁS

Juan D Perón

Perón

Bartolomé Mitre

Bartolomé Mitre

see MAP 5
San Nicolás &
the Microcentro

Congreso

Rivadavia

Palacio del
Congreso

Plaza
del Congreso

Sáenz
Peña

Av de Mayo

Hipólito Yrigoyen

Congreso

Alsina

see MAP 6
Balvanera

Moreno

Av Belgrano

Venezuela

México

Chile

MONTSERRAT

Moreno

Av Independencia

Independencia

Independencia

CONSTITUCIÓN

see MAP 9
Constitución
& Barracas

Montserrat

0   100   200 m
0   100   200 yards

Av Callao · Rodríguez Peña · Montevideo · Paraná · Uruguay · Talcahuano · Cerrito · Lima · Av 9 de Julio · Av de Mayo · Salta · Santiago del Estero · San José · Luis Sáenz Peña · Virrey Cevallos · Solís · Av Entre Ríos · Bernardo de Irigoyen · Tacuarí

PLACES TO STAY		OTHER
1 Hotel Roma	42 Hotel Nogaró	2 Avila Bar
3 Hotel Napoleón	50 Hotel Cevallos	4 Museo y Archivo Histórico de
6 Nuevo Hotel Mundial	57 Hotel Palace Solís	la Dirección General Impositiva
7 Chile Hotel		9 Teatro Avenida
8 Hotel Marbella	**PLACES TO EAT**	14 El Dorado
11 Hotel Madrid	5 Plaza España	20 Pantheon
12 Castelar Hotel	10 El Hispano	21 Academia Nacional
13 Hotel Reina	33 Rodizio	del Tango
15 Novel Hotel	38 Status	22 Morocco
16 Astoria Hotel	39 Swedish Club	23 Café Tortoni
17 Gran Hotel España	45 Restaurant San Francisco	24 Librería El Túnel
18 Hotel La Argentina	51 Club Vasco Francés	25 Israeli Consulate,
19 Gran Hotel Hispano	65 Campo dei Fiori	Dutch Consulate
26 Turista Hotel	67 Laurak Bat	28 Aerolíneas Argentinas
27 Hotel Avenida	69 Café Bar Alexa	29 London City
37 Hotel Central	76 Almafuerte	30 Museo del Cabildo
	78 Taberna Baska	31 Casa Rosada (Casa de Gobierno)
	83 Moliére	

MAP 7

Microcentro

Av Roque Sáenz Peña

Ped Mall

Gal Goemes

Av Leandro N Alem

Av Rosales

Av Eduardo Madero

Esmeralda

Maipú

Florida

San Martín

Reconquista

25 de Mayo

Catedral (S)

Rivadavia

Catedral
Metropolitana

Rivadavia

Av La Rábida

Av Ing Huergo

21 23 24 25 ⌂ 26 ■ 27 ■ 28 29 30 ⌂

Piedras Chacabuco Perú

Av de Mayo

Plaza
de Mayo

● 31

Plaza
de Mayo

(S)

Parque
Colón

▼ 33

Piedras
20

● 22

Hipólito Yrigoyen

35 ● 41 ● 42

Bolívar (S)

Bolívar

36 ⌂ 44 ⌟ 43 ⌂ 54 ● 46 ✝

Defensa

▼ 45

Balcarce

● 47

32 ⌂

Hipólito Yrigoyen

PUERTO
MADERO

Adolfo Alsina

● 48

Moreno

Diagonal Presidente Julio A Roca

Manzana
de las
Luces

● 53

🗎 60 ⌂ 61

⌂ 59

58 ●

● 55

62 ●

Plaza
AP Justo

To Reserva Ecológica
Costanera Sur

elgrano (S)

Av Belgrano

Piedras Chacabuco Perú

68 ●

Bolívar

69 ▼

✝ 71 ● 74 ●
70 72 ●

5 de Julio

Defensa

● 73

Balcarce

Av Paseo Colón

Av Ing Huergo

Av Alicia Moreau de Justo

Venezuela

México

● 75

▼ 76

● 77

Azopardo

● 80

81 ●

● 82
▼ 83

⌂ 79

Chile

SAN TELMO

see MAP 8
San Telmo

Pasaje San Lorenzo

Av Independencia

32 Museo de la Casa de Gobierno
34 Biblioteca del Congreso
35 Asociación Argentina de Polo
36 Belgian Consulate
39 Swedish Consulate
40 Tercer Milenio
41 MasterCard
42 Museo de la Ciudad, Farmacia
de la Estrella
43 Museo de la Ciudad, Farmacia
de la Estrella
44 Bar del Museo
46 Capilla San Roque
47 Ministerio de Economía
48 Edificio Libertador
49 Mercado del Congreso
52 DHL International
53 El Querandí
54 Fundación Vida Silvestre Argentina

55 Dominguín
56 Automóvil Club Argentino (ACA)
58 Cámara de Limportadores de
la República Argentina
(Argentine Chamber of
Importers)
59 Museo Nacional del Grabado
(Casa de la Defensa)
60 Viejos Tiempos
61 Museo Etnográfico Juan
Ambrosetti
62 Administración Nacional
de Aduanas
63 Bolivian Consulate
64 Gays por Derechos Civiles
66 Teatro del Sur
68 Federación Argentina de Pato

70 Iglesia y Convento de Santo
Domingo (Iglesia de Nuestra Señora
del Rosario), Instituto Nacional
Belgraniano
71 La Ventana
72 Michelangelo
73 La Trastienda
74 Teatro Colonial
75 Biblioteca Nacional
(Centro National de la Música)
77 ex-Casa de la Moneda (Instituto
de Estudios Históricos del Ejército)
79 Museo del Traje
80 Plazoleta Rudolfo Walsh
81 Anexo Casa de la Moneda
(Archivo del Ejército)
82 Casa Blanca

Belgrano J A Roca

(S) Av Belgrano

MONTSERRAT

Venezuela

Piedras
Chacabuco
Perú
Bolívar
Defensa
Balcarce
5 de Julio

México

Av Paseo Colón
Azopardo
Av Ing Huergo
Av Alicia Moreau de Justo

Plaza
AP Justo

Chile

1 ■   ● 4
2 ■ ■ 3

▼ 6   ▼ 9 ● 10
● 7

5 ●

Pasaje San Lorenzo
8 ●

see MAP 7
Montserrat

11 ●   12
▼

Av Independencia

13 ▼

● 20

15 ●   18 ▼
16 ▼   Pasaje Giuffra
■ 14

Balcarce

Plazoleta
Olazábal

Estados Unidos

17 ▼   19 ▼

21 ▼

22 ●   24 ●
27 ▼
26 ●
23 ▼   25 ●   33 ● 34 ▼ 35 †
31 ▼ 32 ●

Paseo Colón

Carlos Calvo

❖❖ 29   30 ▼

36 ■

▼ 37

42 ●

38 ●   39 40   41   43 ●
▼ ▼   Plaza   ● 44
Dorrego

45 ●

Humberto Primo

CONSTITUCIÓN

46 ■   47 ▼   🏛 51   ● 52

Balcarce

48 ● 50 ▼
49 ●

Av San Juan

🏛 55
🏛 54

Autopista 25 de Mayo

Cochabamba

56 ●

Piedras
Chacabuco
Perú
Bolívar
Defensa

SAN TELMO

Av Juan de Garay

■ 57

■ 58   † 59
Av Brasil
▼ 60

61 ▼

see MAP 10
La Boca

To Subte
(Constitución)

62 ●

see MAP 9
Constitución &
Barracas

Av Caseros

🏛 63   **Parque**
Lezama

LA BOCA

BARRACAS

Av Martín García
Pilcomayo
Av Ing Huer

MAP 8

San Telmo

0   100   200 m
0   100   200 yards

Reserva Ecológica
Costanera Sur

PUERTO MADERO

Calabria

Av. Tristán Achával Rodríguez

Av. España

Dique No 2

Dique No 1

28

Ciudad Deportiva
Boca Juniors

To Hydrofoils
to Uruguay

Av Brasil

Av Don Pedro de Mendoza

A D'Esposito

M Gálvez

PLACES TO STAY
1 Hotel Oxford
2 Hotel Embajador
3 Hotel Victoria
14 Hotel Bolívar
36 El Hostal de San Telmo
46 Residencial Carly
57 Hotel Zavalia
58 Albergue Juvenil

PLACES TO EAT
6 Nicole de Marseille
9 Calle de Angeles
12 El Viejo Almacén
13 Hostal del Canigó
16 DesNivel
17 Jerónimo
18 La Scala de San Telmo
19 Candombe de Buenos Aires
21 Federación de
    Sociedades Gallegos
23 Las Marías II
27 Bar Sur
30 La Vieja Rotisería
31 La Casa de Estéban de Luca
34 La Carbonera

37 El Repecho de San Telmo
39 El Virrey de San Telmo
40 Mitos Argentinos
    de Buenos Aires
44 Bar Plaza Dorrego
47 Café del Arbol
50 Ming Li
60 La Carretería
61 Heladería Florencia

OTHER
4 Líneas Aéreas del Estado (LADE)
5 Carnaval Mural
7 La Casa del Pueblo
8 Casa Mínima
10 La Cumparsita
11 El Viejo Almacén
13 Teatro Margarita Xirgu
    (Casal de Catalunya)
15 Galería Cecil
20 Facultad de Ingeniería, Universidad
    de Buenos Aires (ex-Fundación
    Eva Perón)
22 Mabel Matto
24 Jorge Muscia
25 Claroscuro

26 Coco Bahiano
28 Museo Corbeta Uruguay
29 Mercado San Telmo
32 La Convención
33 Teatro La Carbonera
35 Dansk Kirke
38 Martiniano Arce
41 El Balcón de San Telmo
42 Churriche Antigüedades
43 Galería French,
    Loreto Antigüedades
45 Galería del Viejo Hotel
48 Arte Antica Antigüedades
49 Pasaje de la Defensa
    (Galería de la Defensa)
51 Museo Penitenciario Nacional
    (Iglesia Nuestra Señora de Belén)
52 Modern Conventillo
53 Cinemark Puerto Madero 1-8
54 Museo del Cine Pablo
    Ducrós Hicken
55 Museo de Arte Moderno
56 Arpegios
59 Iglesia Apostólica Ortodoxa Rusa
62 Centro Cultural Torquato Tasso
63 Museo Histórico Nacional

Constitución & Barracas

see MAP 8
San Telmo

SAN TELMO

Perú

Av Brasil

Chacabuco

Piedras

San Juan

Tacuari

Cochabamba

Bernardo de Irigoyen

Lima Este

Lima Oeste

Plaza Constitución

Autopista 25 de Mayo

Av Juan de Garay

4

5

MONTSERRAT

Independencia

Av Independencia

Estados Unidos

Carlos Calvo

Humberto Primo

Bernardo de Irigoyen

Av 9 de Julio

Lima

Salta

Santiago del Estero

San José

Pte Luis Sáenz Peña

Virrey Cevallos

Solís

San José

1

2

CONSTITUCIÓN

Plaza Garay

Autopista 25 de Mayo

Av San Juan

see MAP 7
Montserrat

see MAP 6
Balvanera

SAN CRISTÓBAL

Av Independencia

Av Entre Ríos

Estados Unidos

Carlos Calvo

Humberto Primo

Entre Ríos

Combate de los Pozos

Av San Juan

Cochabamba

Constitución

Pavón

Filiberto

Av Juan de Garay

3

200 m

200 yards

0   100   200

0   100   200

MAP 9

PLACES TO STAY
2   Hotel Carlos I
3   Che Lagarto
6   Hotel Central
7   Hotel Brasil
8   Residencia Universitaria
    Los Amigos

PLACES TO EAT
10 La Petit

OTHER
1   Cemento
4   Lesbianas a la Vista
5   Transporte Aéreo Costa
    Atlántica (TACA)
9   Centro Cultural del Sur
11 Hospital Británico
12 Cooperación, Información
    y Ayuda al Enfermo de
    SIDA (Coinsida)

Peru
Piedras
Tacuarí
Dr E Finochietto
Salguero
Brando
Av M Tedín
Av Caseros
Av Brasil
Av Manuel Montes de Oca
Hornos
Av 9 de Julio
Estación Constitución
(Transportes Metropolitanos
General Roca, Ferrocarril Roca)
Constitución
Paracas
Av Brasil
Salta
O'Brien
Santiago del Estero
San José
Pte Luis Sáenz Peña
Virrey Cevallos
Solís
Antiquera
Mompox
Echagüe
15 de Noviembre de 1889
Rondeau
Av Entre Ríos
Combate de los Pozos
PARQUE
PATRICIOS

Dr E Finochietto
Herrera
Guanahani
Paracas
Barracas
Av Armando Alcorta
Dr E Finochietto
Av Amancio Alcorta
Plaza
España
Jardín Botanico
del Sur
Balcom
Perdriel
Anchons
Av Vélez Sarsfield
Luzuriaga
Patagones
Uspallata
Ciudad
de Gualeguay
Los Patos

BARRACAS

▼10
● 12
● 9
✿ 11
■ 8
■ 6
■ 7

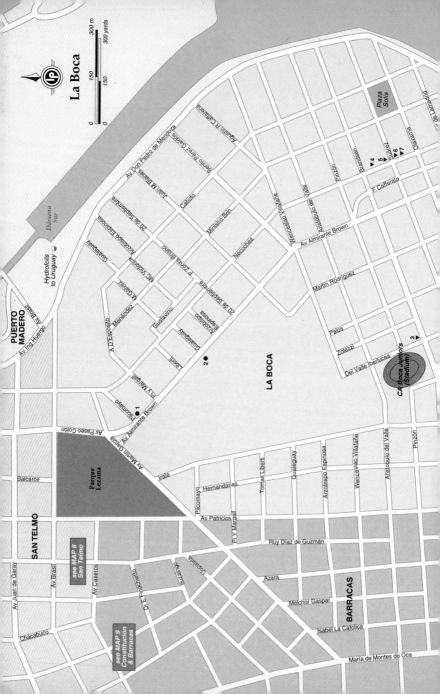

La Boca

PUERTO MADERO

SAN TELMO

LA BOCA

BARRACAS

see MAP 8
San Telmo

see MAP 9
Constitución
& Barracas

Parque
Lezama

CA Boca Juniors
(Stadium)

Plaza
Solís

Dársena
Sur

Hydrofoils
to Uruguay

Avellaneda

Puente Nicolás Avellaneda

Riachuelo

Riachuelo

see inset map

Caminito Ped Mall

Palos

Av Don Pablo de Mendoza

24

23

12

Del Valle Iberlucea

19 20 21 22

25 26

13 14

15

18

17

Olavarría

Moussy

Caminito

Garibaldi

16

Ped Mall

Magallanes

Áraoz de Lamadrid

0   75   150 m
0   75   150 yards

Sargento Ponce
La Plata
Las Heras
Av Almirante Brown
Martín Rodríguez
9
8
Ayolas
Av Don Pedro de Mendoza
California
Daniel Cerri
Carbonari
Salvadores
Alvarado
Quinquela Martín
Rocha
Benito
Vespucio
Garibaldi
10 11
Práctico Póliza
Carlos F Melo
Magallanes
Alvar Núñez
Río Cuarto
Plaza Almirante Brown
Irala
Suárez
Olavarría
Áraoz de Lamadrid
Plaza Matheu
Hernandarias
Av Patricios
Azara
Melchor Gaspar
Isabel La Católica
María de Montes de Oca

PLACES TO EAT
3 La Cancha
4 Spadavecchia
5 Il Piccolo Vapore
6 Tres Amigos
7 Gennarino
9 El Viejo Puente de Mario
10 Puerto Viejo
12 Helados Sorrento
15 Campo e Mare
19 Los Angeles de Caminito
20 El Samovar de Rasputín
25 El Corsario
26 La Barbería

OTHER
1 Blues Special Club
2 Casa de Almirante Brown
8 La Barca bas reliefs
11 Barracas Descours y
   Cabaud (Teatro Espejo)
13 Cambalache Artesanías
14 Caminito Tango Club
16 Siglo XX Cambalache
17 Centro de Exposiciones
   Caminito
18 Vía Caminito
21 Museo de Cera
22 La Vuelta de los Tachos
23 Museo de Bellas Artes de
   La Boca
24 Teatro de la Ribera

Retiro

RECOLETA

Patio Bullrich

see MAP 12
Recoleta &
Barrio Norte

Plaza Pellegrini

RETIRO

Plaza
Vicente
López

Barrio Norte

San Martín

Plaza
Libertad

see MAP 5
San Nicolás &
the Microcentro

SAN NICOLÁS

MAP 11

21 Avianca, Iberia
25 Palacio San Martín (Ministerio de Relaciones Exteriores y Culto)
26 American Express
27 Austral Líneas Aéreas
28 TAP (Air Portugal)
31 Alitalia, Malaysia Airlines
32 San Martín Bus
33 Dirección Nacional de Turismo
34 American Airlines
35 Budget (Car Rental)
36 Hertz (Car Rental)
41 Líneas Aéreas Privadas Argentinas (LAPA)
42 Ecuatoriana
43 French Consulate, Swiss Consulate
44 Swissair
45 AeroMéxico, Aeroperú
46 Aeroflot
47 Andesmar

49 South African Airways
50 Manuel Tienda León (Airport buses)
51 Vasp
54 Lo de Alvarado
56 Italian Consulate
58 Transportes Aéreos de Mercosur (TAM)
60 Diner's Club
62 Econo (Car Rental)
63 Círculo Militar (Museo de Armas)
64 Last Residence of Jorge Luis Borges
65 Administración de Parques Nacionales
66 AI (Car Rental)
68 Lufthansa
69 Buenos Aires Así
72 Dollar (Car Rental)
79 Danish Consulate
85 Norwegian Consulate
86 Lihué Expediciones

87 Líneas Aéreas de Entre Ríos (LAER)
90 Historical Tours
91 LanChile
95 United Airlines
96 Localiza (Car Rental)
98 Swan Turismo
99 Unirent (Car Rental)
103 Air France
105 Southern Winds
117 Peruvian Consulate
120 Buquebus
121 Korean Air, Mexicana
122 National (Car Rental)
123 Ferrytur
125 Harrods
126 Asatej/RAAJ, Galería Buenos Aires, Gerardo Föhse (Camera Repair)
127 Centro Naval
129 Telecom

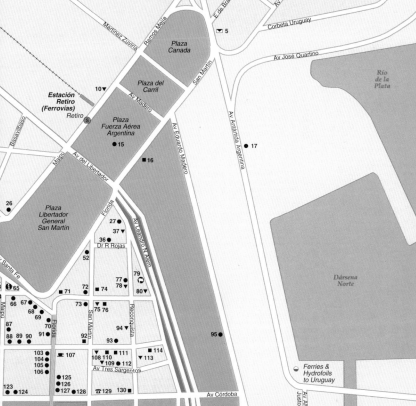

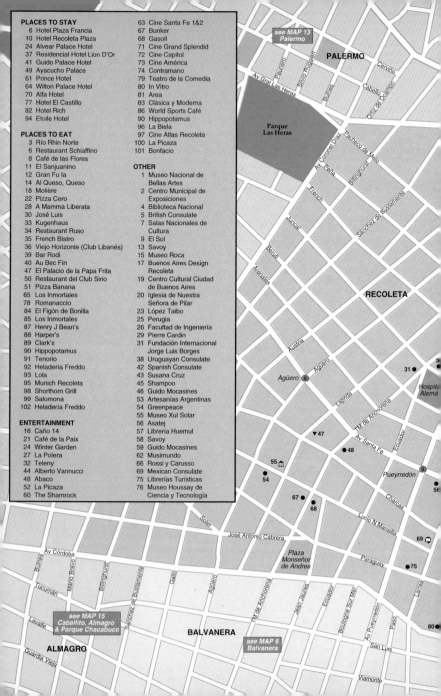

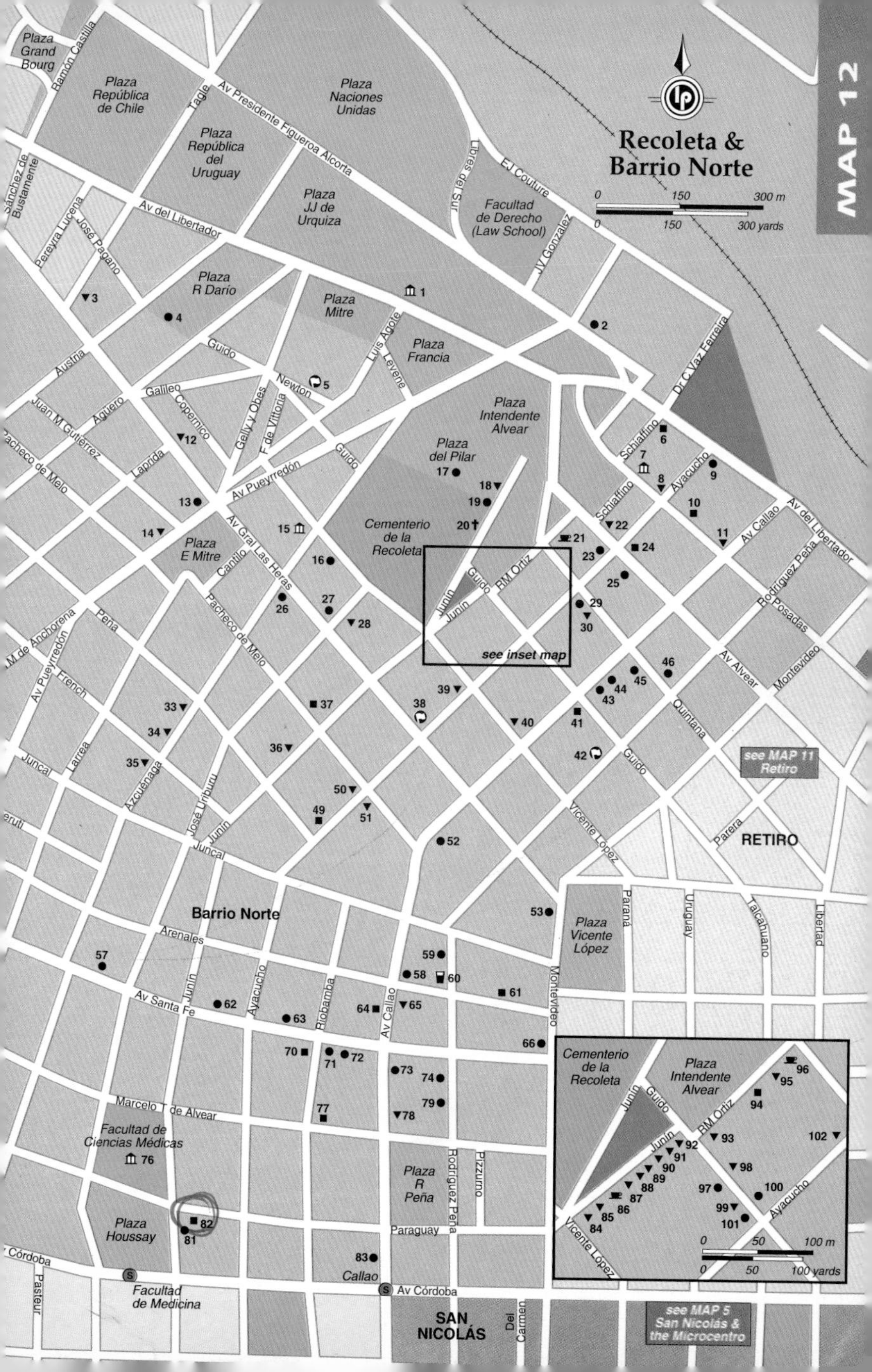

MAP 12

LP

Recoleta & Barrio Norte

0   150   300 m
0   150   300 yards

Plaza Grand Bourg

Plaza República de Chile

Plaza Naciones Unidas

Ramón Castilla

Av Presidente Figueroa Alcorta

Tagle

Libertador

E J Couture

Plaza República del Uruguay

Plaza JJ de Urquiza

Av del Libertador

Plaza Mitre

▲ 1

Facultad de Derecho (Law School)

V J González

Sánchez de Bustamente

de Pagano

Plaza R Darío

● 4

Plaza Francia

● 2

Dr C Vaz Ferreira

▼ 3

Austria

José Pagano

Pereyra Lucena

Guido

Luis Agote

Las Heras

Plaza Intendente Alvear

Newton

⌖ 5

Plaza del Pilar

6 ●

Schiaffino

Galileo

Copérnico

Galv y Obes

F de Vitoria

Guido

17 ●

18 ▼

19 ●

Juan M Gutiérrez

Pacheco de Melo

Agüero

Laprida

Av Pueyrredón

▼ 12

● 13

▼ 14

Plaza E Mitre

15 ⌂

Cementerio de la Recoleta

20 ✝

Schiaffino

7

8

Ayacucho

10 ■

9

● 22

21 ■

23

Av Callao

11 ■

Av del Libertador

16 ●

Capitán Las Heras

27 ●

26 ●

▼ 28

Junín

Guido

R M Ortiz

24 ■

25

29 ●

30

see inset map

Rodríguez Peña

Posadas

M de Anchorena

Peña

Pacheco de Melo

33 ▼

34 ▼

35 ▼

39 ▼

38 ●

37 ■

36 ▼

40 ▼

41 ■

43

44 ●

45 ●

46 ●

Quintana

Av Alvear

Montevideo

see MAP 11 Retiro

Av Pueyrredón

French

Juncal

Larrea

Azcuénaga

José A Cabrera

Junín

42 ⌖

Guido

Vicente López

50 ▼

49 ●

51

● 52

53 ●

Plaza Vicente López

Paraná

Uruguay

Talcahuano

Libertad

RETIRO

Barrio Norte

Arenales

57 ●

62 ●

63 ●

Av Santa Fe

59 ●

58 ●

60 ⌂

64 ■

65 ■

61 ■

66 ●

Montevideo

Ayacucho

Riobamba

Av Callao

70 ●

71

72 ●

73 ●

74 ●

79 ▼

78 ▼

77 ■

Marcelo T de Alvear

Facultad de Ciencias Médicas

⌂ 76

Plaza Houssay

81 ■

82 ■

83 ●

Callao

Plaza R Peña

Rodríguez Peña

Paraguay

Pizzurno

Cementerio de la Recoleta

Plaza Intendente Alvear

96 ▼

95 ●

94 ●

93 ▼

92 ▼

91 ▼

90 ▼

89 ▼

88 ▼

87 ▼

86 ▼

85 ▼

84 ▼

97 ●

98 ▼

100 ●

99 ▼

101 ▼

102 ▼

Junín

Guido

R M Ortiz

Ayacucho

Vicente López

0   50   100 m
0   50   100 yards

Ⓢ

Facultad de Medicina

Av Córdoba

Ⓢ

Córdoba

Pasteur

Del Carmen

SAN NICOLÁS

see MAP 5 San Nicolás & the Microcentro

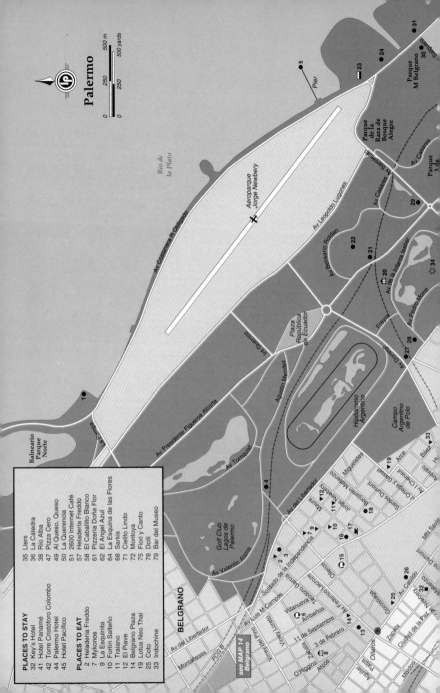

Palermo

0 250 500 m
0 250 500 yards

PLACES TO STAY
32 Key's Hotel
41 Hotel Panamé
42 Torre Cristóforo Colombo
44 Palermo Hotel
45 Hotel Pacífico

PLACES TO EAT
2   Heladería Freddo
7   Mykonos
9   La Esquinita
10 Fortín Salteño
11 Traiano
12 El Piave
14 Belgrano Plaza
19 Lotus Neo Thai
25 Coto
33 Indochine
35 Liers
36 La Cátedra
38 Río Alba
47 Pizza Cero
49 Al Queso, Queso
50 La Querencia
51 2600 Internet Café
57 Heladería Freddo
58 El Caballito Blanco
61 Pizzería Doña Flor
62 El Ángel Azul
64 La Esquina de las Flores
68 Sarkis
71 Cielito Lindo
72 Montoya
75 Fiori y Canto
78 Dolli
79 Bar del Museo

Río de
la Plata

Balneario
Parque
Norte

Aeroparque
Jorge Newbery

Av Costanera R Obligado

Av Presidente Figueroa Alcorta

Av Leopoldo Lugones

Av Belisario Roldán

Int Güemes

Agustín Méndez

Av Tornquist

Golf Club
Lagos de
Palermo

Av Valentín Alsina

Av del Libertador

Hipódromo
Argentino

Plaza
República
de Ecuador

Campo
Argentino
de Polo

Parque
de la
Raza de
Bosque
Alegre

Parque
M Belgrano

Parque
3 de

Av de la Infanta Isabel

Av Pedro Montt

Av Casares

Av Sarmiento

Freyre

Av Dorrego

Arce

Blaz

Baez

Mariscal A Sucre

Jorge Newbery

Av Luis M Campos

Av Federico Lacroze

Teodoro García

Soldado de la Independencia

Olleros

Av del Libertador

Benjamín Matienzo

Santos Dumont

Miñquiletes

L Chenaut

Av J Chenaut

Arribeños

Montañeses

Virrey del Pino

Virrey Loreto

Amenábar

Av Luis M Campos

11 de Septiembre

3 de Febrero

Zapiola

Ciudad de la Paz

Av Cabildo

Av Callao

Maure

Gorostiaga

O'Higgins

Aguilar

Juramento

Echeverría

Villanueva

Arcos

Moldes

Conesa

Zabala

Olazábal

FCG B

BELGRANO

see MAP 14
Belgrano

Pier

5
23
24
30
31
29
22
21
20
28
27
33
26
25
19
18
17
16
15
11
12
13
14
10
9
8
6
3
2
4
1
34

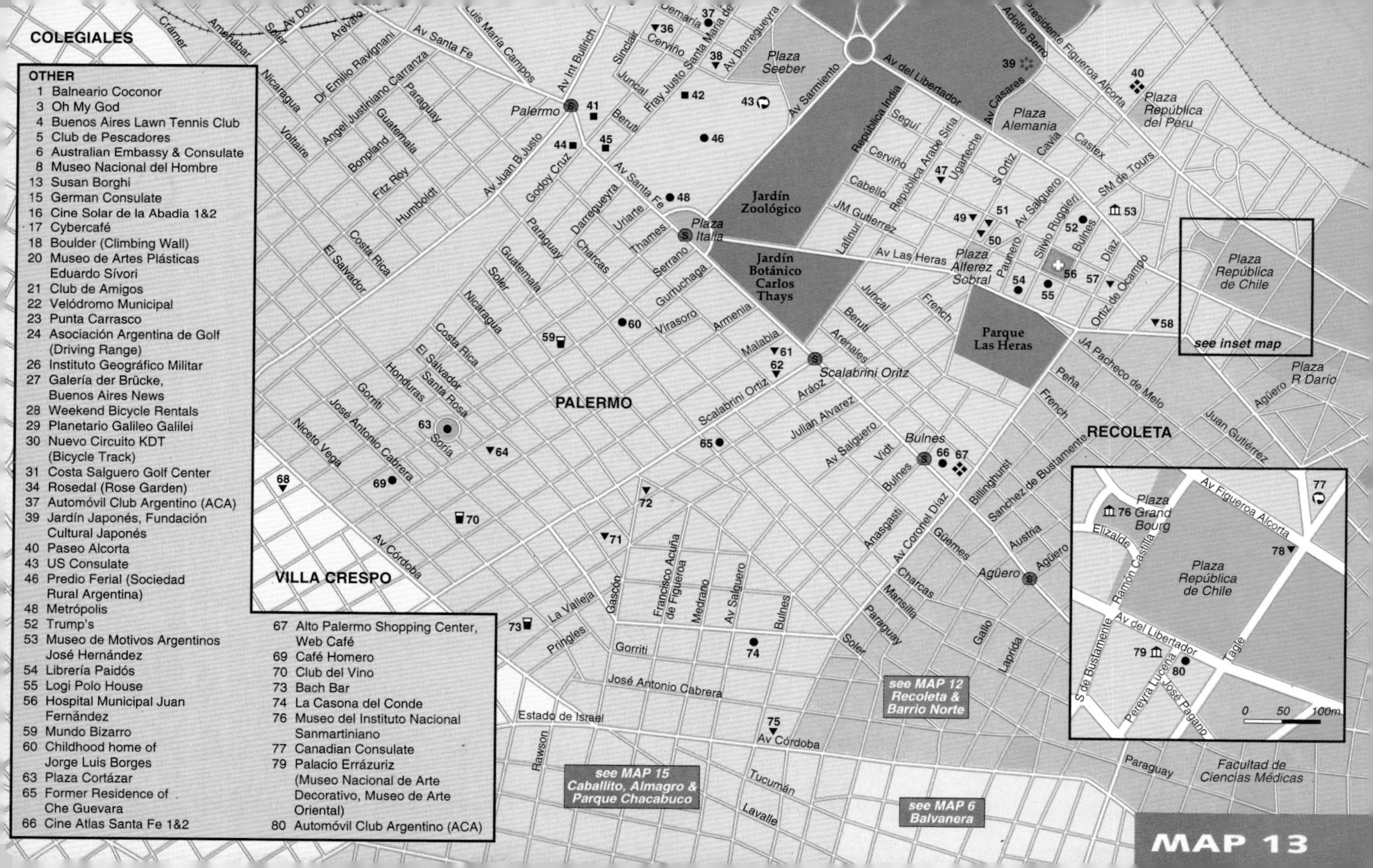
MAP 13
COLEGIALES
PALERMO
RECOLETA
VILLA CRESPO
Jardín Zoológico
Jardín Botánico Carlos Thays
Parque Las Heras
Plaza Seeber
Plaza Alemania
Plaza República del Perú
Plaza República de Chile
Plaza Italia
Plaza Alferez Sobral
Plaza R Darío
Plaza Grand Bourg
Facultad de Ciencias Médicas
see inset map
see MAP 12 Recoleta & Barrio Norte
see MAP 15 Caballito, Almagro & Parque Chacabuco
see MAP 6 Balvanera
Palermo
Scalabrini Oritz
Bulnes
Agüero
Av del Libertador
Av Sarmiento
Av Santa Fe
Av Las Heras
Av Córdoba
Av Casares
Av Figueroa Alcorta
Presidente Figueroa Alcorta
Av Int Bullrich
Av Juan B Justo
Av Coronel Díaz
Av Salguero
Av Darregueyra
Av Dorrego
Luis María Campos
Adolfo Berro
Cavia
Castex
SM de Tours
Ortiz de Ocampo
JA Pacheco de Melo
Juan Gutierrez
Sanchez de Bustamente
S de Bustamente
Ramón Castilla
Elizalde
Tagle
Pereyra Lucena
Jose Pagano
República India
República Arabe Siria
Seguí
Cerviño
Cabello
JM Gutierrez
Lafinur
Ugarteche
S Ortiz
Silvio Ruggieri
Bulnes
Díaz
Paunero
Juncal
French
Beruti
Arenales
Peña
Billinghurst
Austria
Güemes
Charcas
Mansilla
Paraguay
Soler
Gallo
Laprida
Anasgasti
Vidt
Julian Alvarez
Aráoz
Malabia
Armenia
Virasoro
Gurruchaga
Serrano
Thames
Uriarte
Darregueyra
Godoy Cruz
Guatemala
Nicaragua
Costa Rica
El Salvador
Honduras
Santa Rosa
Soria
Gorriti
José Antonio Cabrera
Niceto Vega
Francisco Acuña de Figueroa
Medrano
Gascón
La Valleja
Pringles
Estado de Israel
Rawson
Tucumán
Lavalle
Fray Justo Santa María de Oro
Sinclair
Demaría
Voltaire
Fitz Roy
Humboldt
Bonpland
Angel Justiniano Carranza
Dr Emilio Ravignani
Arévalo
Amenábar
Crámer
0 50 100m
OTHER
1 Balneario Coconor
3 Oh My God
4 Buenos Aires Lawn Tennis Club
5 Club de Pescadores
6 Australian Embassy & Consulate
8 Museo Nacional del Hombre
13 Susan Borghi
15 German Consulate
16 Cine Solar de la Abadia 1&2
17 Cybercafé
18 Boulder (Climbing Wall)
20 Museo de Artes Plásticas Eduardo Sívori
21 Club de Amigos
22 Velódromo Municipal
23 Punta Carrasco
24 Asociación Argentina de Golf (Driving Range)
26 Instituto Geográfico Militar
27 Galería der Brücke, Buenos Aires News
28 Weekend Bicycle Rentals
29 Planetario Galileo Galilei
30 Nuevo Circuito KDT (Bicycle Track)
31 Costa Salguero Golf Center
34 Rosedal (Rose Garden)
37 Automóvil Club Argentino (ACA)
39 Jardín Japonés, Fundación Cultural Japonés
40 Paseo Alcorta
43 US Consulate
46 Predio Ferial (Sociedad Rural Argentina)
48 Metrópolis
52 Trump's
53 Museo de Motivos Argentinos José Hernández
54 Librería Paidós
55 Logi Polo House
56 Hospital Municipal Juan Fernández
59 Mundo Bizarro
60 Childhood home of Jorge Luis Borges
63 Plaza Cortázar
65 Former Residence of Che Guevara
66 Cine Atlas Santa Fe 1&2
67 Alto Palermo Shopping Center, Web Café
69 Café Homero
70 Club del Vino
73 Bach Bar
74 La Casona del Conde
76 Museo del Instituto Nacional Sanmartiniano
77 Canadian Consulate
79 Palacio Errázuriz (Museo Nacional de Arte Decorativo, Museo de Arte Oriental)
80 Automóvil Club Argentino (ACA)

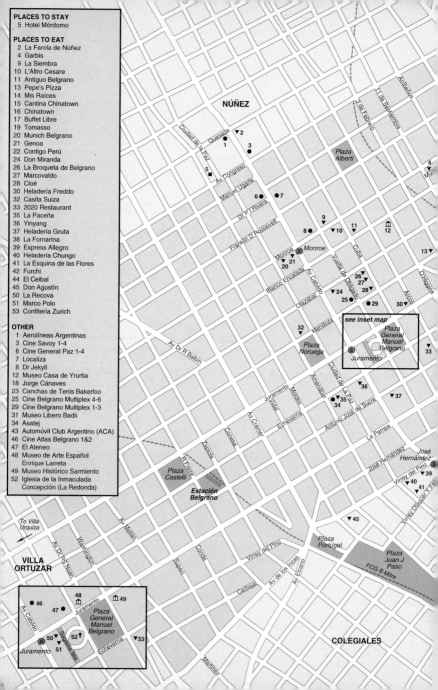

NÚÑEZ

Plaza
Alberti

Quesada

Av Congreso

Manuel Ugarte

Dr P I Rivera

Franklin D Roosevelt

Monroe

Blanco Encalada

Olazábal

Av Cabildo

Vuelta de Obligado

Cuba

Arcos

O'Higgins

Av Dr R Balbin

Mendoza

Plaza
Noruega

see inset map

Plaza
General
Manuel
Belgrano

Juramento

Ciudad de la Paz

Ameirabar

Moldes

Juramento

Av Vidal

Echeverría

Av Cramer

Conesa

Zapiola

11 Freire

Plaza
Castelli

Estación
Belgrano

To Villa
Urquiza

VILLA
ORTÚZAR

Av Dr S Noan

Washington

Av Maipú

Superí

Conde

Carbajal

Av de los Incas

Virrey del Pino

Av Elcano

Antonio José de Sucre

La Paz

La Pampa

José Hernández

Virrey del Pino

Virrey Olázaul L Fu...

José
Hernández

Plaza
Portugal

Plaza
Juan J
Paso

FCG B Mitre

COLEGIALES

Martínez

Plaza
General
Manuel
Belgrano

Juramento

Juramento

Echeverría

Vuelta de ...

MAP 14

To River Plate
Soccer Stadium

Plaza
El Salvador

Manuel Ugarte

Monroe

Blanco Encalada

Olazábal

Mendoza

Castañeda

Ramsay

Int Cantilo

Av. Ezquerra Alcorta

Antonio José de Sucre

La Pampa

BELGRANO

Juramento

Húsares

Dragones

Echeverría

Cazadores

Artilleros

Mitones

Miguéletes

Av. del Libertador

▼15

14 ▼   16 ▼   18 ●
         19 ▼

▼17

22 ▼

23 ●

Montañeses

Arribeños

Zavalía

FCGB Mitre

🏛
31

Barrancas
de
Belgrano

Av. Valentín Alsina

Golf Club
Lagos de
Palermo

Av. Torquist

Av. Luis María Campos

Arribeños

11 de Setiembre

Virrey Loreto

Zabala

Villanueva

3 de Febrero

O'Higgins

Arcos

Virrey Arredondo

Plaza General
Morazán

43
● 44
▼

Vuelta de Obligado

Av. Cabildo

Céspedes

Aguilar

Paroa

Olleros

Teodoro García

Av. Federico Lacroze

Olleros

PALERMO

Miguéletes

Av. del Libertador

Soldado de la Independencia

Gorostiaga

Arce

Maure

Vicente

Jorge Newbery

Benjamín Matienzo

Santos Dumont

J. Ortega y Gasset

Báez

see MAP 13
Palermo

Arribeños

Zapata

Jorge Newbery

B. Matienzo

Av. V. Chenaut

Av. Huergo

LP

Belgrano

0   150   300 m
0   150   300 yards